MAGI
The labyrinth of magic

CONTENTS

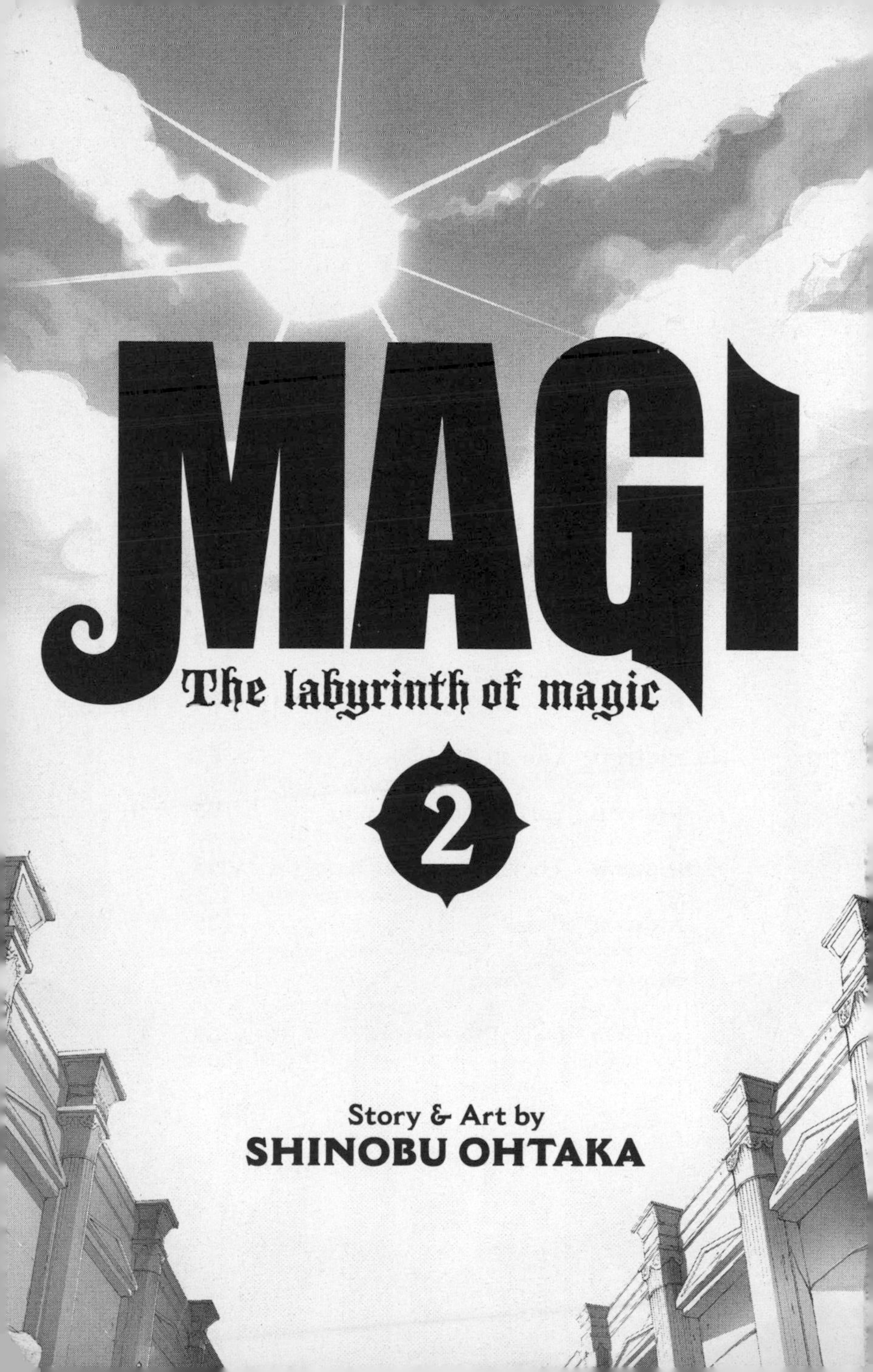

MAGI

The labyrinth of magic

2

Story & Art by

SHINOBU OHTAKA

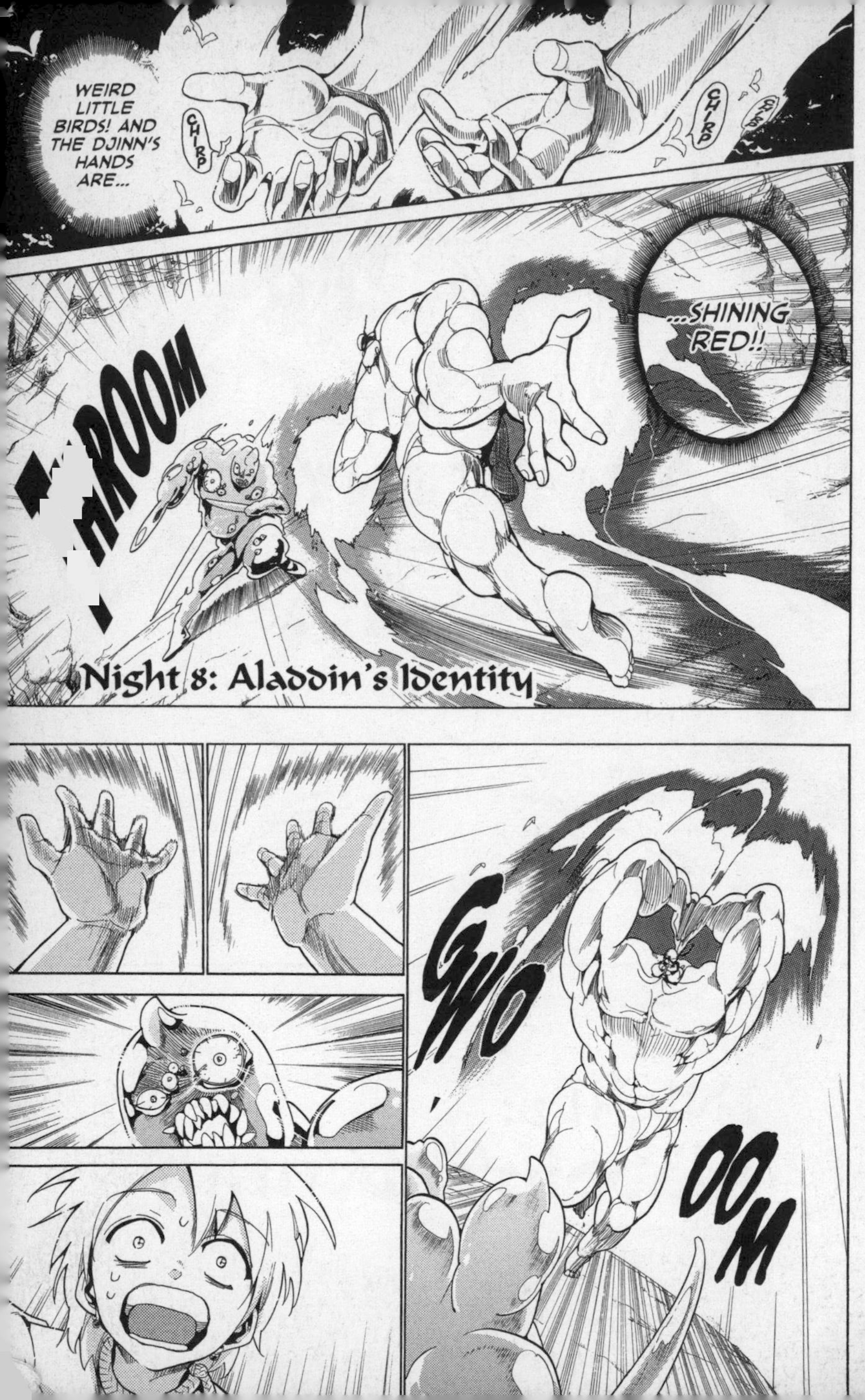
CHIRP
CHIRP
CHIRP
WEIRD LITTLE BIRDS! AND THE DJINN'S HANDS ARE...
...SHINING RED!!
HROOM
Night 8: Aladdin's Identity
GWO
OOM

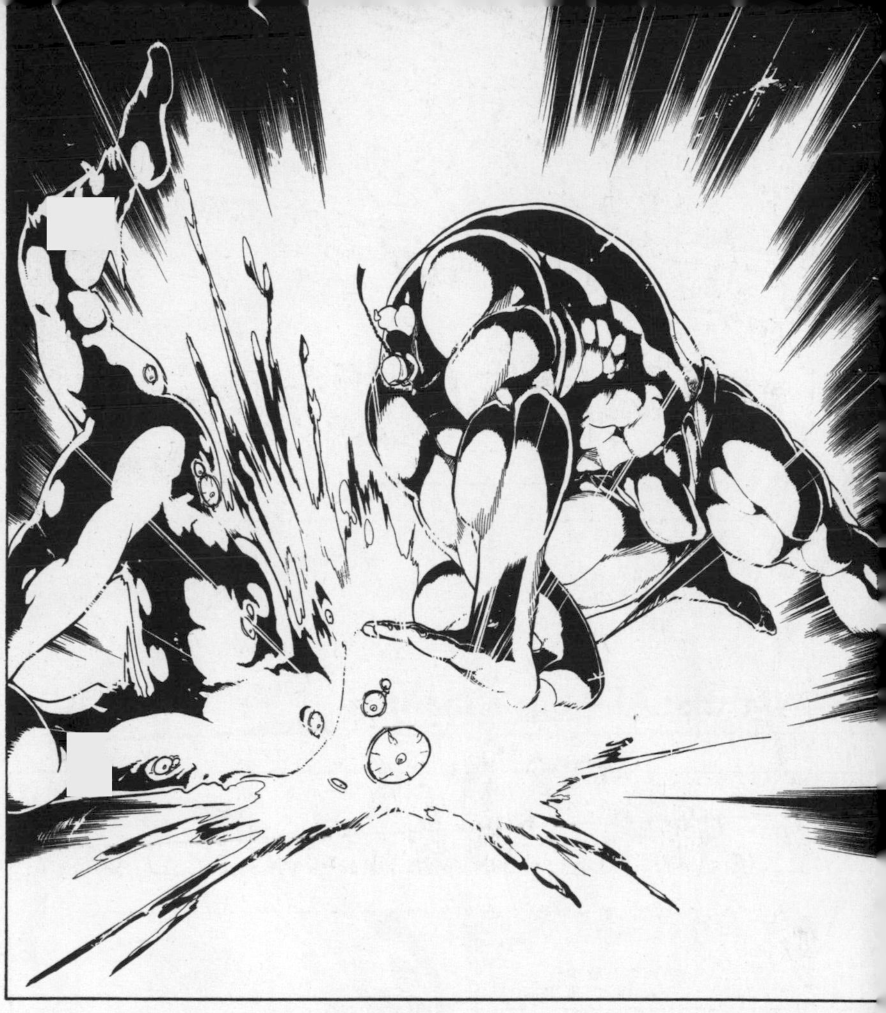

Night 8: Aladdin's Identity

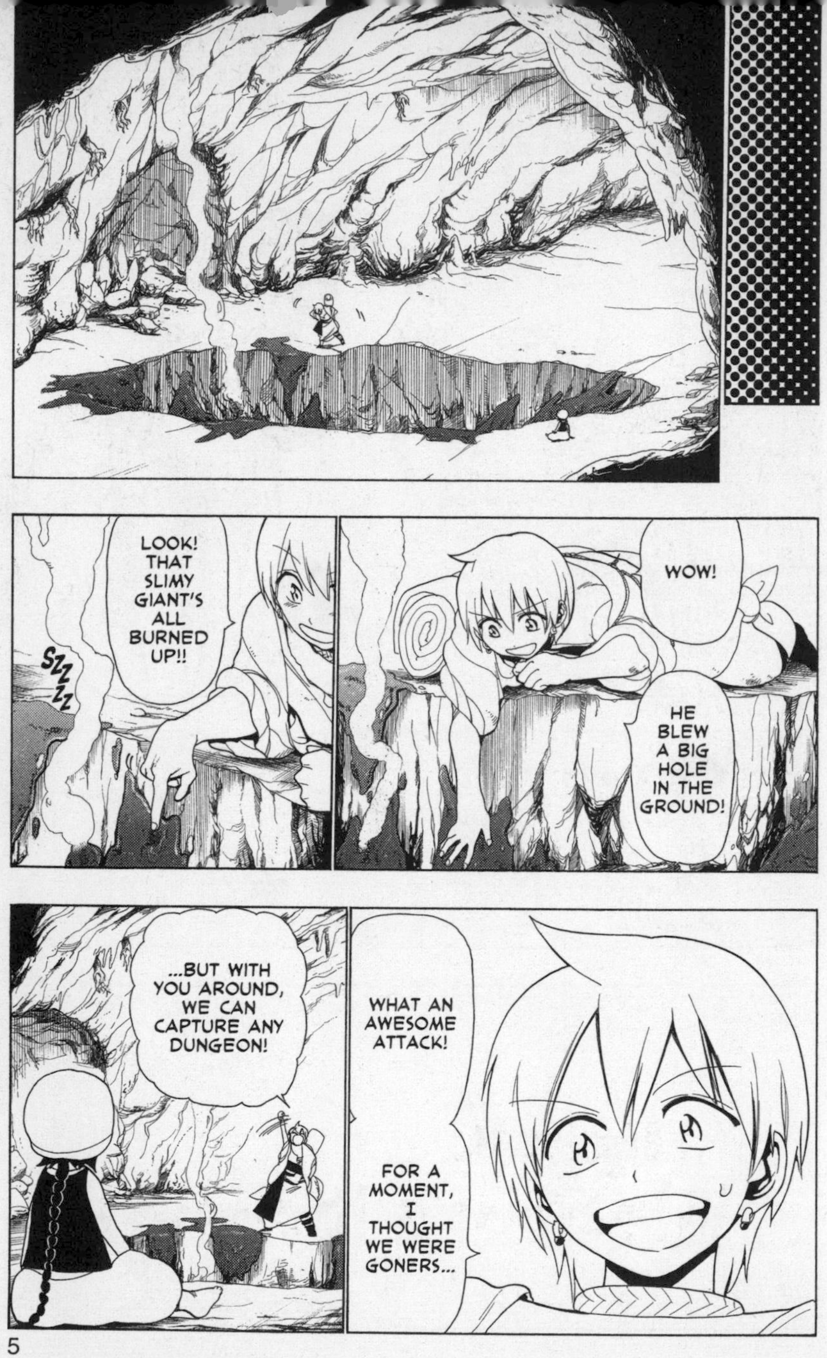
WOW!
HE BLEW A BIG HOLE IN THE GROUND!
SZZZZ
LOOK! THAT SLIMY GIANT'S ALL BURNED UP!!
WHAT AN AWESOME ATTACK!
FOR A MOMENT, I THOUGHT WE WERE GONERS...
...BUT WITH YOU AROUND, WE CAN CAPTURE ANY DUNGEON!

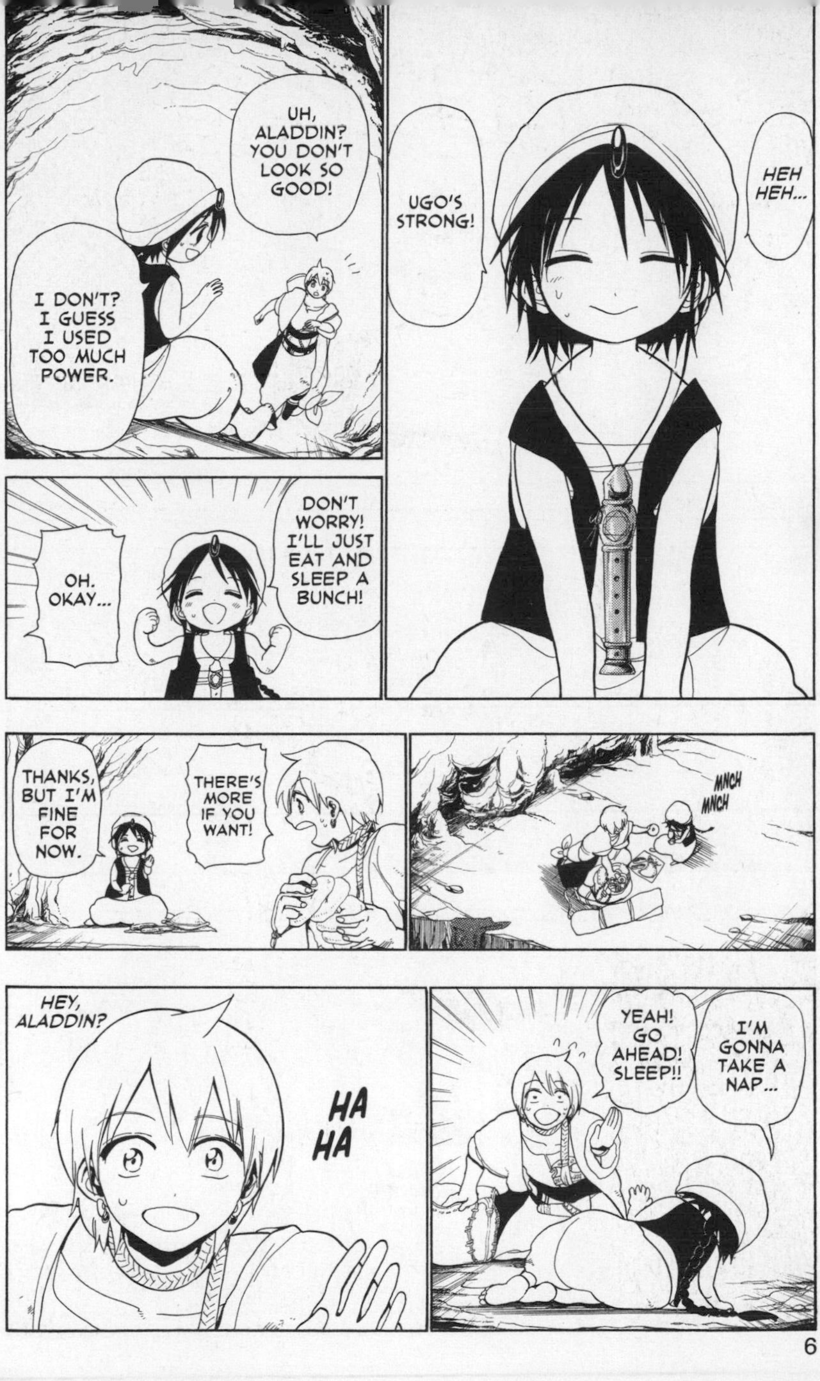
HEH HEH...
UGO'S STRONG!
UH, ALADDIN? YOU DON'T LOOK SO GOOD!
I DON'T? I GUESS I USED TOO MUCH POWER.
DON'T WORRY! I'LL JUST EAT AND SLEEP A BUNCH!
OH. OKAY...
MNCH MNCH
THERE'S MORE IF YOU WANT!
THANKS, BUT I'M FINE FOR NOW.
I'M GONNA TAKE A NAP...
YEAH! GO AHEAD! SLEEP!!
HEY, ALADDIN?
HA HA

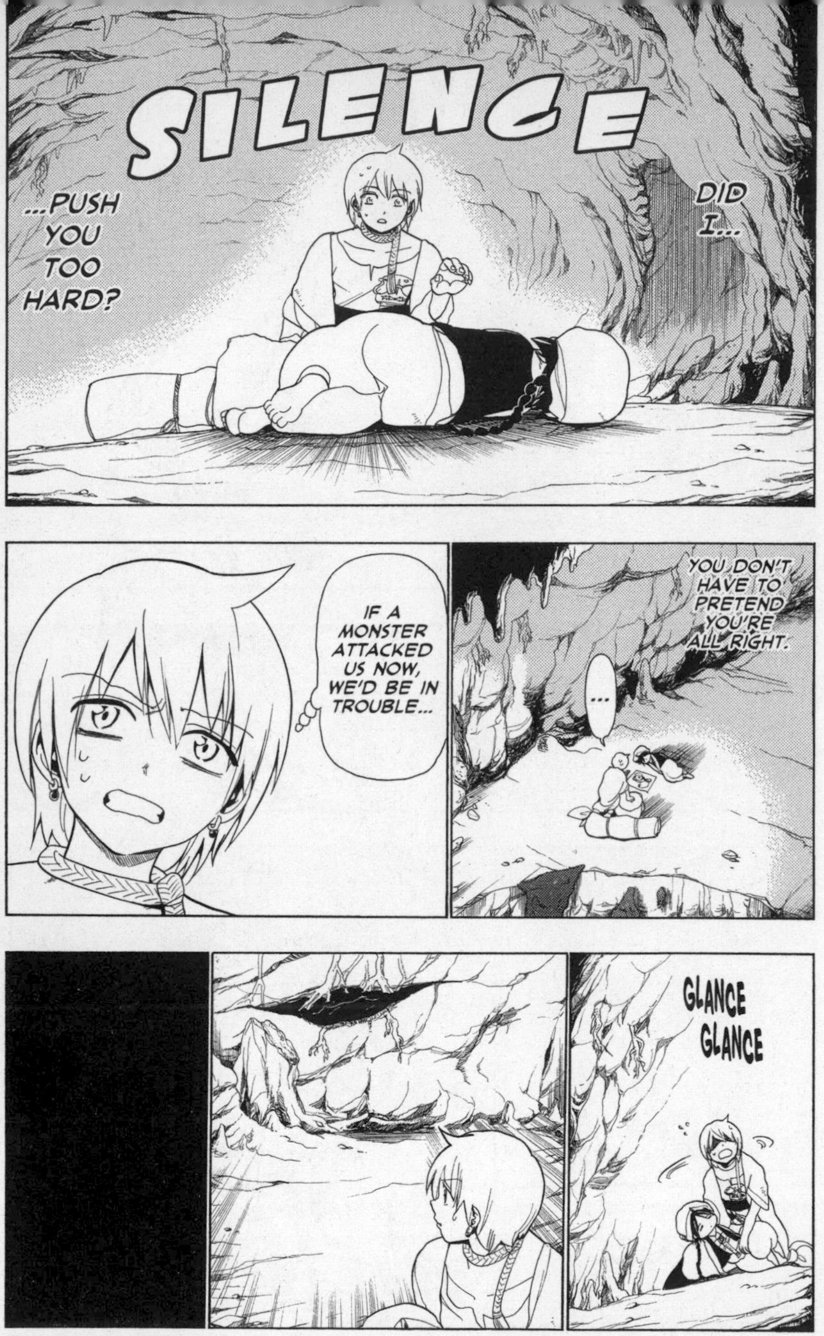
SILENCE
DID I...
...PUSH YOU TOO HARD?
YOU DON'T HAVE TO PRETEND YOU'RE ALL RIGHT.
...
IF A MONSTER ATTACKED US NOW, WE'D BE IN TROUBLE...
GLANCE GLANCE

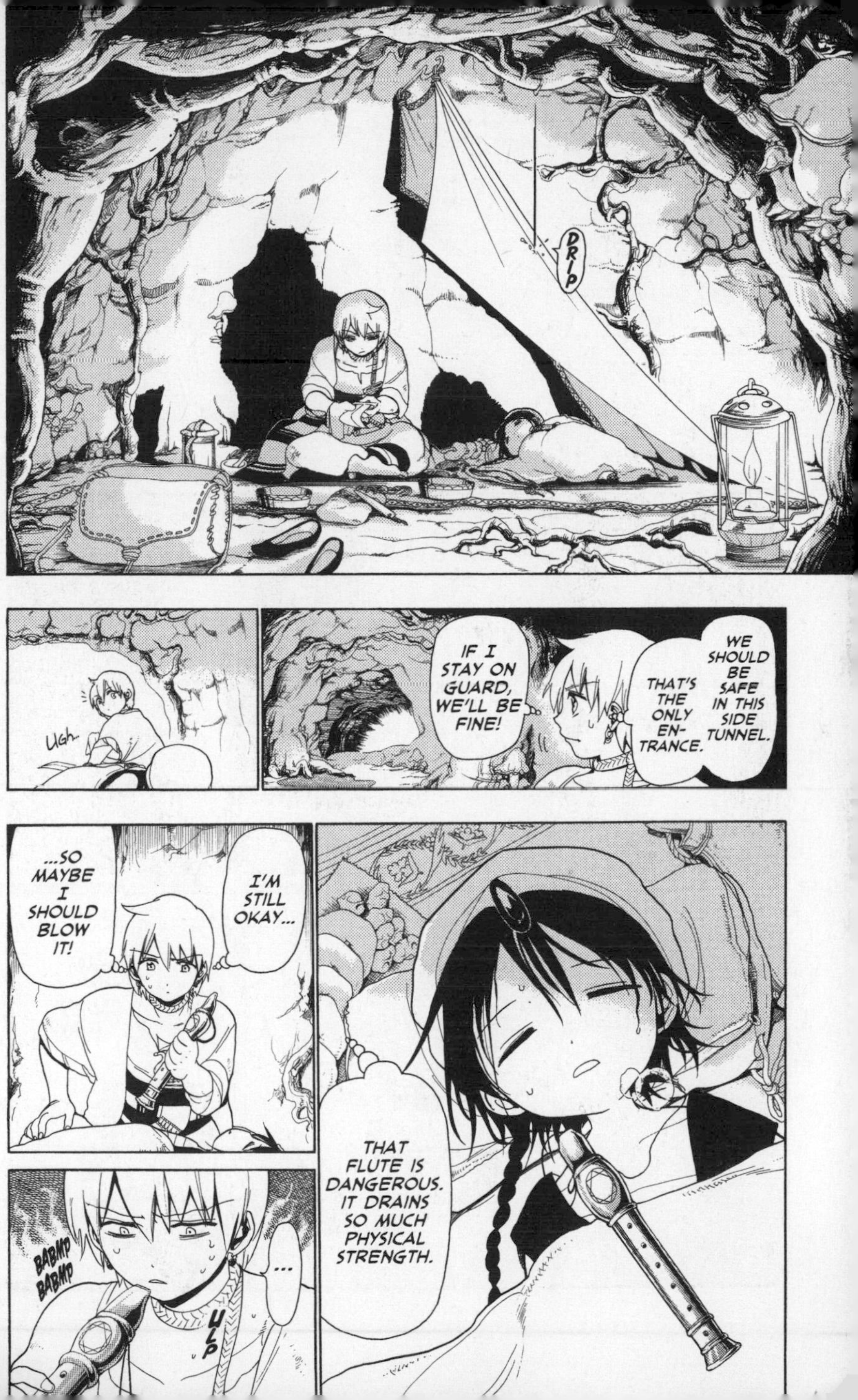
DRIP
WE SHOULD BE SAFE IN THIS SIDE TUNNEL.
THAT'S THE ONLY EN-TRANCE.
IF I STAY ON GUARD, WE'LL BE FINE!
Ugh...
THAT FLUTE IS DANGEROUS. IT DRAINS SO MUCH PHYSICAL STRENGTH.
I'M STILL OKAY...
...SO MAYBE I SHOULD BLOW IT!
...
BABMP BABMP
ULP

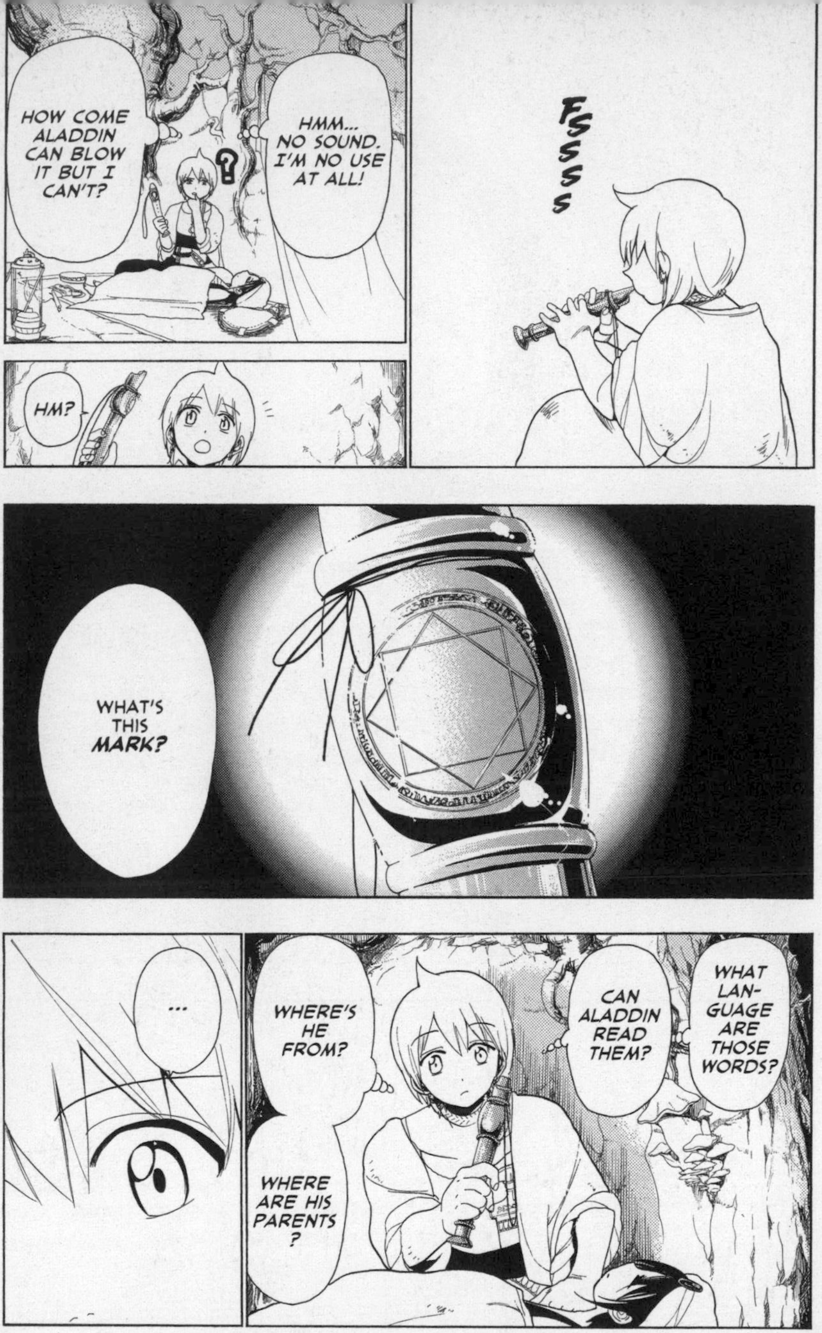
FSSSS
HMM... NO SOUND. I'M NO USE AT ALL!
HOW COME ALADDIN CAN BLOW IT BUT I CAN'T?
HM?
WHAT'S THIS MARK?
WHAT LAN-GUAGE ARE THOSE WORDS?
CAN ALADDIN READ THEM?
WHERE'S HE FROM?
WHERE ARE HIS PARENTS ?
...

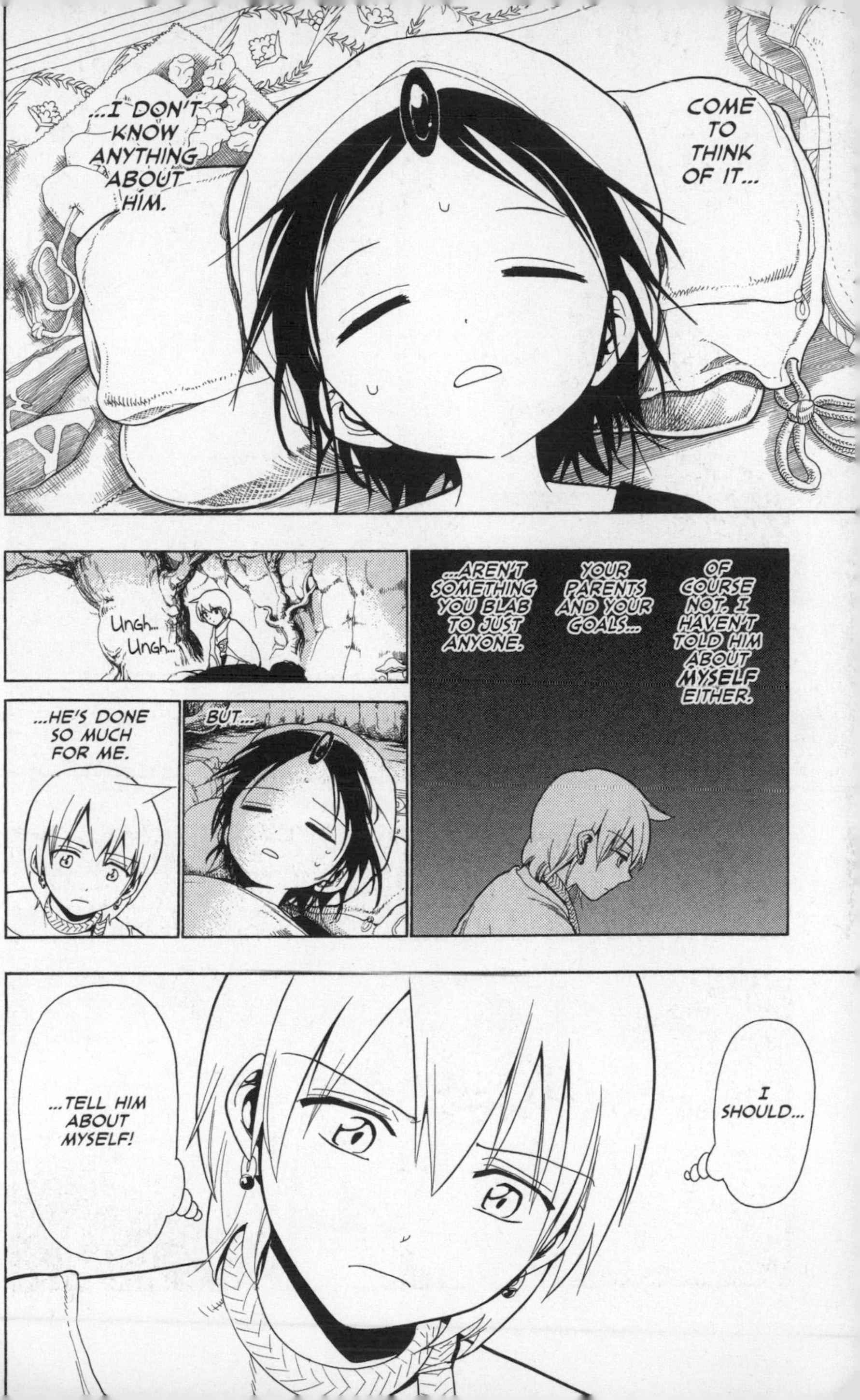
COME TO THINK OF IT...
...I DON'T KNOW ANYTHING ABOUT HIM.
OF COURSE NOT. I HAVEN'T TOLD HIM ABOUT MYSELF EITHER.
YOUR PARENTS AND YOUR GOALS...
...AREN'T SOMETHING YOU BLAB TO JUST ANYONE.
Ungh... Ungh...
BUT...
...HE'S DONE SO MUCH FOR ME.
I SHOULD...
...TELL HIM ABOUT MYSELF!

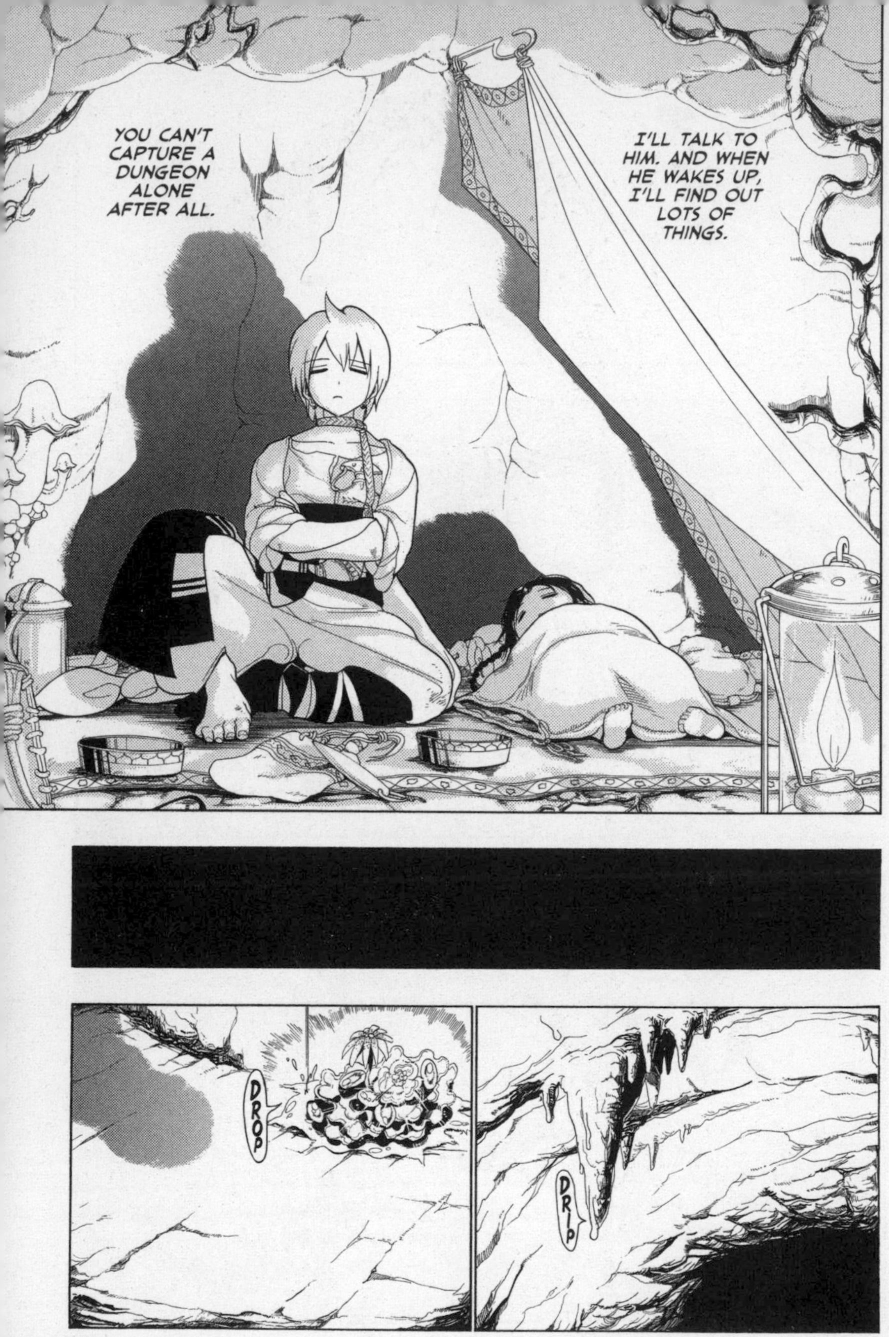
I'LL TALK TO HIM. AND WHEN HE WAKES UP, I'LL FIND OUT LOTS OF THINGS.
YOU CAN'T CAPTURE A DUNGEON ALONE AFTER ALL.
DRIP
DROP

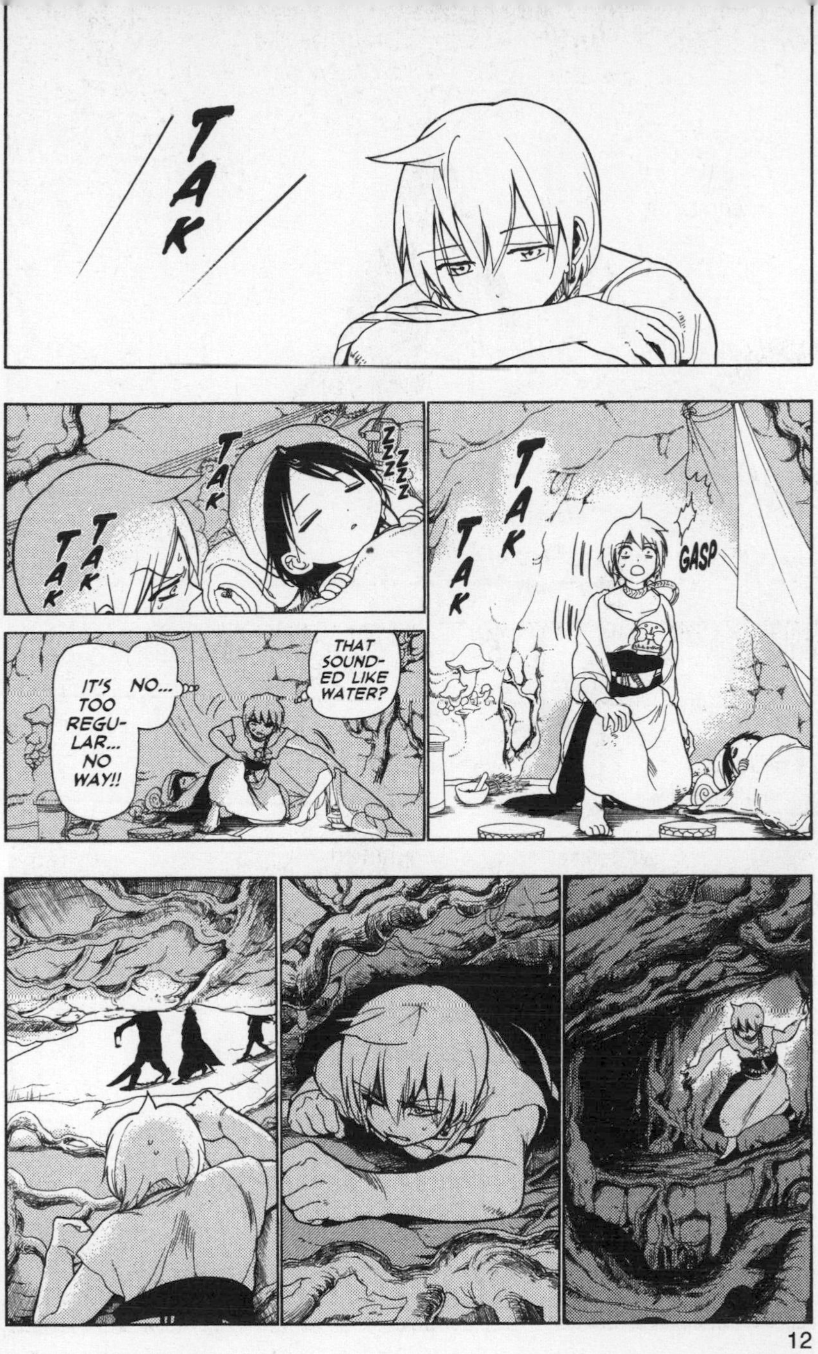
TAK
TAK
TAK
GASP
TAK
TAK
TAK
TAK
ZZZ
ZZZ
THAT SOUNDED LIKE WATER?
NO...
IT'S TOO REGULAR... NO WAY!!

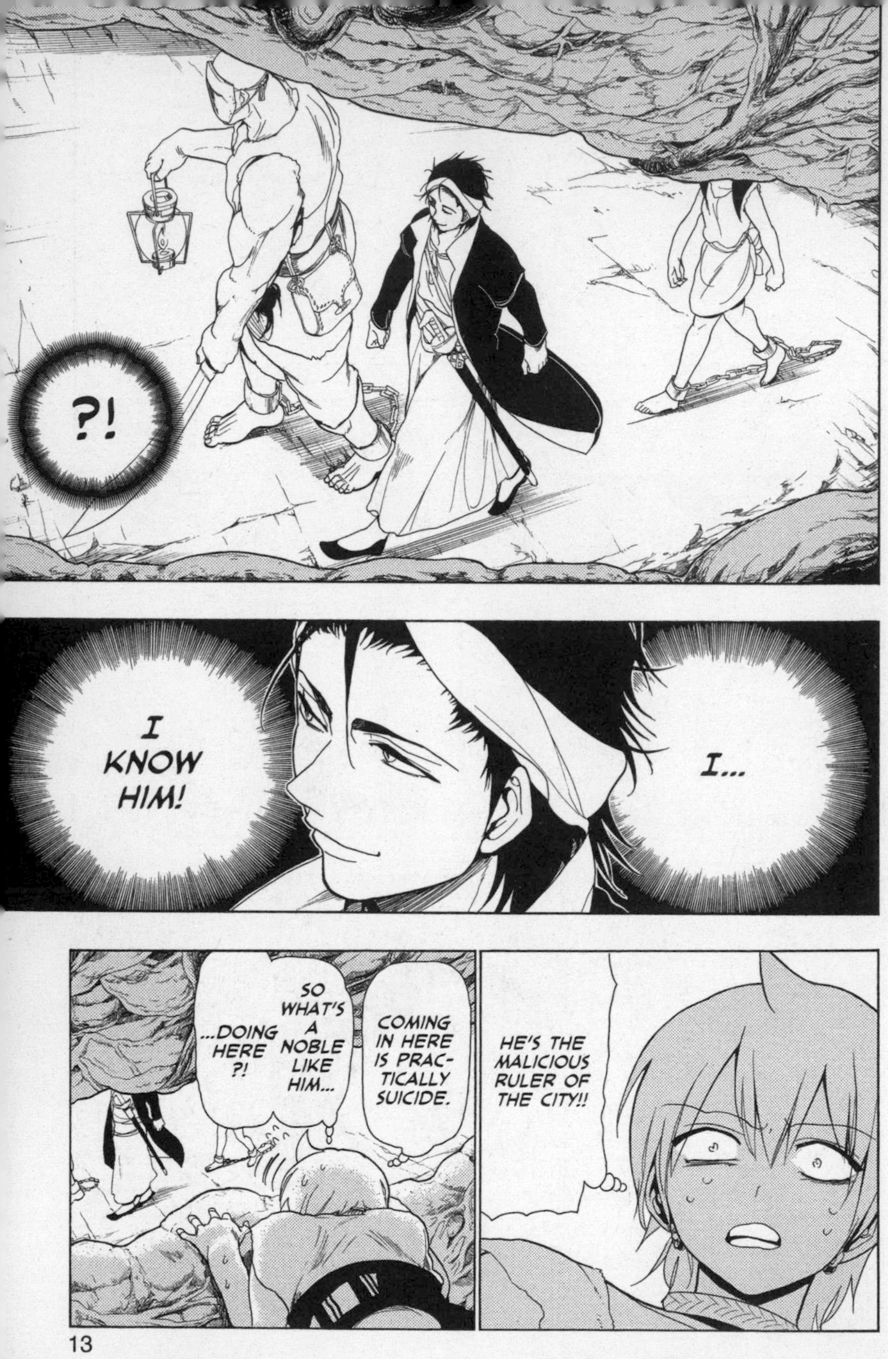
?!
I...
I KNOW HIM!
HE'S THE MALICIOUS RULER OF THE CITY!!
COMING IN HERE IS PRAC-TICALLY SUICIDE.
SO WHAT'S A NOBLE LIKE HIM...
...DOING HERE ?!

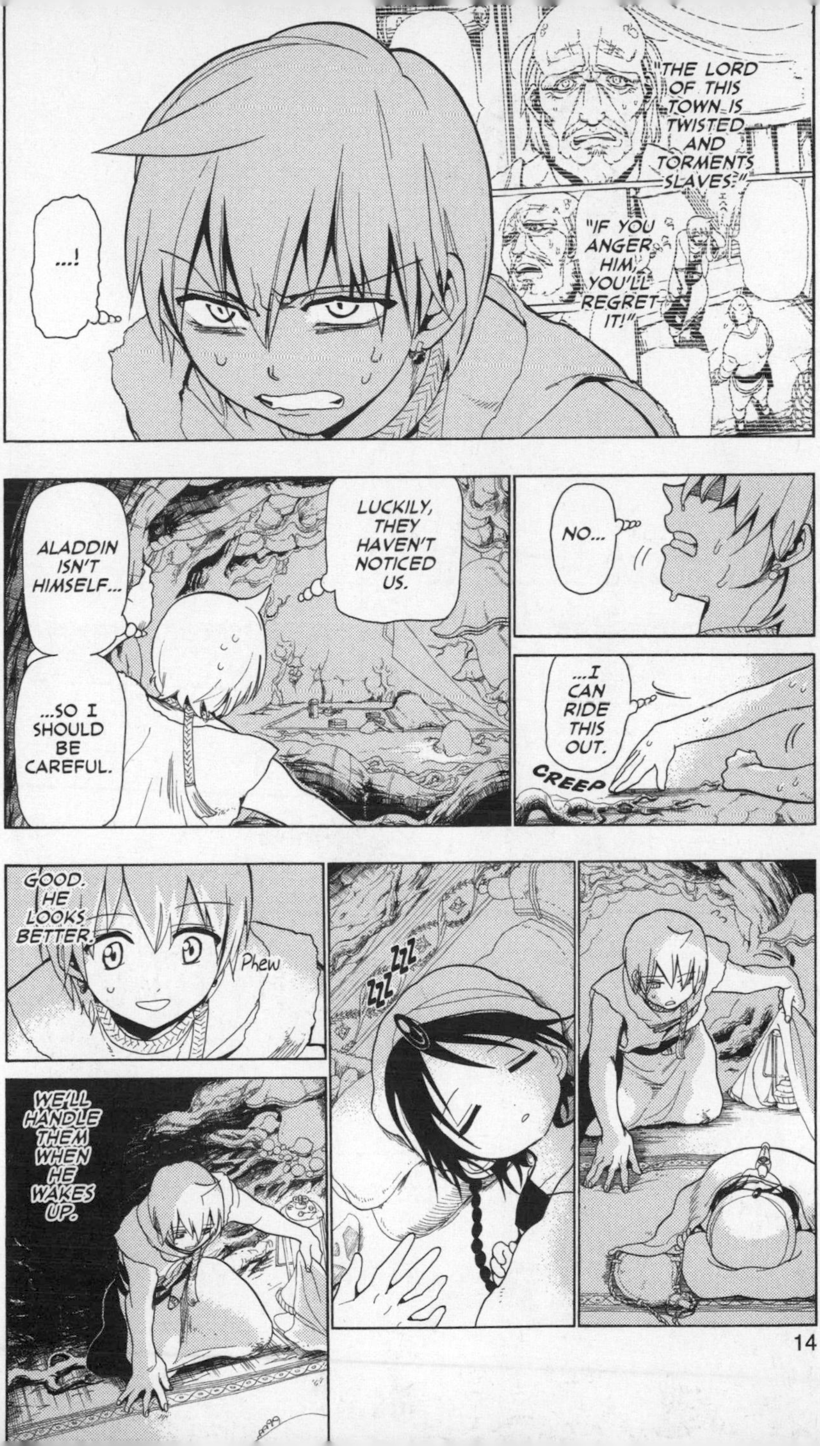
"THE LORD OF THIS TOWN IS TWISTED AND TORMENTS SLAVES."
"IF YOU ANGER HIM, YOU'LL REGRET IT!"
...!
NO...
...I CAN RIDE THIS OUT.
CREEP
LUCKILY, THEY HAVEN'T NOTICED US.
ALADDIN ISN'T HIMSELF...
...SO I SHOULD BE CAREFUL.
ZZZ
ZZZ
GOOD. HE LOOKS BETTER.
Phew
WE'LL HANDLE THEM WHEN HE WAKES UP.

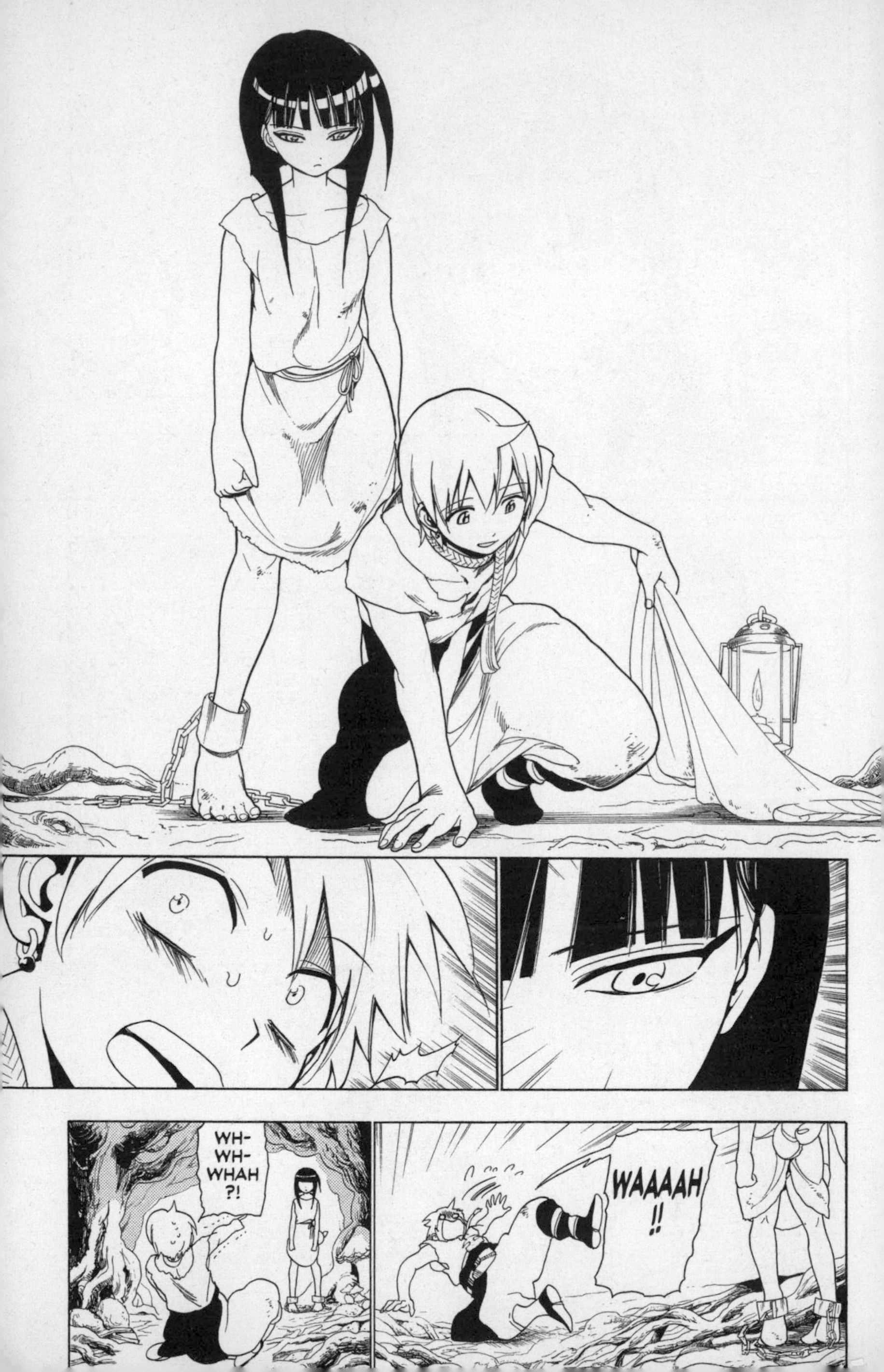
WAAAAH !!
WH- WH- WHAH ?!

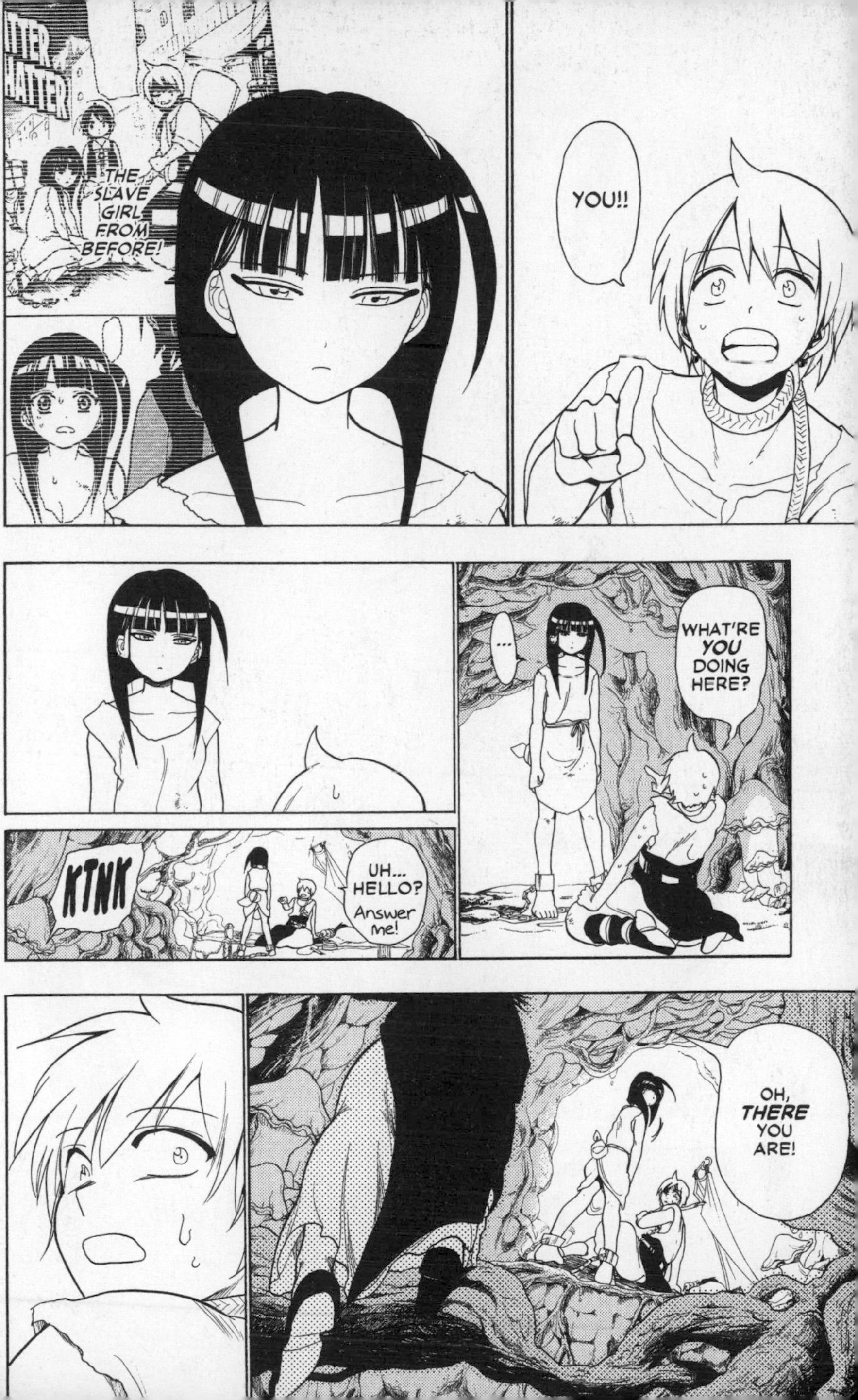
YOU!!
THE SLAVE GIRL FROM BEFORE!
...
WHAT'RE *YOU* DOING HERE?
KTNK
UH... HELLO? Answer me!
OH, *THERE* YOU ARE!

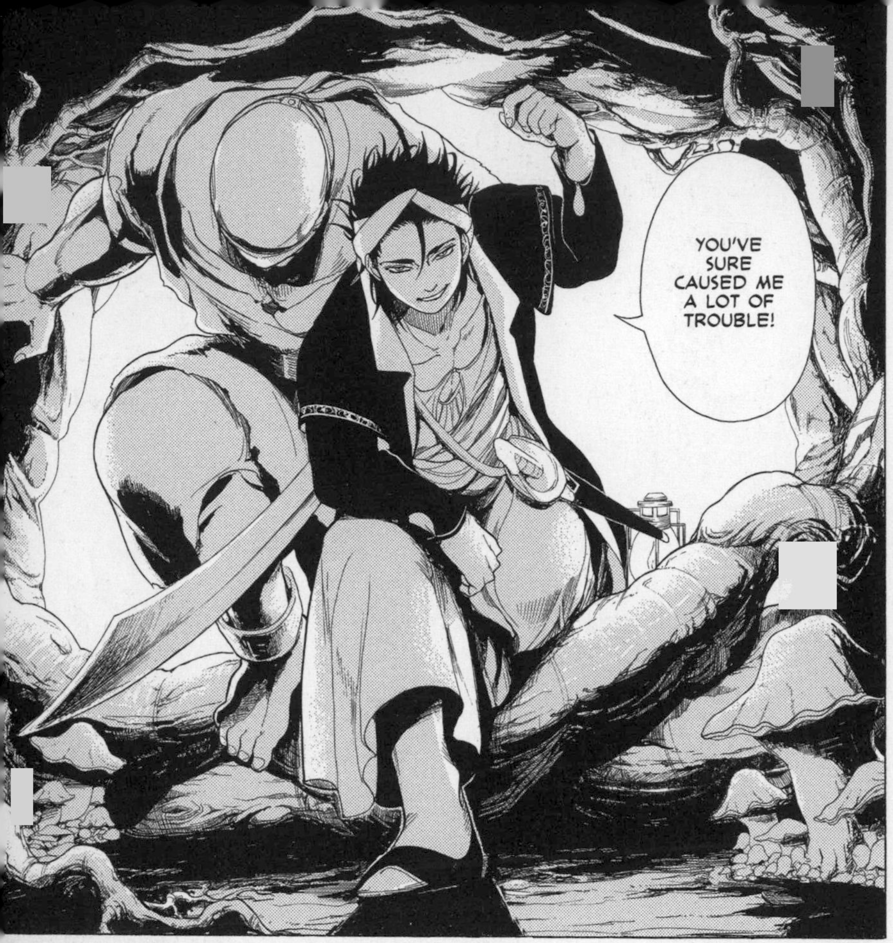
YOU'VE SURE CAUSED ME A LOT OF TROUBLE!

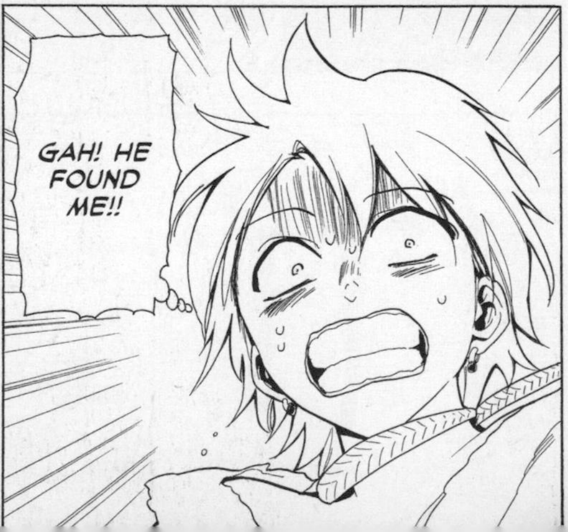
GAH! HE FOUND ME!!

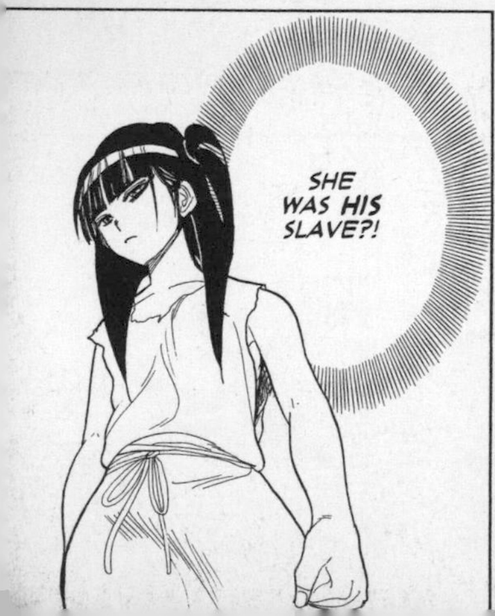
SHE WAS HIS SLAVE?!

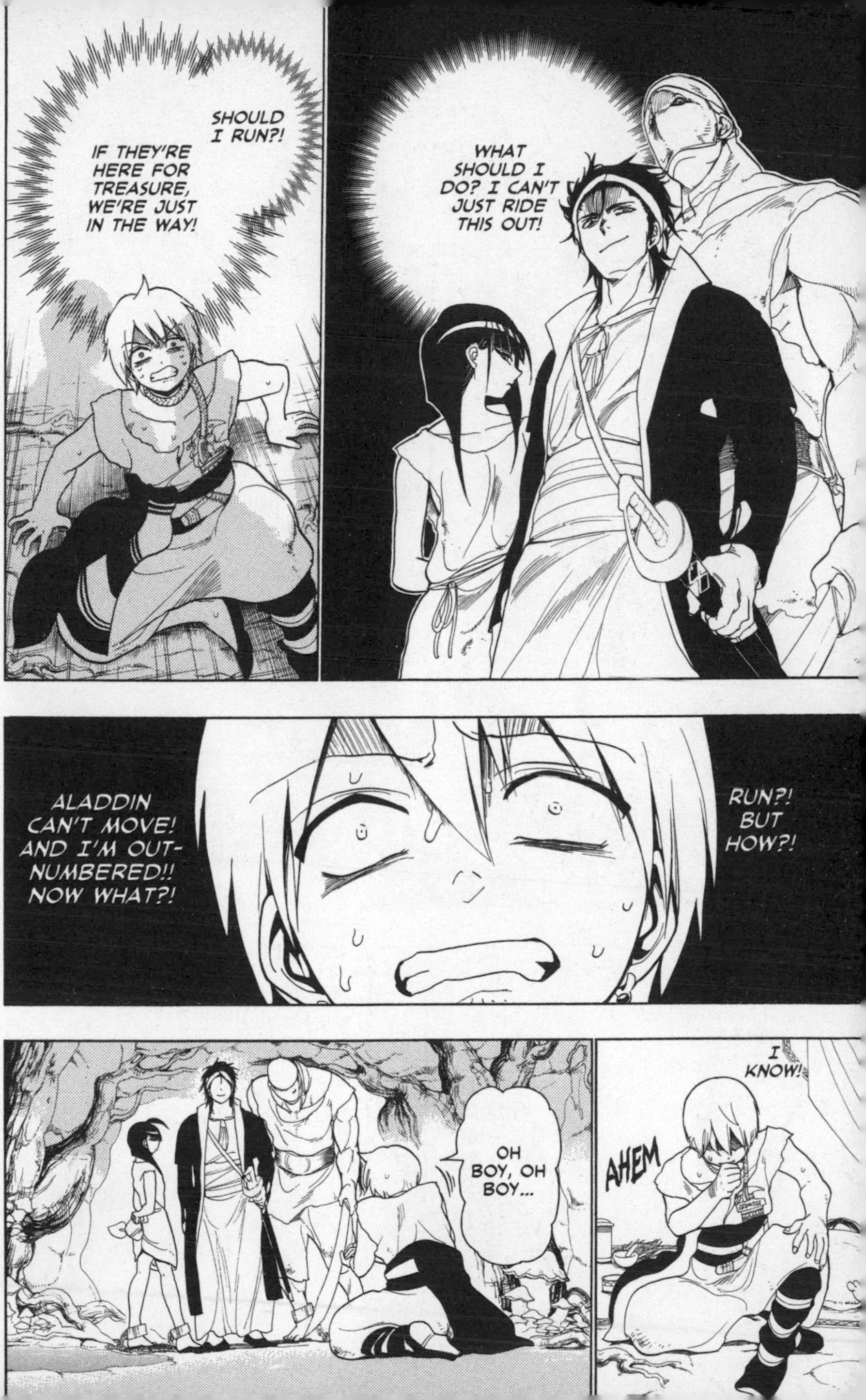
WHAT SHOULD I DO? I CAN'T JUST RIDE THIS OUT!
SHOULD I RUN?!
IF THEY'RE HERE FOR TREASURE, WE'RE JUST IN THE WAY!
RUN?! BUT HOW?!
ALADDIN CAN'T MOVE! AND I'M OUT-NUMBERED!! NOW WHAT?!
I KNOW!
AHEM
OH BOY, OH BOY...

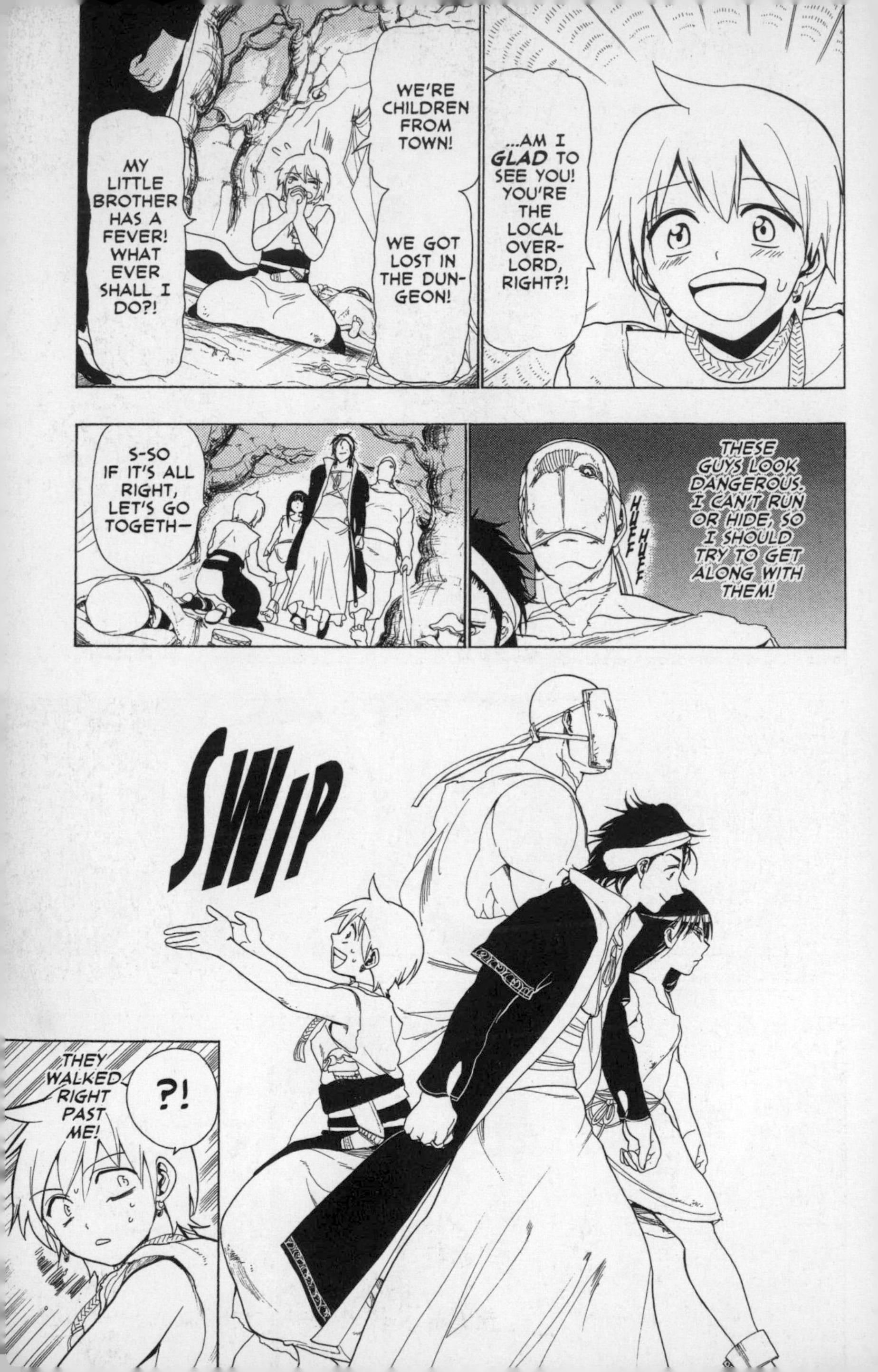
...AM I GLAD TO SEE YOU! YOU'RE THE LOCAL OVER-LORD, RIGHT?!
WE'RE CHILDREN FROM TOWN!
WE GOT LOST IN THE DUN-GEON!
MY LITTLE BROTHER HAS A FEVER! WHAT EVER SHALL I DO?!
HUFF HUFF
THESE GUYS LOOK DANGEROUS. I CAN'T RUN OR HIDE, SO I SHOULD TRY TO GET ALONG WITH THEM!
S-SO IF IT'S ALL RIGHT, LET'S GO TOGETH—
SWIP
?!
THEY WALKED RIGHT PAST ME!

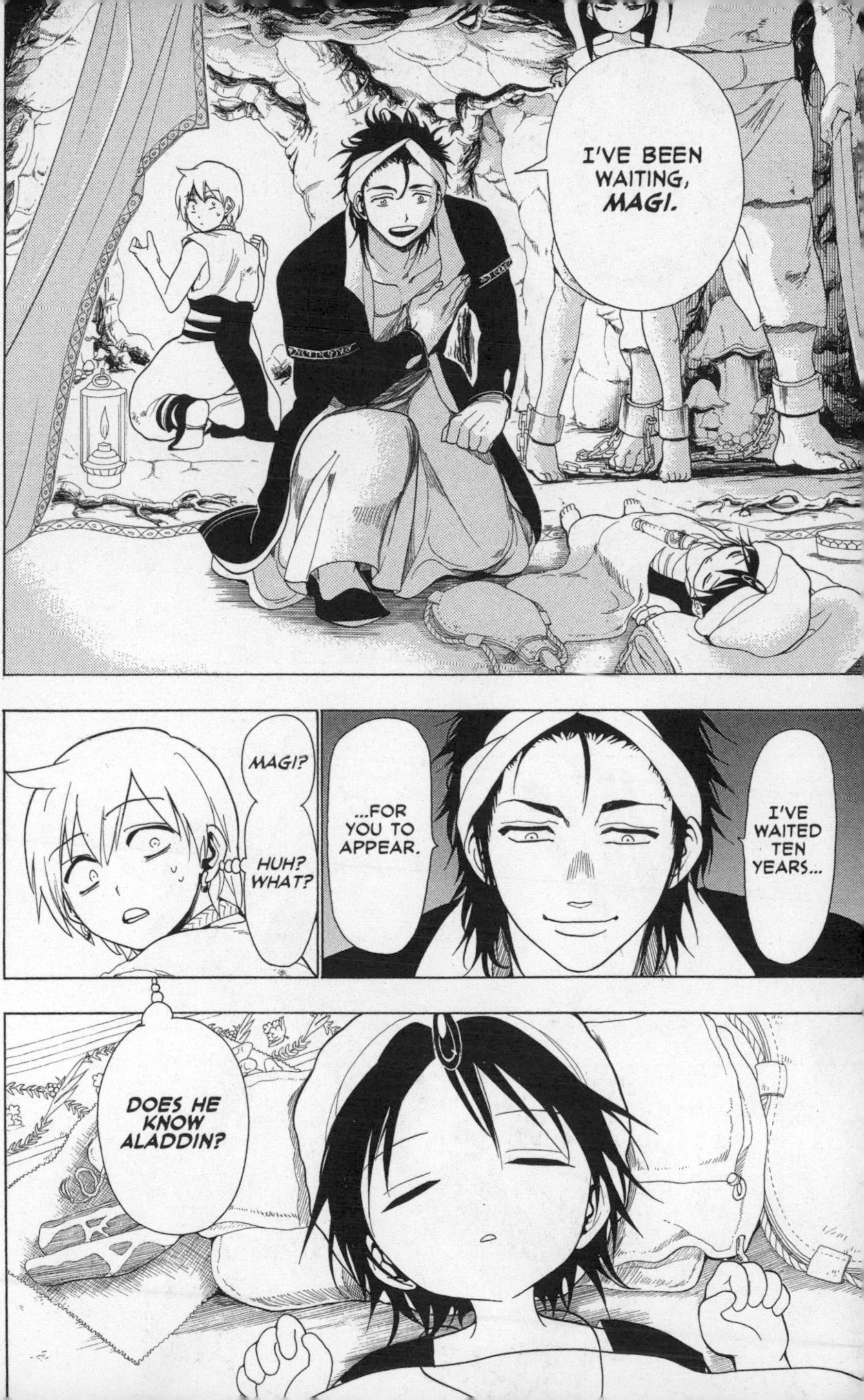
I'VE BEEN WAITING, MAGI.
I'VE WAITED TEN YEARS...
...FOR YOU TO APPEAR.
MAGI?
HUH? WHAT?
DOES HE KNOW ALADDIN?

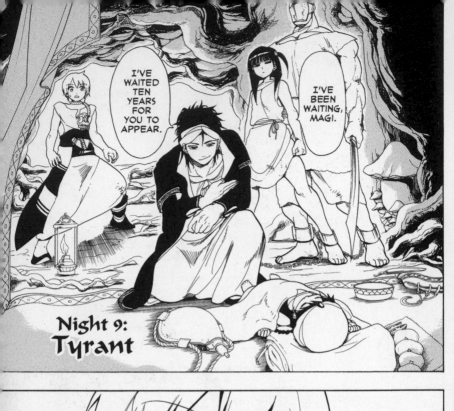

I'VE WAITED TEN YEARS FOR YOU TO APPEAR.

I'VE BEEN WAITING, MAGI.

Night 9: Tyrant

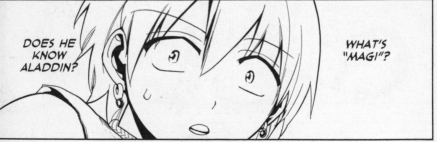

WHAT'S "MAGI"?

DOES HE KNOW ALADDIN?

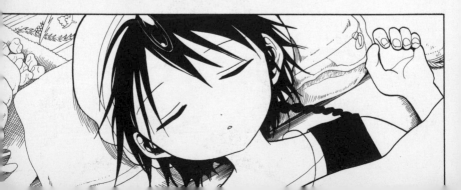

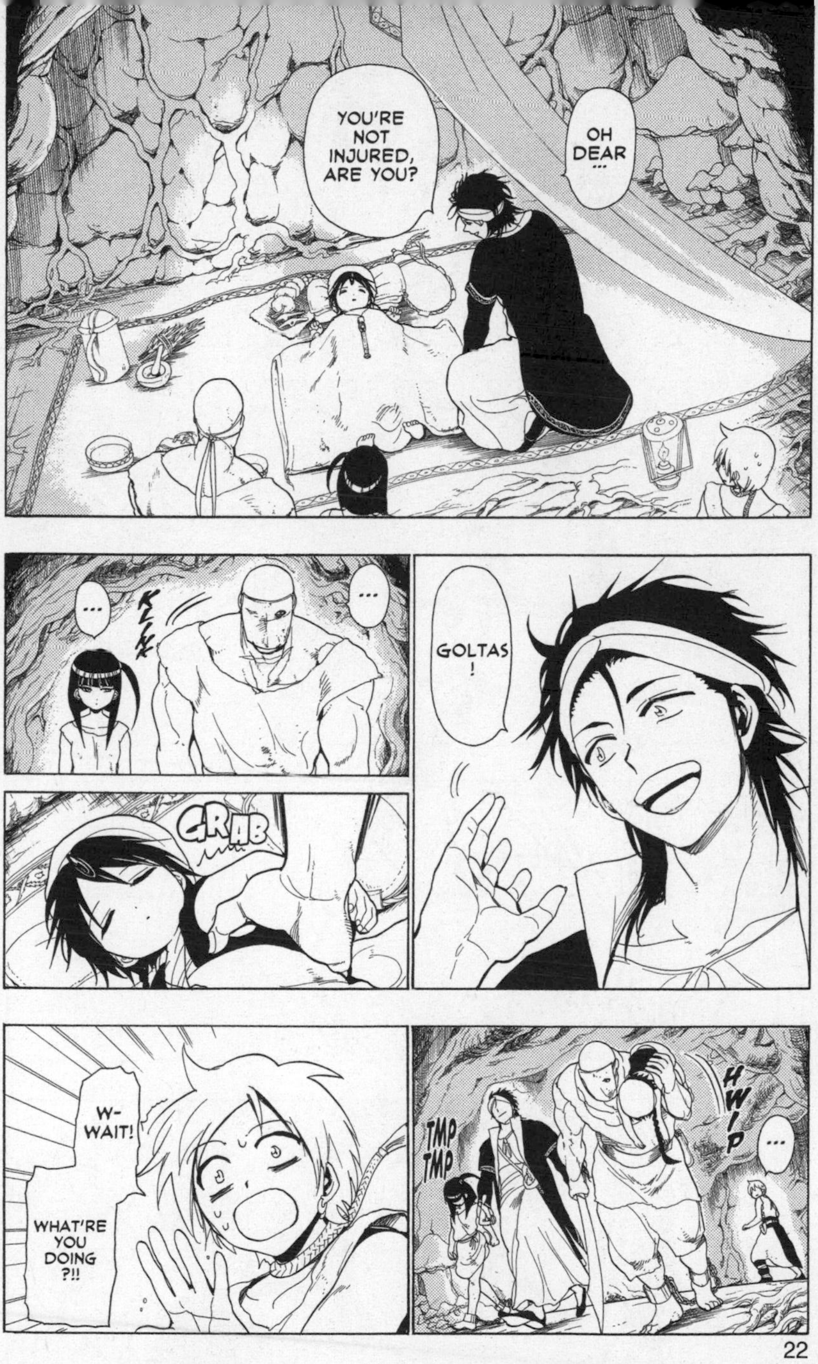
OH DEAR ...
YOU'RE NOT INJURED, ARE YOU?
GOLTAS!
...
...
GRAB
HWIP
...
TMP TMP
W-WAIT!
WHAT'RE YOU DOING?!!

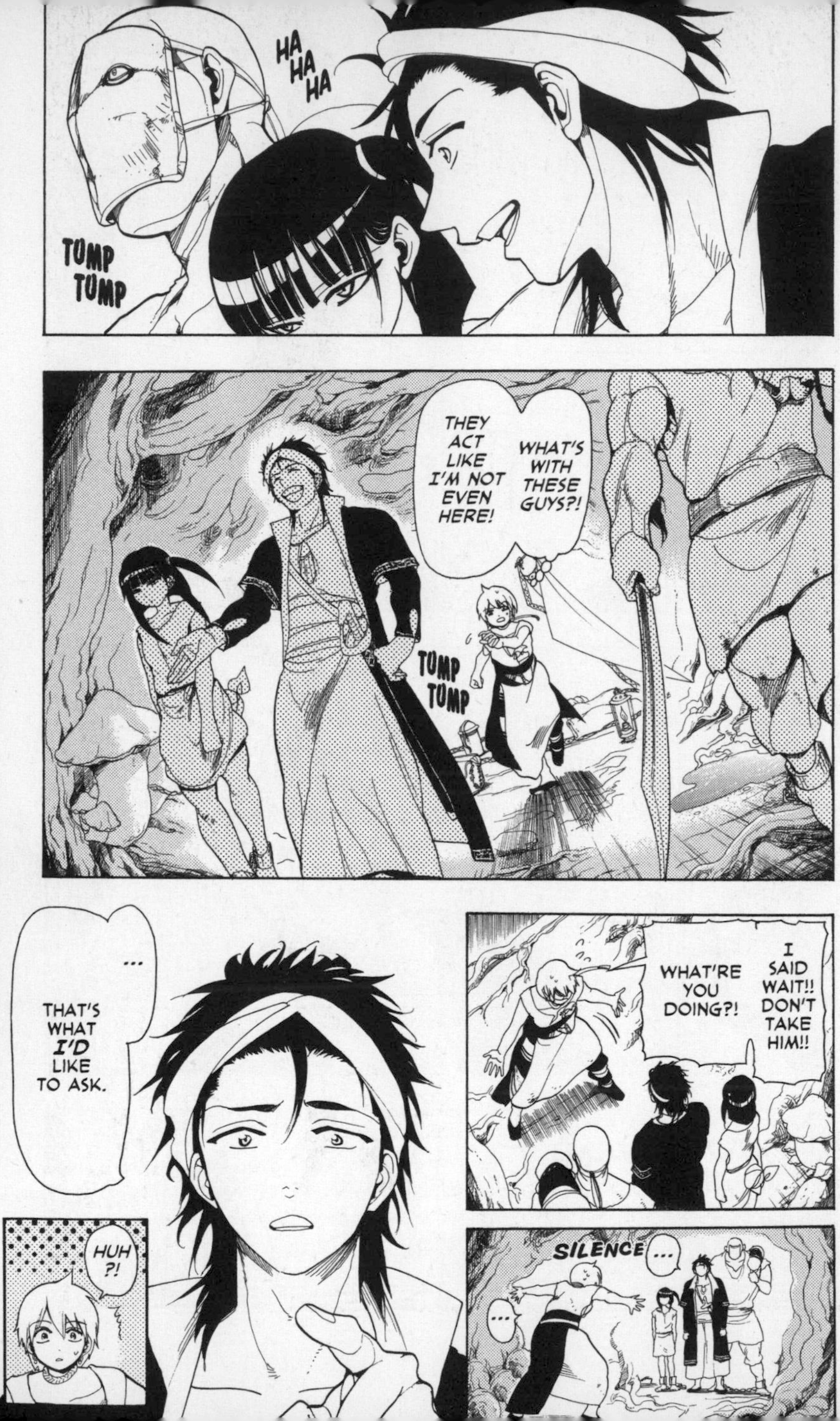
HA HA HA
TUMP TUMP
WHAT'S WITH THESE GUYS?!
THEY ACT LIKE I'M NOT EVEN HERE!
TUMP TUMP
I SAID WAIT!! DON'T TAKE HIM!!
WHAT'RE YOU DOING?!
SILENCE
...
...
...
THAT'S WHAT *I'D* LIKE TO ASK.
HUH ?!

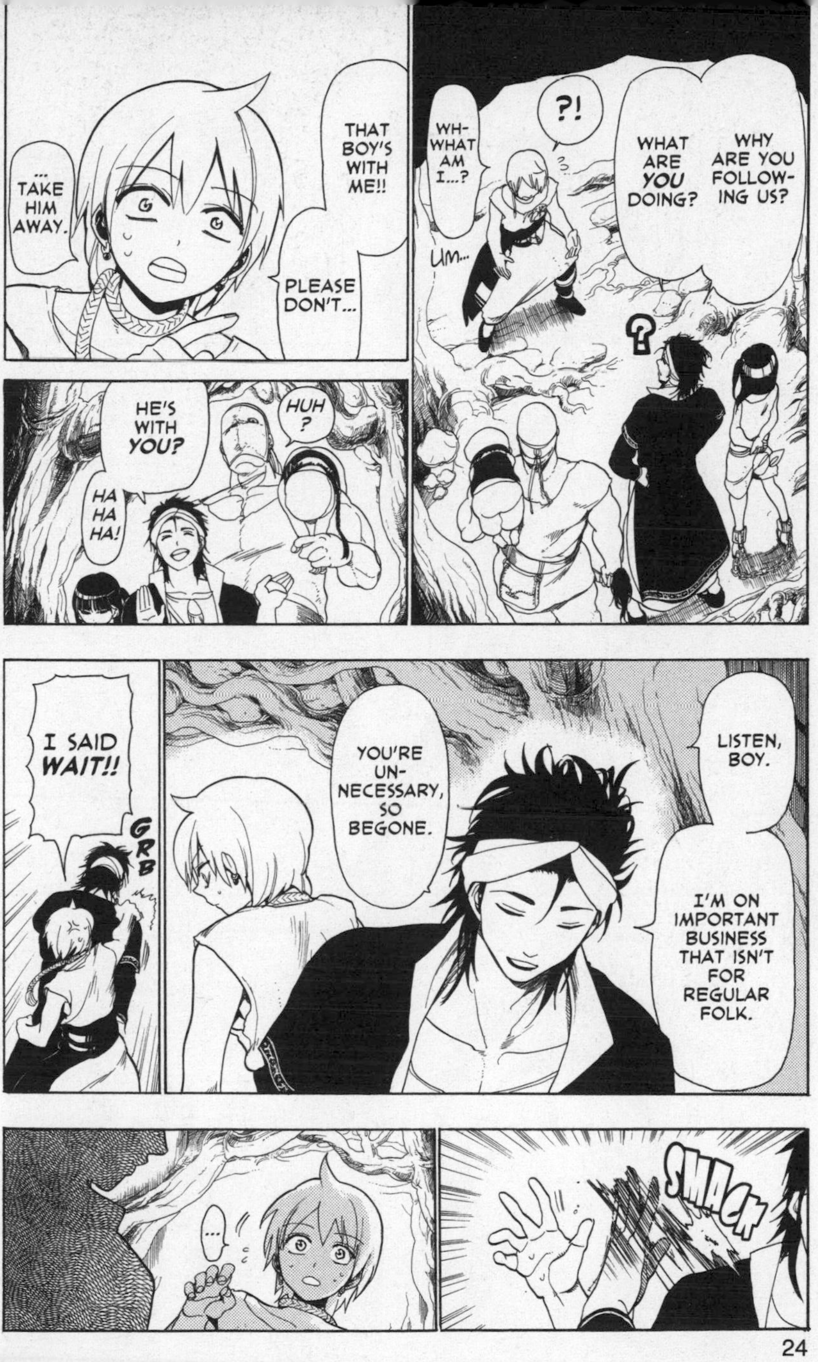
WHY ARE YOU FOLLOW-ING US?
WHAT ARE *YOU* DOING?
?!
WH-WHAT AM I...?
UM...
?
THAT BOY'S WITH ME!!
PLEASE DON'T...
...TAKE HIM AWAY.
HUH?
HE'S WITH *YOU?*
HA HA HA!
LISTEN, BOY.
I'M ON IMPORTANT BUSINESS THAT ISN'T FOR REGULAR FOLK.
YOU'RE UN-NECESSARY, SO BEGONE.
GRB
I SAID *WAIT!!*
SMACK
...

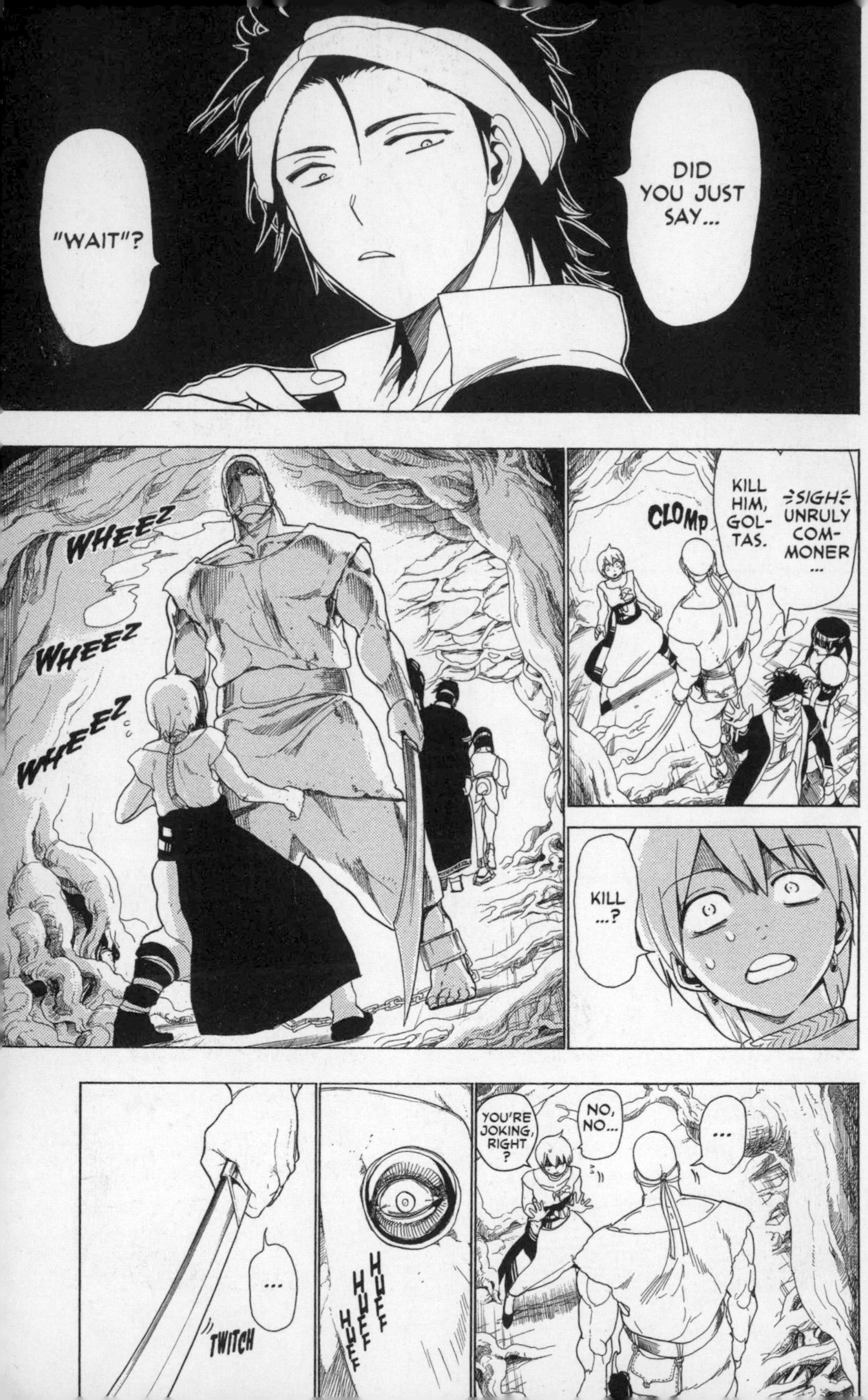
DID YOU JUST SAY...
"WAIT"?
≠SIGH≠ UNRULY COM-MONER...
KILL HIM, GOL-TAS.
CLOMP
KILL...?
WHEEZ
WHEEZ
WHEEZ
...
NO, NO...
YOU'RE JOKING, RIGHT?
HUFF HUFF
HUFF HUFF
...
TWITCH

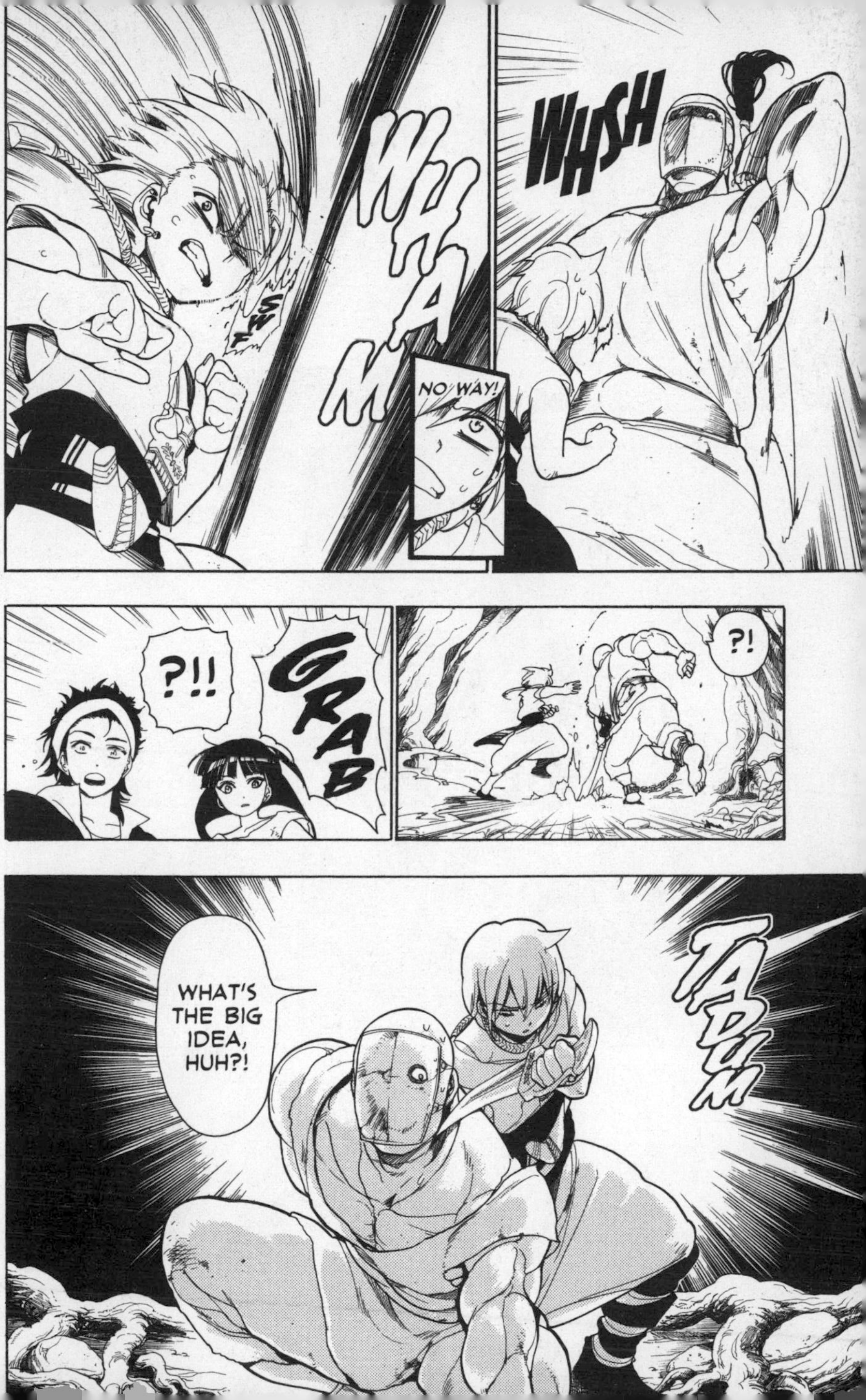
WHSH
WHAM
SWF
NO WAY!
?!
GRAB
?!!
TADUM
WHAT'S THE BIG IDEA, HUH?!

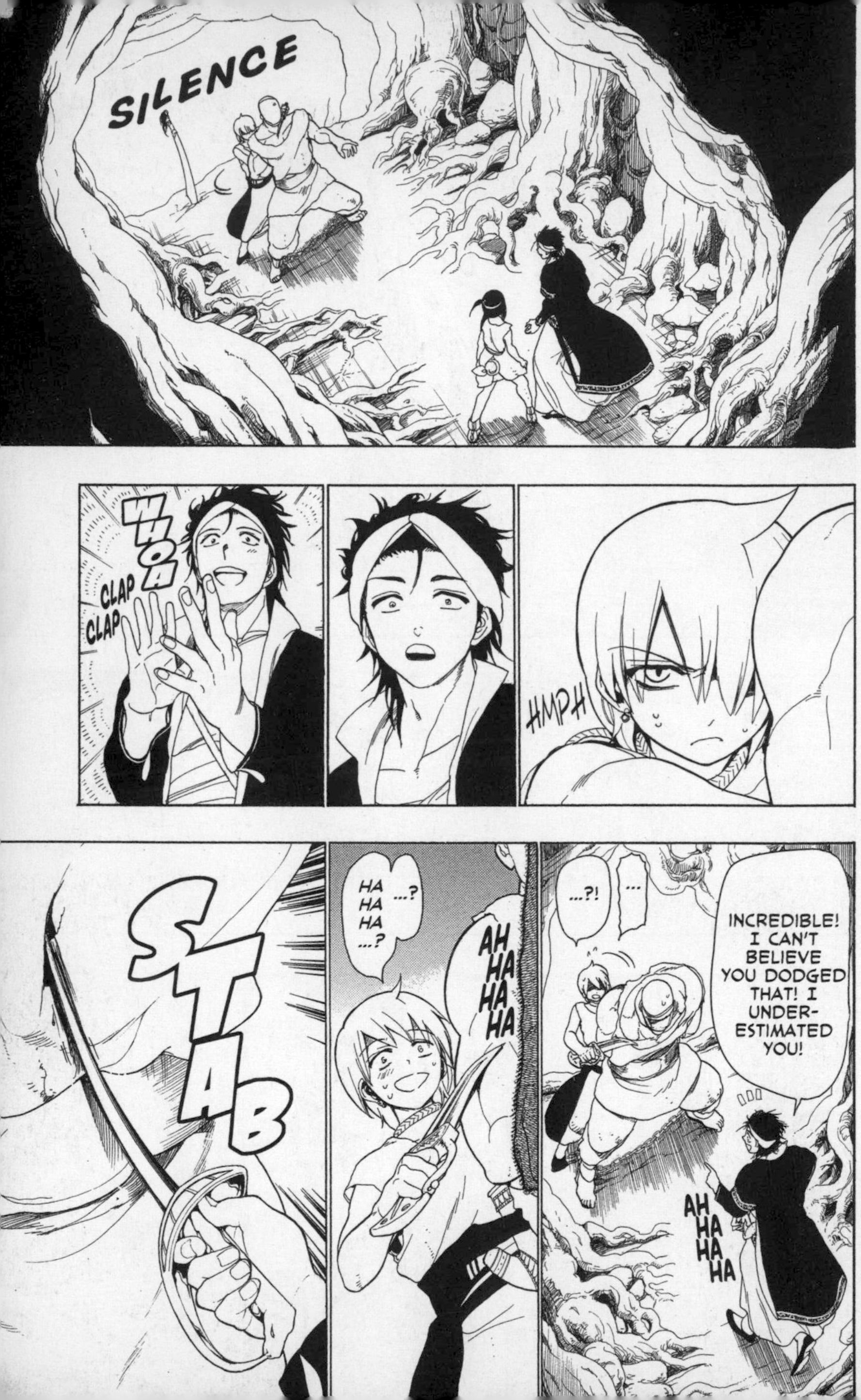
SILENCE
HMPH
WHOA
CLAP CLAP
...
...?!
INCREDIBLE! I CAN'T BELIEVE YOU DODGED THAT! I UNDER-ESTIMATED YOU!
AH HA HA HA HA
...?
HA HA HA ...?
AH HA HA HA HA
STAB

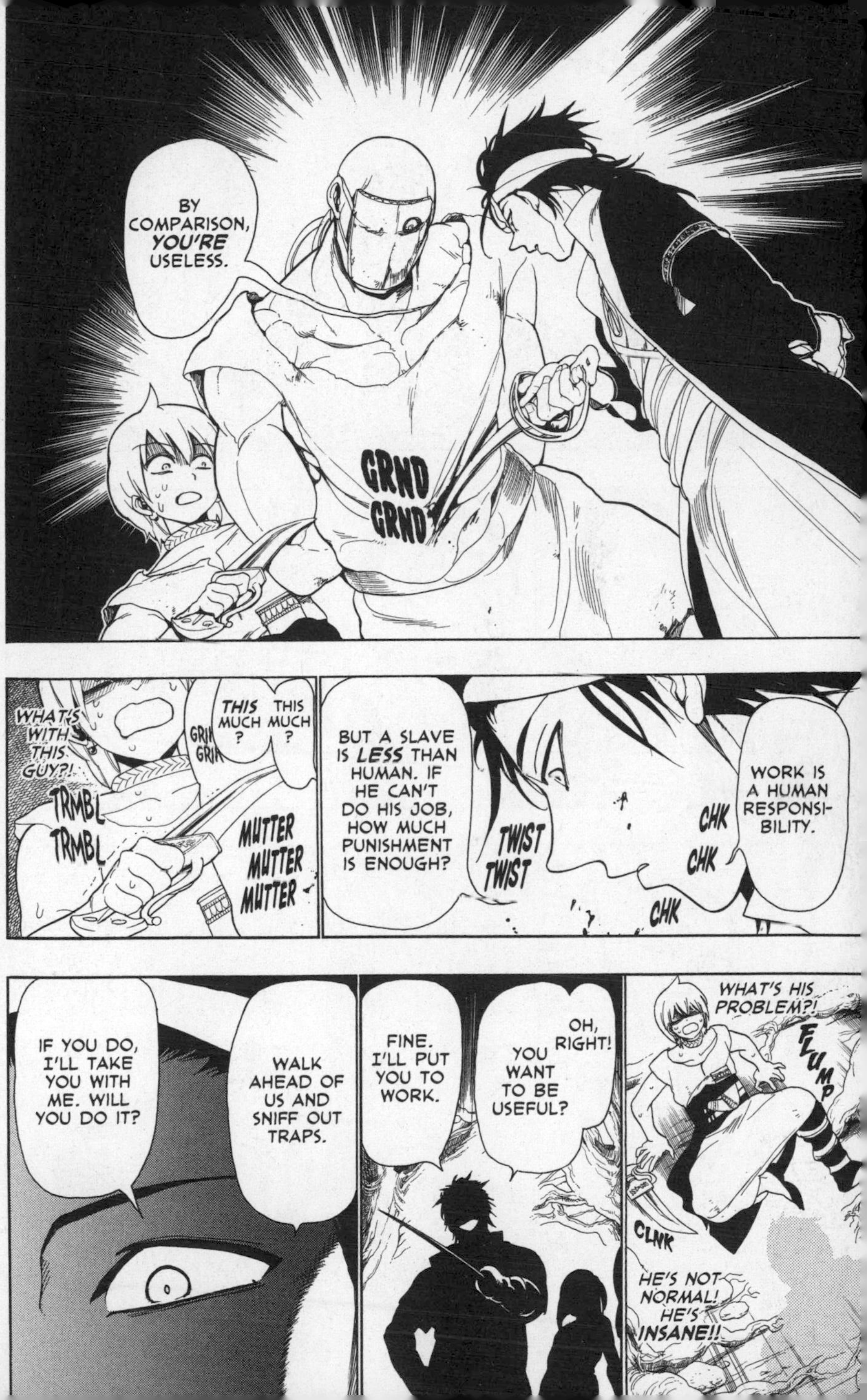
BY COMPARISON, *YOU'RE* USELESS.
GRND GRND
WORK IS A HUMAN RESPONSI-BILITY.
CHK CHK CHK
BUT A SLAVE IS *LESS* THAN HUMAN. IF HE CAN'T DO HIS JOB, HOW MUCH PUNISHMENT IS ENOUGH?
TWIST TWIST
THIS MUCH ?
THIS MUCH ?
WHAT'S WITH THIS GUY?!
TRMBL TRMBL
MUTTER MUTTER MUTTER
WHAT'S HIS PROBLEM?!
FLUMP
CLNK
HE'S NOT NORMAL! HE'S *INSANE!!*
OH, RIGHT!
YOU WANT TO BE USEFUL?
FINE. I'LL PUT YOU TO WORK.
WALK AHEAD OF US AND SNIFF OUT TRAPS.
IF YOU DO, I'LL TAKE YOU WITH ME. WILL YOU DO IT?

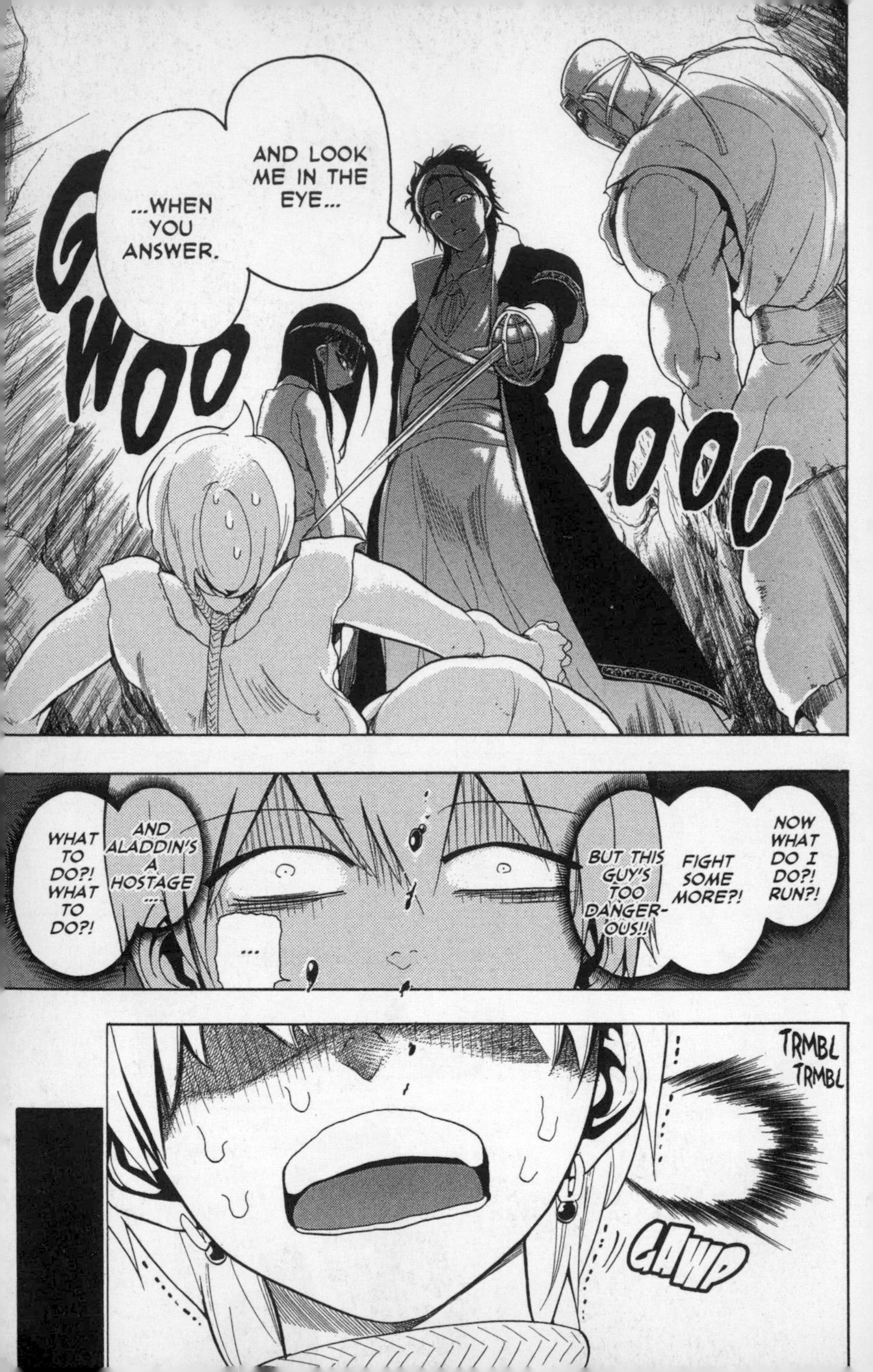
AND LOOK ME IN THE EYE...
...WHEN YOU ANSWER.
GWOOOOOOO
NOW WHAT DO I DO?! RUN?!
FIGHT SOME MORE?!
BUT THIS GUY'S TOO DANGER-OUS!!
...
AND ALADDIN'S A HOSTAGE ...
WHAT TO DO?! WHAT TO DO?!
TRMBL TRMBL
!
GAWP

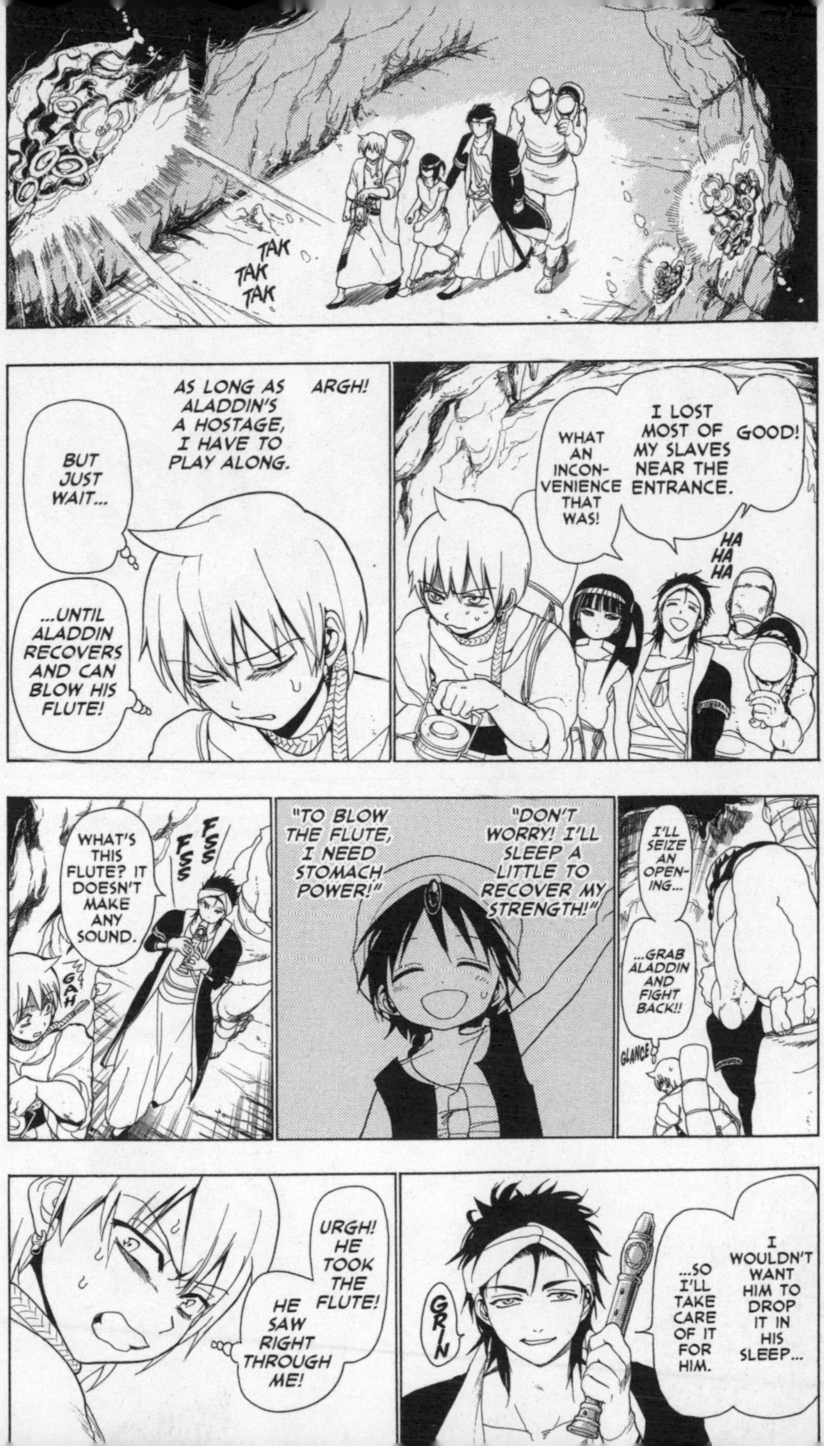
TAK TAK TAK
GOOD!
I LOST MOST OF MY SLAVES NEAR THE ENTRANCE.
WHAT AN INCONVENIENCE THAT WAS!
HA HA HA
ARGH!
AS LONG AS ALADDIN'S A HOSTAGE, I HAVE TO PLAY ALONG.
BUT JUST WAIT...
...UNTIL ALADDIN RECOVERS AND CAN BLOW HIS FLUTE!
I'LL SEIZE AN OPENING...
...GRAB ALADDIN AND FIGHT BACK!!
GLANCE
"DON'T WORRY! I'LL SLEEP A LITTLE TO RECOVER MY STRENGTH!"
"TO BLOW THE FLUTE, I NEED STOMACH POWER!"
FSS FSS
WHAT'S THIS FLUTE? IT DOESN'T MAKE ANY SOUND.
GAH
I WOULDN'T WANT HIM TO DROP IT IN HIS SLEEP...
...SO I'LL TAKE CARE OF IT FOR HIM.
GRIN
URGH! HE TOOK THE FLUTE!
HE SAW RIGHT THROUGH ME!

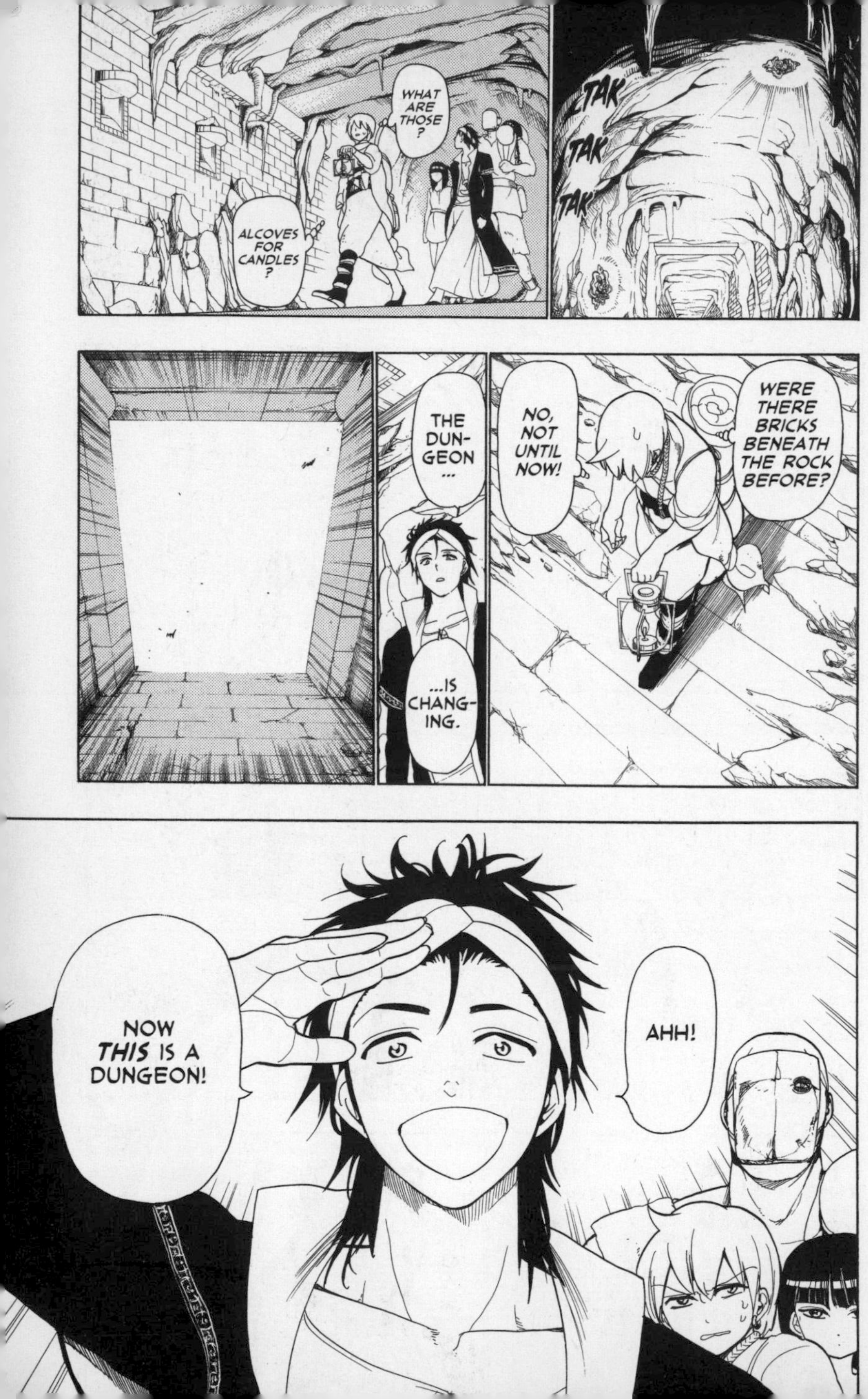
TAK
TAK
TAK
WHAT ARE THOSE?
ALCOVES FOR CANDLES?
WERE THERE BRICKS BENEATH THE ROCK BEFORE?
NO, NOT UNTIL NOW!
THE DUN-GEON...
...IS CHANG-ING.
AHH!
NOW *THIS* IS A DUNGEON!

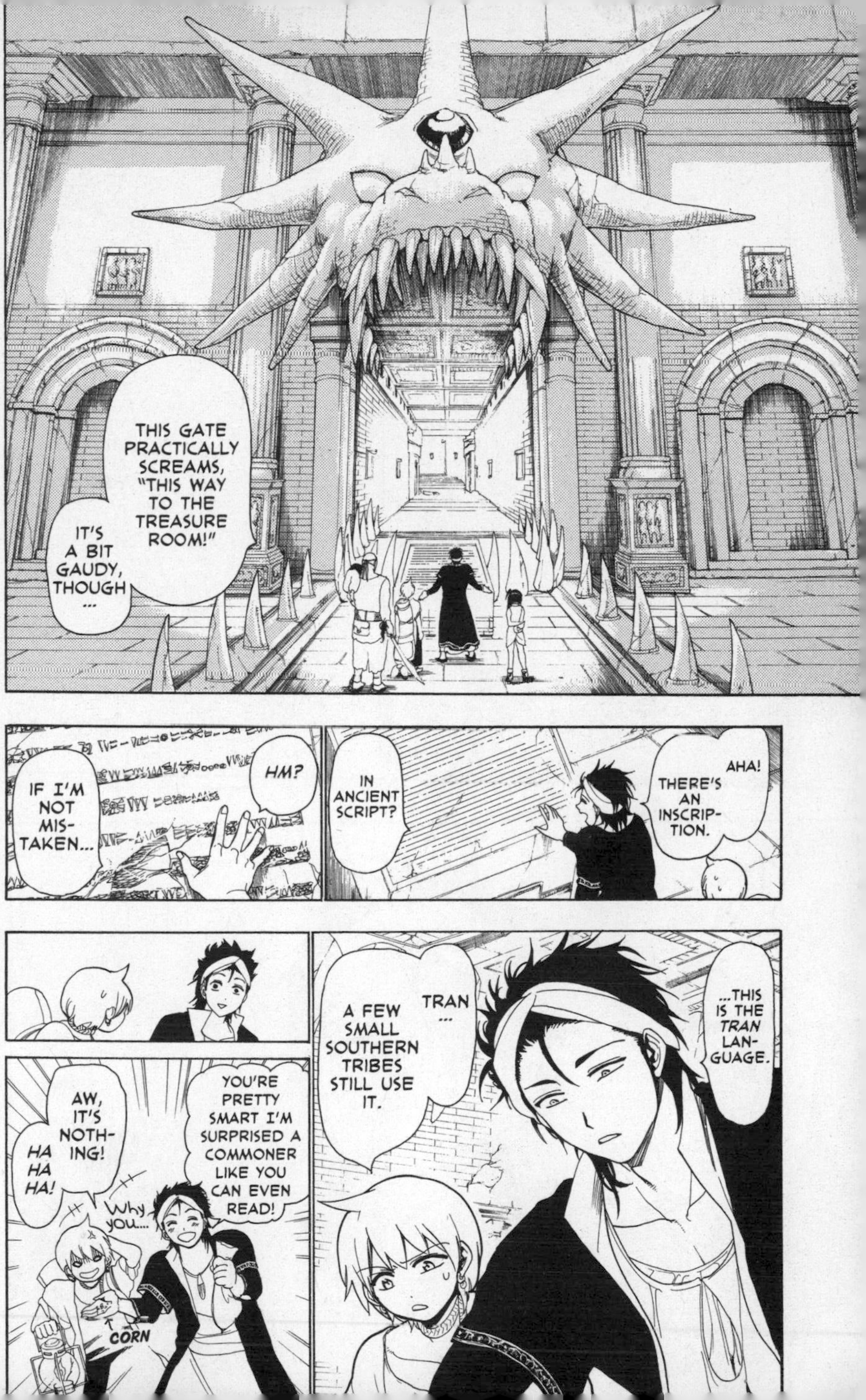
THIS GATE PRACTICALLY SCREAMS, "THIS WAY TO THE TREASURE ROOM!"
IT'S A BIT GAUDY, THOUGH ...
AHA! THERE'S AN INSCRIP- TION.
IN ANCIENT SCRIPT?
HM?
IF I'M NOT MIS- TAKEN...
...THIS IS THE *TRAN* LAN- GUAGE.
TRAN ...
A FEW SMALL SOUTHERN TRIBES STILL USE IT.
YOU'RE PRETTY SMART I'M SURPRISED A COMMONER LIKE YOU CAN EVEN READ!
AW, IT'S NOTH- ING!
HA HA HA!
Why you....
CORN

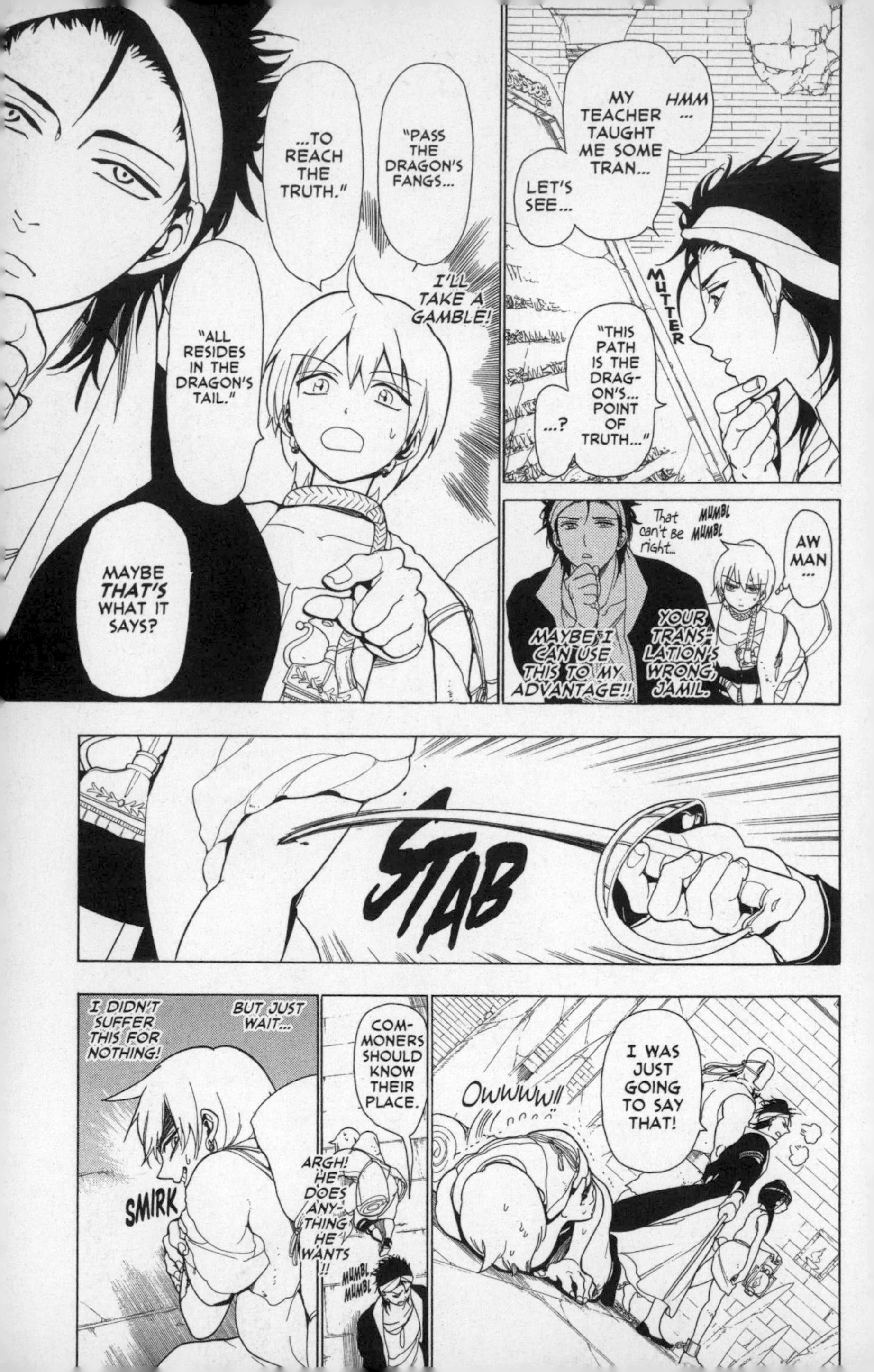
HMM...
MY TEACHER TAUGHT ME SOME TRAN...
LET'S SEE...
MUTTER
"THIS PATH IS THE DRAG-ON'S... POINT OF TRUTH..."
...?
AW MAN...
MUMBL MUMBL
That can't be right...
YOUR TRANS-LATION'S WRONG, JAMIL.
MAYBE I CAN USE THIS TO MY ADVANTAGE!!
"PASS THE DRAGON'S FANGS...
...TO REACH THE TRUTH."
I'LL TAKE A GAMBLE!
"ALL RESIDES IN THE DRAGON'S TAIL."
MAYBE THAT'S WHAT IT SAYS?
STAB
I WAS JUST GOING TO SAY THAT!
OWWWW!!
COM-MONERS SHOULD KNOW THEIR PLACE.
ARGH! HE DOES ANY-THING HE WANTS!!
MUMBL MUMBL
BUT JUST WAIT...
I DIDN'T SUFFER THIS FOR NOTHING!
SMIRK

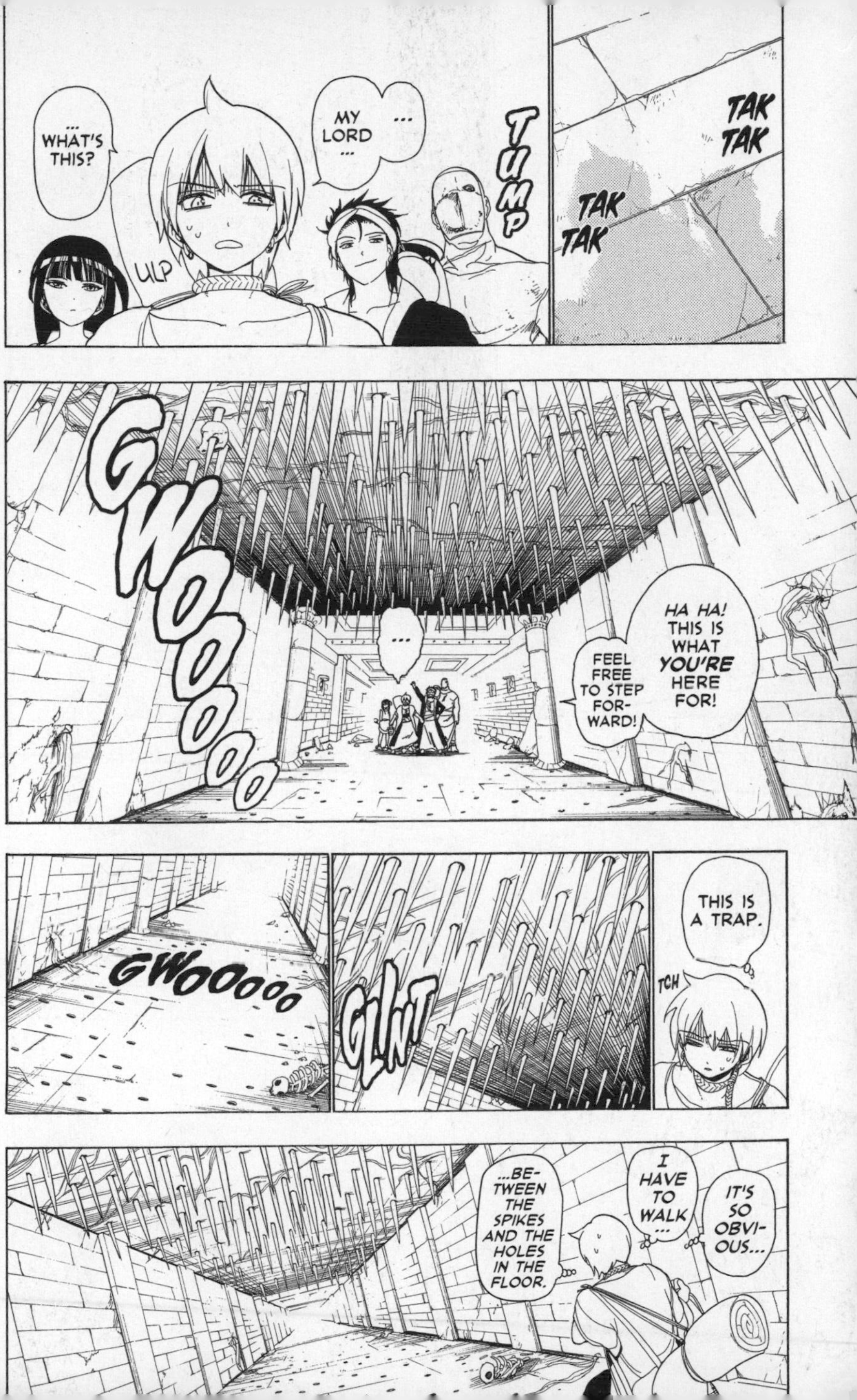
TAK TAK
TAK TAK
TUMP
... MY LORD ...
... WHAT'S THIS?
ULP
HA HA! THIS IS WHAT *YOU'RE* HERE FOR!
FEEL FREE TO STEP FOR-WARD!
...
GWOOOOOO
THIS IS A TRAP.
TCH
GLINT
GWOOOOOO
IT'S SO OBVI-OUS...
I HAVE TO WALK ...
...BE-TWEEN THE SPIKES AND THE HOLES IN THE FLOOR.

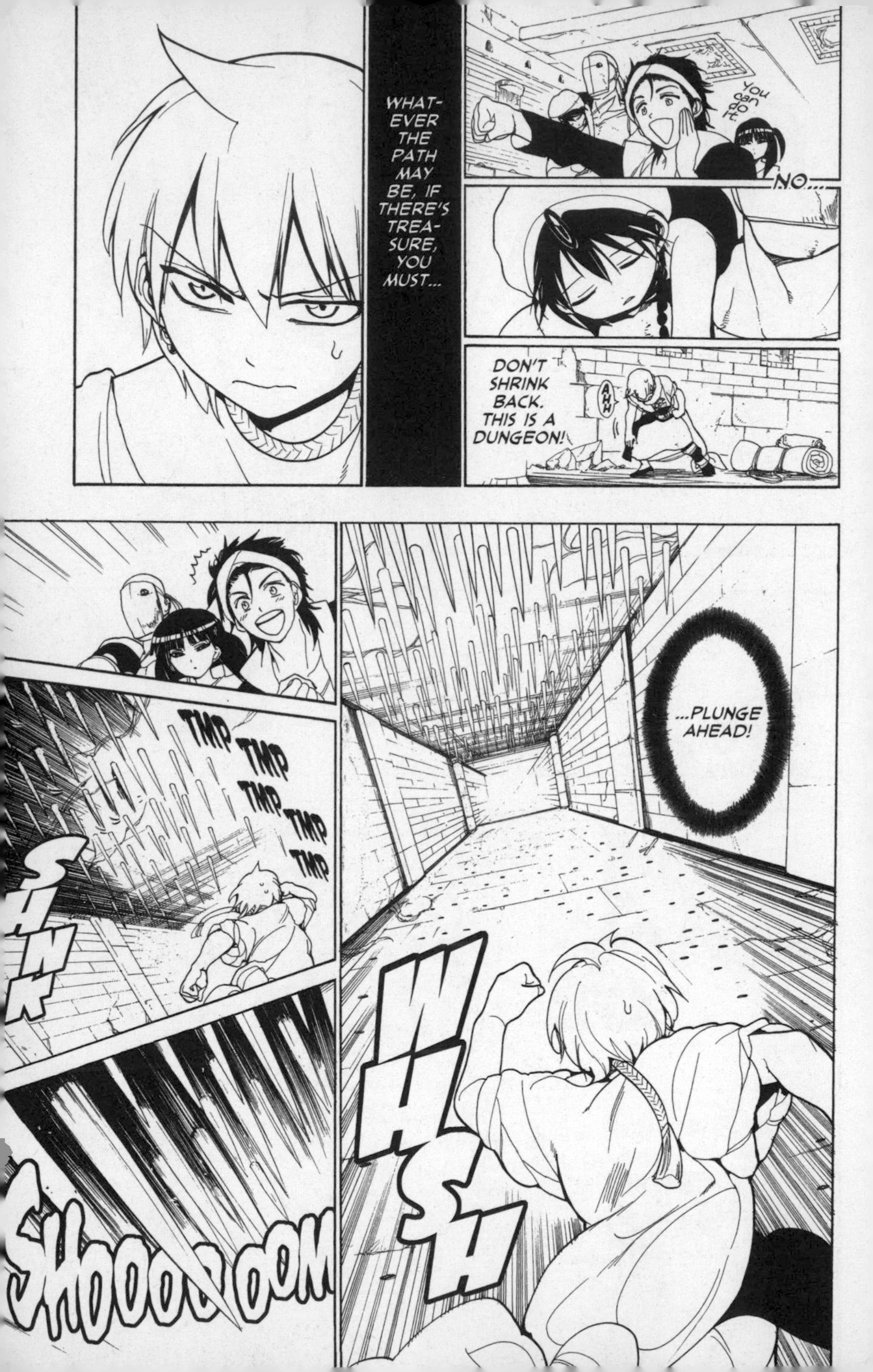
You can do it.
NO...
AHH
DON'T SHRINK BACK. THIS IS A DUNGEON!
WHATEVER THE PATH MAY BE, IF THERE'S TREASURE, YOU MUST...
...PLUNGE AHEAD!
WHSH
TMP TMP TMP TMP TMP
SHNK
SHOOOOOOM

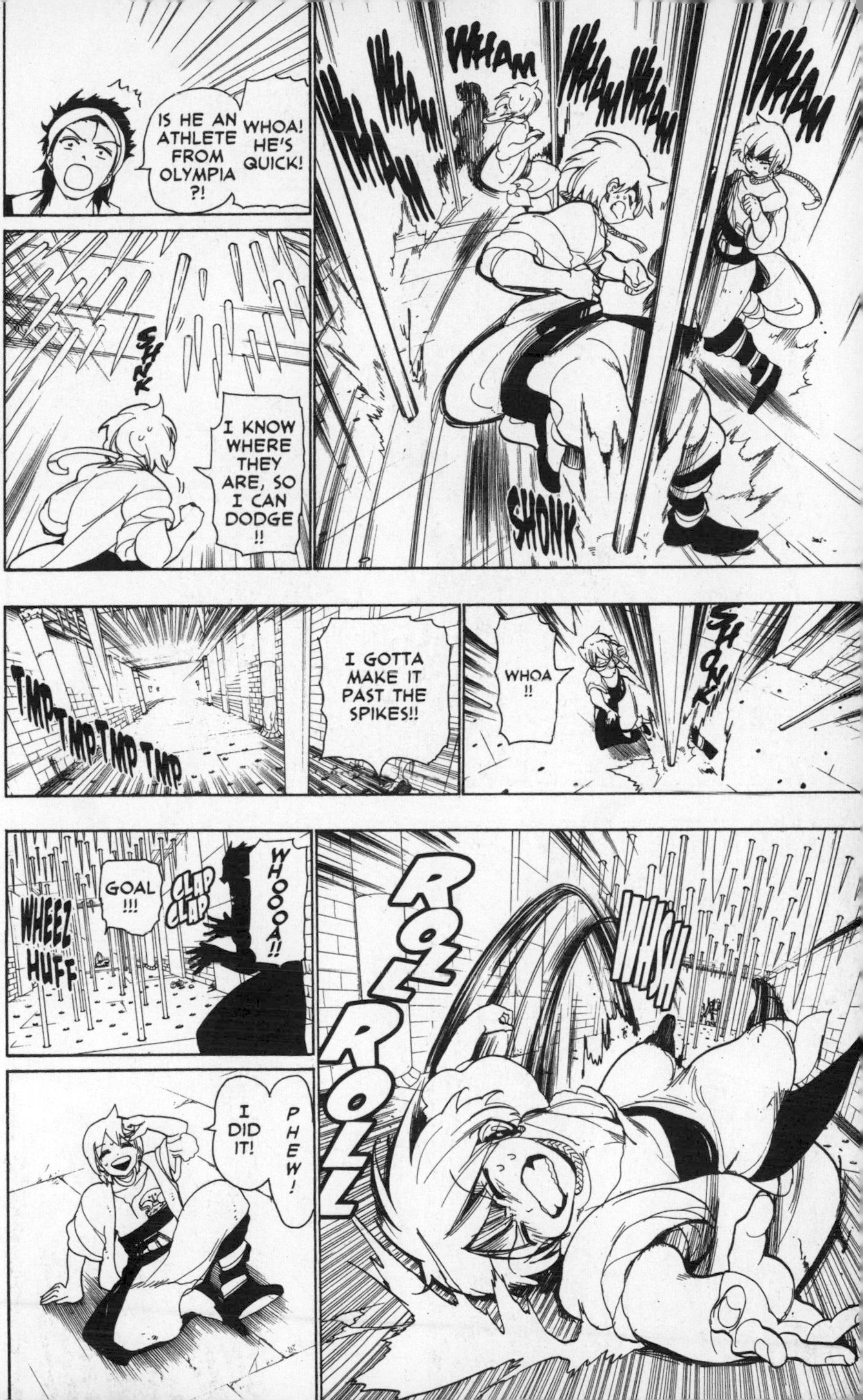
WHAM
WHAM
WHAM
WHAM WHAM WHAM
WHAM
SHONK
WHOA! HE'S QUICK!
IS HE AN ATHLETE FROM OLYMPIA ?!
SHINK
I KNOW WHERE THEY ARE, SO I CAN DODGE !!
SHONK
WHOA !!
I GOTTA MAKE IT PAST THE SPIKES!!
TMP TMP TMP TMP TMP
ROLL ROLL
WHSH
WHOOOA!!
CLAP CLAP
GOAL !!!
WHEEZ HUFF
PHEW!
I DID IT!

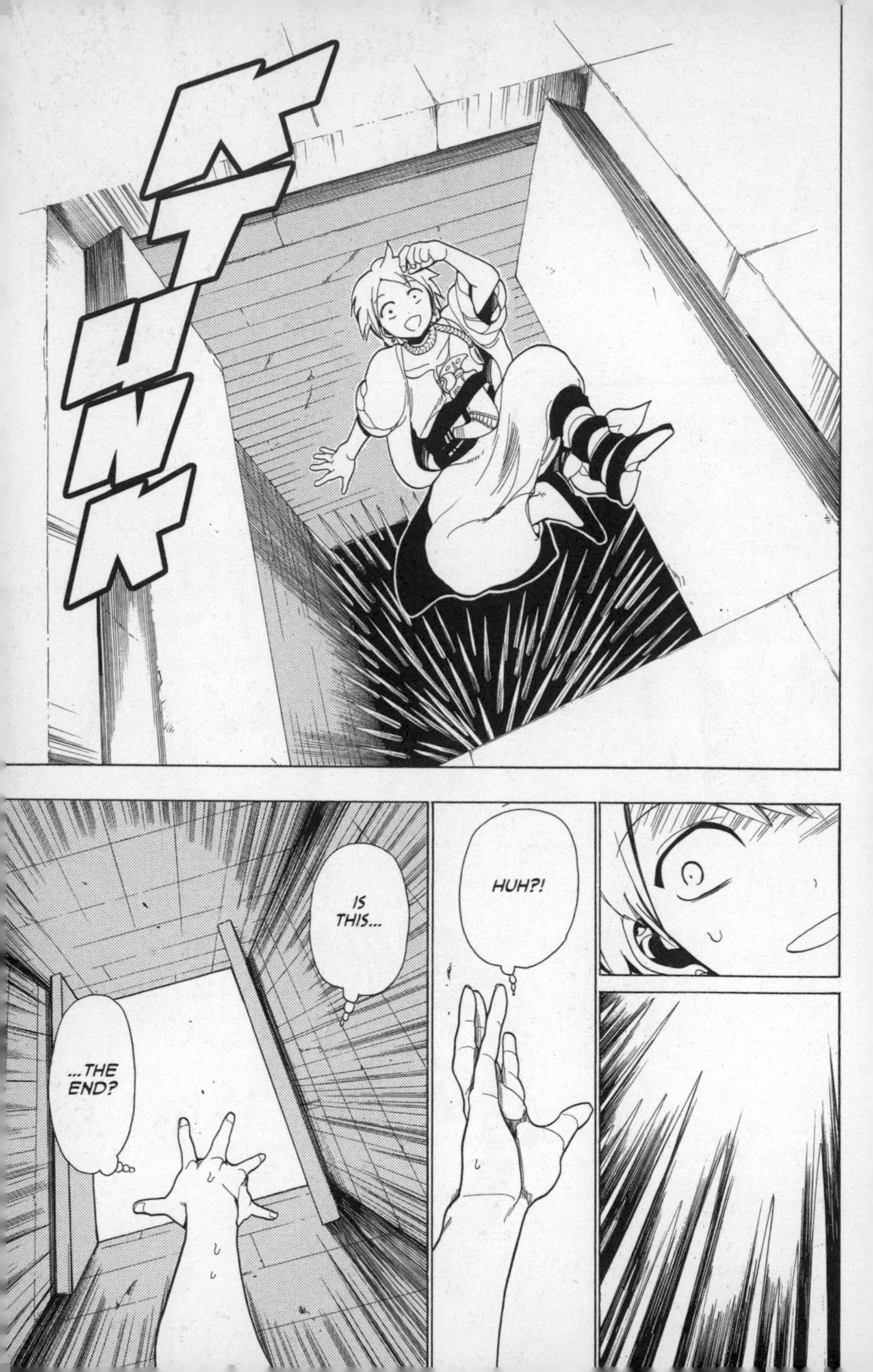
STUNK
HUH?!
IS THIS...
...THE END?

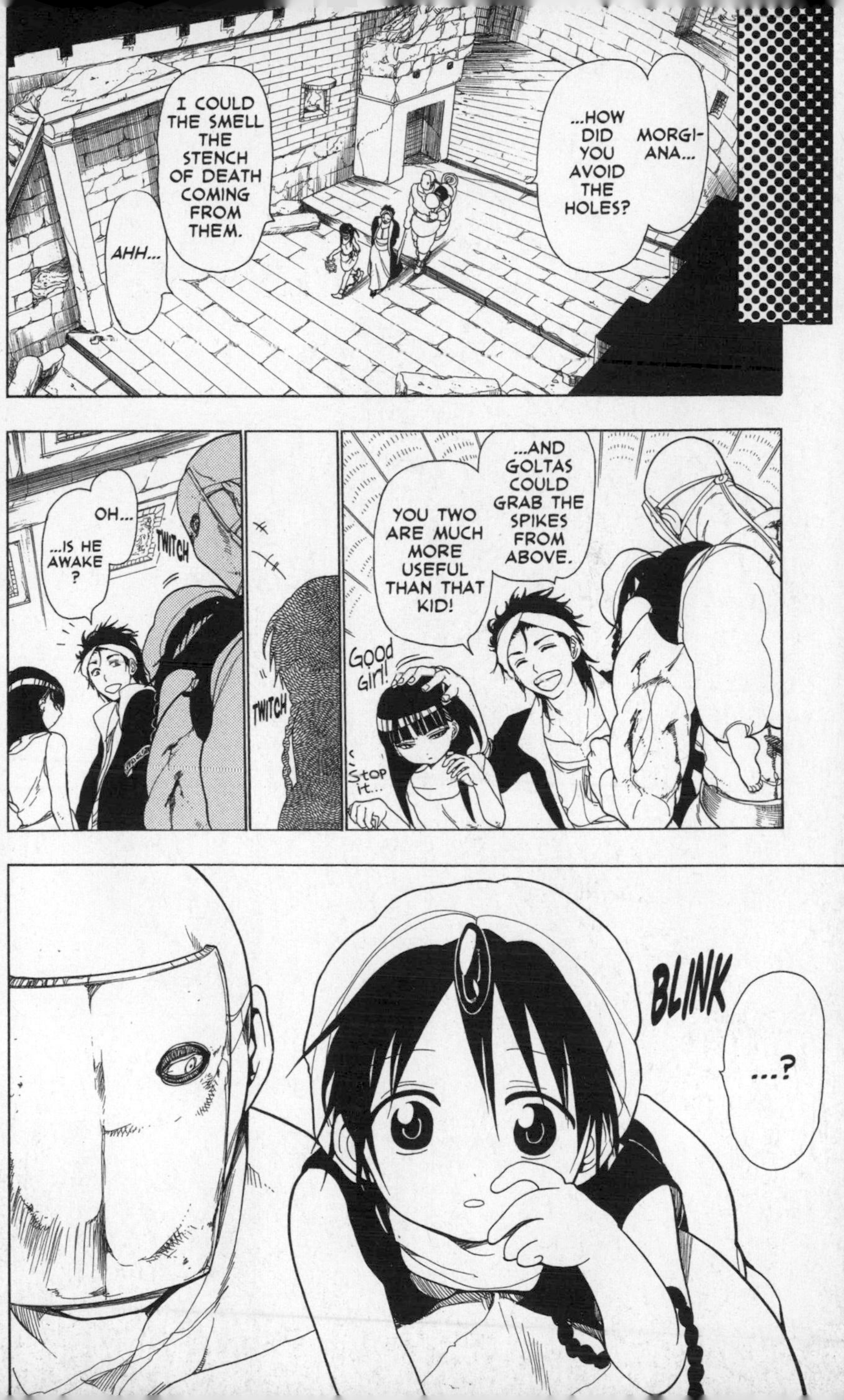
MORGIANA... ...HOW DID YOU AVOID THE HOLES?
I COULD THE SMELL THE STENCH OF DEATH COMING FROM THEM.
AHH...
...AND GOLTAS COULD GRAB THE SPIKES FROM ABOVE.
YOU TWO ARE MUCH MORE USEFUL THAN THAT KID!
Good Girl!
Stop it...
TWITCH
TWITCH
OH...
...IS HE AWAKE?
BLINK
...?

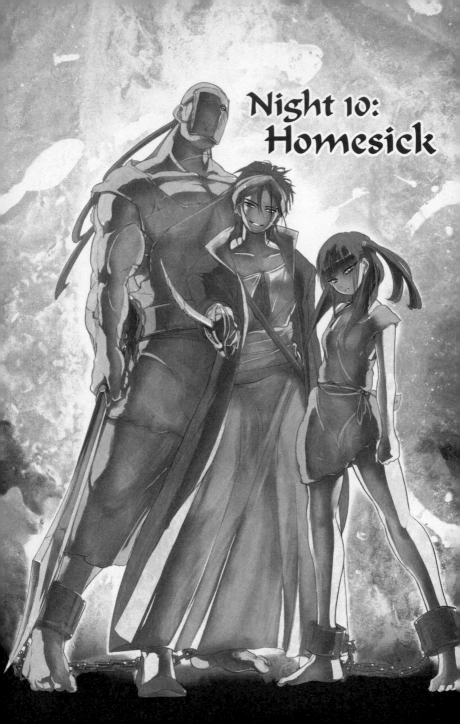

Night 10:
Homesick

About Me-Shinobu Ohtaka ③

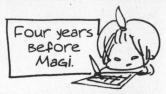

Four years Before Magi.

The magazine that picked up my *debut work* was Square Enix's *Young Gangan,* where I started my first series. It was a romantic comedy called *Sumomomo Momomo: The Strongest Bride on Earth.*

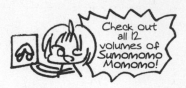

Check out all 12 volumes of Sumomomo Momomo!

The editor who supported me, from the time I debuted until my first series started up, won a prize and is the *current editor of Magi.* His name is *Ishibashi.* I didn't have a series, but when I suddenly quit university and showed up, he felt responsible somehow and carried me along until I got a series.

After three years of serialization, Ishibashi transferred to the editorial department at Shogakukan's *Weekly Shonen Sunday.* And that was all for a while, but then, about the time *Sumomo* ended, I received an invitation to *try for Sunday.*

Ever since I started submitting scripts as a high school student, I *wanted to get into a weekly shonen magazine,* but I never had any luck. I was unsure of my talent, but *it had been my dream ever since I was a child* for my work to appear in a weekly shonen magazine. I thought if I didn't try, I would regret it on my deathbed, so I drew up layouts for a one-shot. I think *I often do things because I'll regret it afterward if I don't.*

Later, that became the *prototype for the first chapter of Magi.*

Continued on page 116.

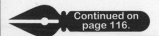

Shinobu Ohtaka History

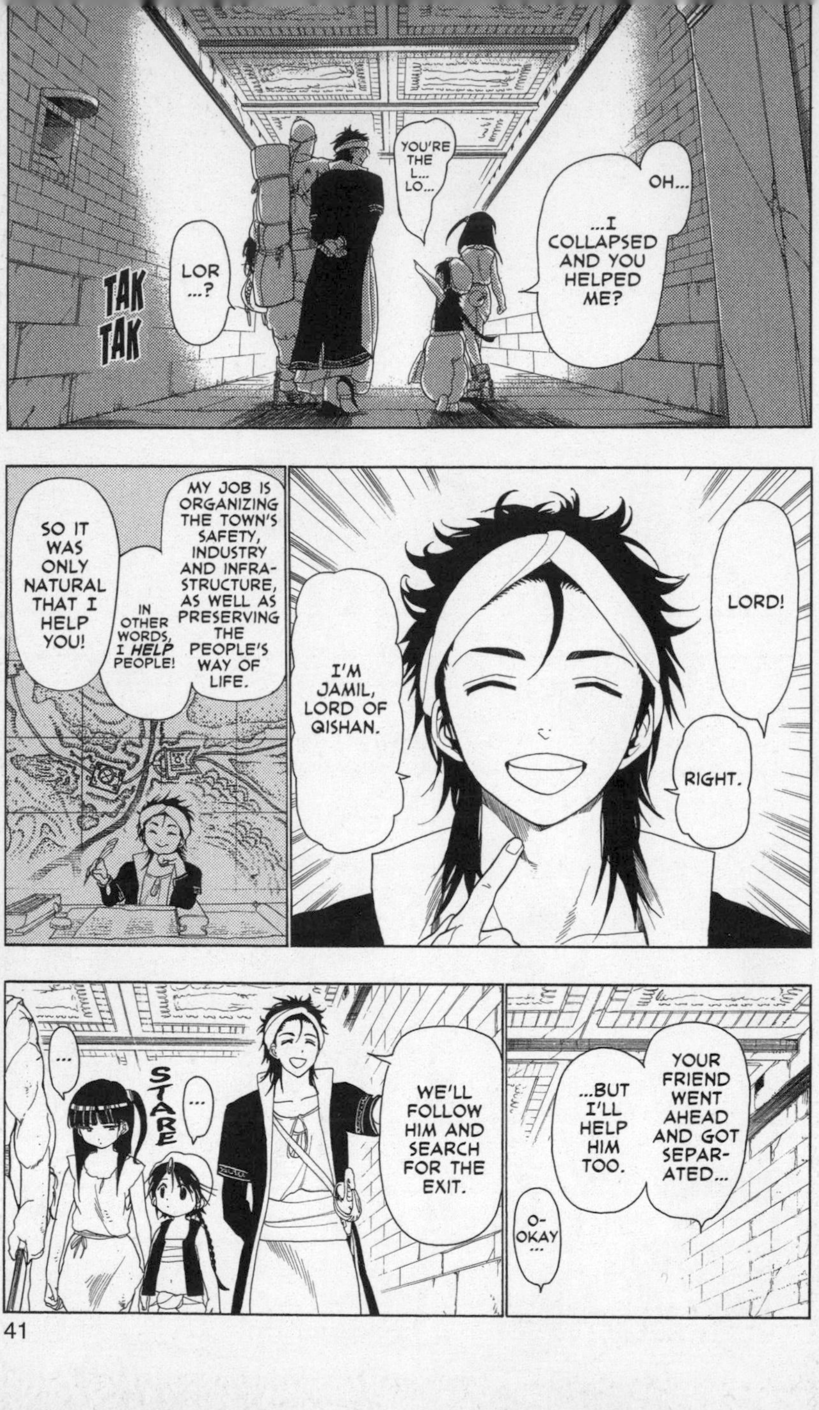
OH...
...I COLLAPSED AND YOU HELPED ME?
YOU'RE THE L... LO...
LOR ...?
TAK TAK
LORD!
RIGHT.
I'M JAMIL, LORD OF QISHAN.
MY JOB IS ORGANIZING THE TOWN'S SAFETY, INDUSTRY AND INFRA-STRUCTURE, AS WELL AS PRESERVING THE PEOPLE'S WAY OF LIFE.
IN OTHER WORDS, I *HELP* PEOPLE!
SO IT WAS ONLY NATURAL THAT I HELP YOU!
YOUR FRIEND WENT AHEAD AND GOT SEPAR-ATED...
...BUT I'LL HELP HIM TOO.
O-OKAY...
WE'LL FOLLOW HIM AND SEARCH FOR THE EXIT.
...
STARE
...

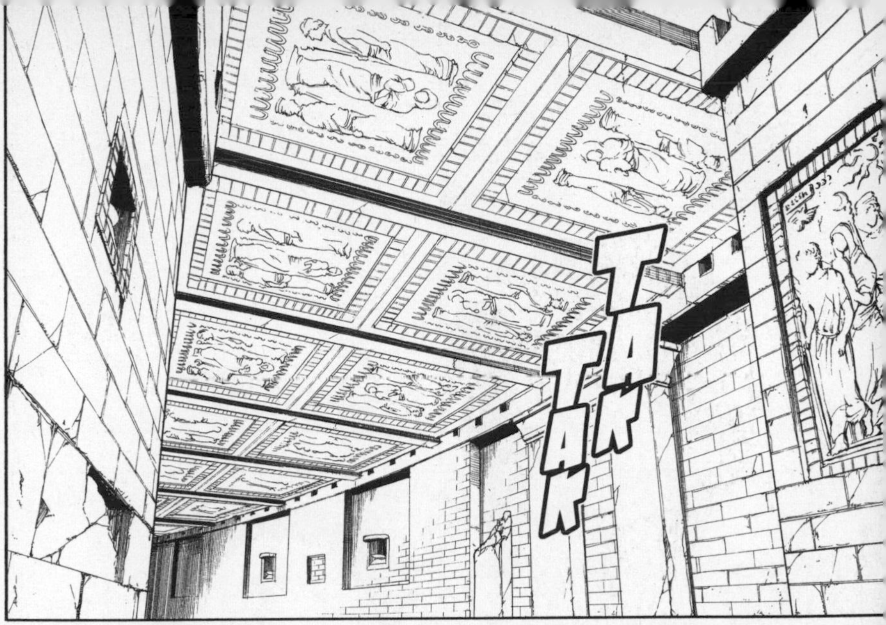
TAK
TAK

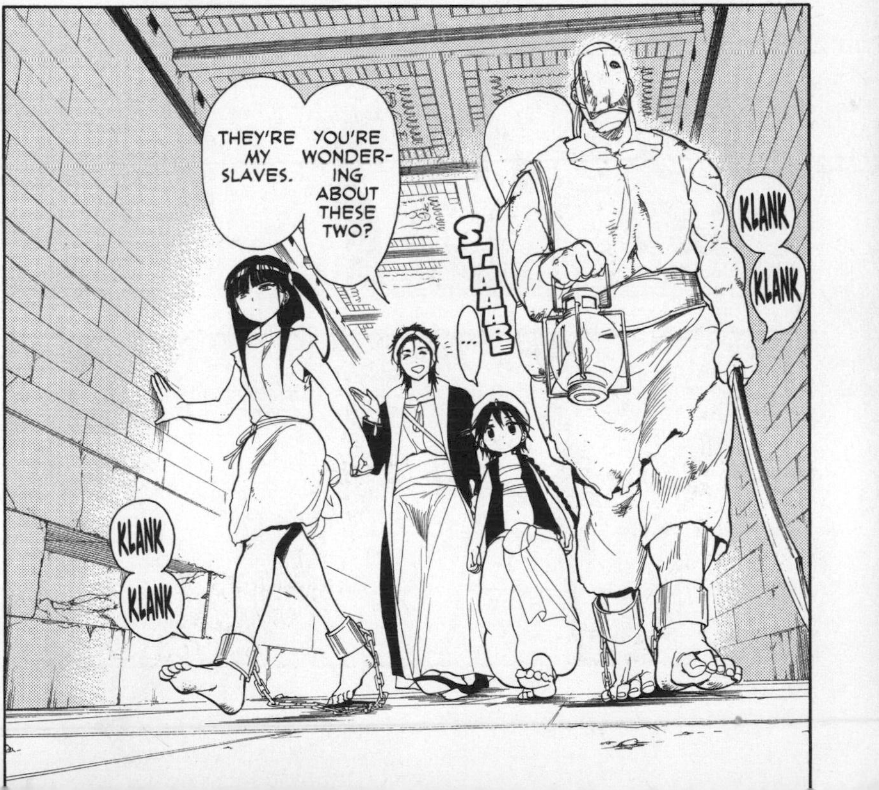
YOU'RE WONDERING ABOUT THESE TWO?
THEY'RE MY SLAVES.
KLANK
KLANK
STAAAARE
...
KLANK
KLANK

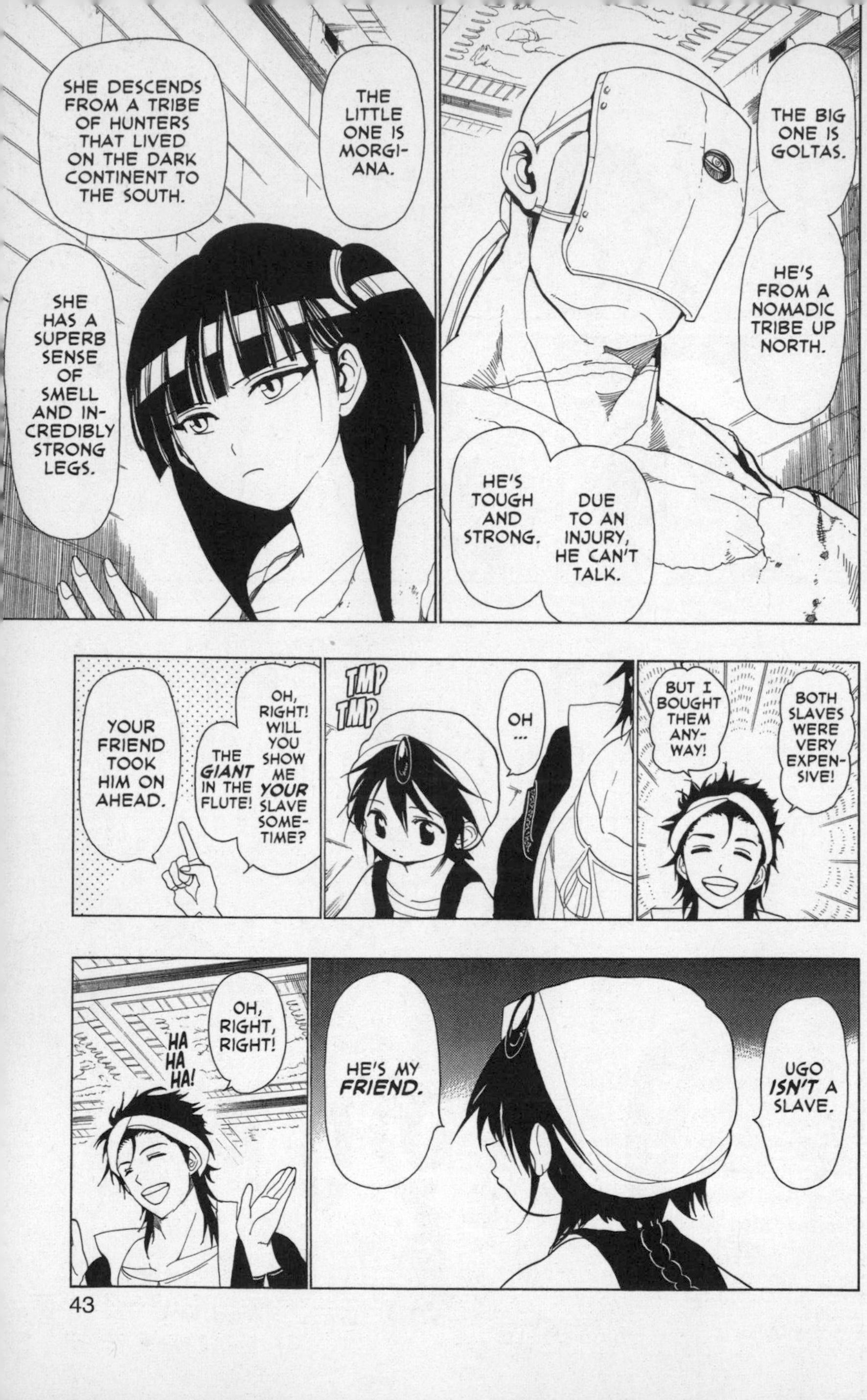
THE BIG ONE IS GOLTAS.
HE'S FROM A NOMADIC TRIBE UP NORTH.
DUE TO AN INJURY, HE CAN'T TALK.
HE'S TOUGH AND STRONG.
THE LITTLE ONE IS MORGI-ANA.
SHE DESCENDS FROM A TRIBE OF HUNTERS THAT LIVED ON THE DARK CONTINENT TO THE SOUTH.
SHE HAS A SUPERB SENSE OF SMELL AND IN-CREDIBLY STRONG LEGS.
BOTH SLAVES WERE VERY EXPEN-SIVE!
BUT I BOUGHT THEM ANY-WAY!
TMP TMP
OH ...
OH, RIGHT! WILL YOU SHOW ME *YOUR* SLAVE SOME-TIME?
THE *GIANT* IN THE FLUTE!
YOUR FRIEND TOOK HIM ON AHEAD.
UGO *ISN'T* A SLAVE.
HE'S MY *FRIEND.*
OH, RIGHT, RIGHT!
HA HA HA!

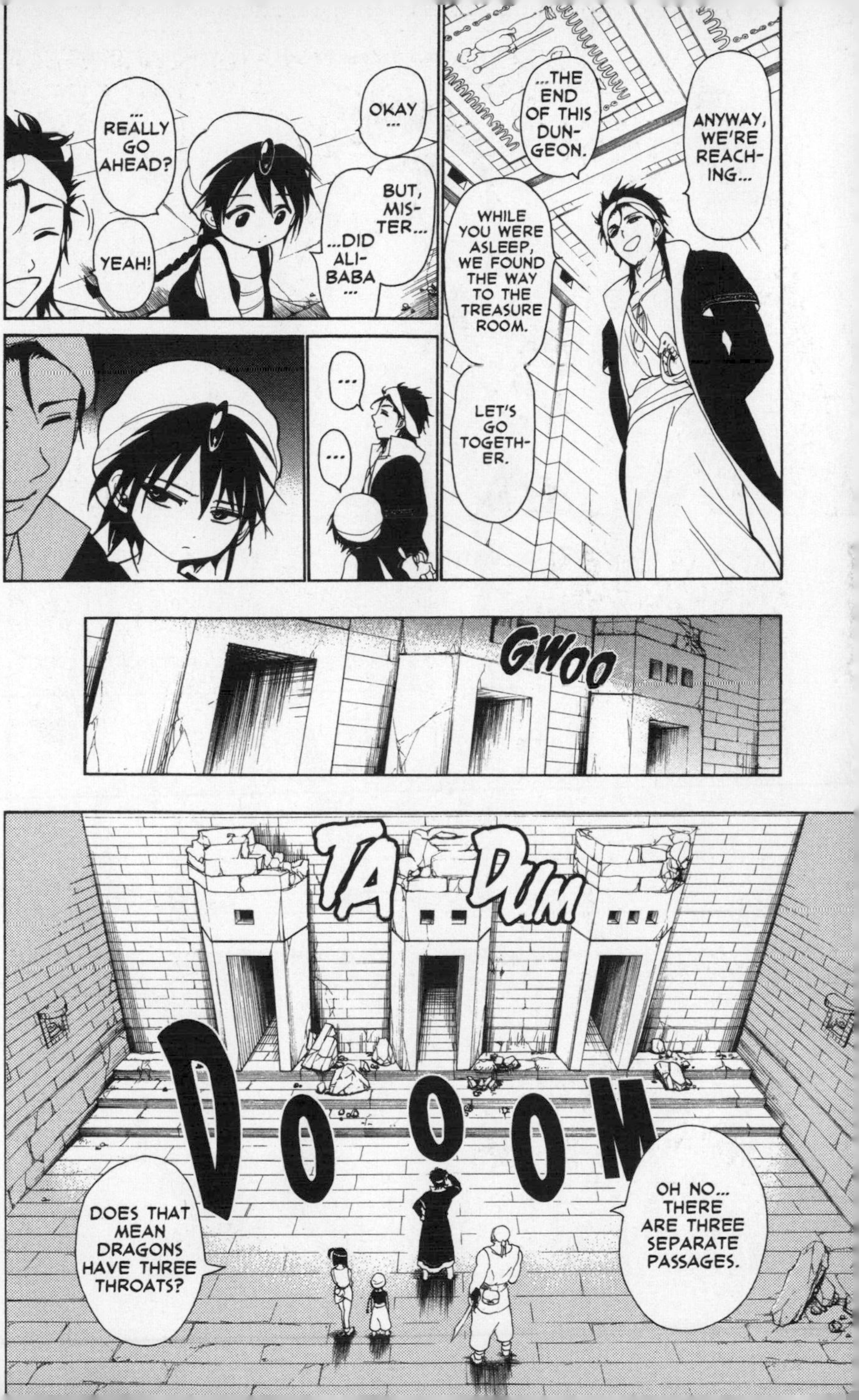
ANYWAY, WE'RE REACHING...
...THE END OF THIS DUNGEON.
WHILE YOU WERE ASLEEP, WE FOUND THE WAY TO THE TREASURE ROOM.
LET'S GO TOGETHER.
OKAY...
BUT, MISTER... ...DID ALI-BABA...
...REALLY GO AHEAD?
YEAH!
...
...
GWOO
TA DUM
DOOOM
OH NO... THERE ARE THREE SEPARATE PASSAGES.
DOES THAT MEAN DRAGONS HAVE THREE THROATS?

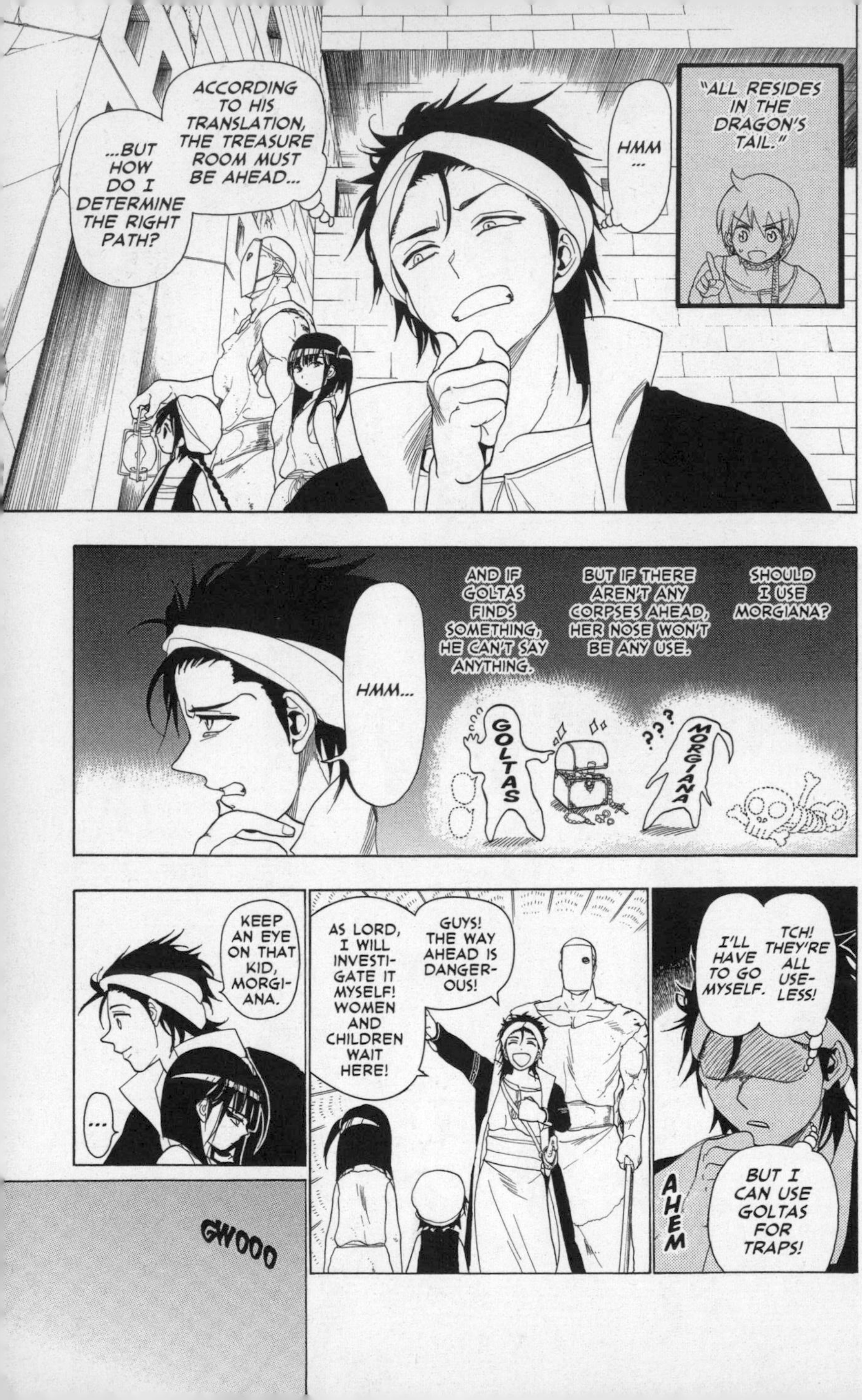
"ALL RESIDES IN THE DRAGON'S TAIL."
HMM...
ACCORDING TO HIS TRANSLATION, THE TREASURE ROOM MUST BE AHEAD...
...BUT HOW DO I DETERMINE THE RIGHT PATH?
SHOULD I USE MORGIANA?
BUT IF THERE AREN'T ANY CORPSES AHEAD, HER NOSE WON'T BE ANY USE.
AND IF GOLTAS FINDS SOMETHING, HE CAN'T SAY ANYTHING.
HMM...
GOLTAS
MORGIANA
TCH! THEY'RE ALL USE-LESS!
I'LL HAVE TO GO MYSELF.
BUT I CAN USE GOLTAS FOR TRAPS!
AHEM
GUYS! THE WAY AHEAD IS DANGER-OUS!
AS LORD, I WILL INVESTI-GATE IT MYSELF! WOMEN AND CHILDREN WAIT HERE!
KEEP AN EYE ON THAT KID, MORGI-ANA.
...
GWOOO

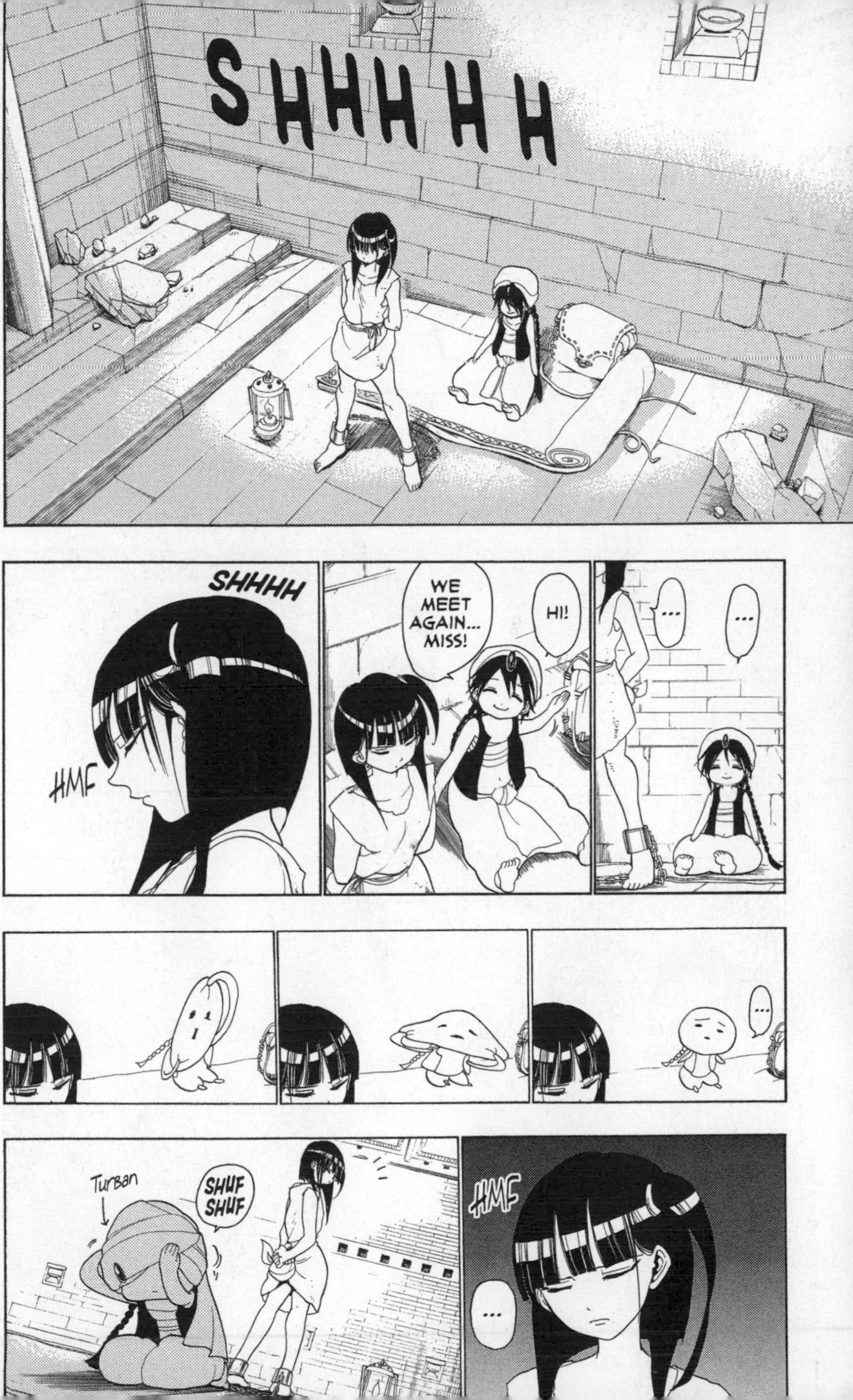
SHHHHH
...
...
HI!
WE MEET AGAIN... MISS!
SHHHH
HMF
...
HMF
...
SHUF SHUF
Turban

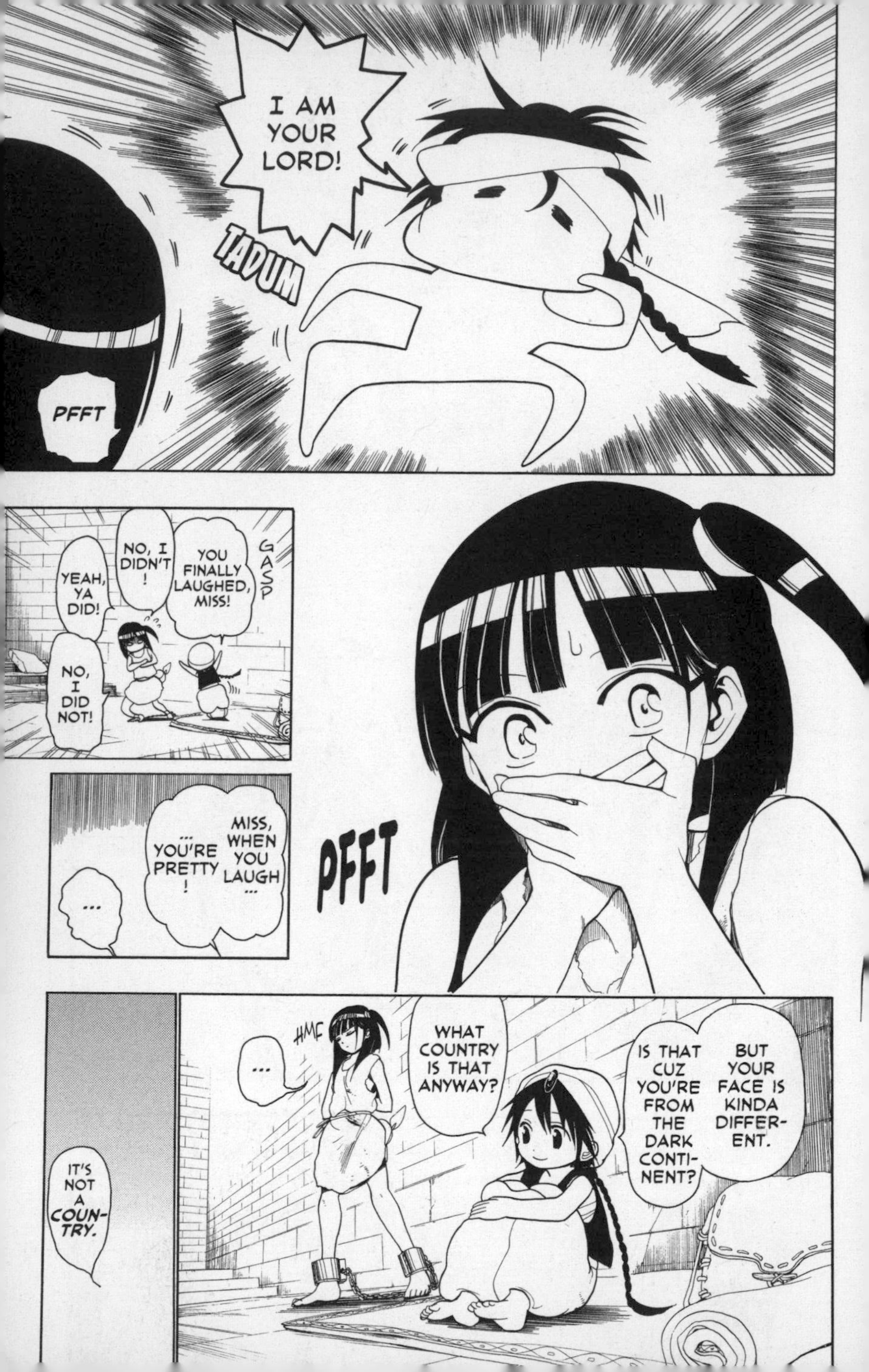
I AM YOUR LORD!
TADUM
PFFT
PFFT
GASP
YOU FINALLY LAUGHED, MISS!
NO, I DIDN'T!
YEAH, YA DID!
NO, I DID NOT!
MISS, WHEN YOU LAUGH...
...YOU'RE PRETTY!
...
BUT YOUR FACE IS KINDA DIFFERENT.
IS THAT CUZ YOU'RE FROM THE DARK CONTINENT?
WHAT COUNTRY IS THAT ANYWAY?
HMF
...
IT'S NOT A COUNTRY.

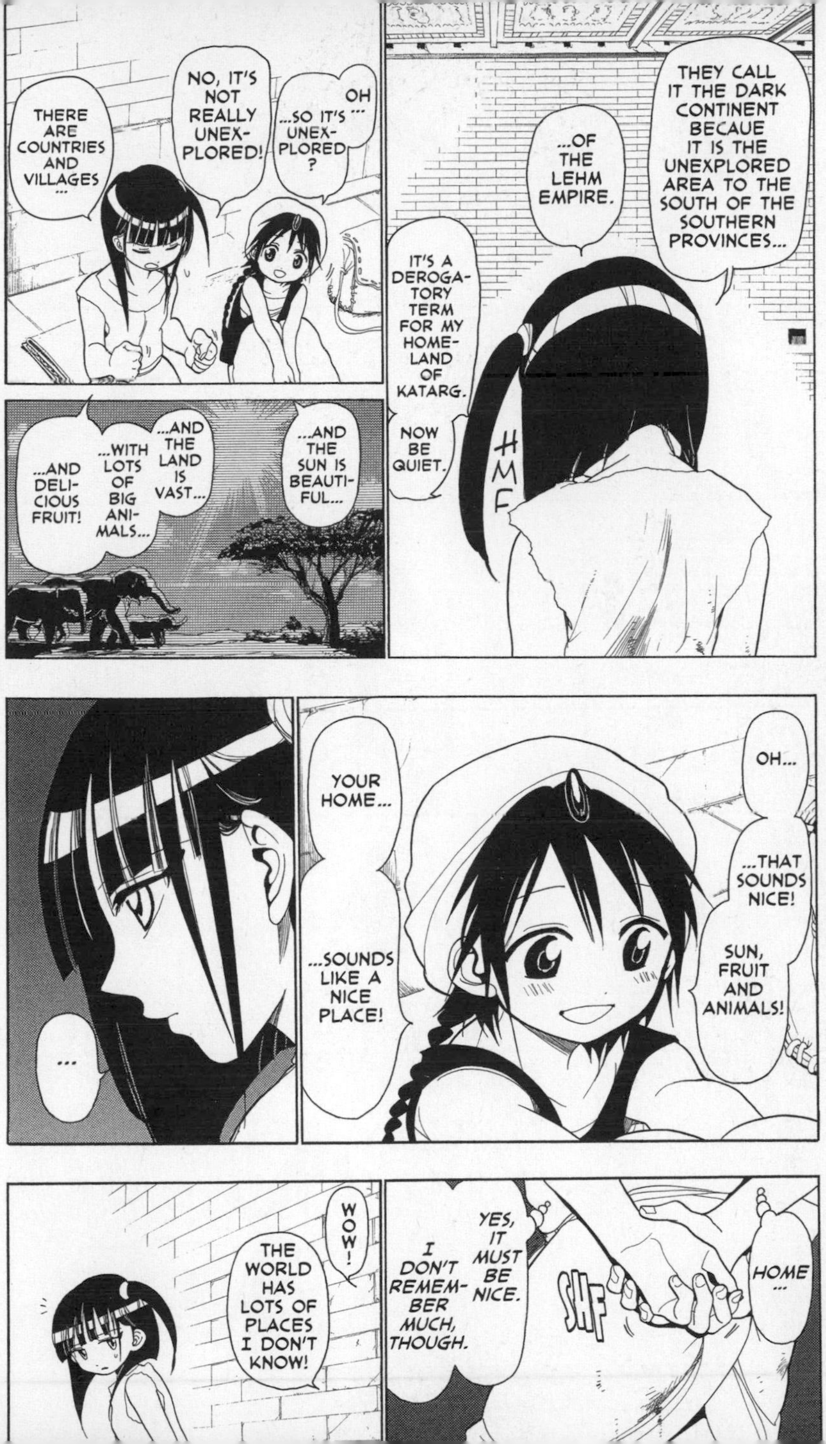
THEY CALL IT THE DARK CONTINENT BECAUE IT IS THE UNEXPLORED AREA TO THE SOUTH OF THE SOUTHERN PROVINCES...
...OF THE LEHM EMPIRE.
IT'S A DEROGATORY TERM FOR MY HOMELAND OF KATARG.
NOW BE QUIET.
HMF
OH ...
...SO IT'S UNEXPLORED?
NO, IT'S NOT REALLY UNEXPLORED!
THERE ARE COUNTRIES AND VILLAGES ...
...AND THE SUN IS BEAUTIFUL...
...AND THE LAND IS VAST...
...WITH LOTS OF BIG ANIMALS...
...AND DELICIOUS FRUIT!
OH...
...THAT SOUNDS NICE!
SUN, FRUIT AND ANIMALS!
YOUR HOME...
...SOUNDS LIKE A NICE PLACE!
...
HOME ...
SHF
YES, IT MUST BE NICE.
I DON'T REMEMBER MUCH, THOUGH.
WOW!
THE WORLD HAS LOTS OF PLACES I DON'T KNOW!

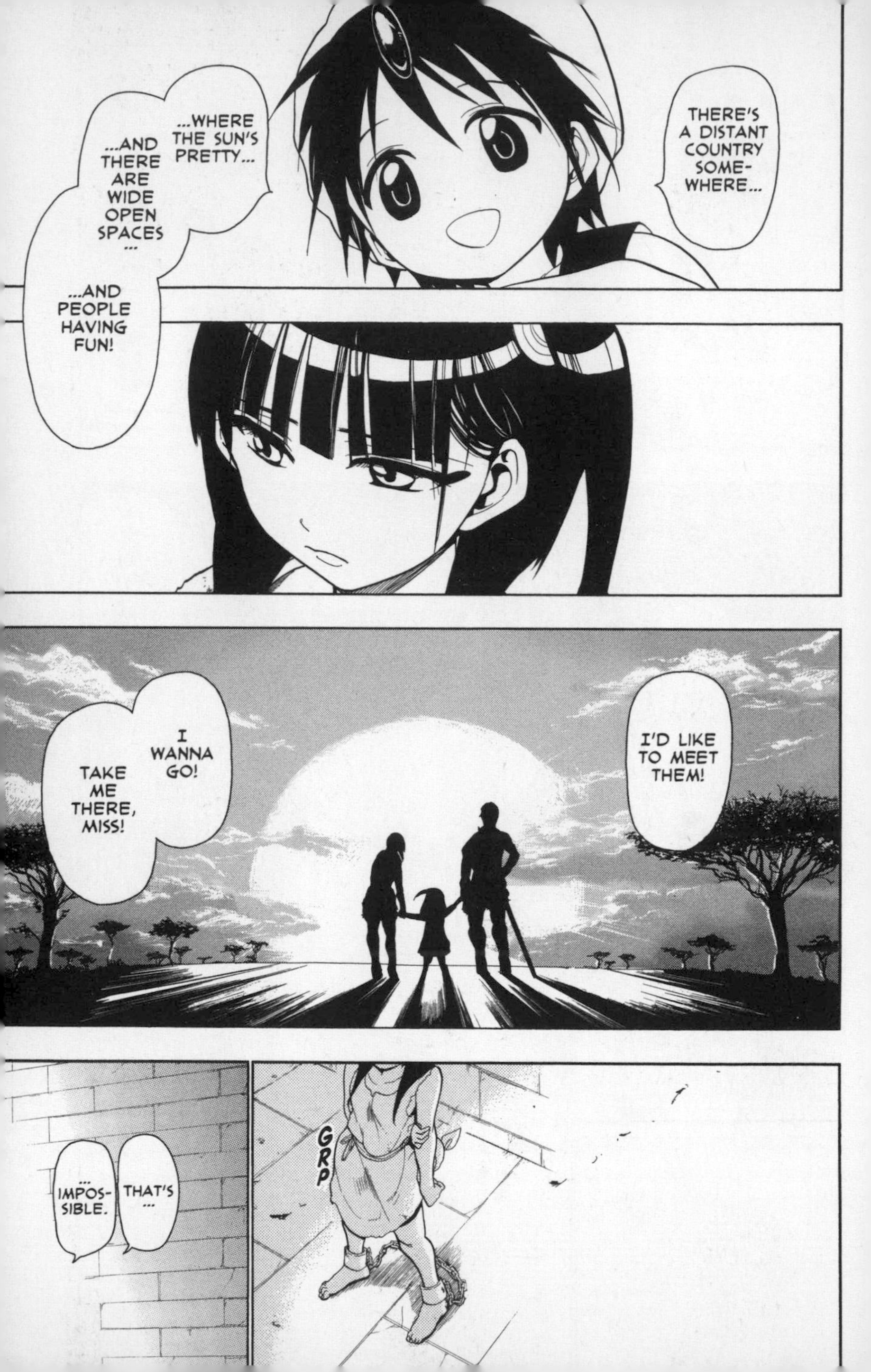
THERE'S A DISTANT COUNTRY SOME-WHERE...
...WHERE THE SUN'S PRETTY...
...AND THERE ARE WIDE OPEN SPACES ...
...AND PEOPLE HAVING FUN!
I'D LIKE TO MEET THEM!
I WANNA GO!
TAKE ME THERE, MISS!
GRP
THAT'S ...
... IMPOS-SIBLE.

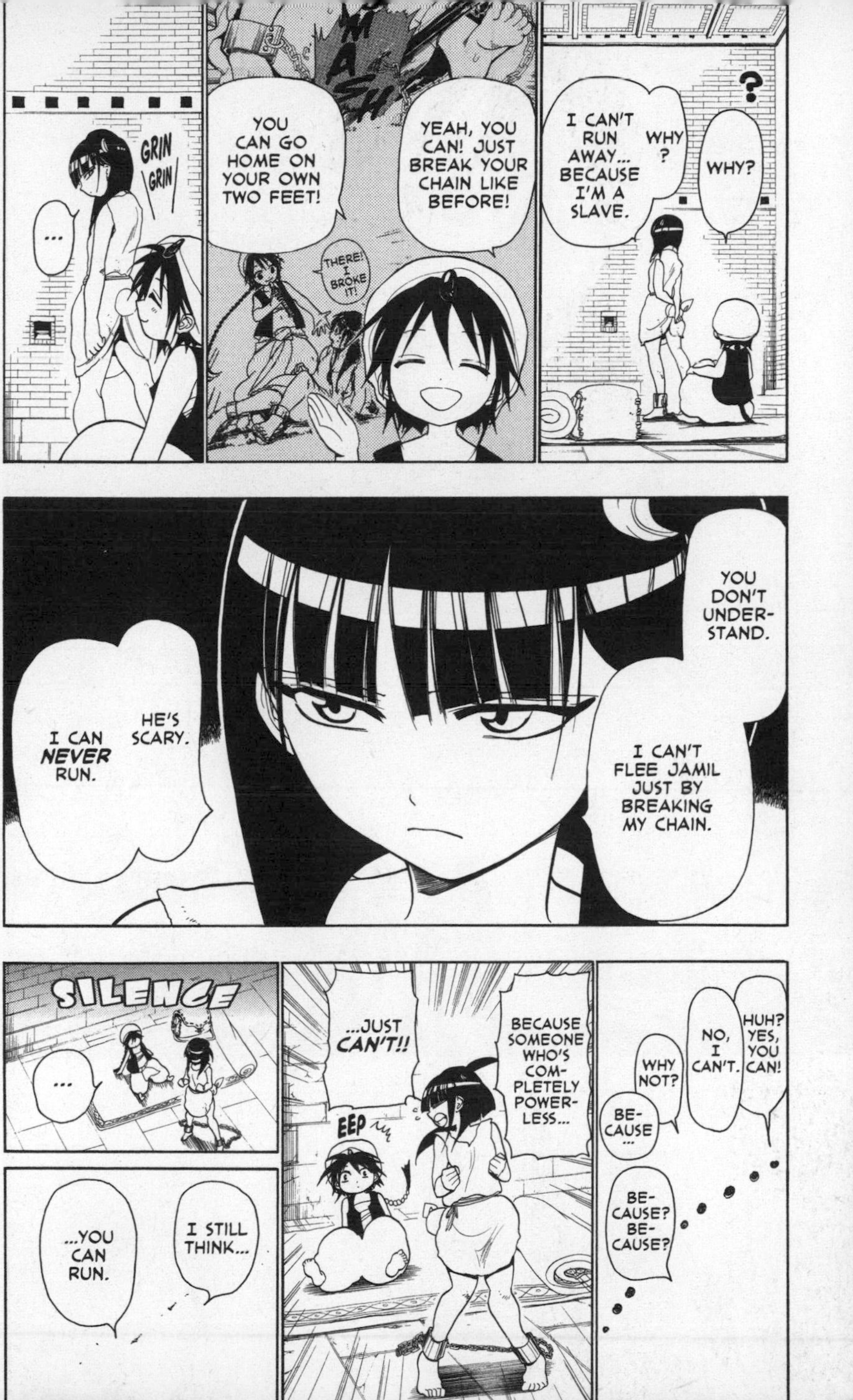
?
WHY?
I CAN'T RUN AWAY... BECAUSE I'M A SLAVE.
WHY?
SMASH
YEAH, YOU CAN! JUST BREAK YOUR CHAIN LIKE BEFORE!
THERE! I BROKE IT!
YOU CAN GO HOME ON YOUR OWN TWO FEET!
GRIN GRIN
...
YOU DON'T UNDER-STAND.
I CAN'T FLEE JAMIL JUST BY BREAKING MY CHAIN.
HE'S SCARY.
I CAN *NEVER* RUN.
HUH? YES, YOU CAN!
NO, I CAN'T.
WHY NOT?
BE-CAUSE...
BE-CAUSE? BE-CAUSE?
BECAUSE SOMEONE WHO'S COM-PLETELY POWER-LESS...
...JUST *CAN'T!!*
EEP
SILENCE
...
I STILL THINK...
...YOU CAN RUN.

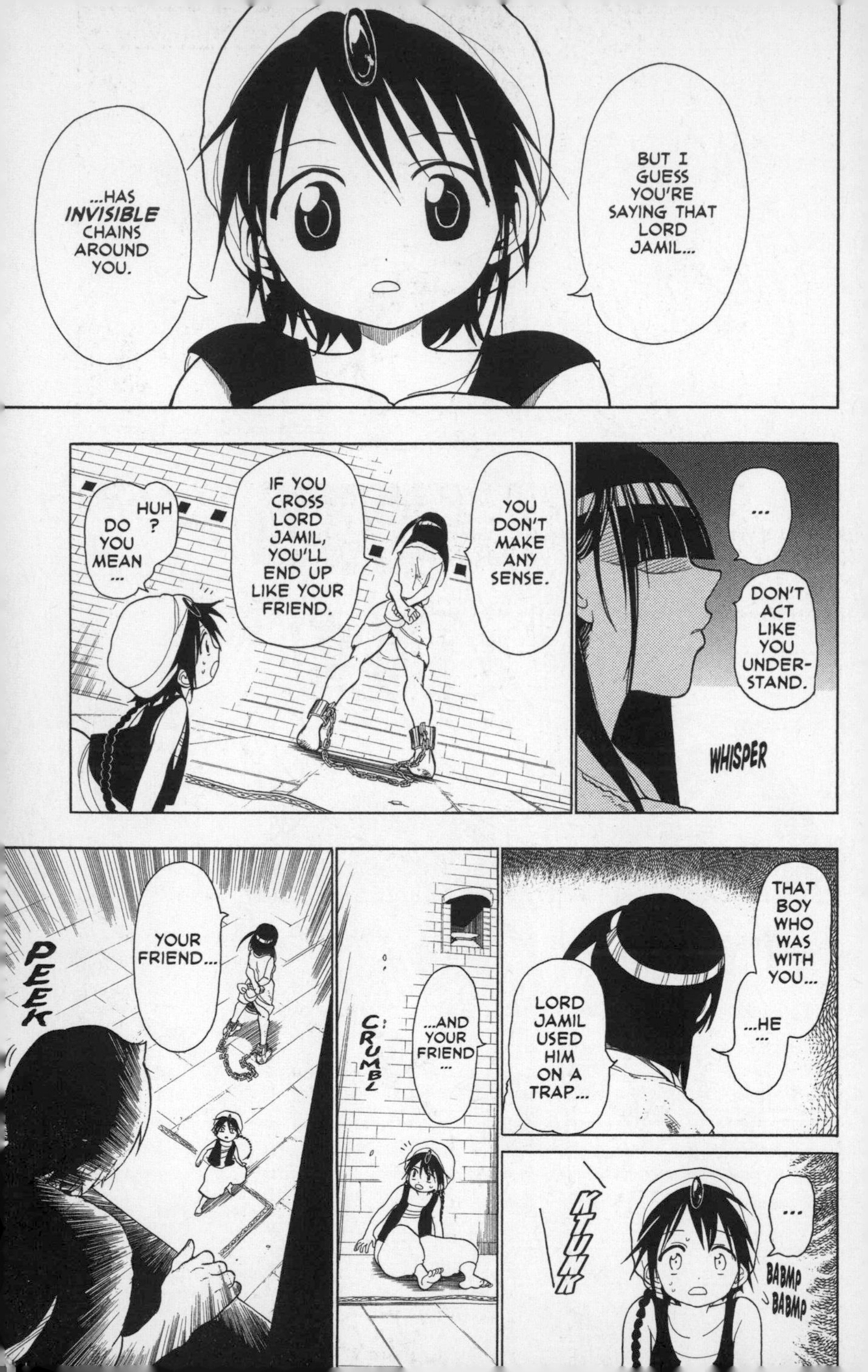
BUT I GUESS YOU'RE SAYING THAT LORD JAMIL...
...HAS *INVISIBLE* CHAINS AROUND YOU.
...
DON'T ACT LIKE YOU UNDER-STAND.
WHISPER
YOU DON'T MAKE ANY SENSE.
IF YOU CROSS LORD JAMIL, YOU'LL END UP LIKE YOUR FRIEND.
HUH? DO YOU MEAN ...
THAT BOY WHO WAS WITH YOU...
...HE ...
LORD JAMIL USED HIM ON A TRAP...
KTUNK
...
BABMP BABMP
CRUMBL
...AND YOUR FRIEND ...
YOUR FRIEND...
PEEK

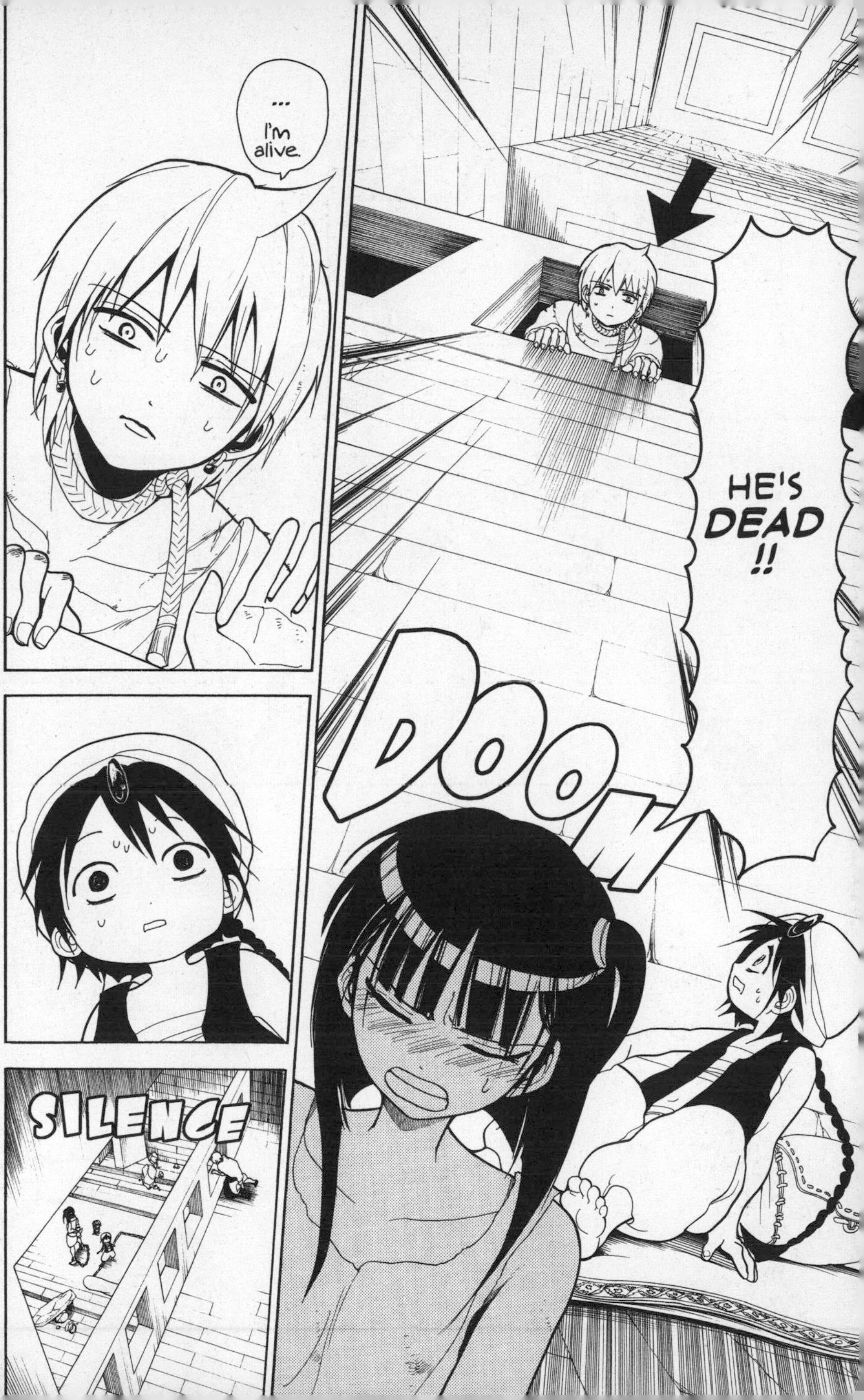
HE'S DEAD!!
DOOM
... I'm alive.
SILENCE

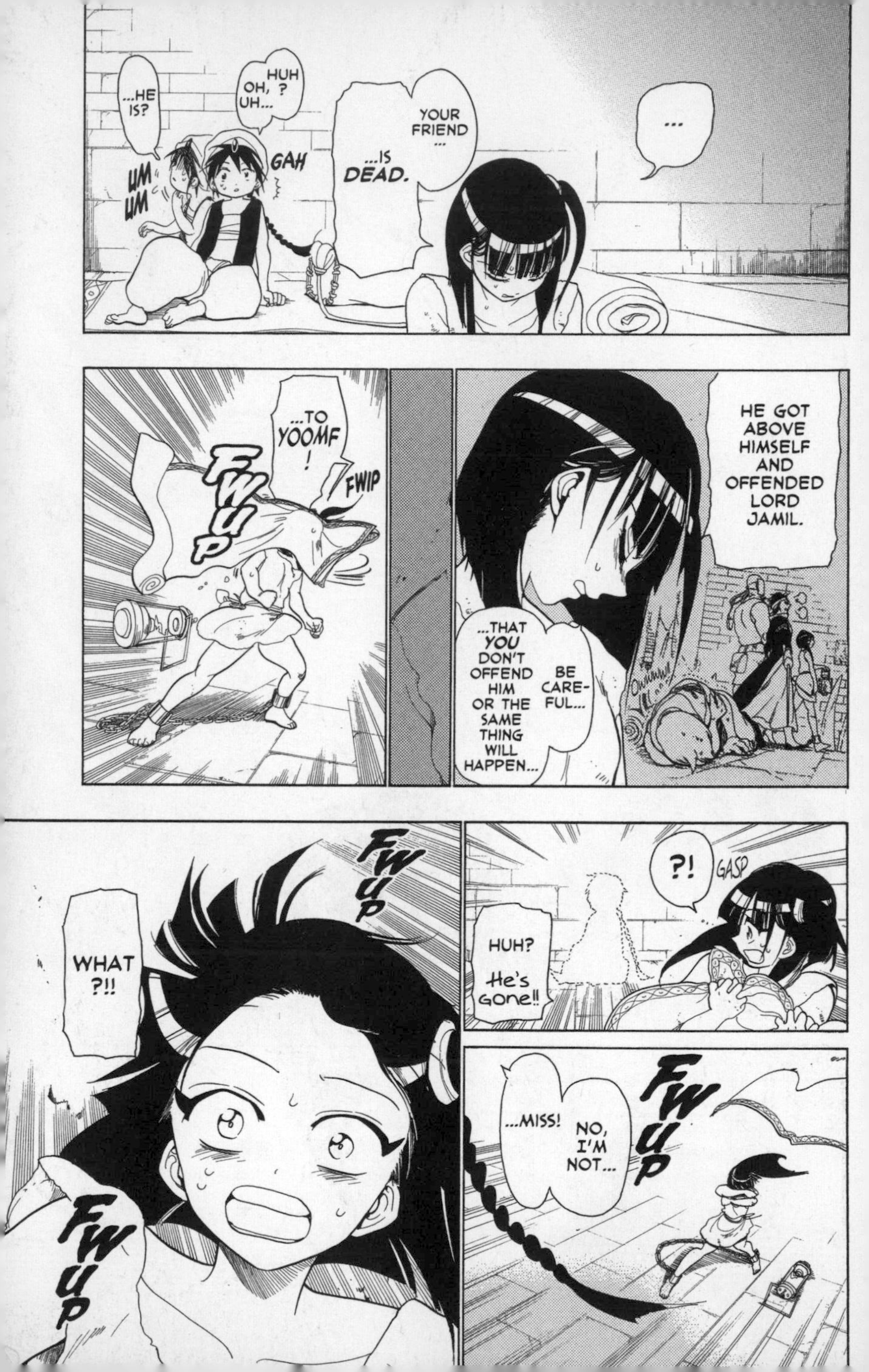
...
YOUR FRIEND ...
...IS DEAD.
OH, UH... HUH?
GAH
...HE IS?
UM UM
HE GOT ABOVE HIMSELF AND OFFENDED LORD JAMIL.
BE CAREFUL...
...THAT YOU DON'T OFFEND HIM OR THE SAME THING WILL HAPPEN...
FWIP
...TO YOOMF!
FWUP
GASP
?!
HUH? He's Gone!!
FWUP
NO, I'M NOT...
...MISS!
FWUP
WHAT?!!
FWUP

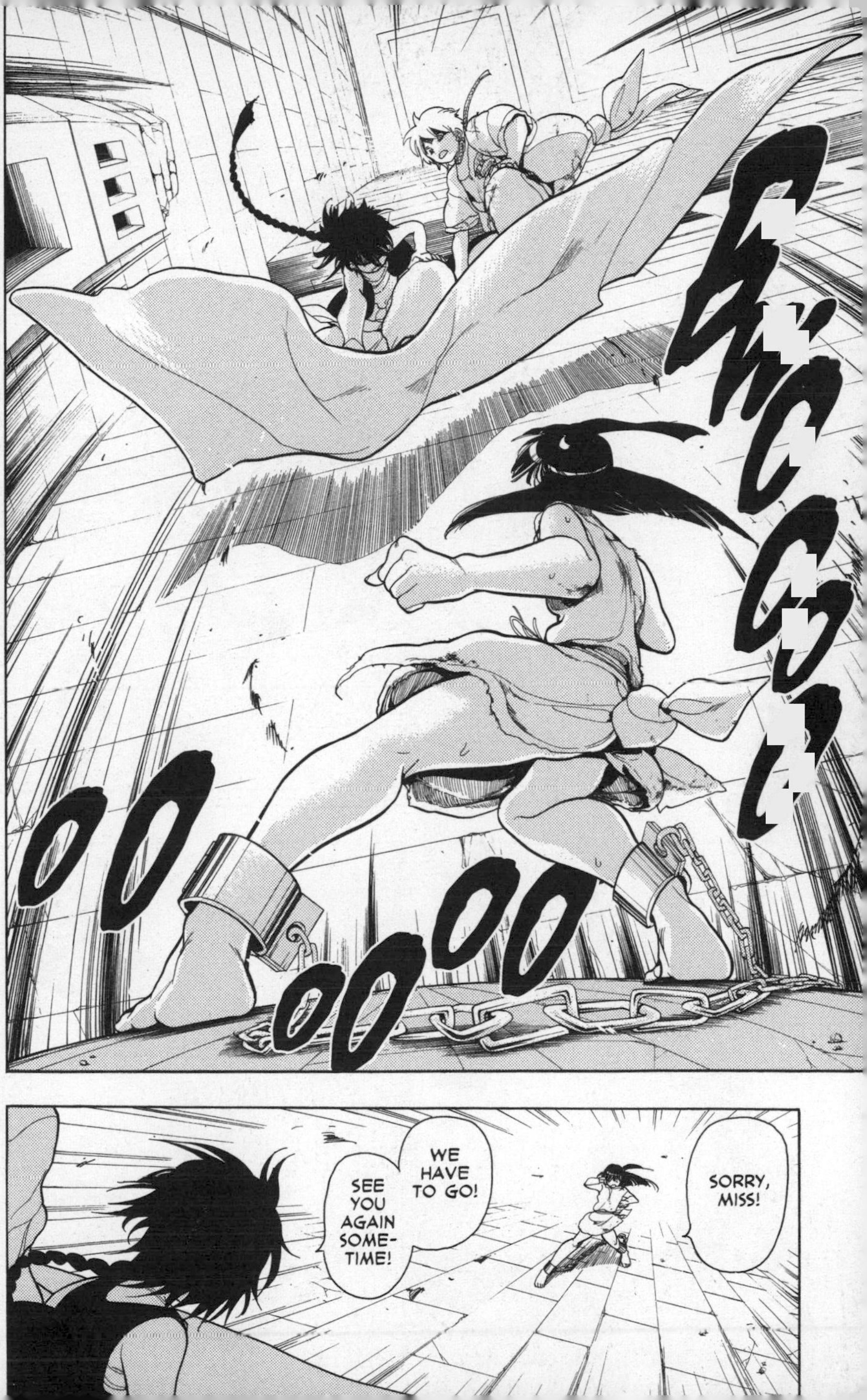
SORRY, MISS!
WE HAVE TO GO!
SEE YOU AGAIN SOME-TIME!

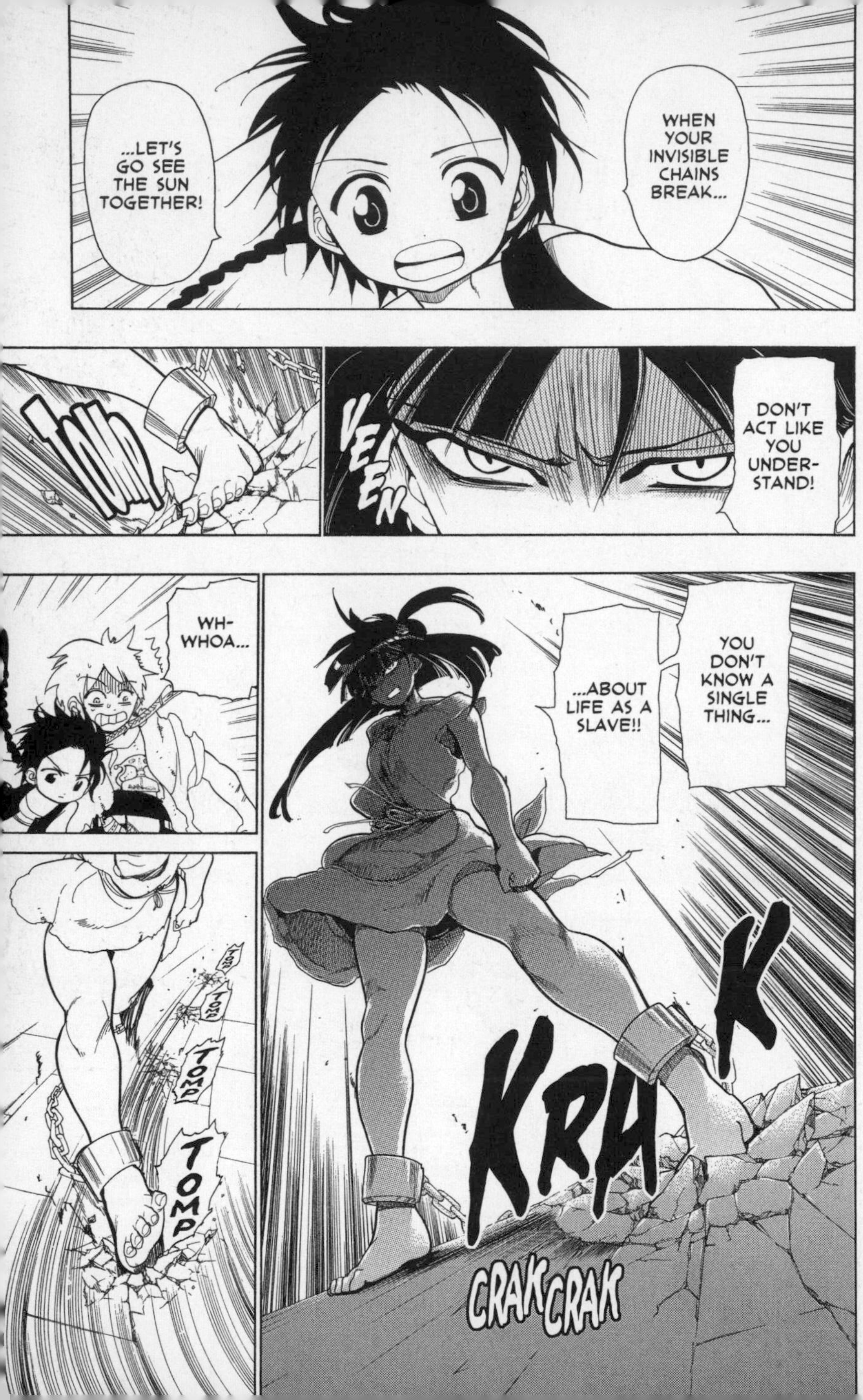
WHEN YOUR INVISIBLE CHAINS BREAK...
...LET'S GO SEE THE SUN TOGETHER!
VEEEN.
DON'T ACT LIKE YOU UNDER-STAND!
YOU DON'T KNOW A SINGLE THING...
...ABOUT LIFE AS A SLAVE!!
KRAK
CRAKCRAK
WH-WHOA...
TOMP
TOMP
TOMP
TOMP

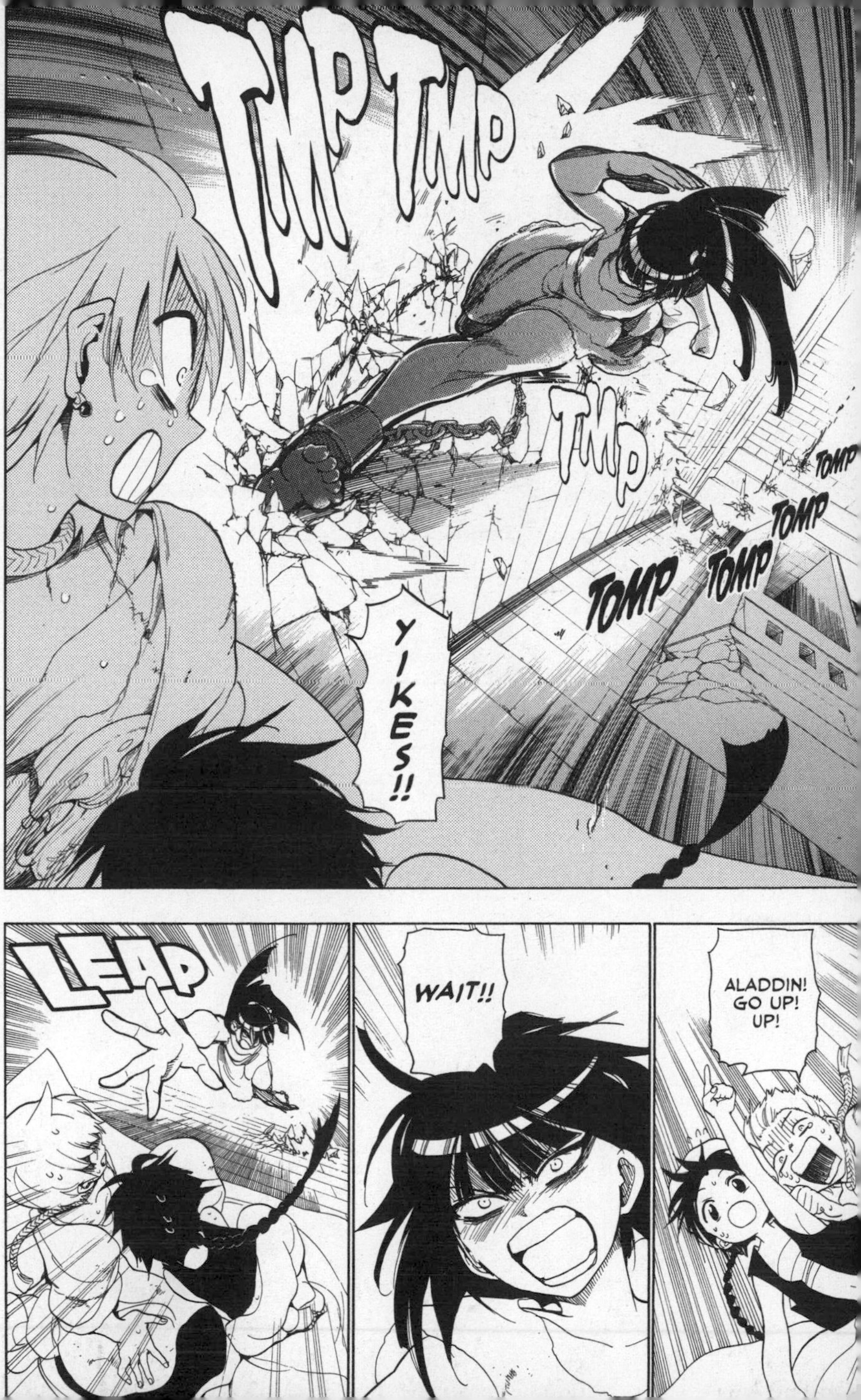
TMP TMP
TOMP
TOMP
TOMP
TOMP
TMP
YIKES!!
ALADDIN! GO UP! UP!
WAIT!!
LEAP

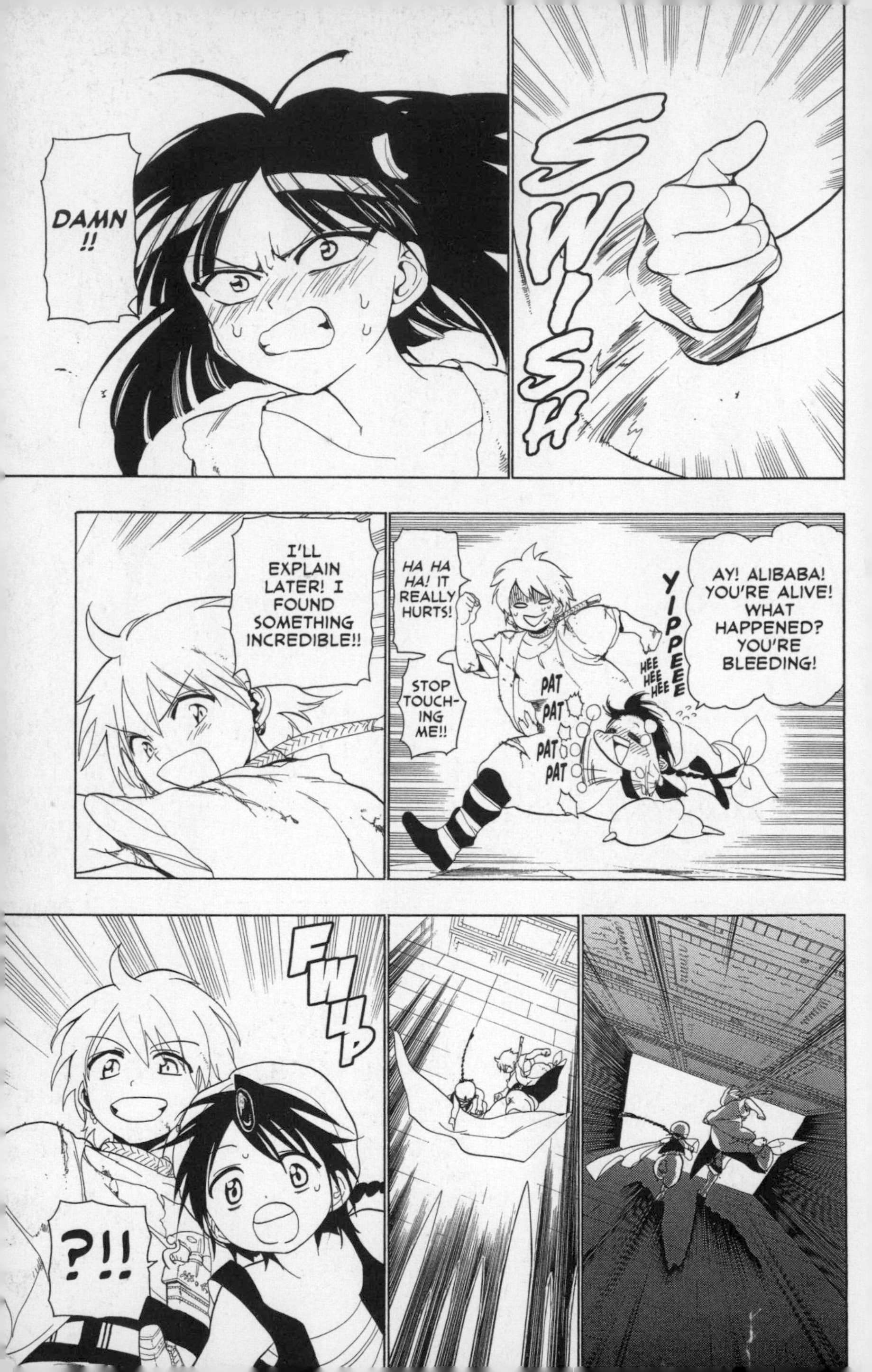
SWISH
DAMN!!
AY! ALIBABA! YOU'RE ALIVE! WHAT HAPPENED? YOU'RE BLEEDING!
YIPPEEE
HEE HEE HEE
PAT PAT PAT PAT
HA HA HA! IT REALLY HURTS!
STOP TOUCHING ME!!
I'LL EXPLAIN LATER! I FOUND SOMETHING INCREDIBLE!!
FWUP
?!!

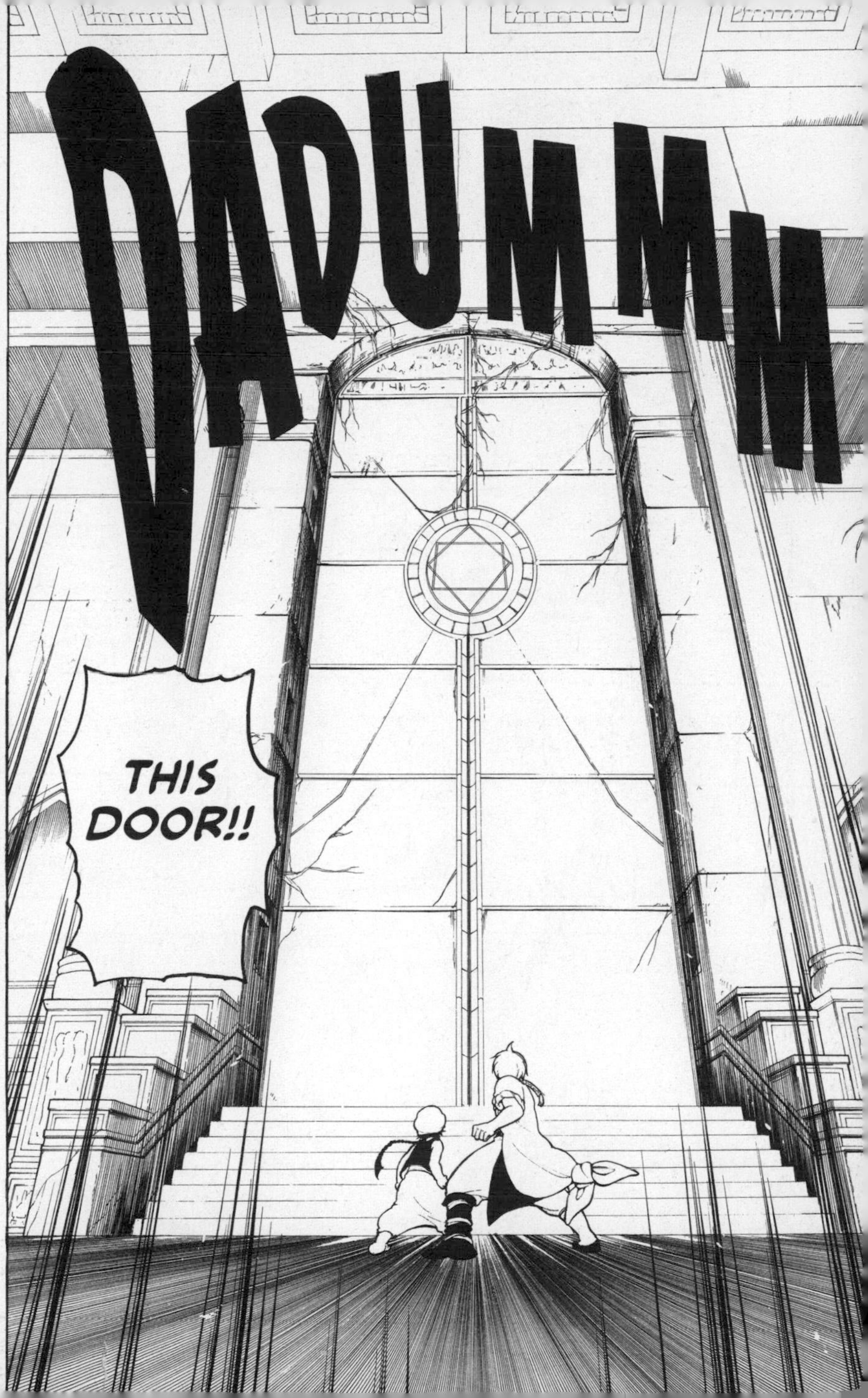
DADUMMM
THIS DOOR!!

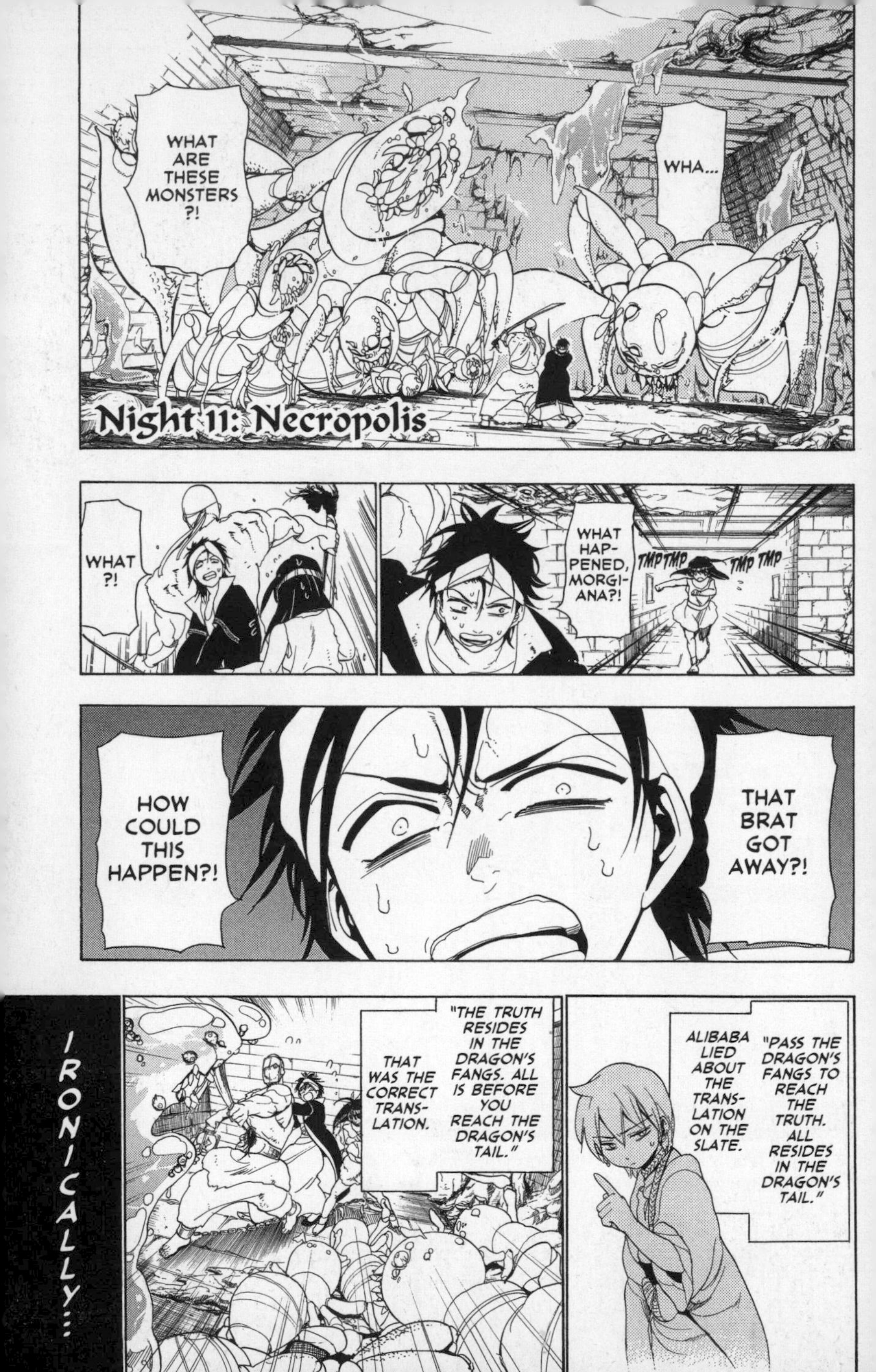
Night 11: Necropolis
WHA...
WHAT ARE THESE MONSTERS?!
TMP TMP
TMPTMP
WHAT HAP-PENED, MORGI-ANA?!
WHAT?!
THAT BRAT GOT AWAY?!
HOW COULD THIS HAPPEN?!
"PASS THE DRAGON'S FANGS TO REACH THE TRUTH. ALL RESIDES IN THE DRAGON'S TAIL."
ALIBABA LIED ABOUT THE TRANS-LATION ON THE SLATE.
"THE TRUTH RESIDES IN THE DRAGON'S FANGS. ALL IS BEFORE YOU REACH THE DRAGON'S TAIL."
THAT WAS THE CORRECT TRANS-LATION.
IRONICALLY...

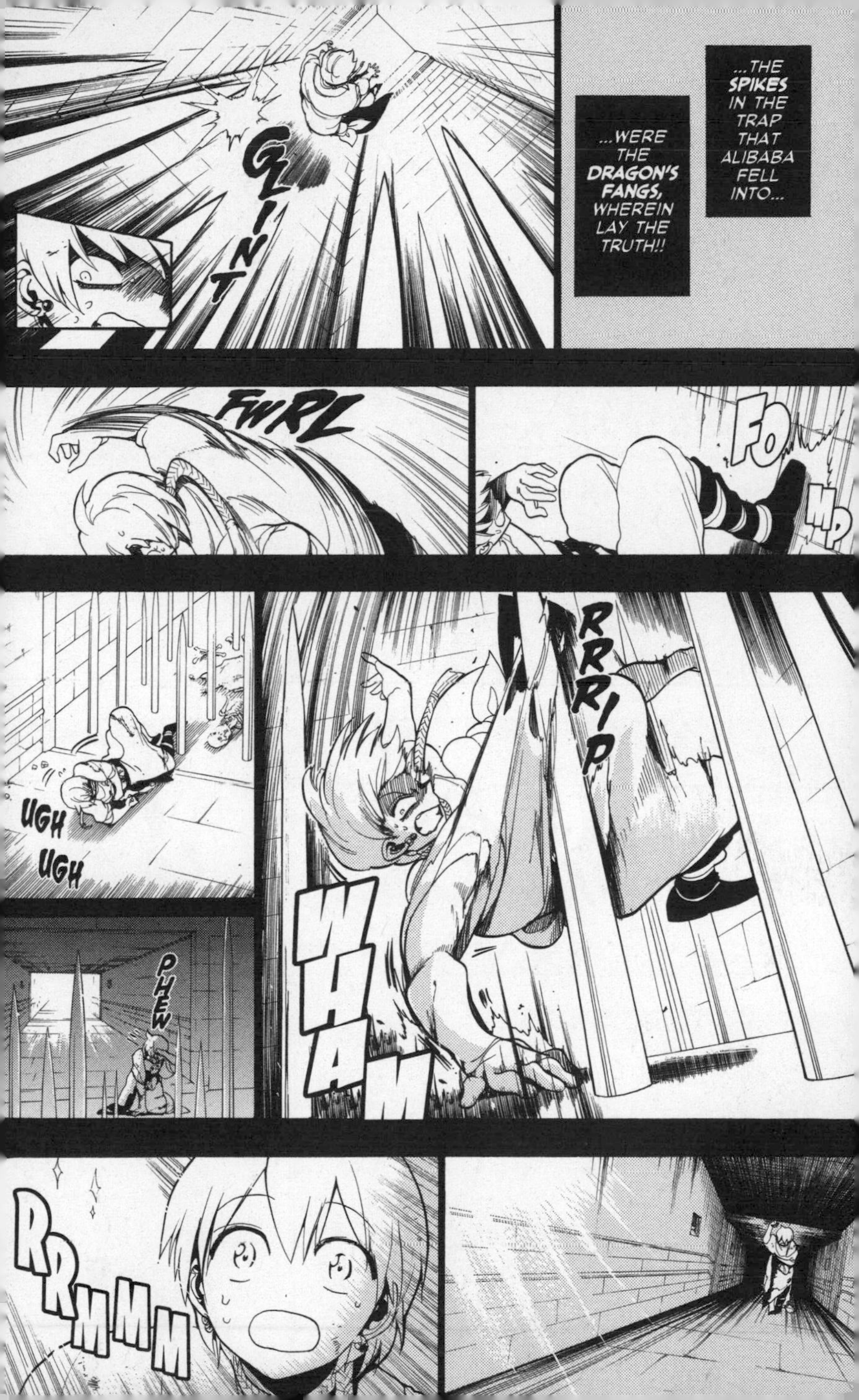
...THE SPIKES IN THE TRAP THAT ALIBABA FELL INTO...
...WERE THE DRAGON'S FANGS, WHEREIN LAY THE TRUTH!!
GLINT
FOMP
FWRL
RRRIP
WHAM
UGH UGH
PHEW
RRMMMM

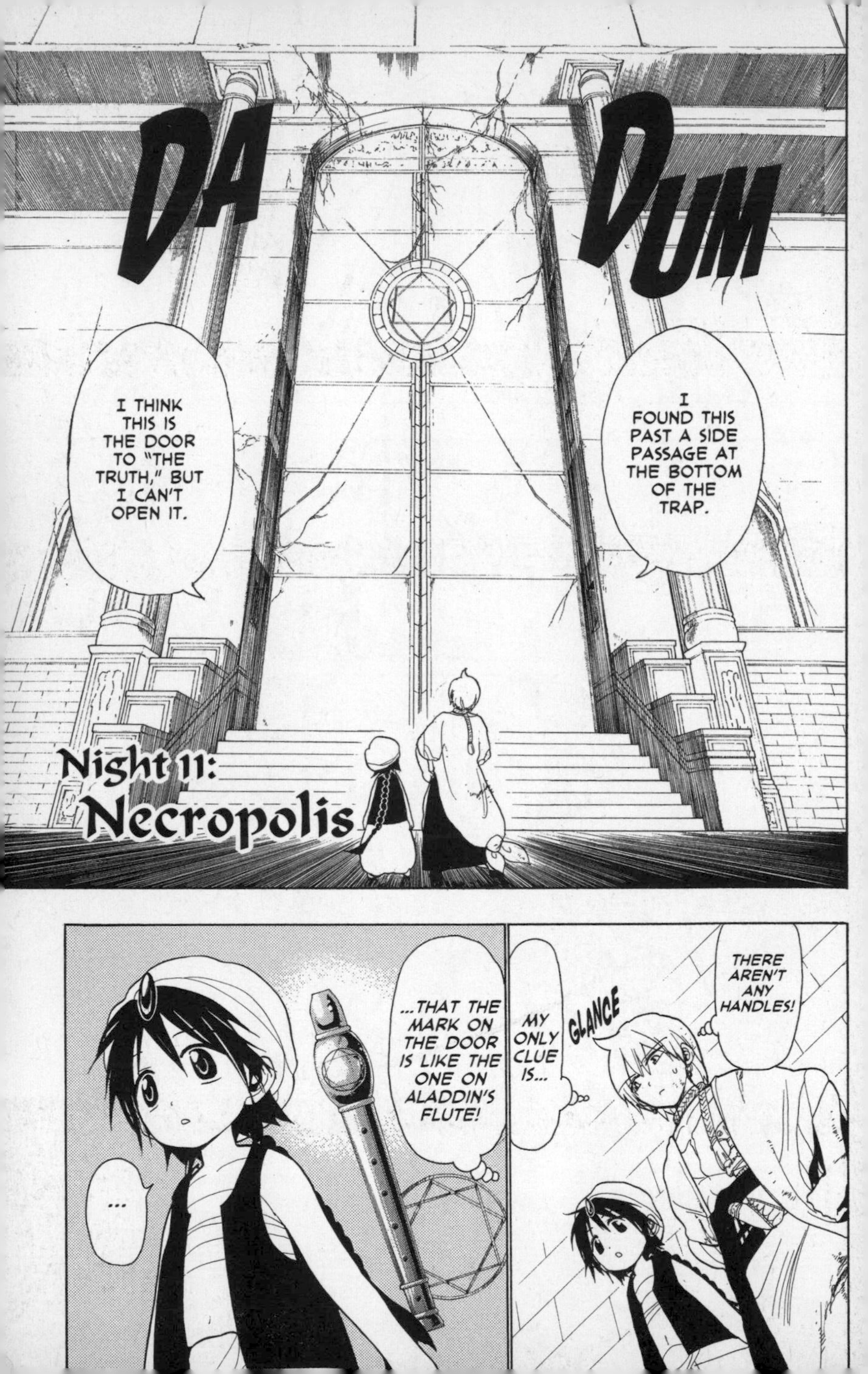
DA DUM
I FOUND THIS PAST A SIDE PASSAGE AT THE BOTTOM OF THE TRAP.
I THINK THIS IS THE DOOR TO "THE TRUTH," BUT I CAN'T OPEN IT.
Night 11: Necropolis
THERE AREN'T ANY HANDLES!
GLANCE
MY ONLY CLUE IS...
...THAT THE MARK ON THE DOOR IS LIKE THE ONE ON ALADDIN'S FLUTE!
...

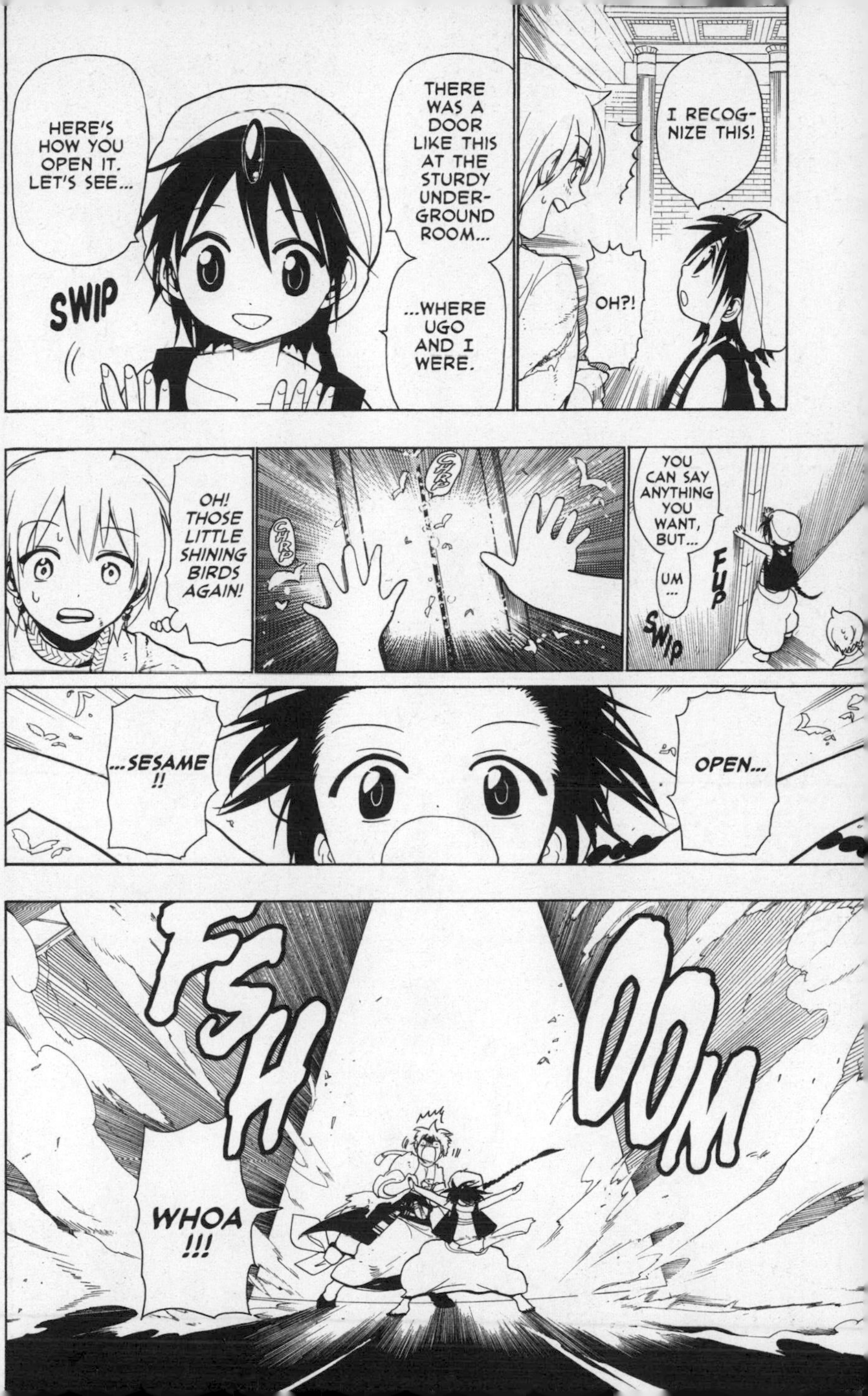
I RECOGNIZE THIS!
OH?!
THERE WAS A DOOR LIKE THIS AT THE STURDY UNDERGROUND ROOM...
...WHERE UGO AND I WERE.
HERE'S HOW YOU OPEN IT. LET'S SEE...
SWIP
YOU CAN SAY ANYTHING YOU WANT, BUT...
UM ...
FUP
SWIP
OH! THOSE LITTLE SHINING BIRDS AGAIN!
OPEN...
...SESAME !!
FSH
OOM
WHOA !!!

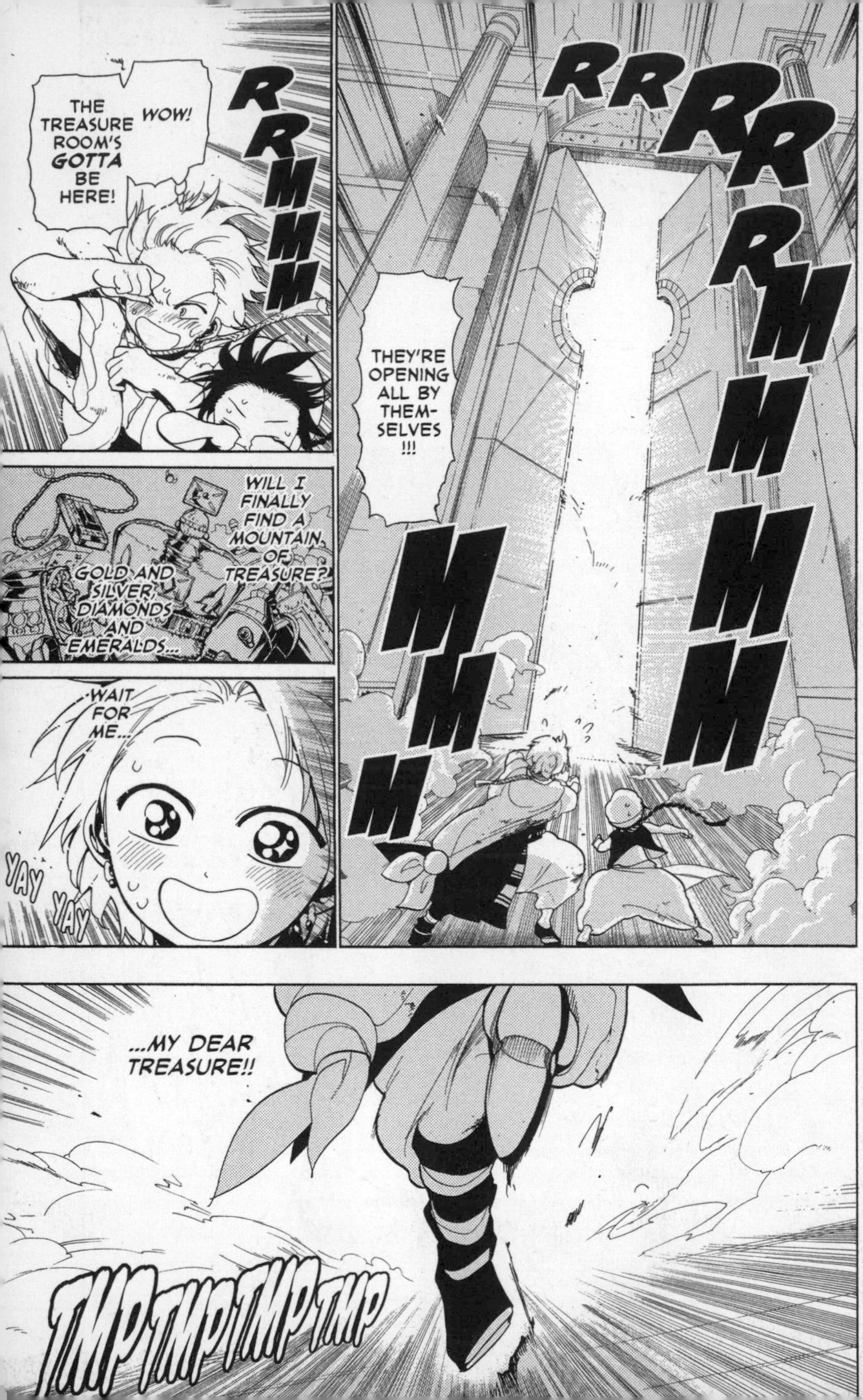
RRRRRRMMMMMM
THEY'RE OPENING ALL BY THEM-SELVES!!!
MMMM
WOW!
THE TREASURE ROOM'S GOTTA BE HERE!
RRMMMM
WILL I FINALLY FIND A MOUNTAIN OF TREASURE?
GOLD AND SILVER, DIAMONDS AND EMERALDS...
WAIT FOR ME...
YAY YAY
...MY DEAR TREASURE!!
TMP TMP TMP TMP

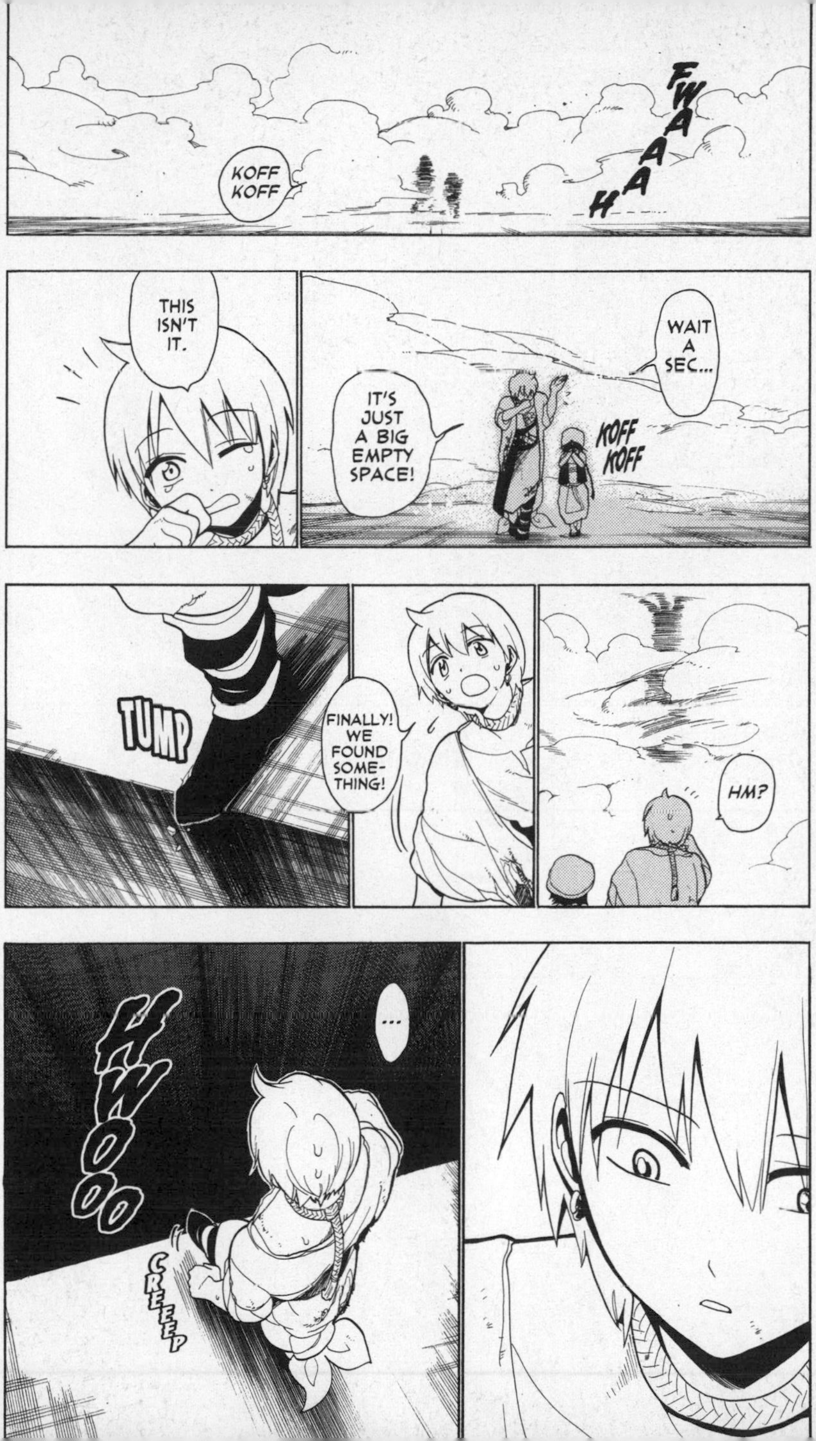
FWAAAH
KOFF KOFF
WAIT A SEC...
KOFF KOFF
IT'S JUST A BIG EMPTY SPACE!
THIS ISN'T IT.
HM?
FINALLY! WE FOUND SOME-THING!
TUMP
...
HWOOO
CREEEP

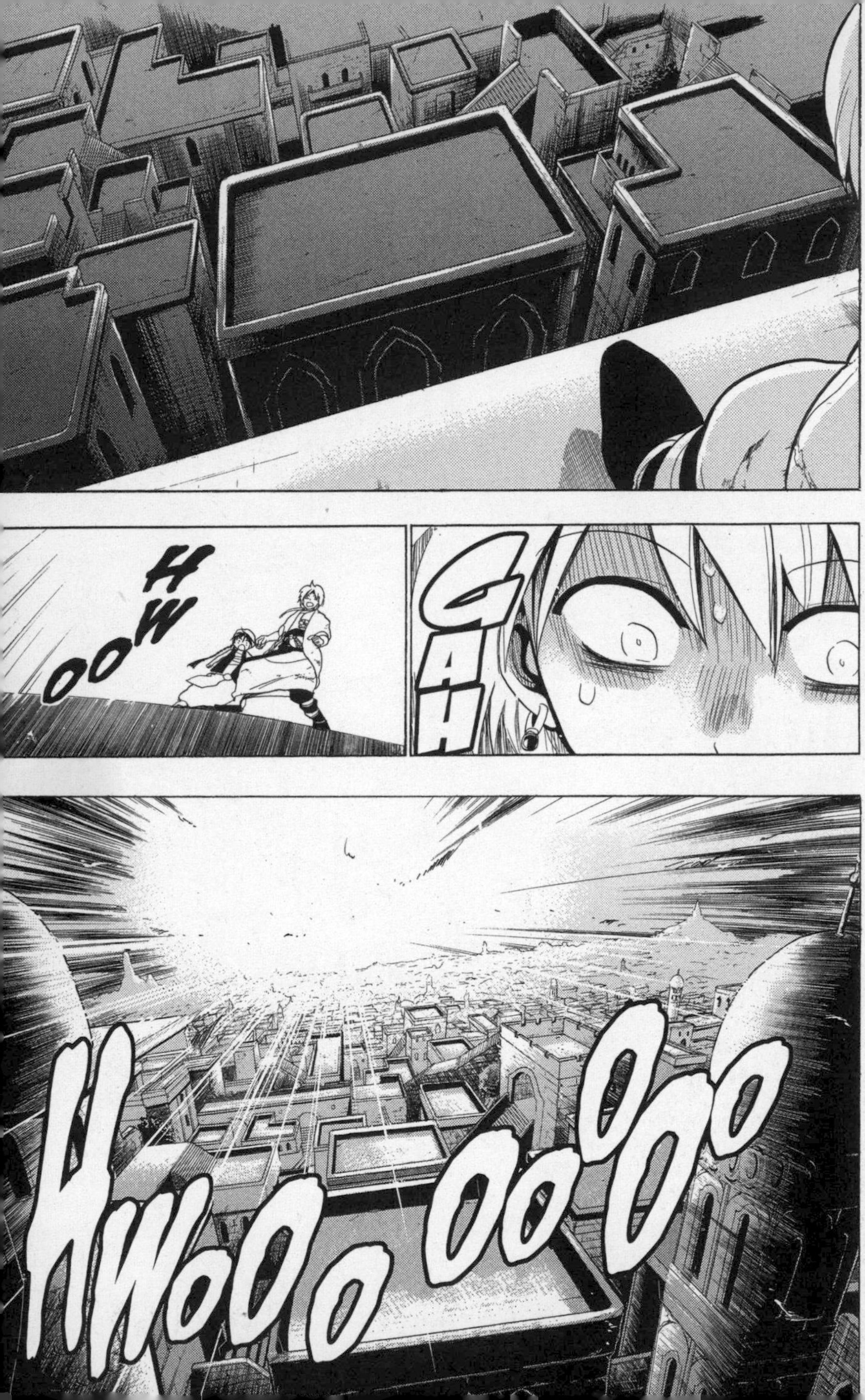
GAH
HWOOO
HWOOOOOOOOOO

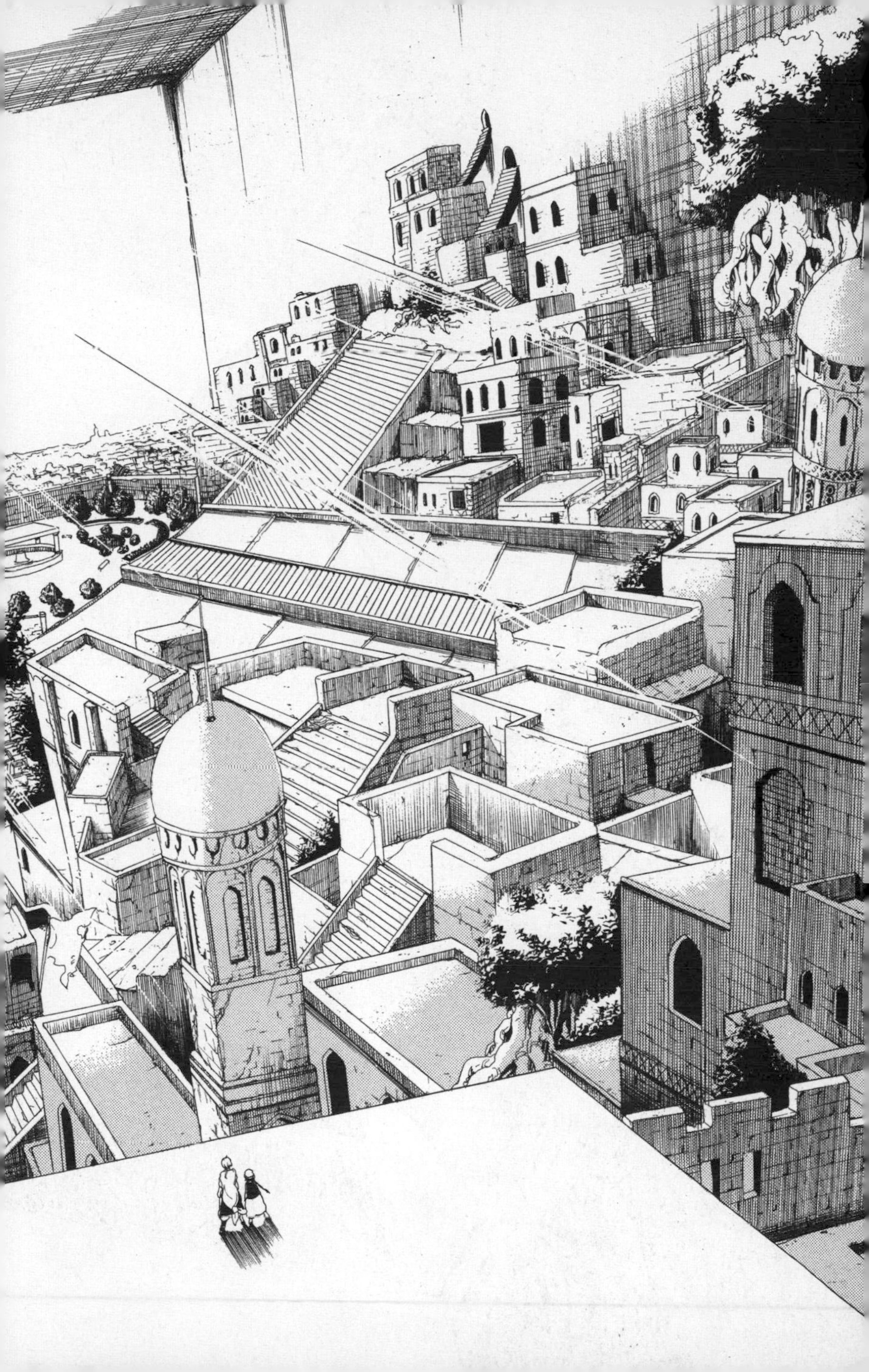

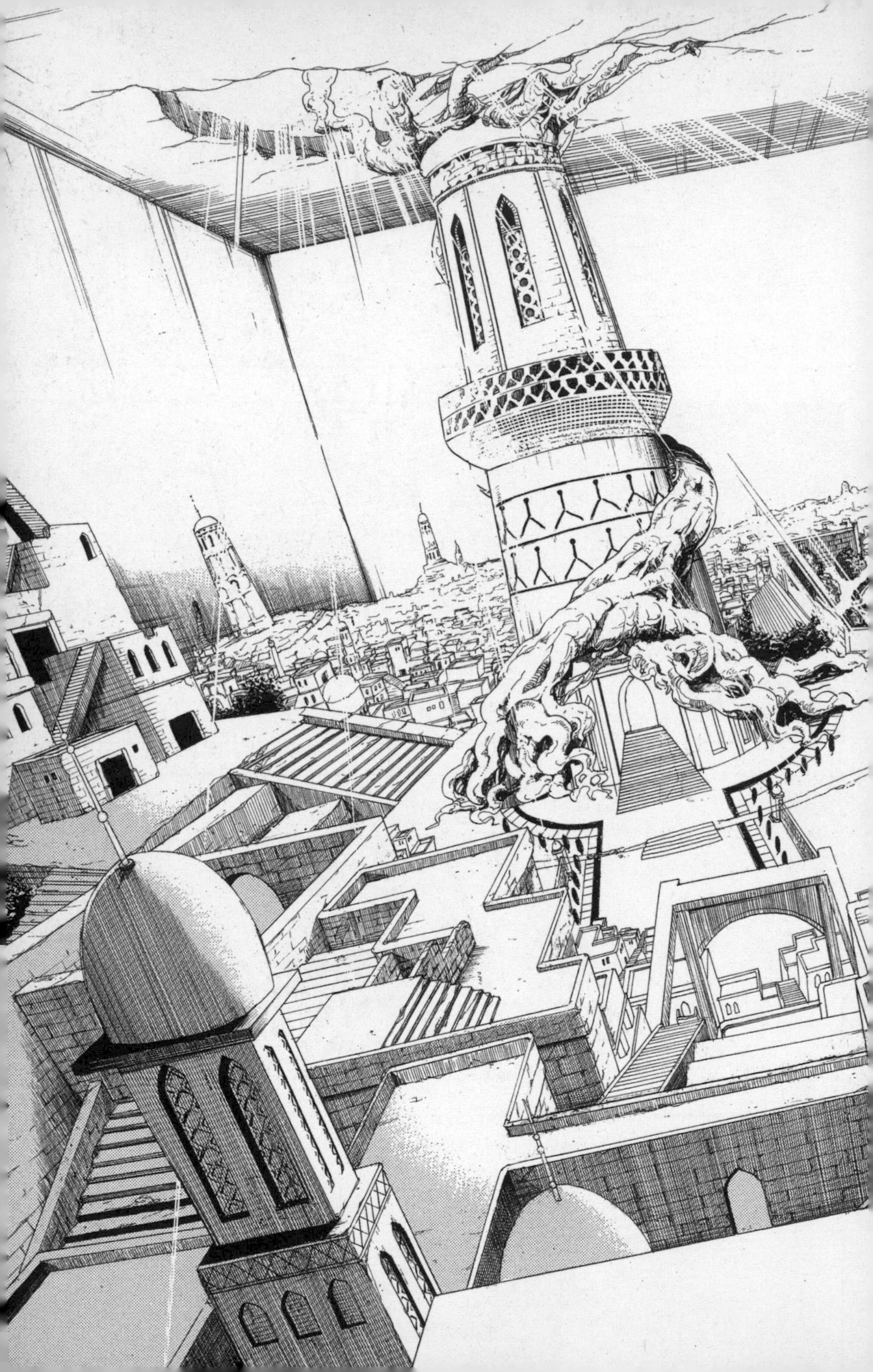

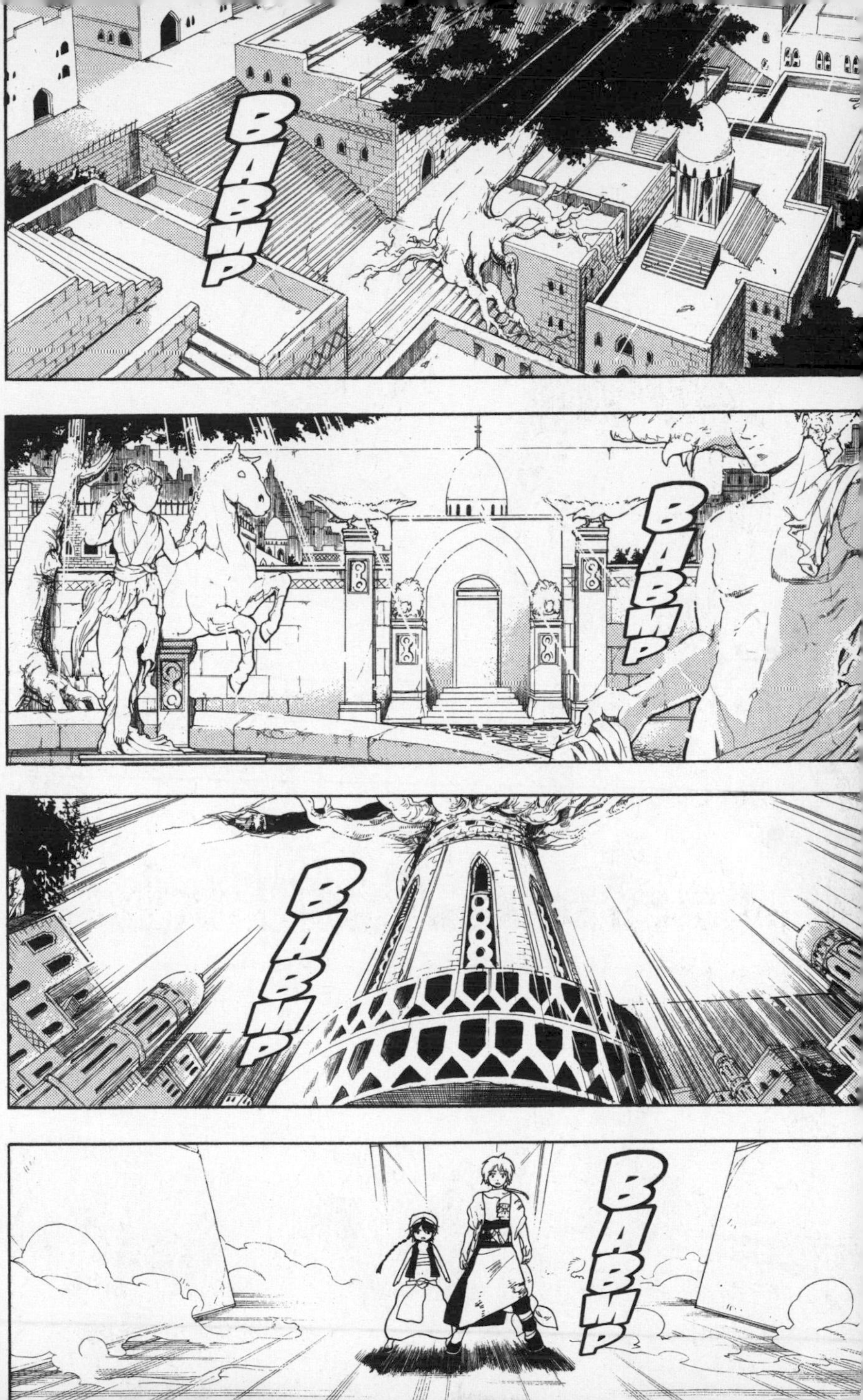
BABMP
BABMP
BABMP
BABMP

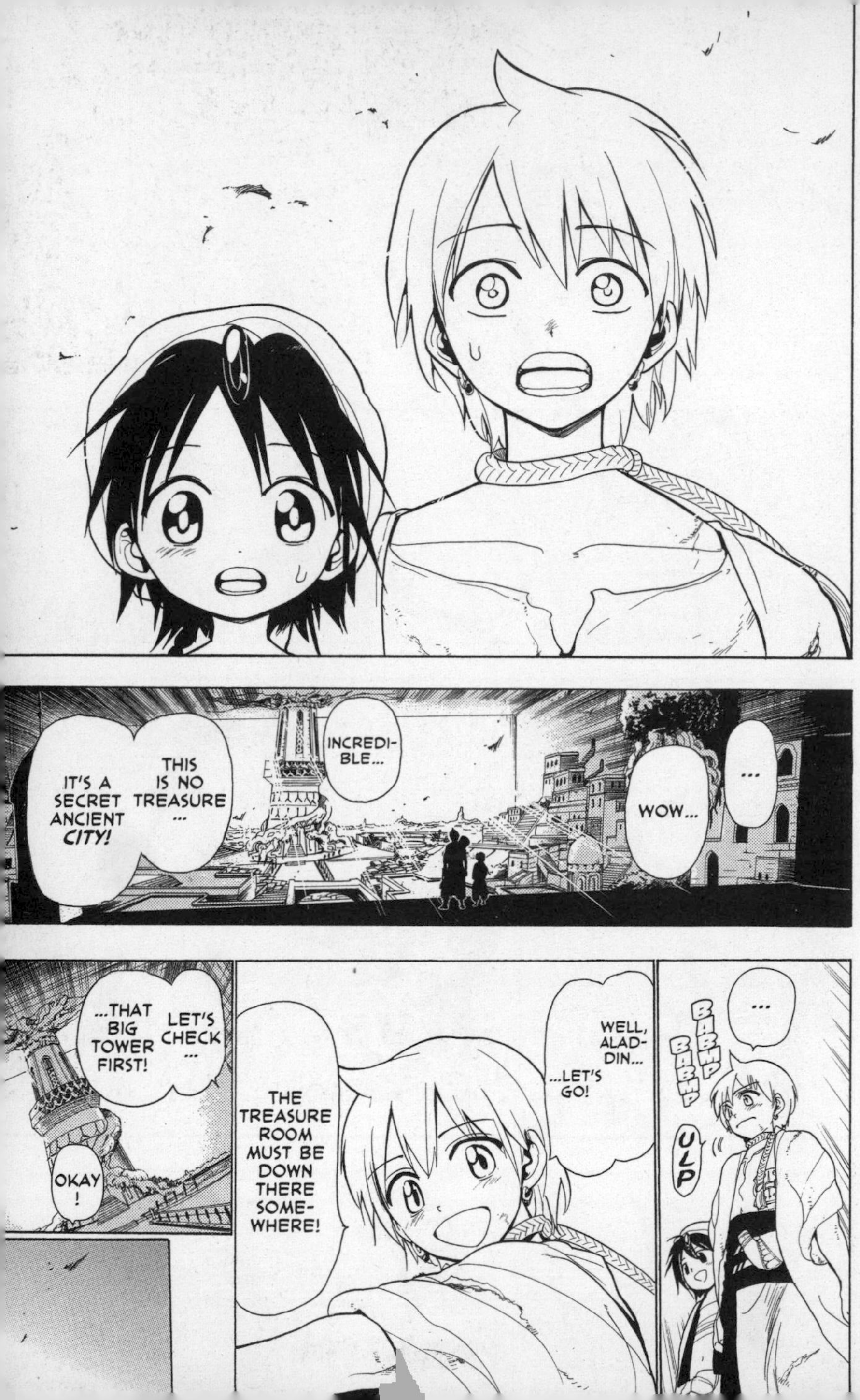
...
WOW...
INCREDI-BLE...
THIS IS NO TREASURE...
IT'S A SECRET ANCIENT CITY!
...
BABMP BABMP
ULP
WELL, ALAD-DIN...
...LET'S GO!
THE TREASURE ROOM MUST BE DOWN THERE SOME-WHERE!
LET'S CHECK...
...THAT BIG TOWER FIRST!
OKAY!

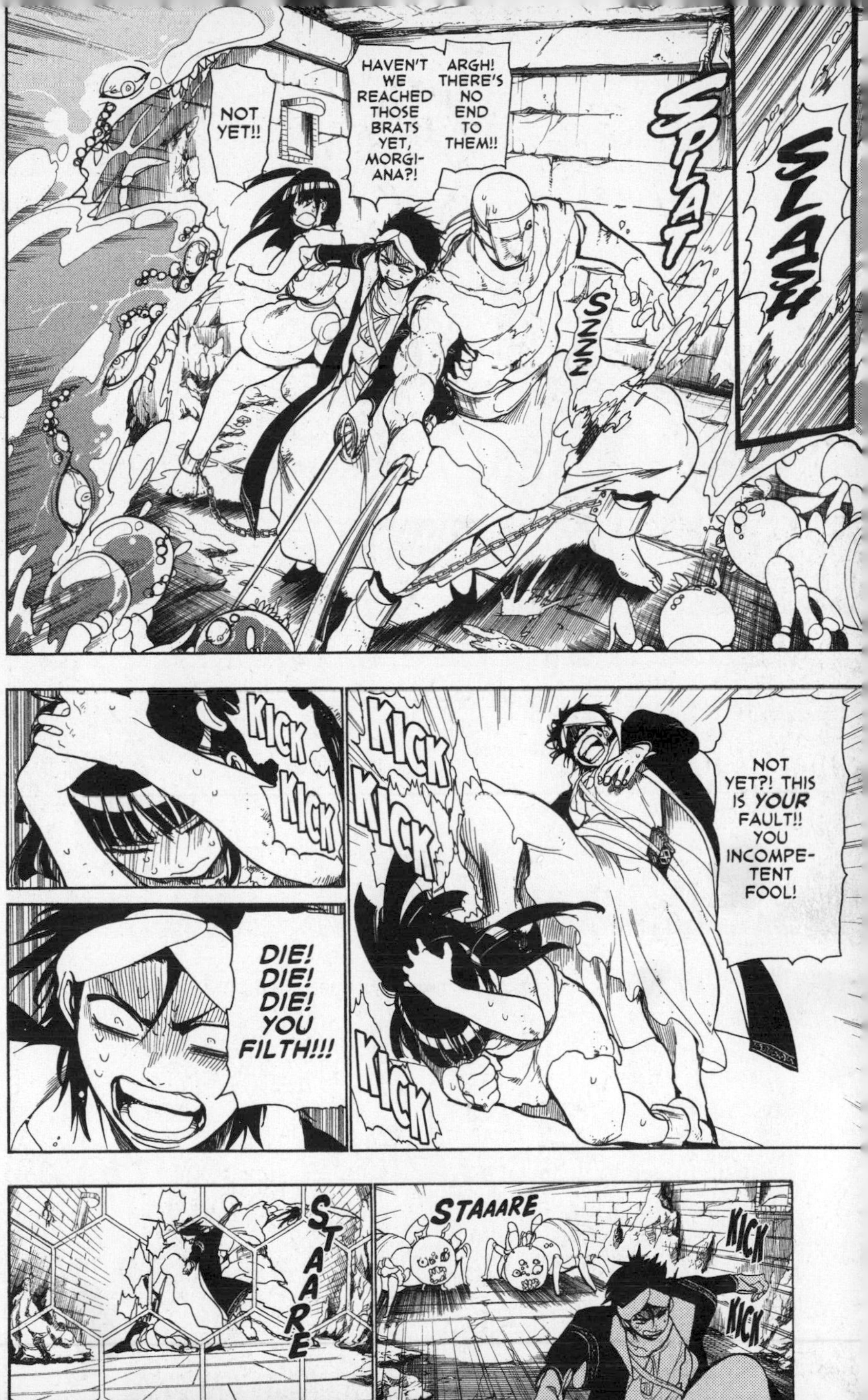
SLASH
SPLAT
ARGH! THERE'S NO END TO THEM!!
HAVEN'T WE REACHED THOSE BRATS YET, MORGIANA?!
NOT YET!!
SZZZ
NOT YET?! THIS IS *YOUR* FAULT!! YOU INCOMPETENT FOOL!
KICK KICK KICK
KICK KICK
DIE! DIE! DIE! YOU FILTH!!!
KICK KICK
STAAARE
STAAARE

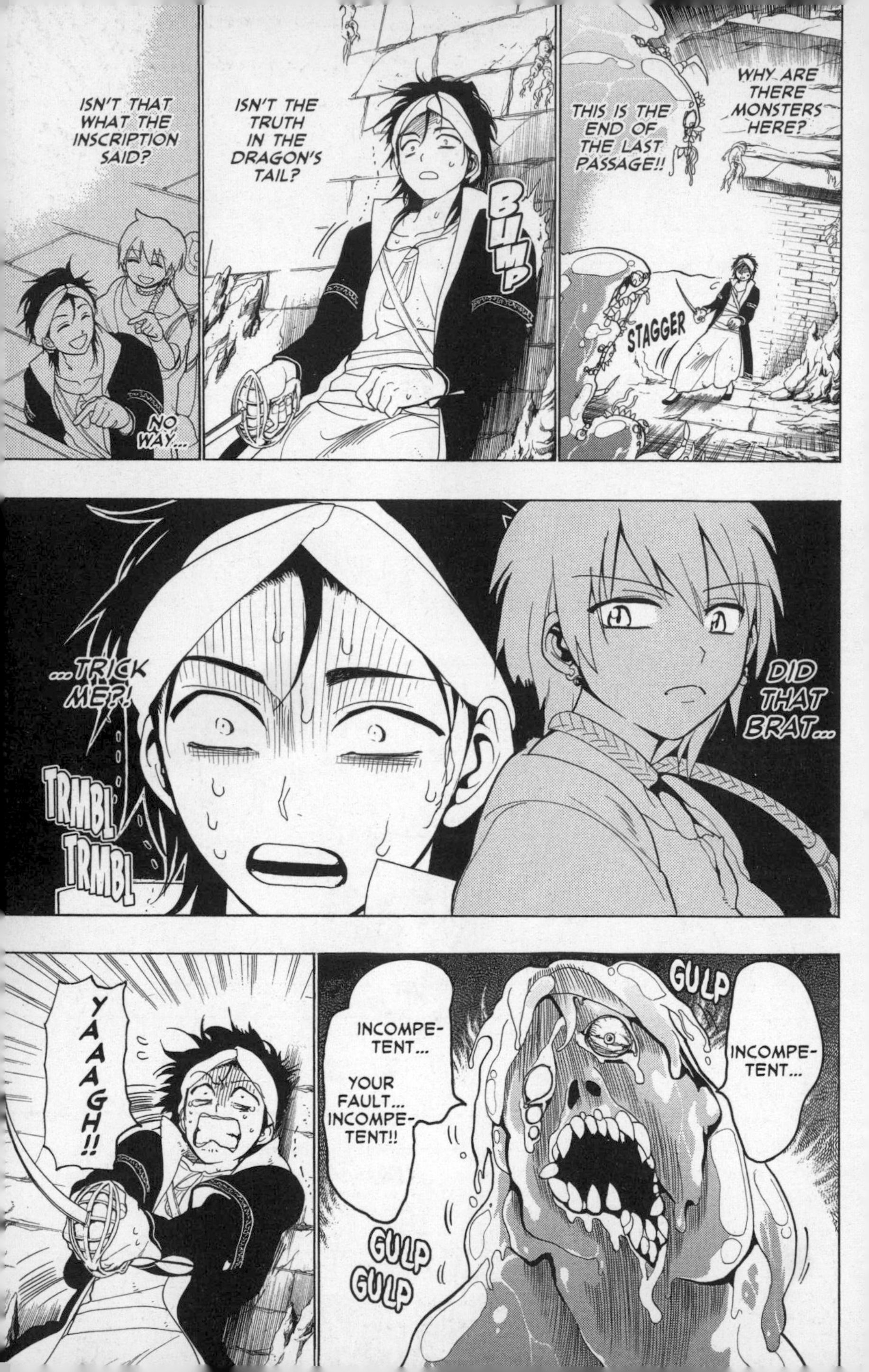
WHY ARE THERE MONSTERS HERE?
THIS IS THE END OF THE LAST PASSAGE!!
STAGGER
BUMP
ISN'T THE TRUTH IN THE DRAGON'S TAIL?
ISN'T THAT WHAT THE INSCRIPTION SAID?
NO WAY...
DID THAT BRAT...
...TRICK ME?!
TRMBL TRMBL
GULP
INCOMPETENT...
INCOMPETENT...
YOUR FAULT... INCOMPETENT!!
GULP GULP
YAAAGH!!

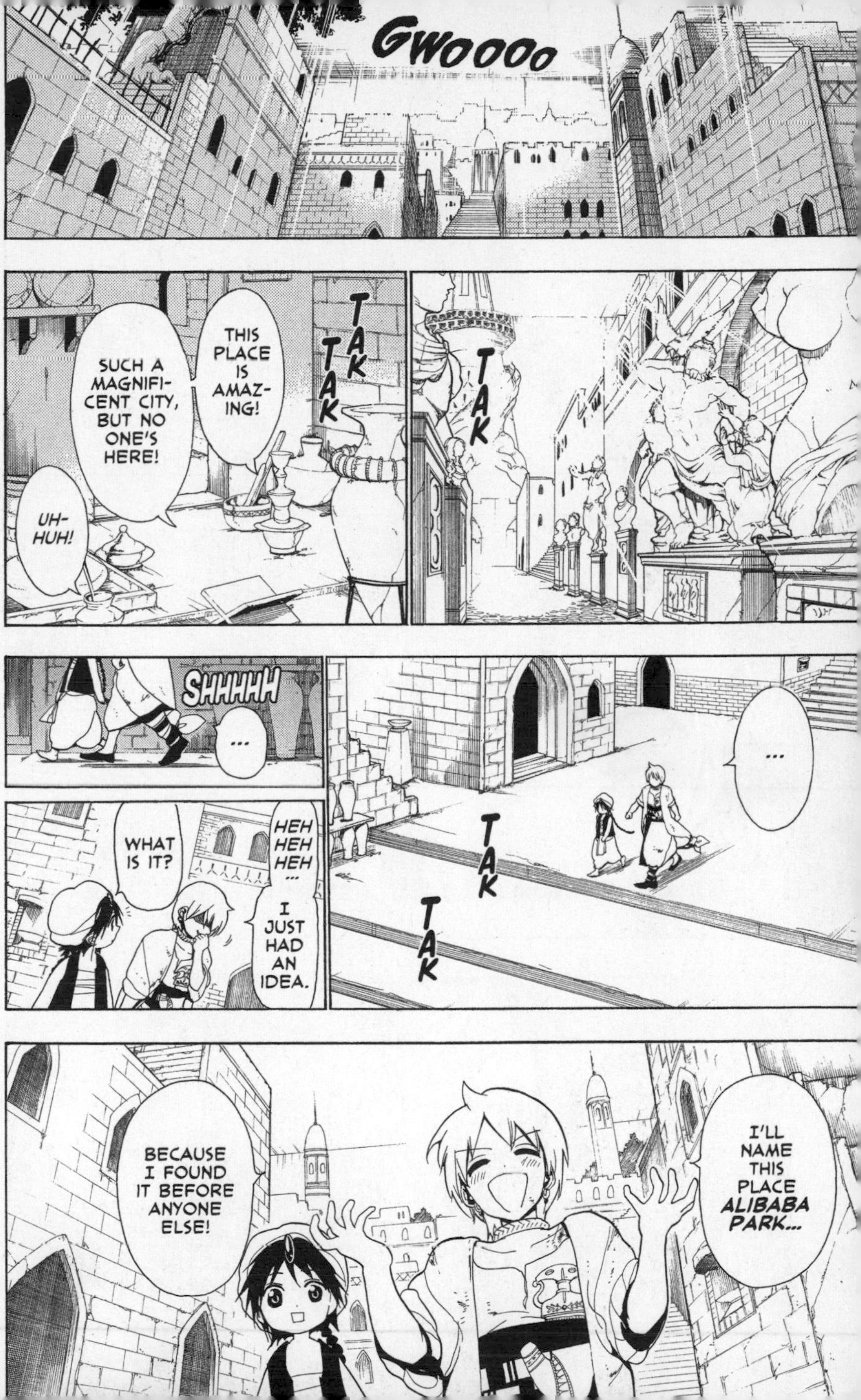
GWOOOO
TAK
TAK
TAK
THIS PLACE IS AMAZING!
SUCH A MAGNIFICENT CITY, BUT NO ONE'S HERE!
UH-HUH!
...
TAK
TAK
SHHHHH
...
HEH HEH HEH... I JUST HAD AN IDEA.
WHAT IS IT?
I'LL NAME THIS PLACE ALIBABA PARK...
BECAUSE I FOUND IT BEFORE ANYONE ELSE!

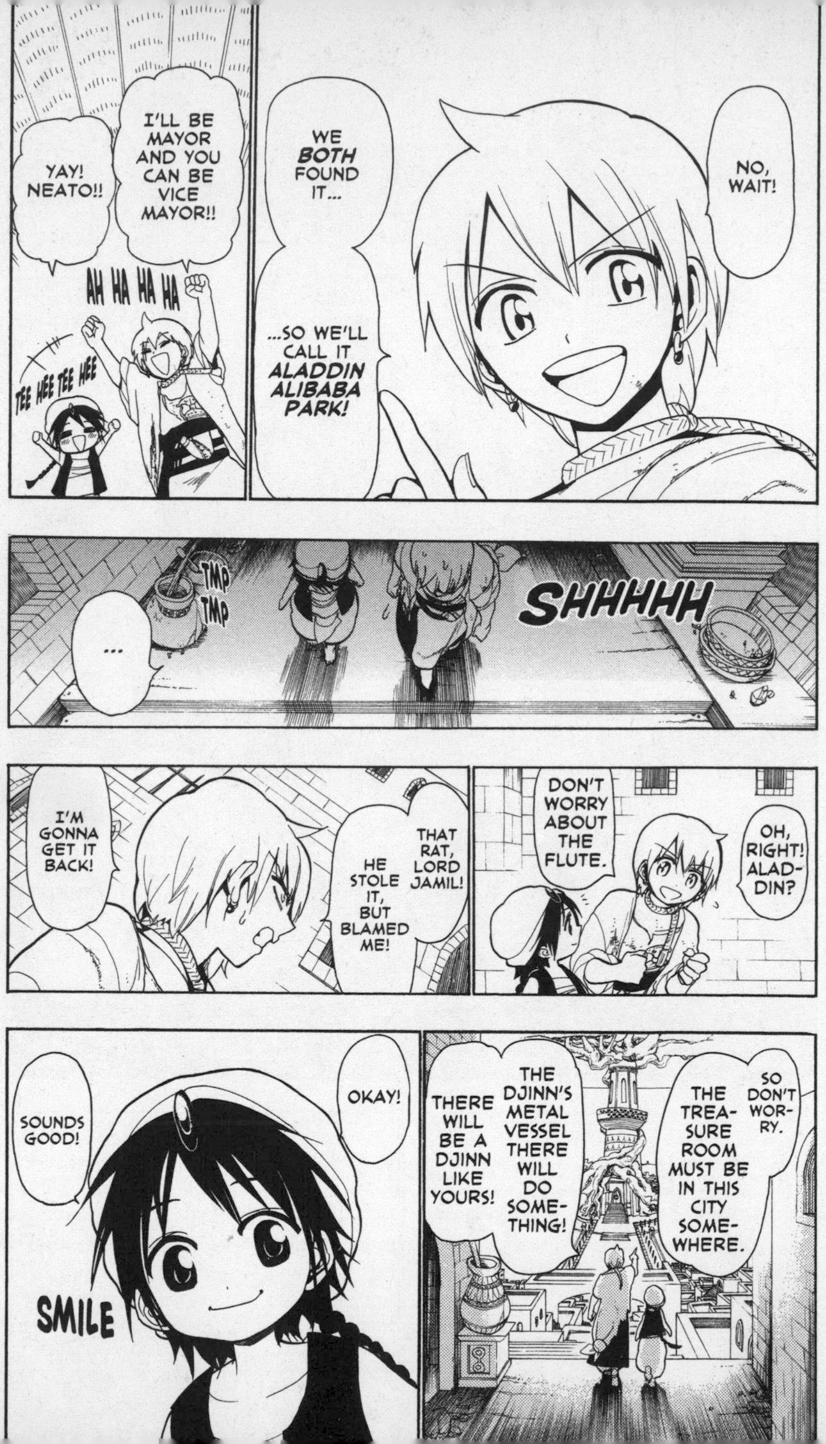
NO, WAIT!
WE BOTH FOUND IT...
...SO WE'LL CALL IT ALADDIN ALIBABA PARK!
I'LL BE MAYOR AND YOU CAN BE VICE MAYOR!!
AH HA HA HA
YAY! NEATO!!
TEE HEE TEE HEE
SHHHHH
TMP TMP
...
OH, RIGHT! ALADDIN?
DON'T WORRY ABOUT THE FLUTE.
THAT RAT, LORD JAMIL!
HE STOLE IT, BUT BLAMED ME!
I'M GONNA GET IT BACK!
SO DON'T WORRY.
THE TREASURE ROOM MUST BE IN THIS CITY SOMEWHERE.
THE DJINN'S METAL VESSEL THERE WILL DO SOMETHING!
THERE WILL BE A DJINN LIKE YOURS!
OKAY!
SOUNDS GOOD!
SMILE

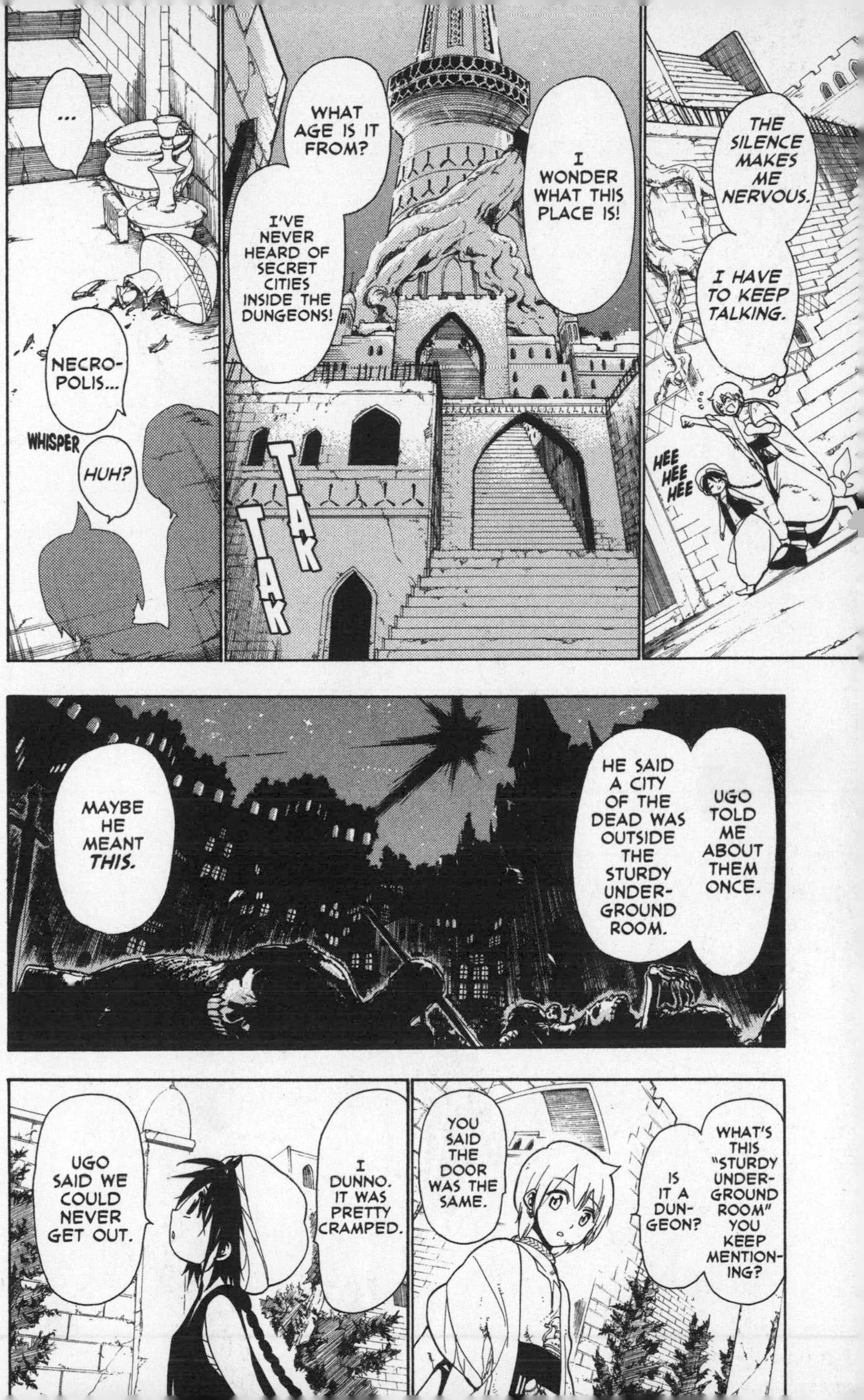
THE SILENCE MAKES ME NERVOUS.
I HAVE TO KEEP TALKING.
HEE HEE HEE
I WONDER WHAT THIS PLACE IS!
WHAT AGE IS IT FROM?
I'VE NEVER HEARD OF SECRET CITIES INSIDE THE DUNGEONS!
TAK TAK
...
NECROPOLIS...
WHISPER
HUH?
UGO TOLD ME ABOUT THEM ONCE.
HE SAID A CITY OF THE DEAD WAS OUTSIDE THE STURDY UNDERGROUND ROOM.
MAYBE HE MEANT THIS.
WHAT'S THIS "STURDY UNDERGROUND ROOM" YOU KEEP MENTIONING?
IS IT A DUNGEON?
YOU SAID THE DOOR WAS THE SAME.
I DUNNO. IT WAS PRETTY CRAMPED.
UGO SAID WE COULD NEVER GET OUT.

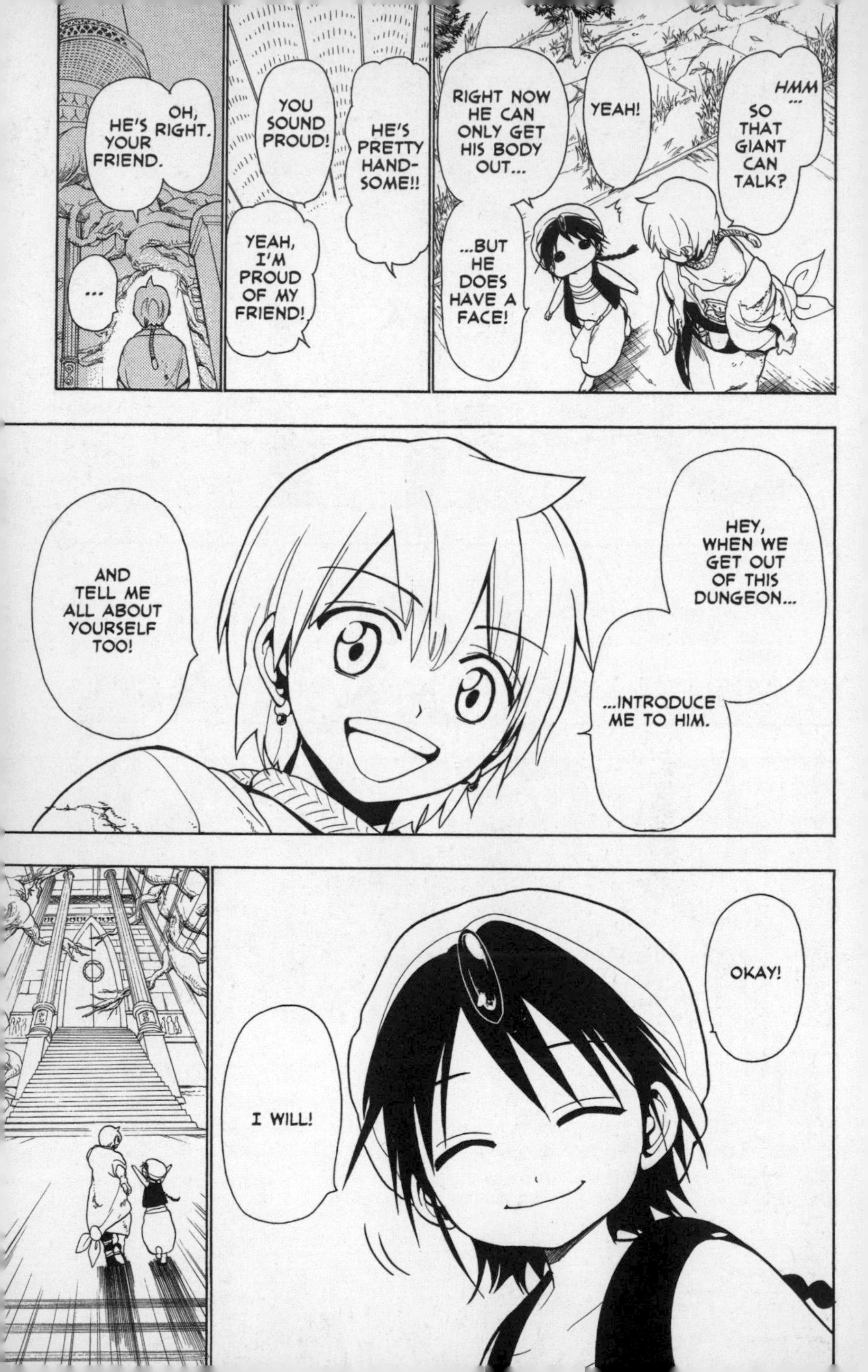
HMM... SO THAT GIANT CAN TALK?
YEAH!
RIGHT NOW HE CAN ONLY GET HIS BODY OUT...
...BUT HE DOES HAVE A FACE!
HE'S PRETTY HANDSOME!!
YOU SOUND PROUD!
YEAH, I'M PROUD OF MY FRIEND!
OH, HE'S RIGHT. YOUR FRIEND.
...
HEY, WHEN WE GET OUT OF THIS DUNGEON...
...INTRODUCE ME TO HIM.
AND TELL ME ALL ABOUT YOURSELF TOO!
OKAY!
I WILL!

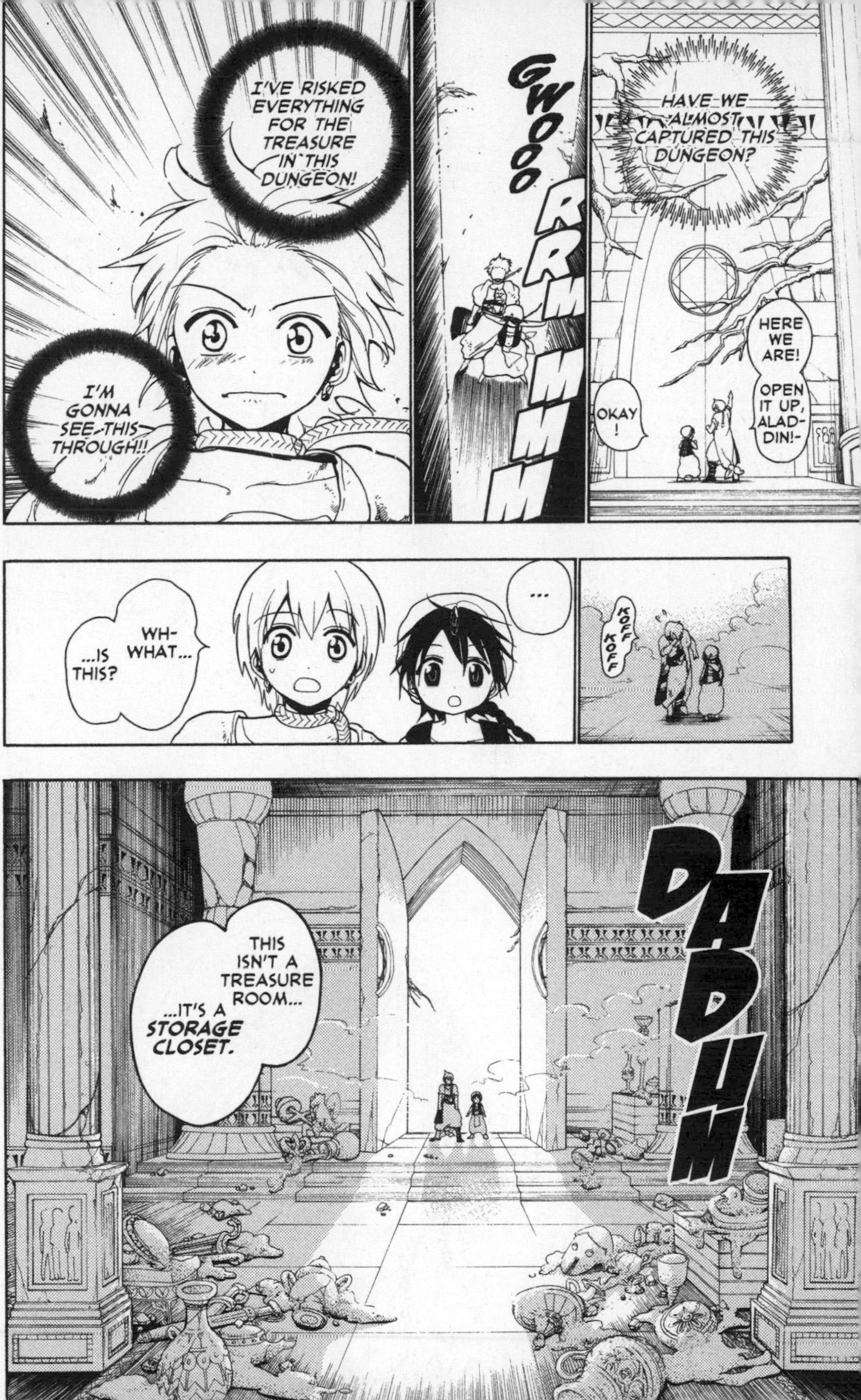
HAVE WE ALMOST CAPTURED THIS DUNGEON?
HERE WE ARE!
OPEN IT UP, ALADDIN!
OKAY!
GWOOOO
RRMMMMM
I'VE RISKED EVERYTHING FOR THE TREASURE IN THIS DUNGEON!
I'M GONNA SEE THIS THROUGH!!
KOFF KOFF
...
WH-WHAT...
...IS THIS?
DADUM
THIS ISN'T A TREASURE ROOM...
...IT'S A STORAGE CLOSET.

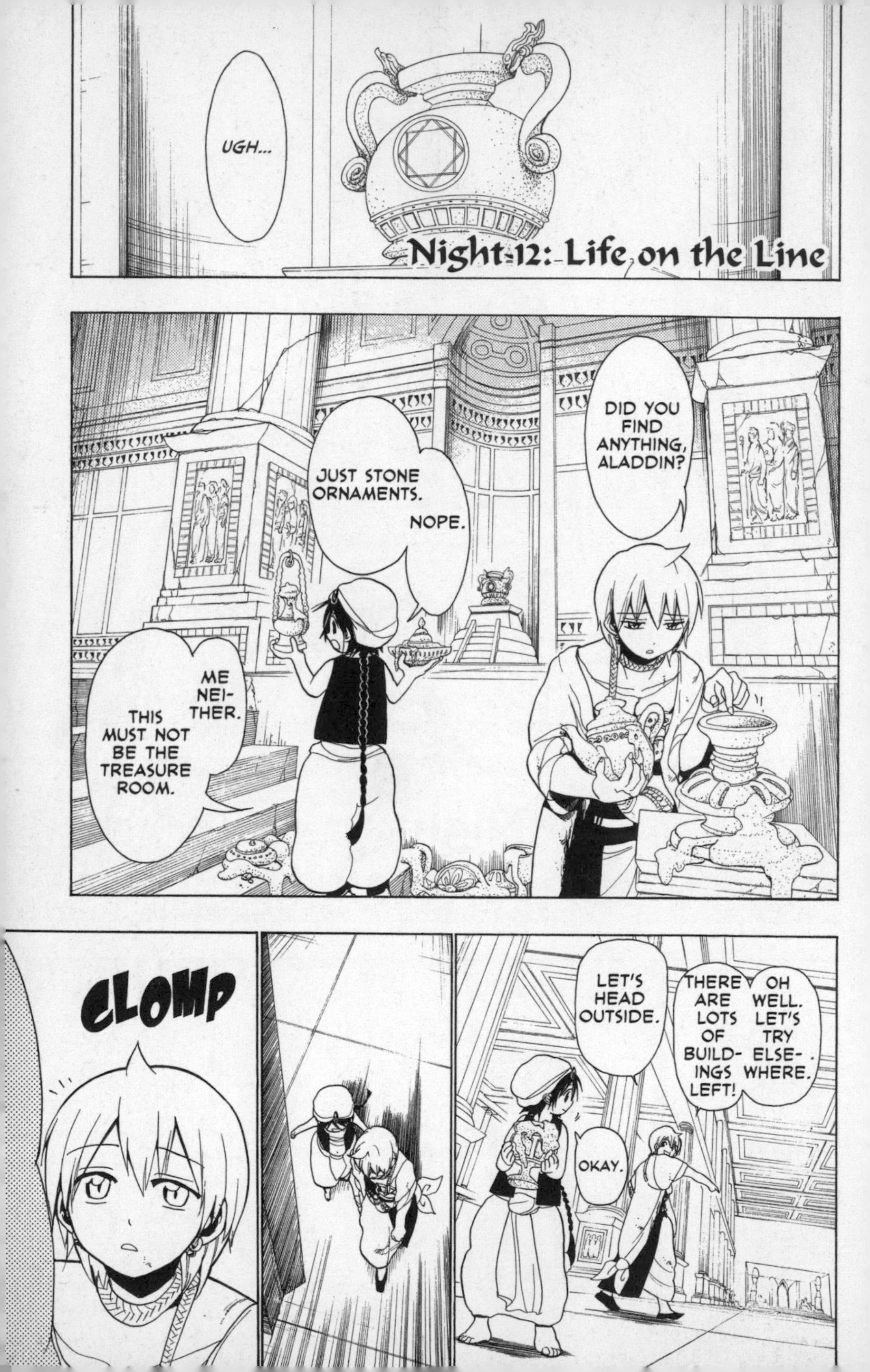
UGH...
Night 12: Life on the Line
DID YOU FIND ANYTHING, ALADDIN?
NOPE.
JUST STONE ORNAMENTS.
ME NEITHER.
THIS MUST NOT BE THE TREASURE ROOM.
OH WELL. LET'S TRY ELSEWHERE.
THERE ARE LOTS OF BUILDINGS LEFT!
LET'S HEAD OUTSIDE.
OKAY.
CLOMP

Night 12: Life on the Line

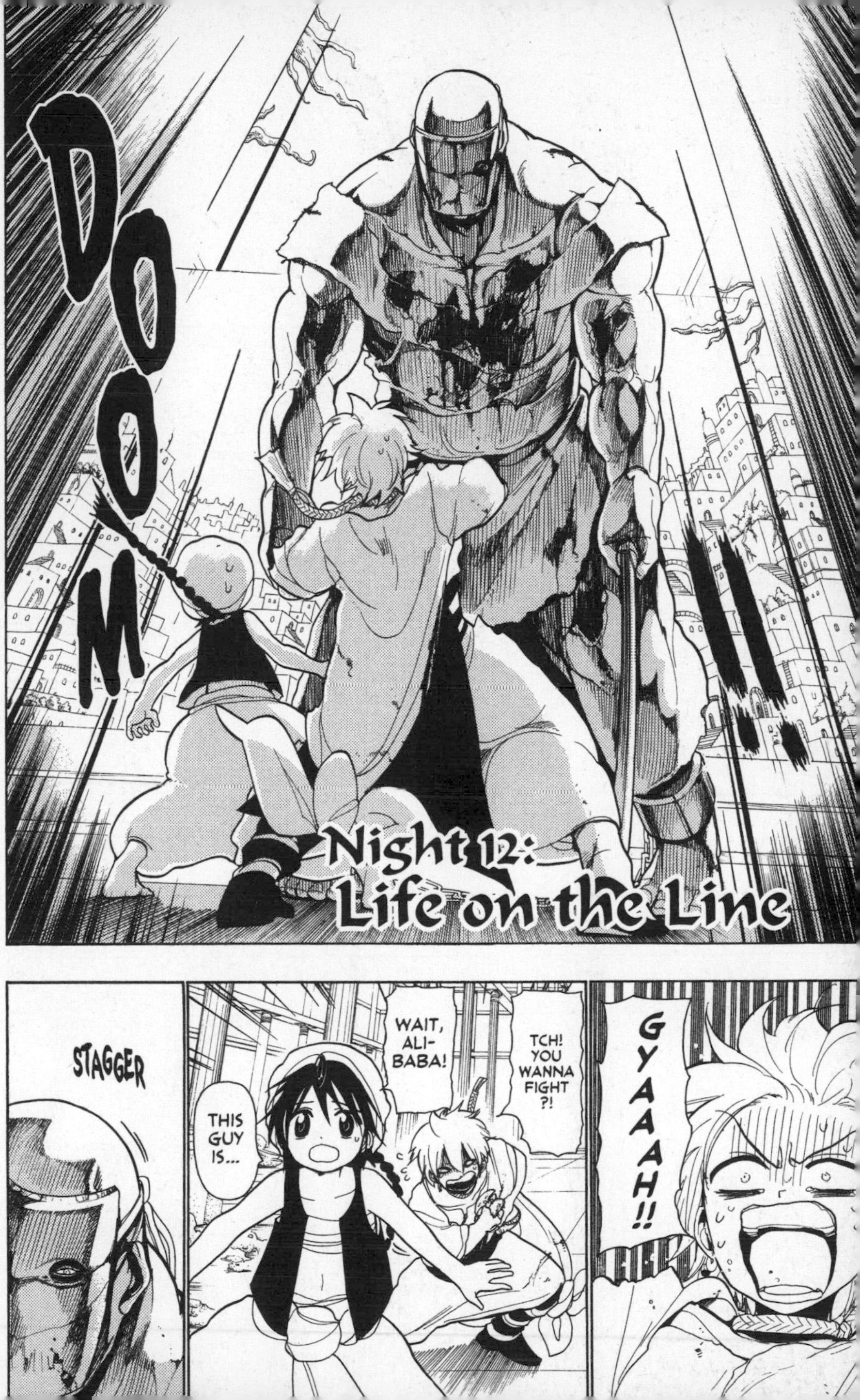
DOOM
!!
GYAAAH!!
TCH! YOU WANNA FIGHT?!
WAIT, ALI-BABA!
THIS GUY IS...
STAGGER

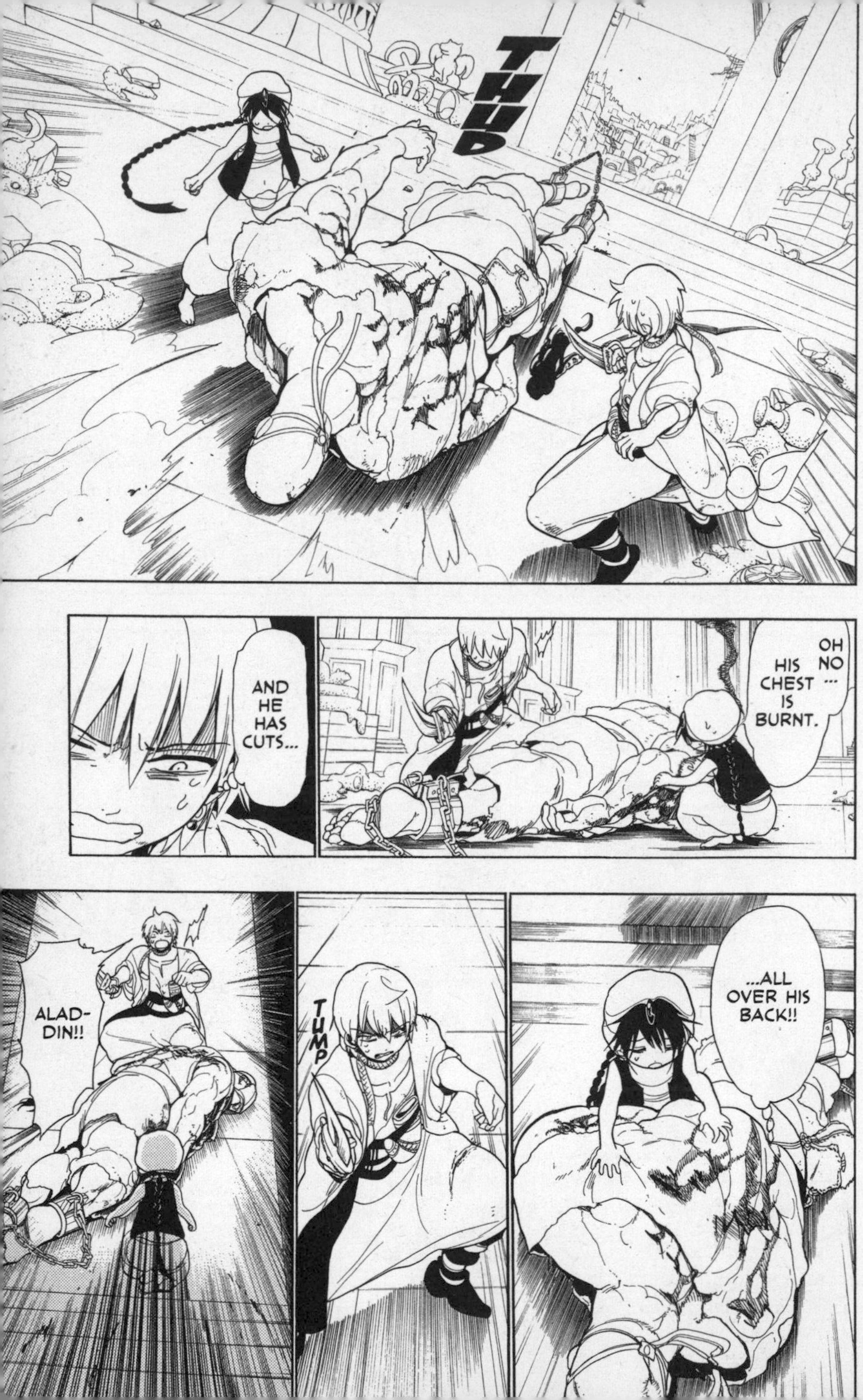
THUD
OH NO... HIS CHEST IS BURNT.
AND HE HAS CUTS...
...ALL OVER HIS BACK!!
TUMP
ALAD-DIN!!

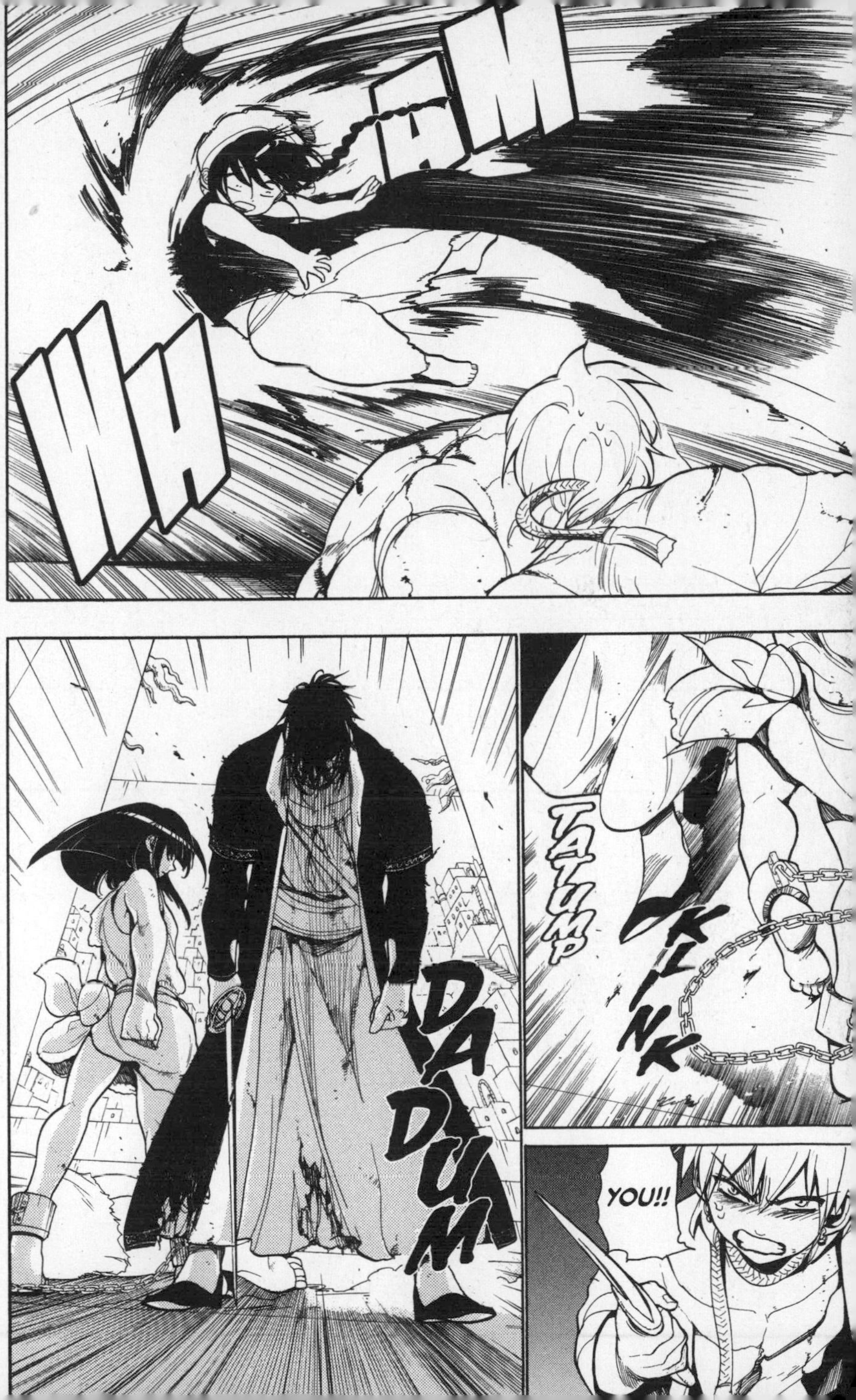
WHAM
TATUMP
KLINK
YOU!!
DADUM

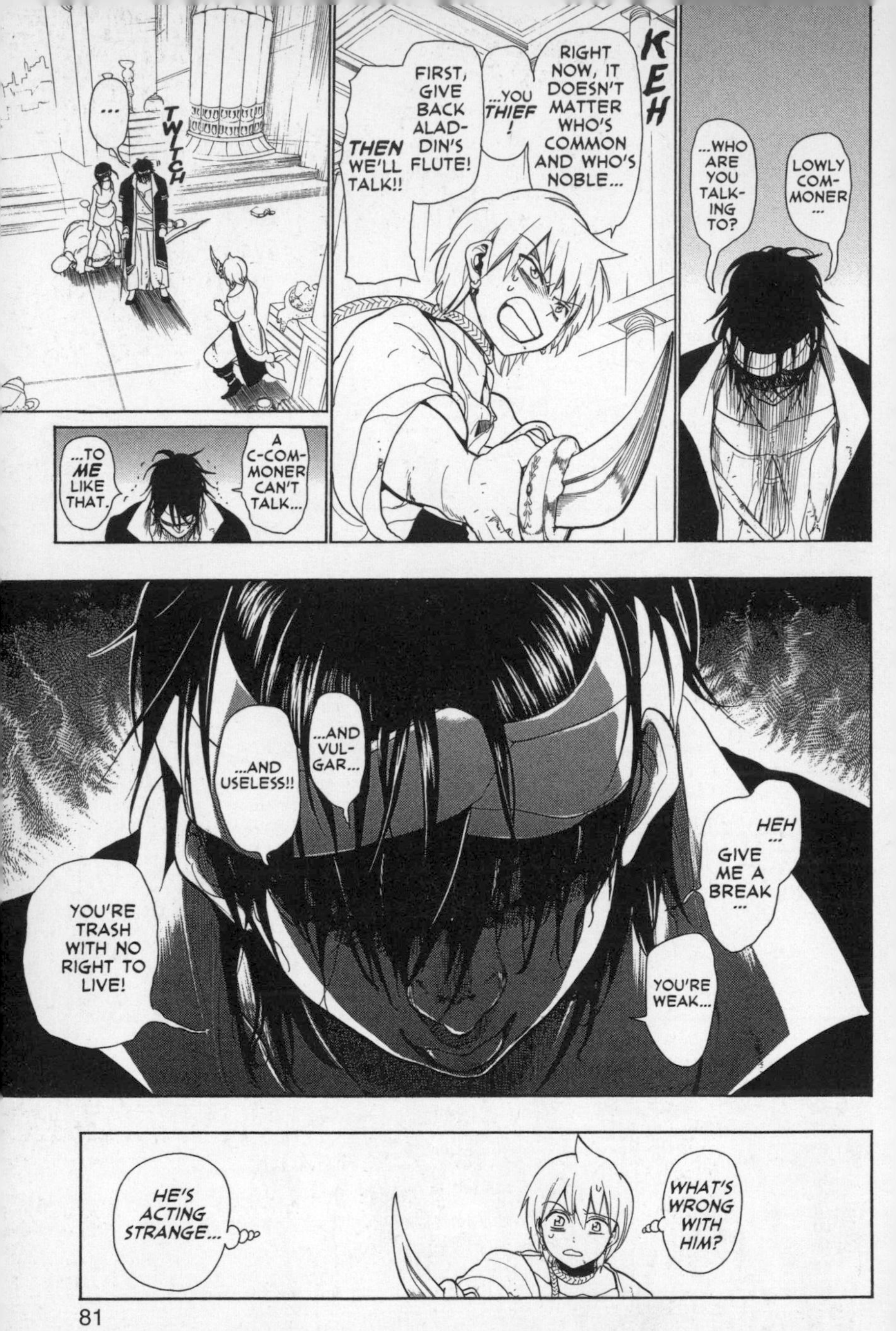
LOWLY COMMONER...
...WHO ARE YOU TALKING TO?
KEH
RIGHT NOW, IT DOESN'T MATTER WHO'S COMMON AND WHO'S NOBLE...
...YOU THIEF!
FIRST, GIVE BACK ALADDIN'S FLUTE!
THEN WE'LL TALK!!
...
TWITCH
A C-COMMONER CAN'T TALK...
...TO ME LIKE THAT.
HEH... GIVE ME A BREAK...
YOU'RE WEAK...
...AND VULGAR...
...AND USELESS!!
YOU'RE TRASH WITH NO RIGHT TO LIVE!
WHAT'S WRONG WITH HIM?
HE'S ACTING STRANGE...

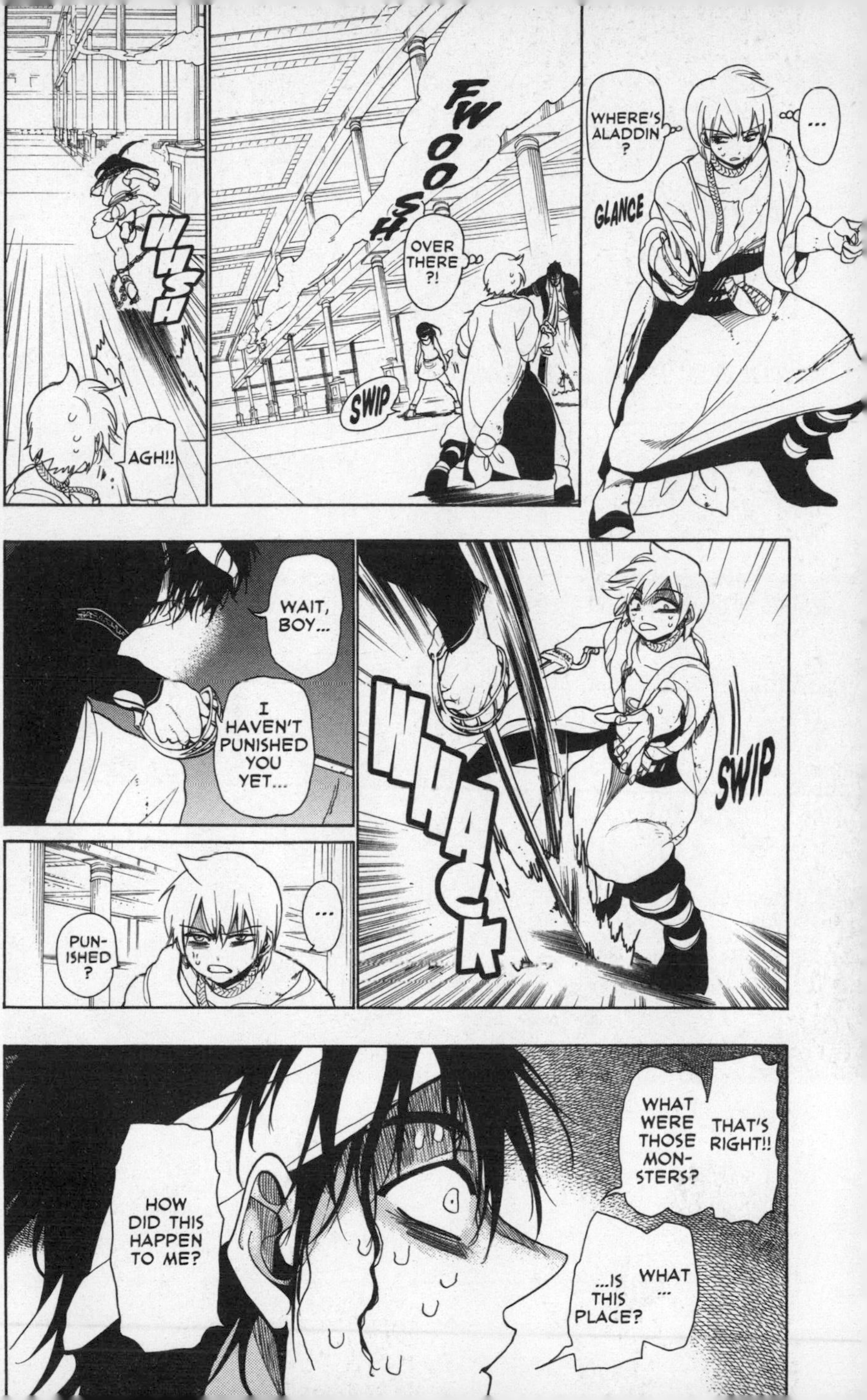
WHERE'S ALADDIN?
...
GLANCE
FWOOSH
OVER THERE?!
SWIP
WHSH
AGH!!
WHACK
SWIP
WAIT, BOY...
I HAVEN'T PUNISHED YOU YET...
...
PUN-ISHED?
THAT'S RIGHT!!
WHAT WERE THOSE MON-STERS?
WHAT...
...IS THIS PLACE?
HOW DID THIS HAPPEN TO ME?

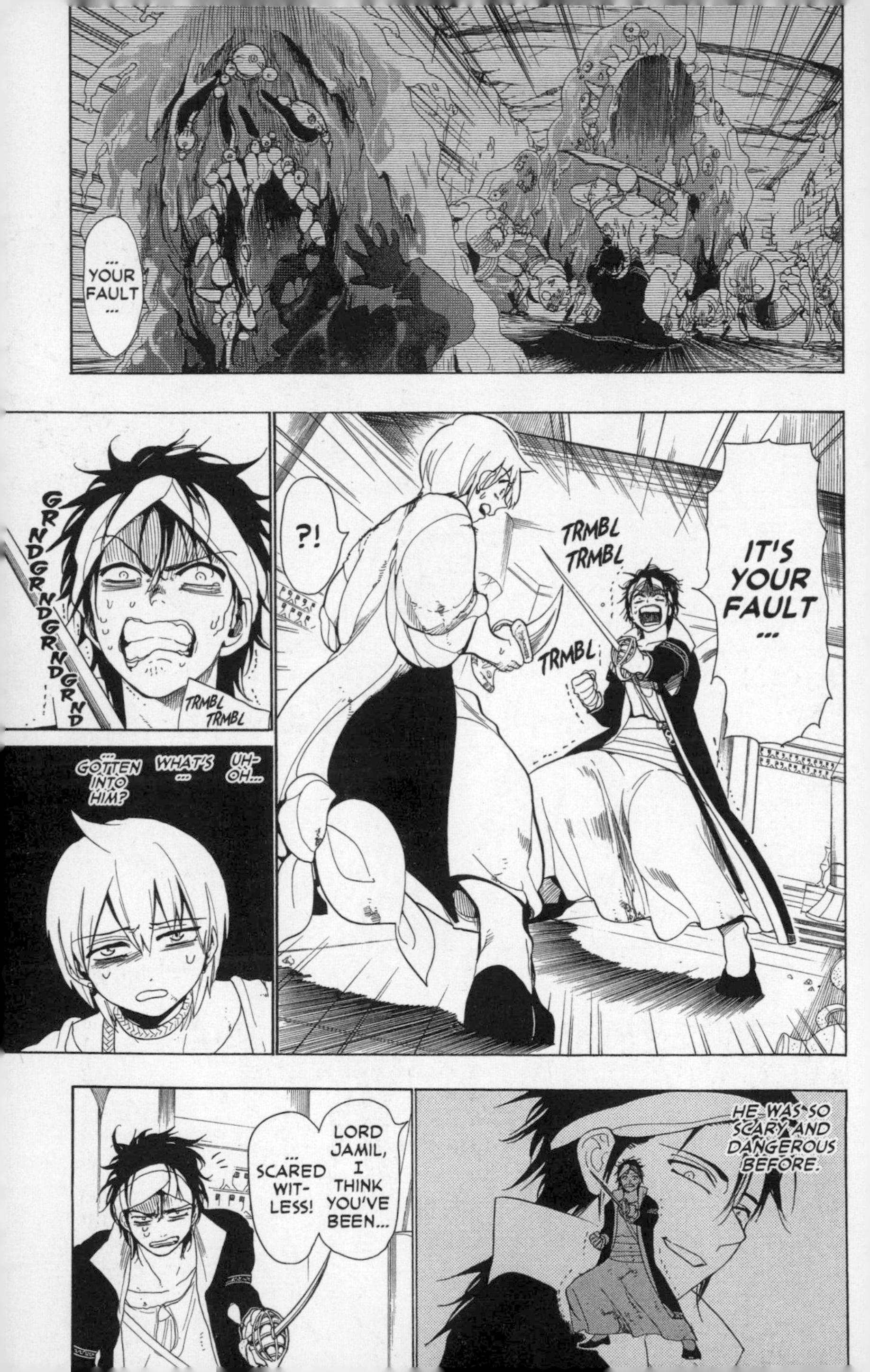
... YOUR FAULT ...
IT'S YOUR FAULT ...
TRMBL TRMBL
?!
TRMBL
GRNDGRNDGRNDGRNDGRND
TRMBL TRMBL
UH-OH...
WHAT'S ...
... GOTTEN INTO HIM?
HE WAS SO SCARY AND DANGEROUS BEFORE.
LORD JAMIL, I THINK YOU'VE BEEN...
... SCARED WIT-LESS!

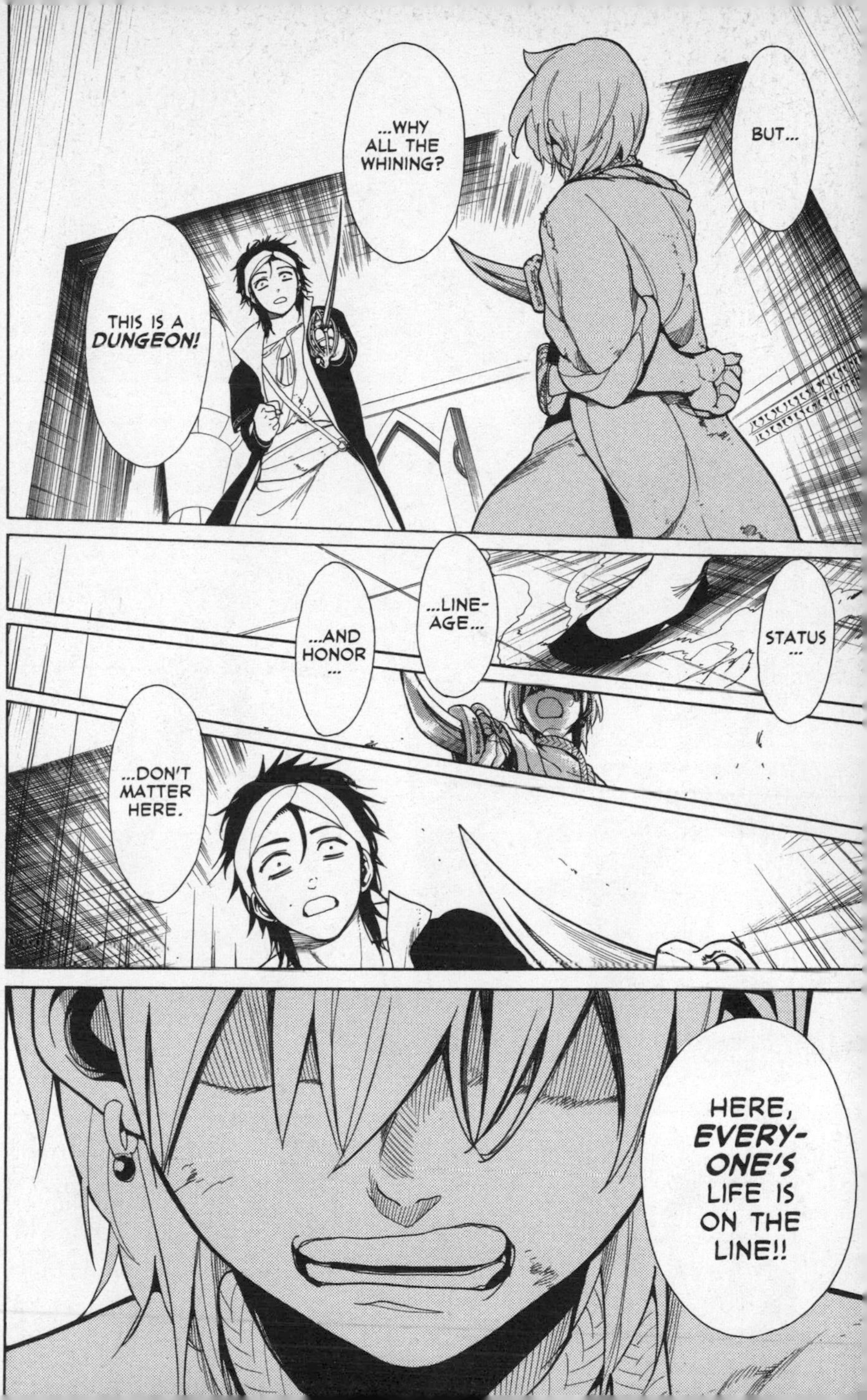
BUT...
...WHY ALL THE WHINING?
THIS IS A *DUNGEON!*
STATUS...
...LINE-AGE...
...AND HONOR...
...DON'T MATTER HERE.
HERE, *EVERY-ONE'S* LIFE IS ON THE LINE!!

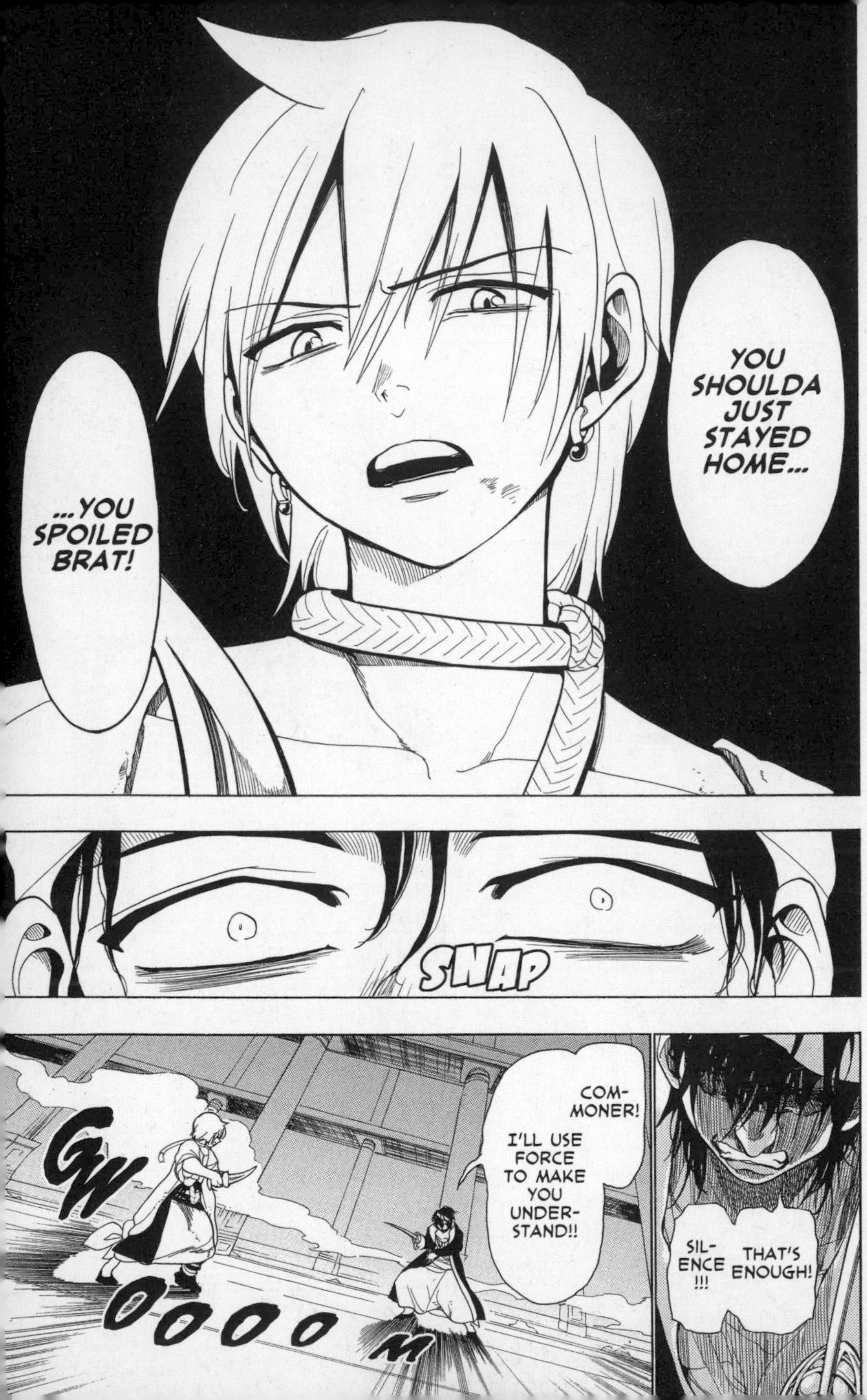
YOU SHOULDA JUST STAYED HOME...
...YOU SPOILED BRAT!
SNAP
THAT'S ENOUGH!
SIL-ENCE!!!
COM-MONER!
I'LL USE FORCE TO MAKE YOU UNDER-STAND!!
GWOOOOOM

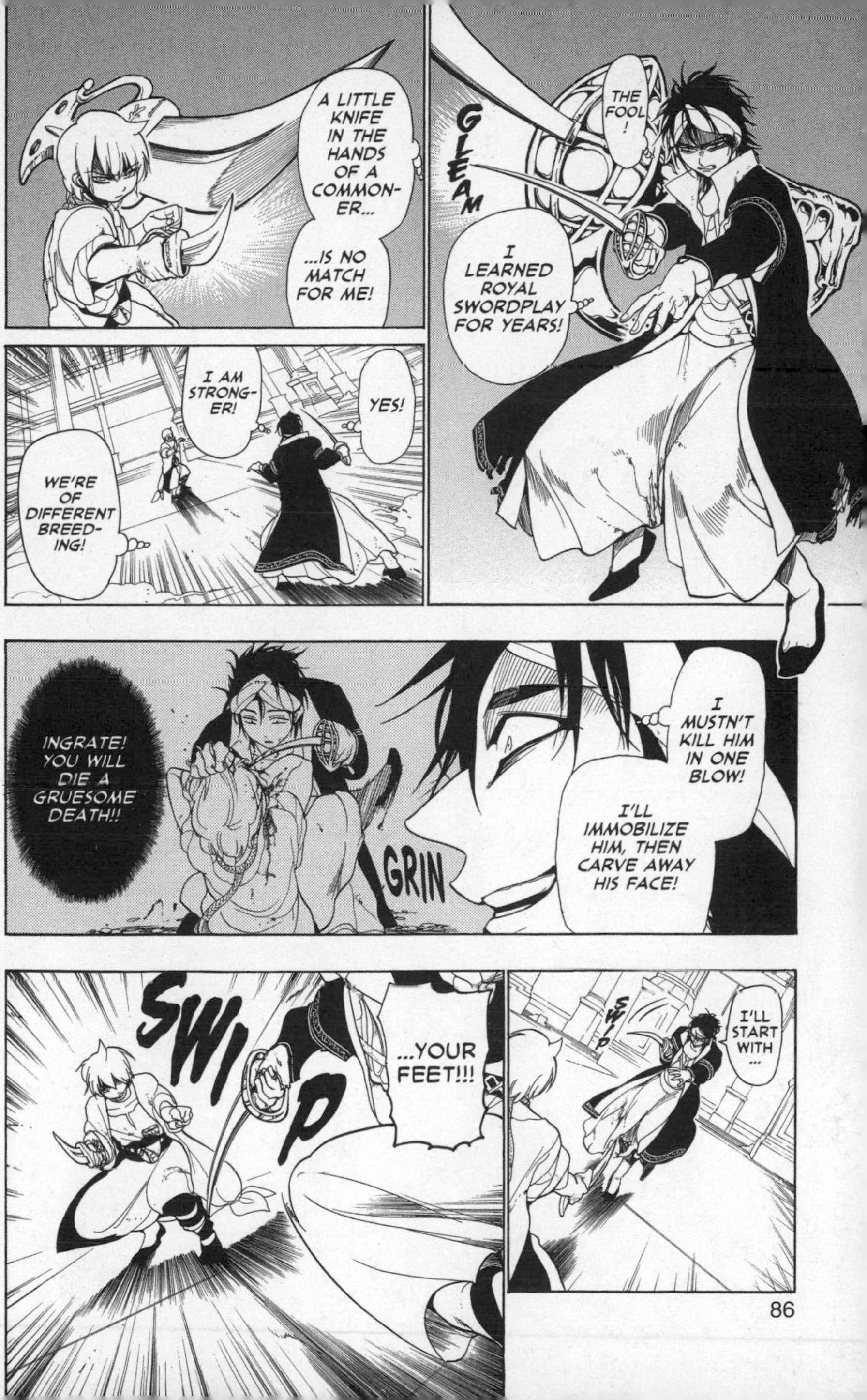
THE FOOL!
GLEAM
I LEARNED ROYAL SWORDPLAY FOR YEARS!
A LITTLE KNIFE IN THE HANDS OF A COMMONER...
...IS NO MATCH FOR ME!
YES!
I AM STRONGER!
WE'RE OF DIFFERENT BREEDING!
I MUSTN'T KILL HIM IN ONE BLOW!
I'LL IMMOBILIZE HIM, THEN CARVE AWAY HIS FACE!
GRIN
INGRATE! YOU WILL DIE A GRUESOME DEATH!!
SWIP
I'LL START WITH ...
...YOUR FEET!!!
SWIP

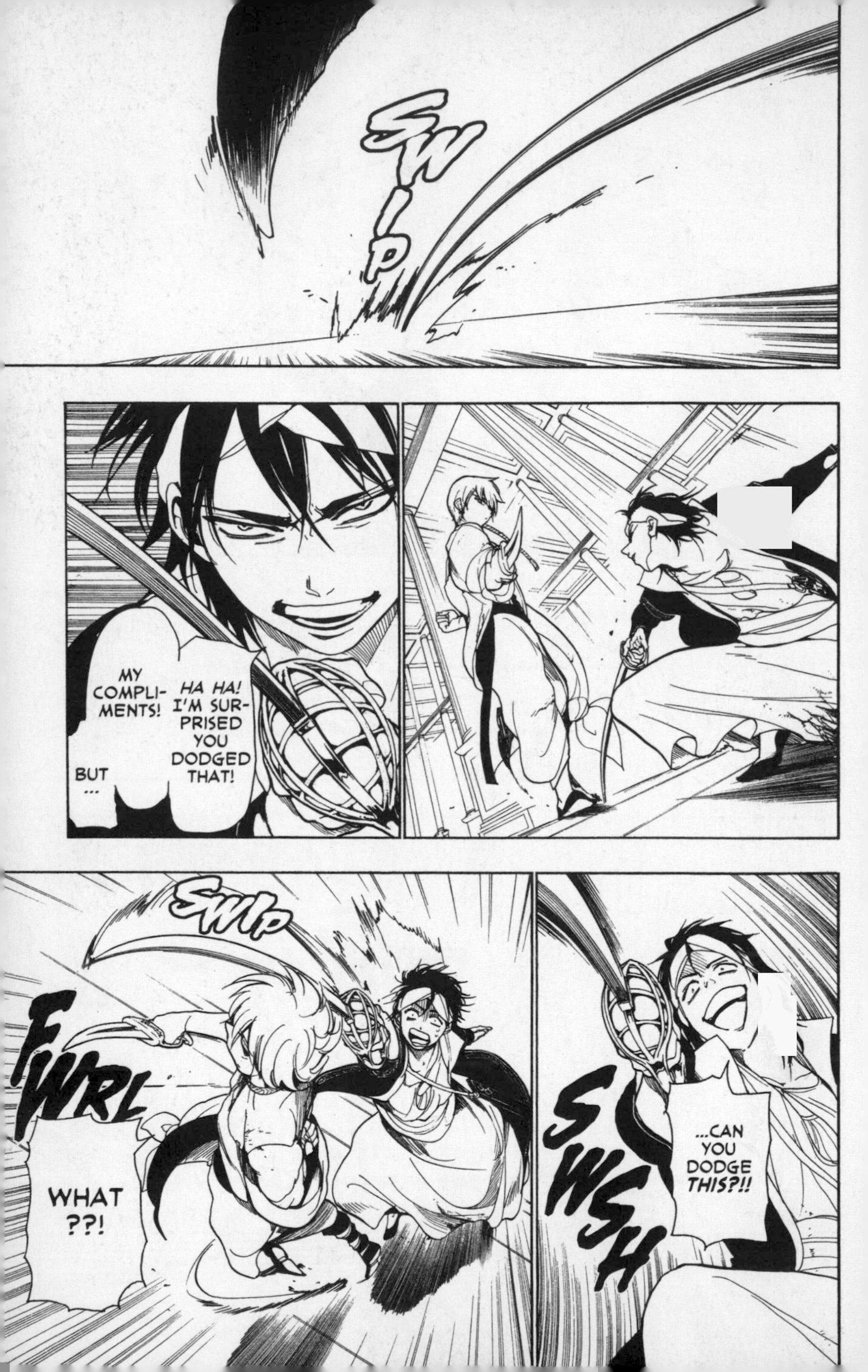
SWIP
HA HA! I'M SURPRISED YOU DODGED THAT!
MY COMPLIMENTS!
BUT ...
SWSH
...CAN YOU DODGE THIS?!!
SWIP
FWRL
WHAT ??!

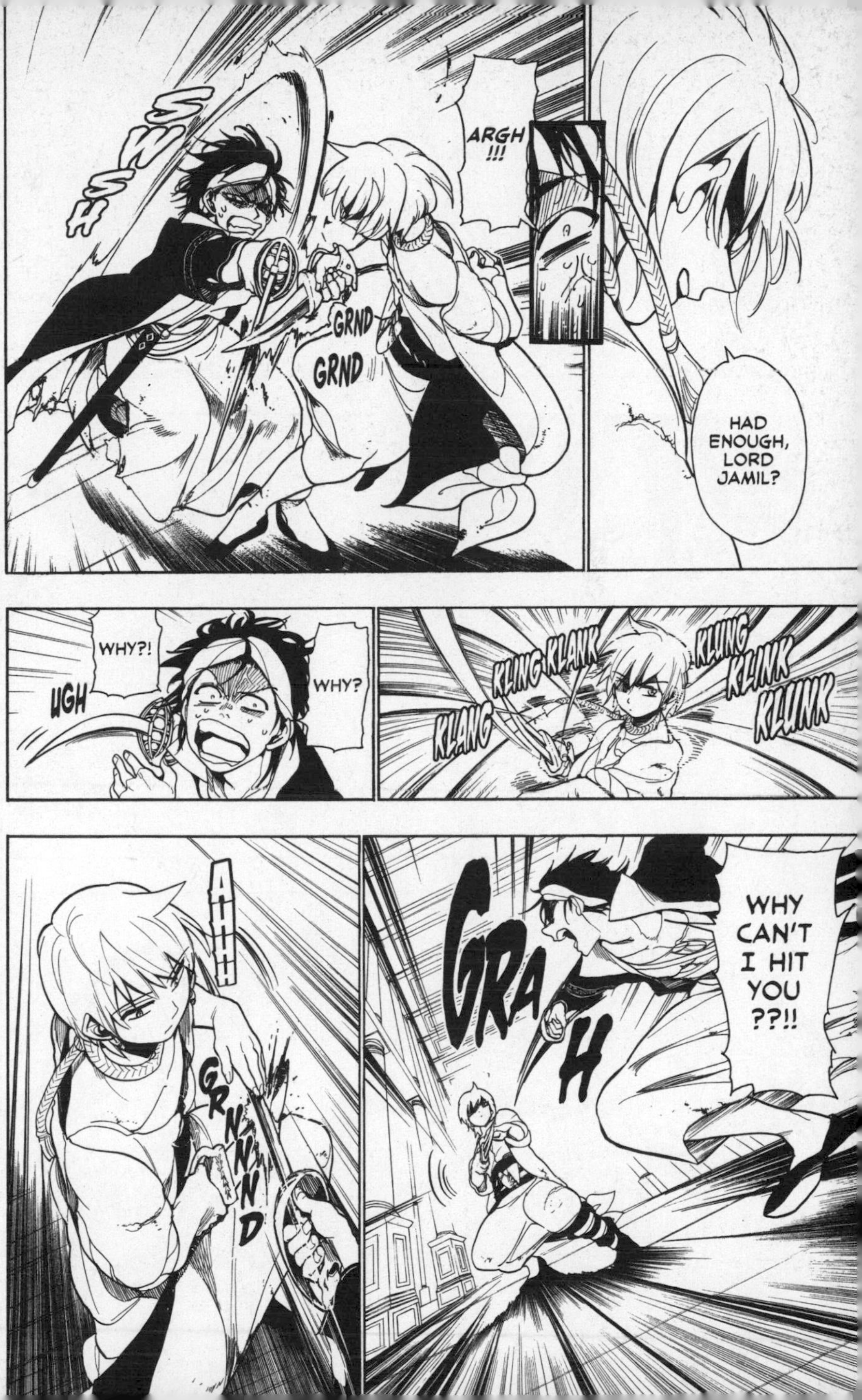
HAD ENOUGH, LORD JAMIL?
ARGH!!!
SWISH
GRND
GRND
KLUNG
KLINK
KLUNK
KLING KLANK
KLANG
WHY?
WHY?!
UGH
WHY CAN'T I HIT YOU??!!
GRAH
AHHH
GRNNNND

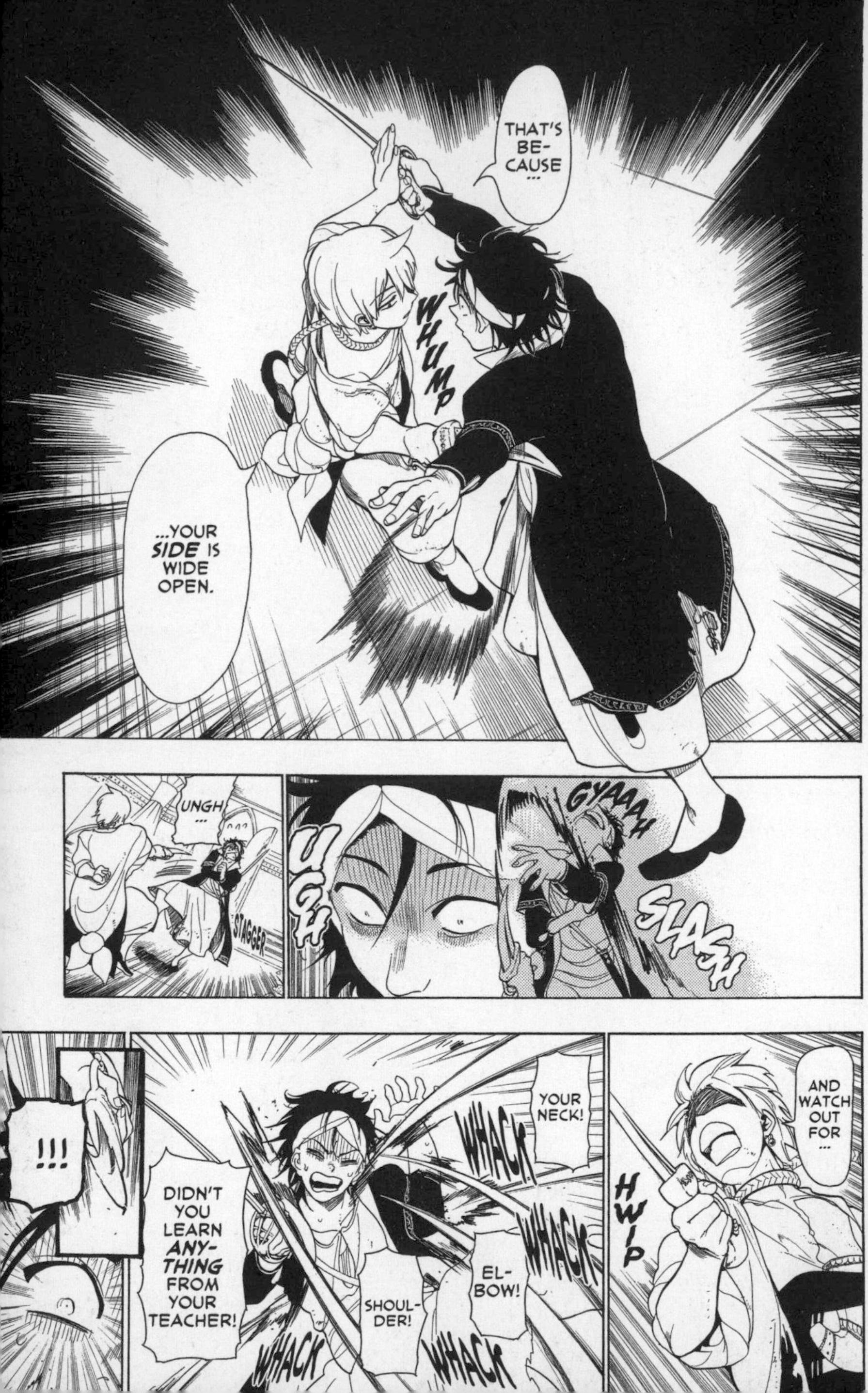
THAT'S BE-CAUSE ...
WHUMP
...YOUR SIDE IS WIDE OPEN.
GYAAAH
SLASH
UGH
UNGH ...
STAGGER
AND WATCH OUT FOR ...
HWIP
YOUR NECK!
WHACK
WHACK
EL-BOW!
WHACK
SHOUL-DER!
WHACK
DIDN'T YOU LEARN ANYTHING FROM YOUR TEACHER!
!!!

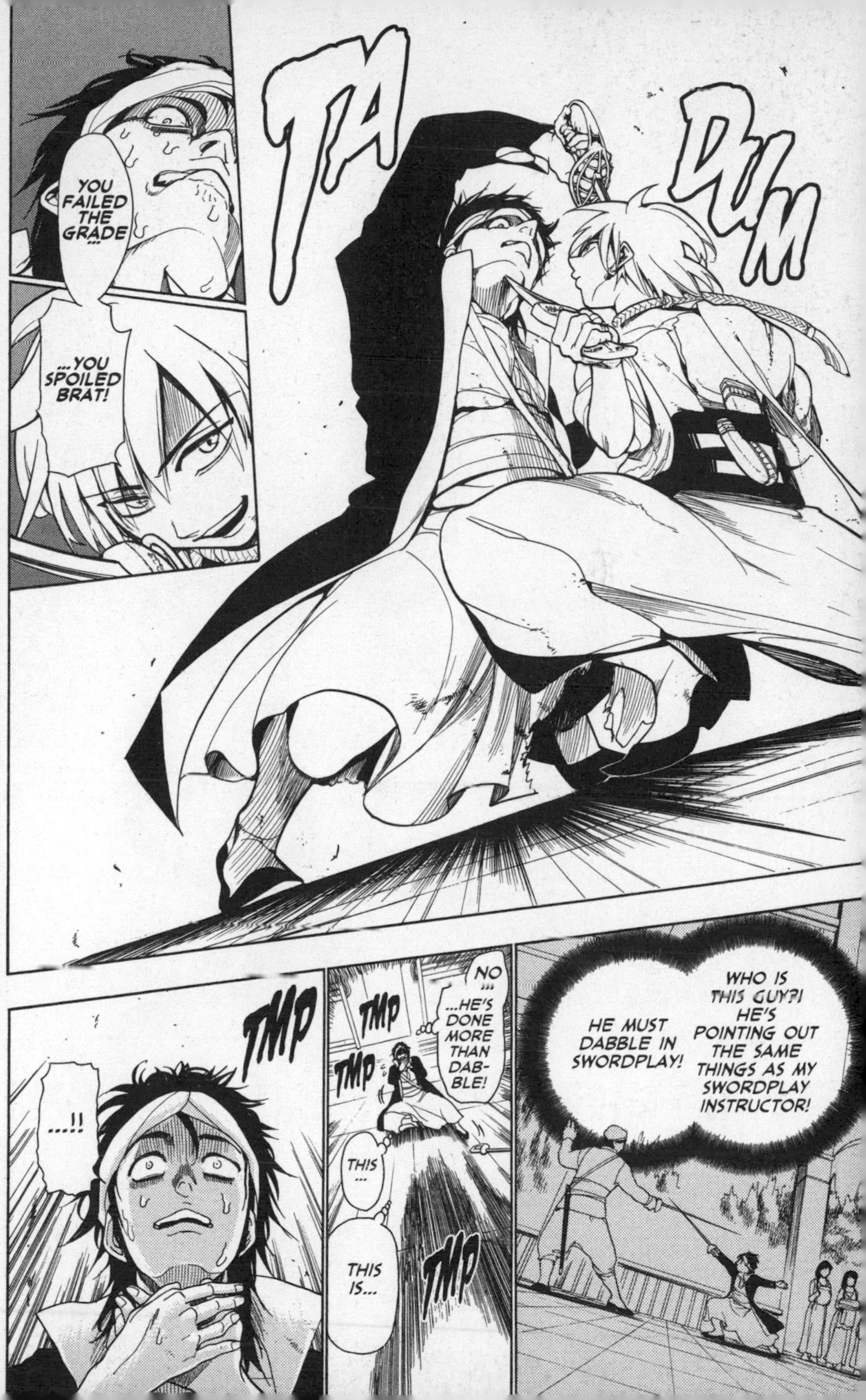
TA
DUM
YOU FAILED THE GRADE...
...YOU SPOILED BRAT!
WHO IS THIS GUY?! HE'S POINTING OUT THE SAME THINGS AS MY SWORDPLAY INSTRUCTOR!
HE MUST DABBLE IN SWORDPLAY!
NO...
...HE'S DONE MORE THAN DAB-BLE!
TMP
TMP
THIS...
THIS IS...
TMP
TMP
...!!

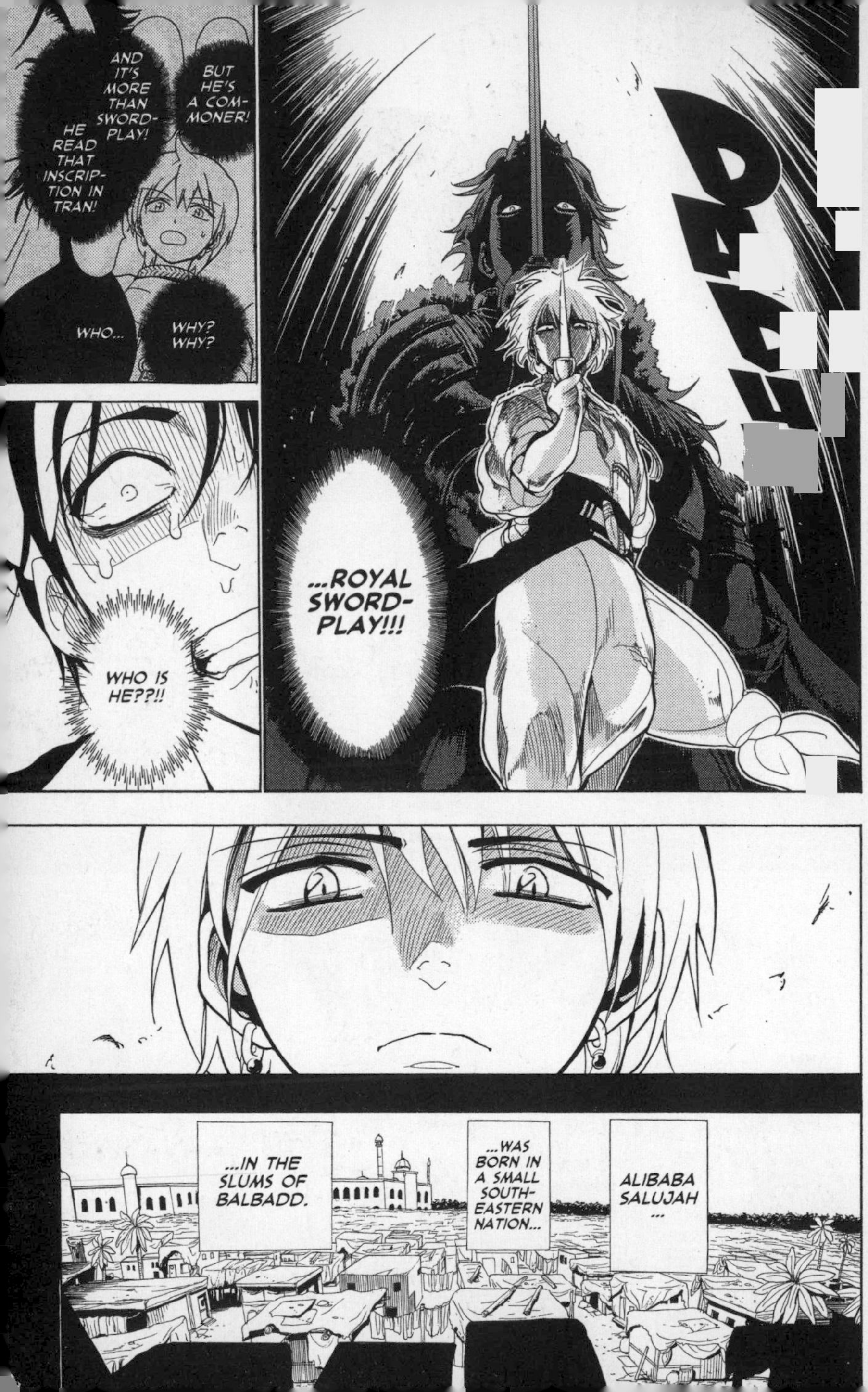
...ROYAL SWORD-PLAY!!!
BUT HE'S A COM-MONER!
AND IT'S MORE THAN SWORD-PLAY!
HE READ THAT INSCRIP-TION IN TRAN!
WHY? WHY?
WHO...
WHO IS HE??!!
ALIBABA SALUJAH ...
...WAS BORN IN A SMALL SOUTH-EASTERN NATION...
...IN THE SLUMS OF BALBADD.

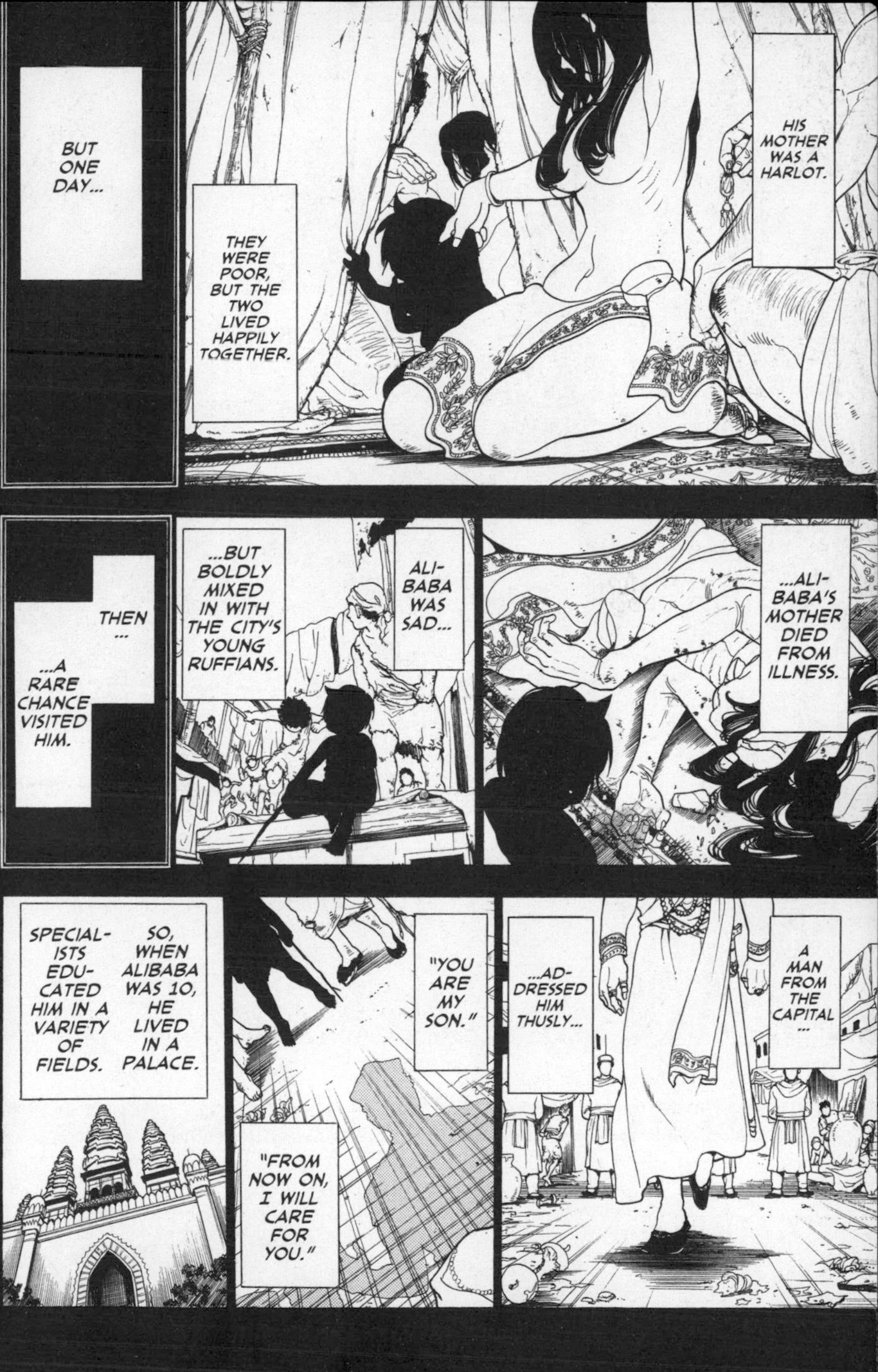
HIS MOTHER WAS A HARLOT.
THEY WERE POOR, BUT THE TWO LIVED HAPPILY TOGETHER.
BUT ONE DAY...
...ALI-BABA'S MOTHER DIED FROM ILLNESS.
ALI-BABA WAS SAD...
...BUT BOLDLY MIXED IN WITH THE CITY'S YOUNG RUFFIANS.
THEN...
...A RARE CHANCE VISITED HIM.
A MAN FROM THE CAPITAL...
...ADDRESSED HIM THUSLY...
"YOU ARE MY SON."
"FROM NOW ON, I WILL CARE FOR YOU."
SO, WHEN ALIBABA WAS 10, HE LIVED IN A PALACE.
SPECIALISTS EDUCATED HIM IN A VARIETY OF FIELDS.

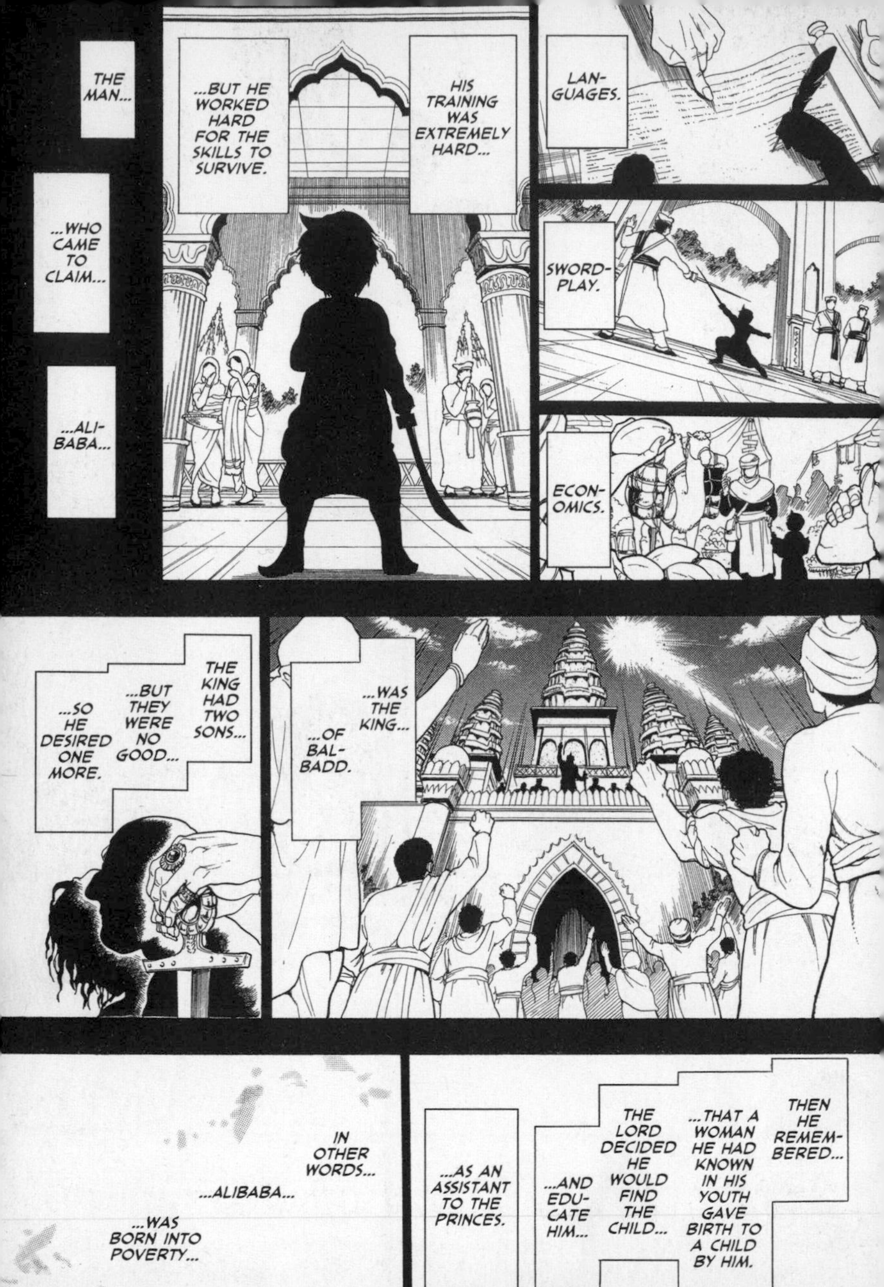
LAN-GUAGES.
SWORD-PLAY.
ECON-OMICS.
HIS TRAINING WAS EXTREMELY HARD...
...BUT HE WORKED HARD FOR THE SKILLS TO SURVIVE.
THE MAN...
...WHO CAME TO CLAIM...
...ALI-BABA...
...WAS THE KING...
...OF BAL-BADD.
THE KING HAD TWO SONS...
...BUT THEY WERE NO GOOD...
...SO HE DESIRED ONE MORE.
THEN HE REMEM-BERED...
...THAT A WOMAN HE HAD KNOWN IN HIS YOUTH GAVE BIRTH TO A CHILD BY HIM.
THE LORD DECIDED HE WOULD FIND THE CHILD...
...AND EDU-CATE HIM...
...AS AN ASSISTANT TO THE PRINCES.
IN OTHER WORDS...
...ALIBABA...
...WAS BORN INTO POVERTY...

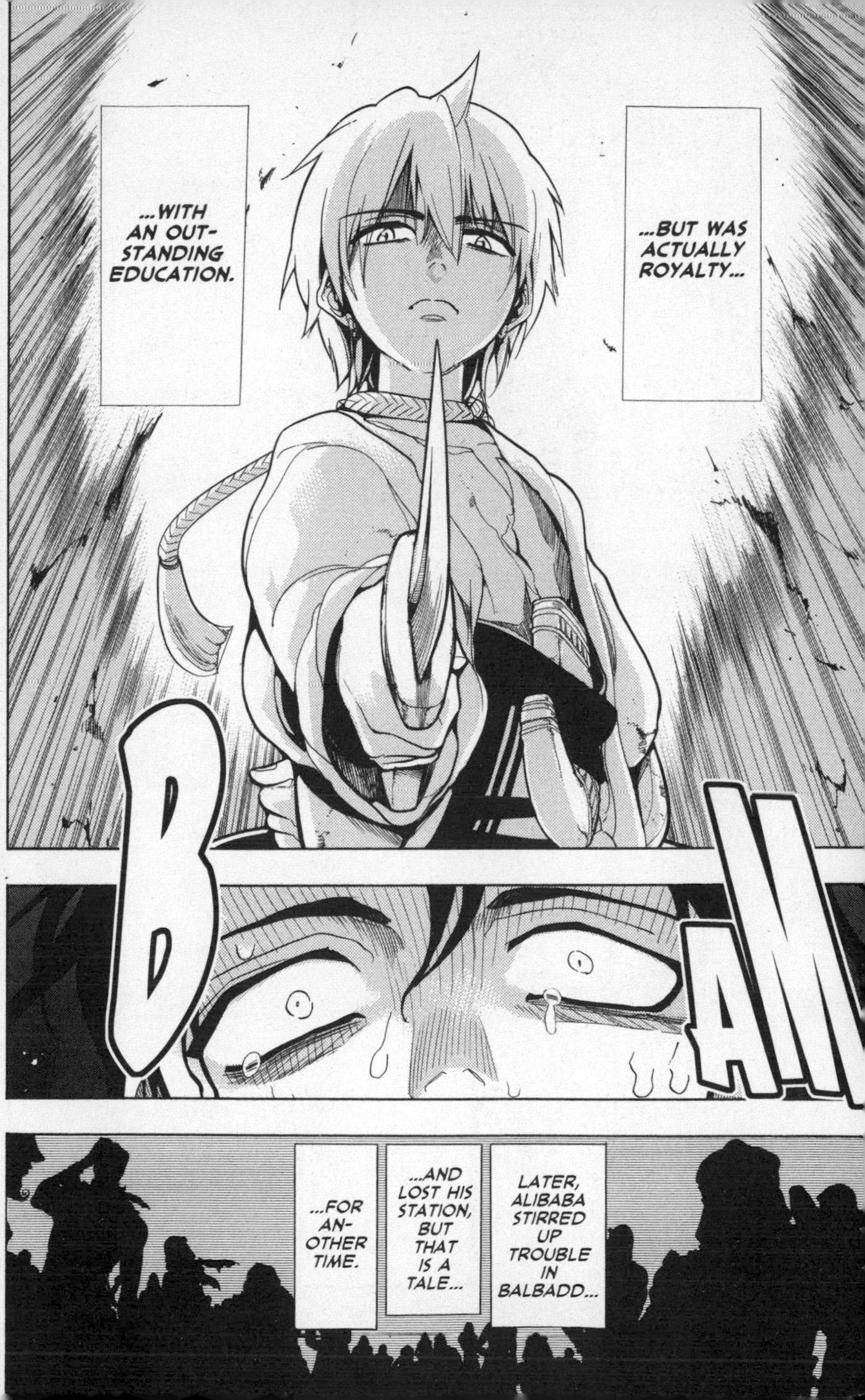
...BUT WAS ACTUALLY ROYALTY...
...WITH AN OUT-STANDING EDUCATION.
BAM
LATER, ALIBABA STIRRED UP TROUBLE IN BALBADD...
...AND LOST HIS STATION, BUT THAT IS A TALE...
...FOR AN-OTHER TIME.

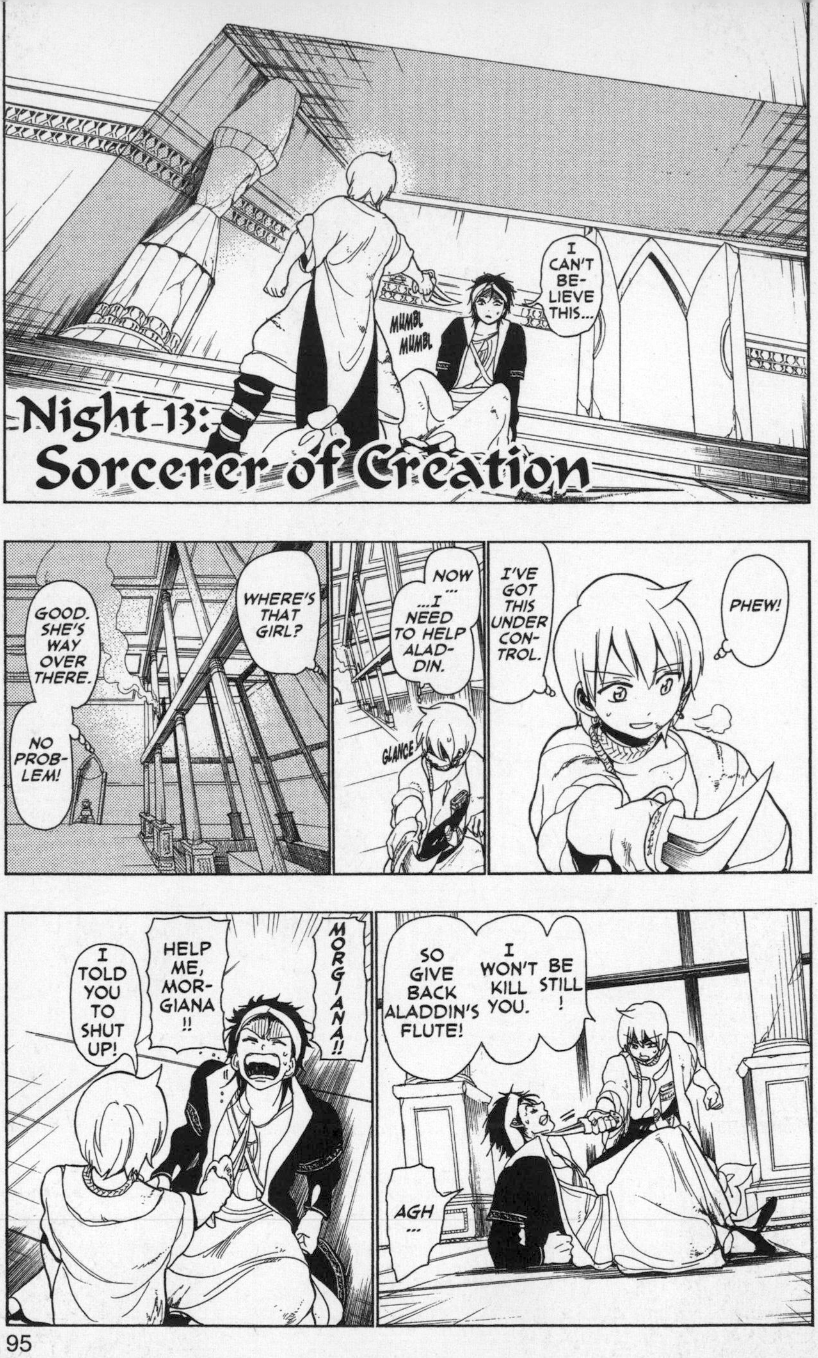
I CAN'T BE-LIEVE THIS...
MUMBL MUMBL
Night 13: Sorcerer of Creation
PHEW!
I'VE GOT THIS UNDER CON-TROL.
NOW... ...I NEED TO HELP ALAD-DIN.
GLANCE
WHERE'S THAT GIRL?
GOOD. SHE'S WAY OVER THERE.
NO PROB-LEM!
BE STILL!
I WON'T KILL YOU.
SO GIVE BACK ALADDIN'S FLUTE!
AGH...
MORGIANA!!
HELP ME, MOR-GIANA!!
I TOLD YOU TO SHUT UP!

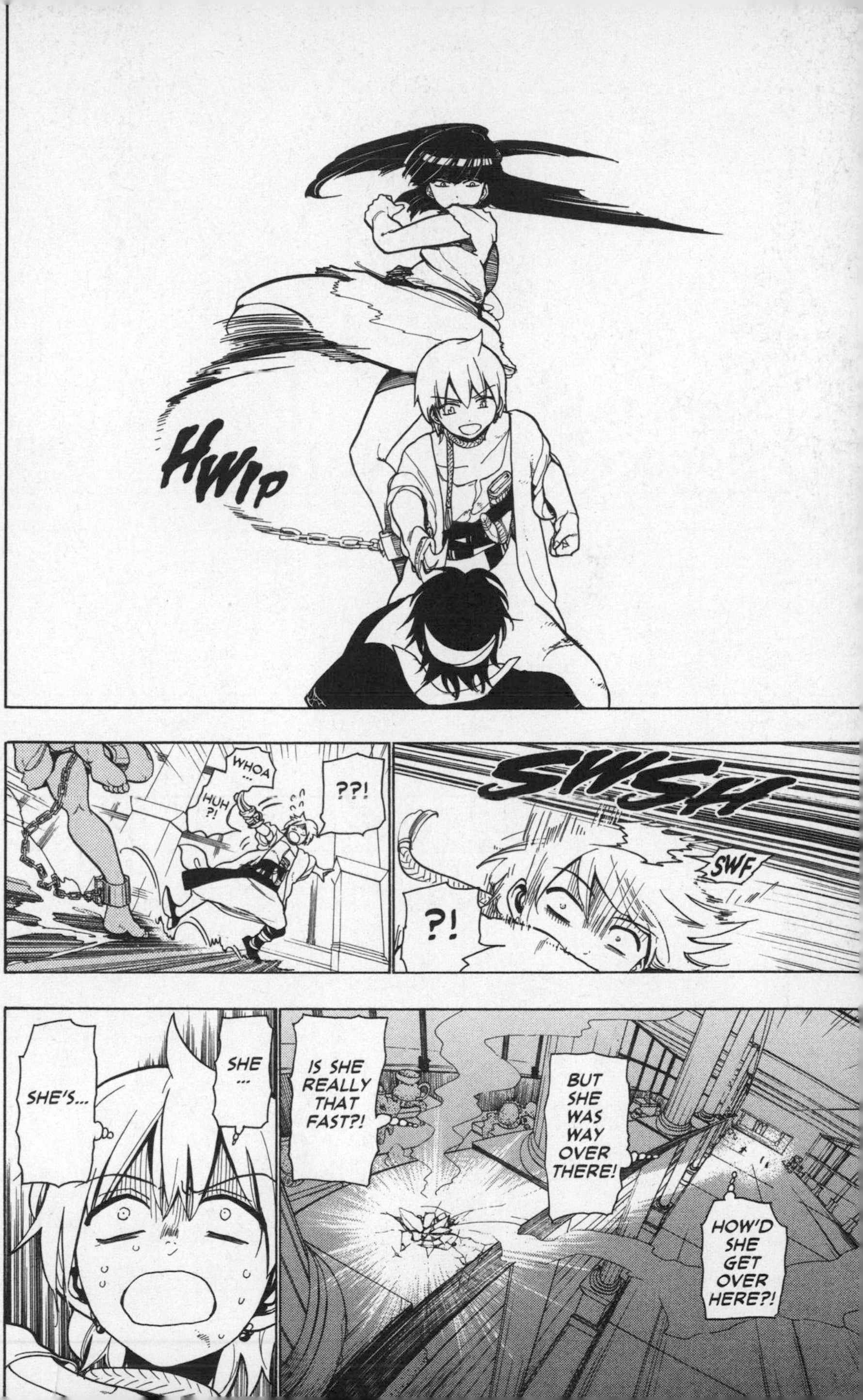
HWIP
SWSH
SWF
?!
??!
WHOA ...
HUH ?!
BUT SHE WAS WAY OVER THERE!
IS SHE REALLY THAT FAST?!
HOW'D SHE GET OVER HERE?!
SHE ...
SHE'S...

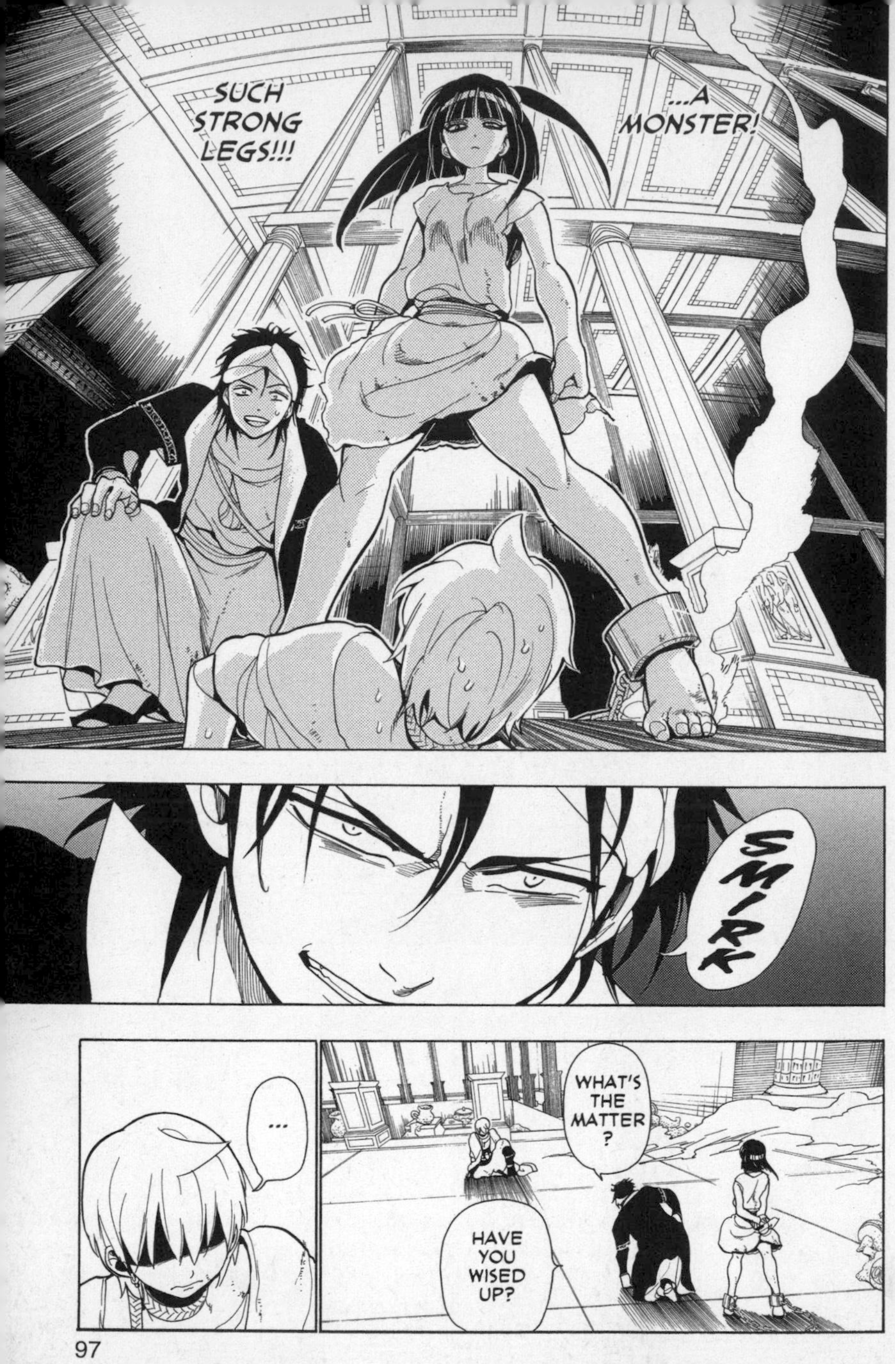
...A MONSTER!
SUCH STRONG LEGS!!!
SMIRK
WHAT'S THE MATTER?
HAVE YOU WISED UP?
...

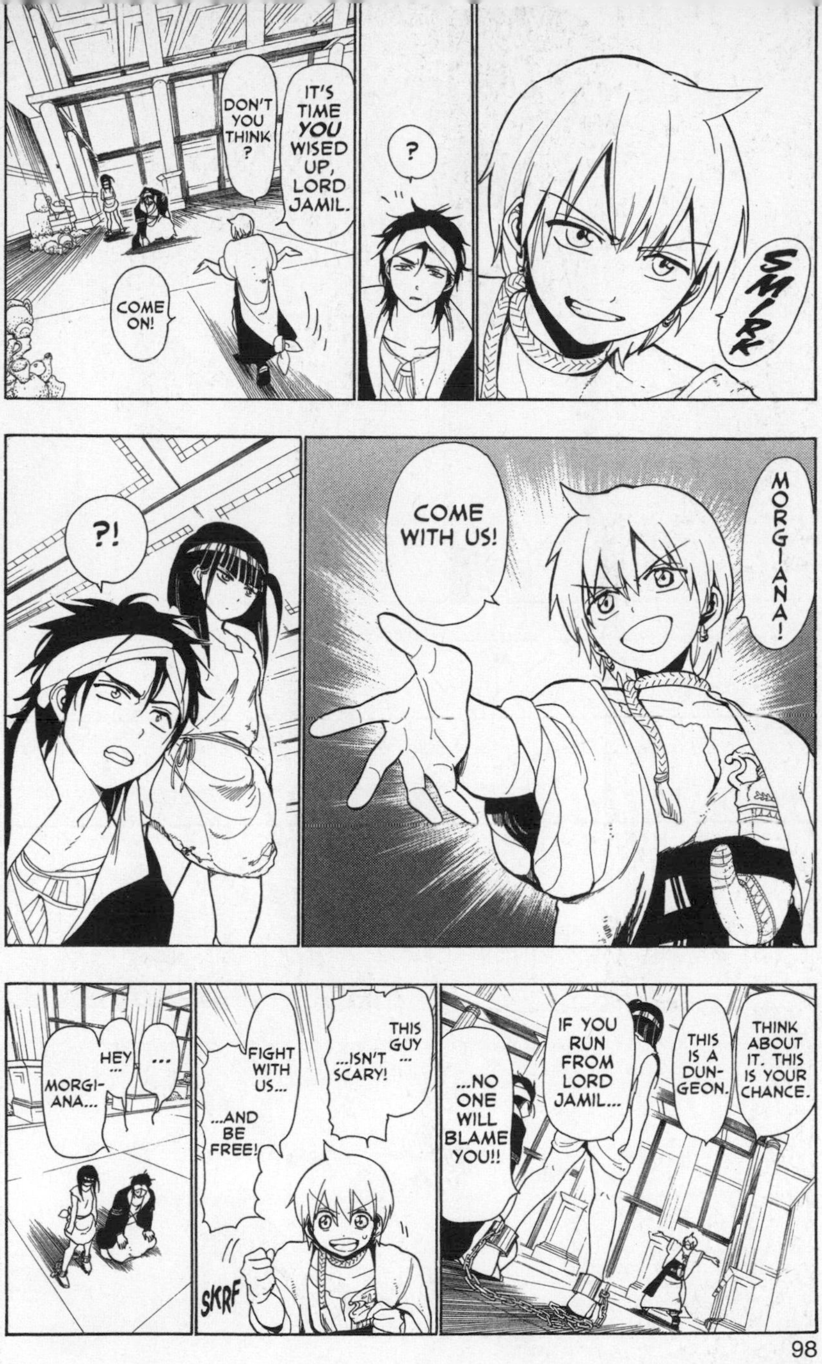
SMIRK
?
IT'S TIME *YOU* WISED UP, LORD JAMIL.
DON'T YOU THINK?
COME ON!
MORGIANA!
COME WITH US!
?!
THINK ABOUT IT. THIS IS YOUR CHANCE.
THIS IS A DUN-GEON.
IF YOU RUN FROM LORD JAMIL...
...NO ONE WILL BLAME YOU!!
THIS GUY...
...ISN'T SCARY!
FIGHT WITH US...
...AND BE FREE!
SKRF
...
HEY... MORGI-ANA...

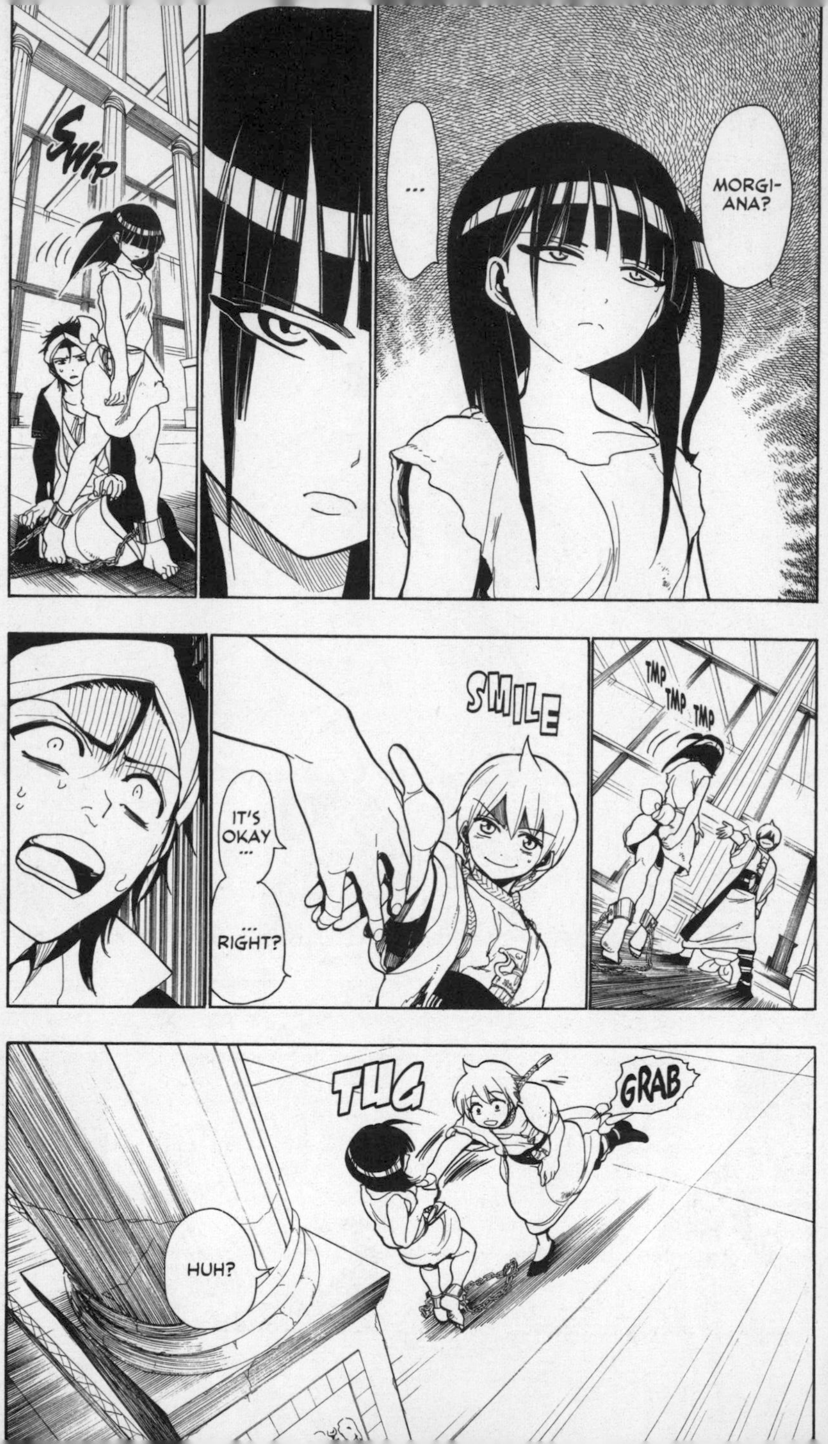
MORGI-
ANA?
...
SWIP
TMP
TMP
TMP
TMP
SMILE
IT'S OKAY ...
... RIGHT?
GRAB
TUG
HUH?

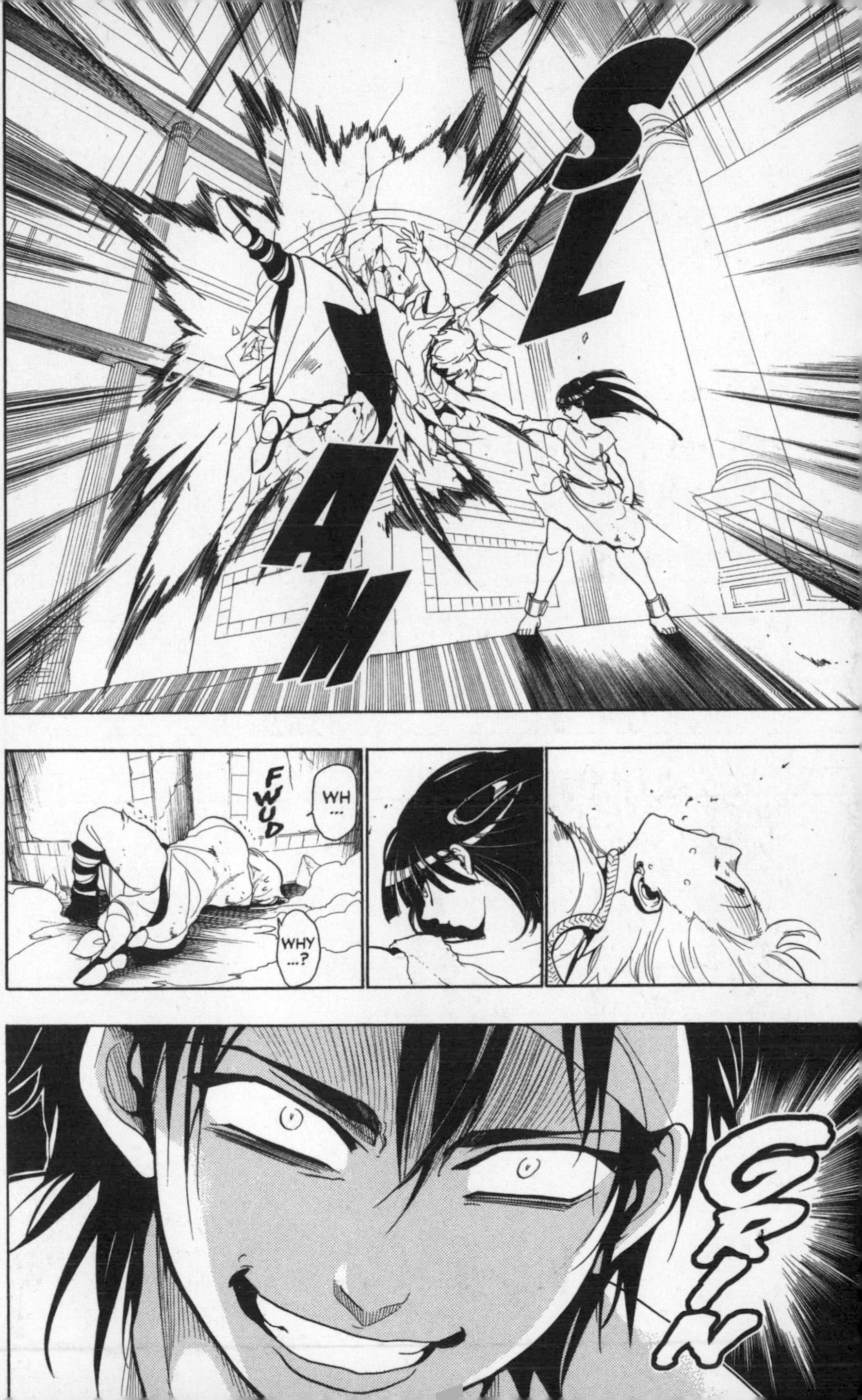
SLAM
WH ...
FWUD
WHY ...?
GRIN

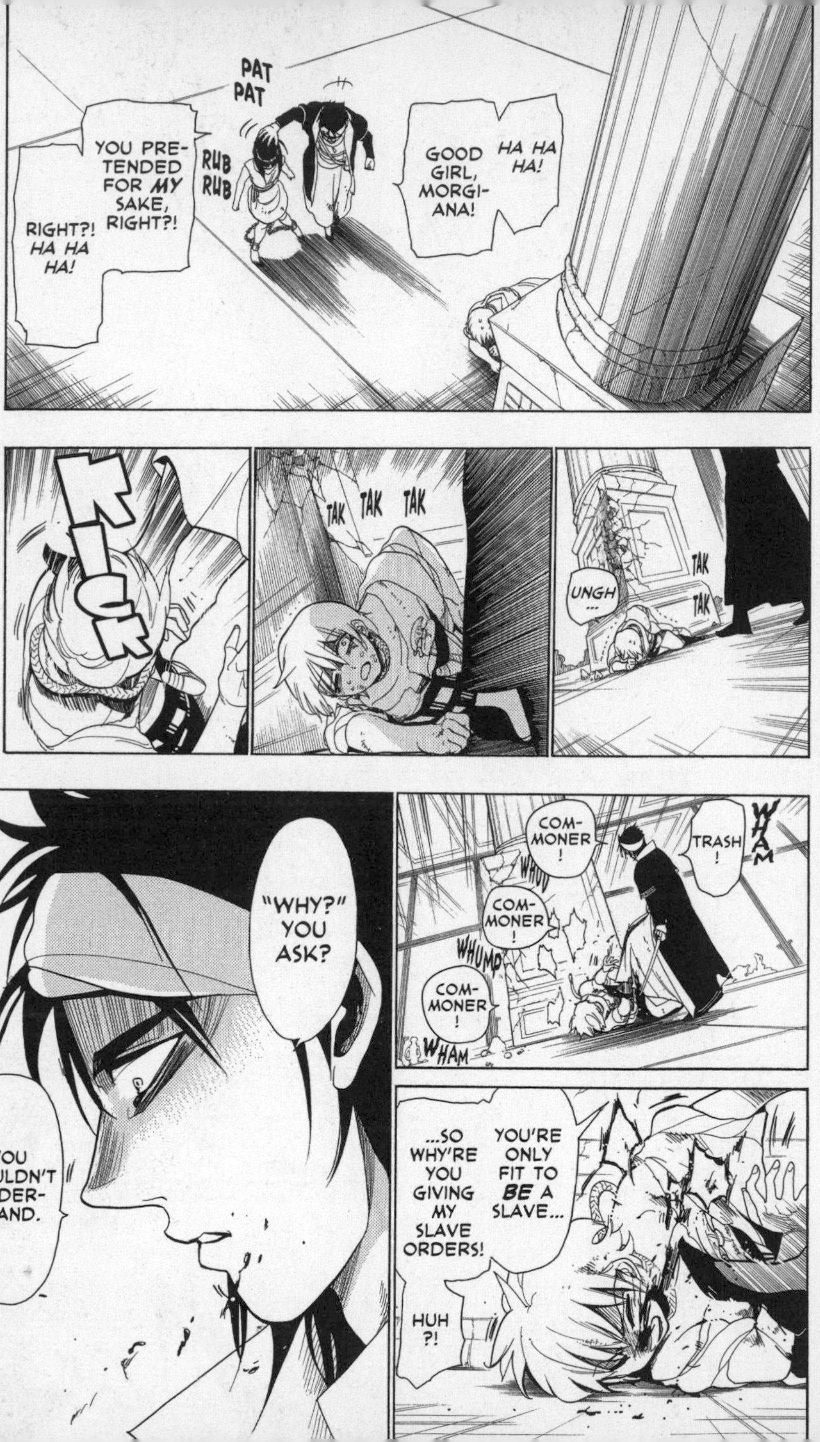
HA HA HA!
GOOD GIRL, MORGIANA!
PAT PAT
RUB RUB
YOU PRETENDED FOR MY SAKE, RIGHT?!
RIGHT?! HA HA HA!
TAK TAK
UNGH ...
TAK TAK TAK
KICK
WHAM
TRASH!
COMMONER!
WHUD
COMMONER!
WHUMP
COMMONER!
WHAM
YOU'RE ONLY FIT TO BE A SLAVE...
...SO WHY'RE YOU GIVING MY SLAVE ORDERS!
HUH?!
"WHY?" YOU ASK?
YOU WOULDN'T UNDERSTAND.

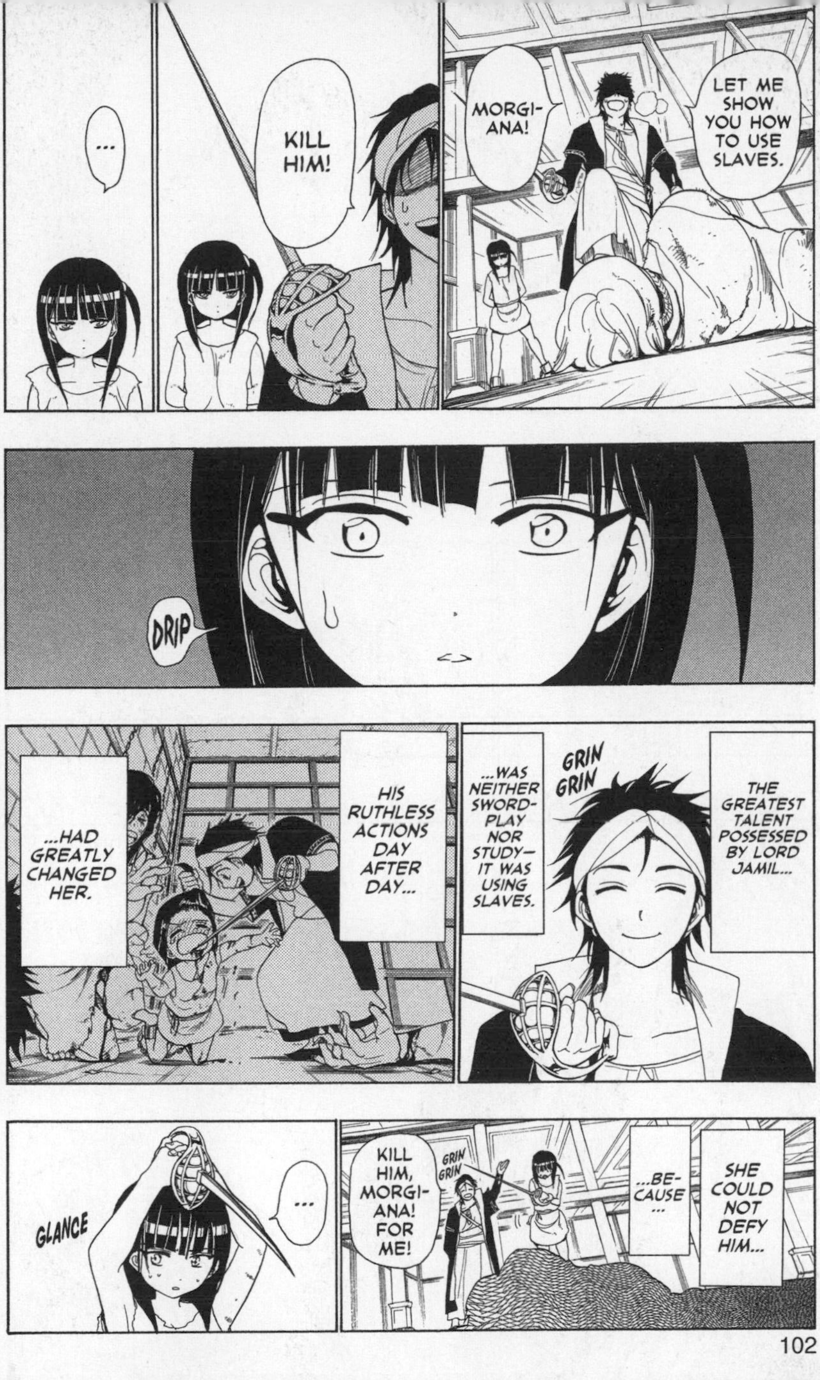
LET ME SHOW YOU HOW TO USE SLAVES.
MORGI-ANA!
KILL HIM!
...
DRIP
THE GREATEST TALENT POSSESSED BY LORD JAMIL...
GRIN GRIN
...WAS NEITHER SWORD-PLAY NOR STUDY— IT WAS USING SLAVES.
HIS RUTHLESS ACTIONS DAY AFTER DAY...
...HAD GREATLY CHANGED HER.
SHE COULD NOT DEFY HIM...
...BE-CAUSE ...
GRIN GRIN
KILL HIM, MORGI-ANA! FOR ME!
...
GLANCE

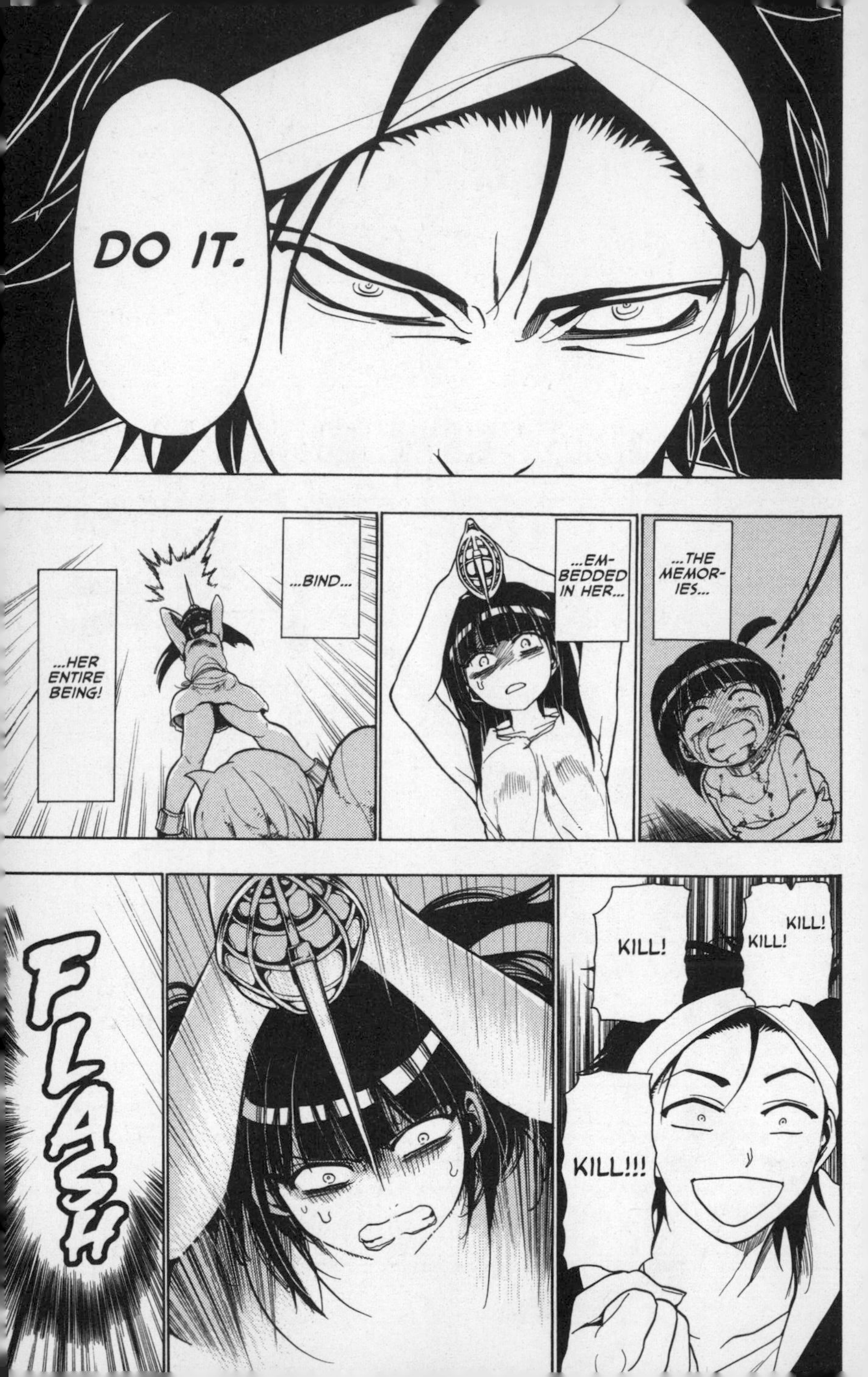
DO IT.
...THE MEMORIES...
...EMBEDDED IN HER...
...BIND...
...HER ENTIRE BEING!
KILL!
KILL!
KILL!
KILL!!!
FLASH

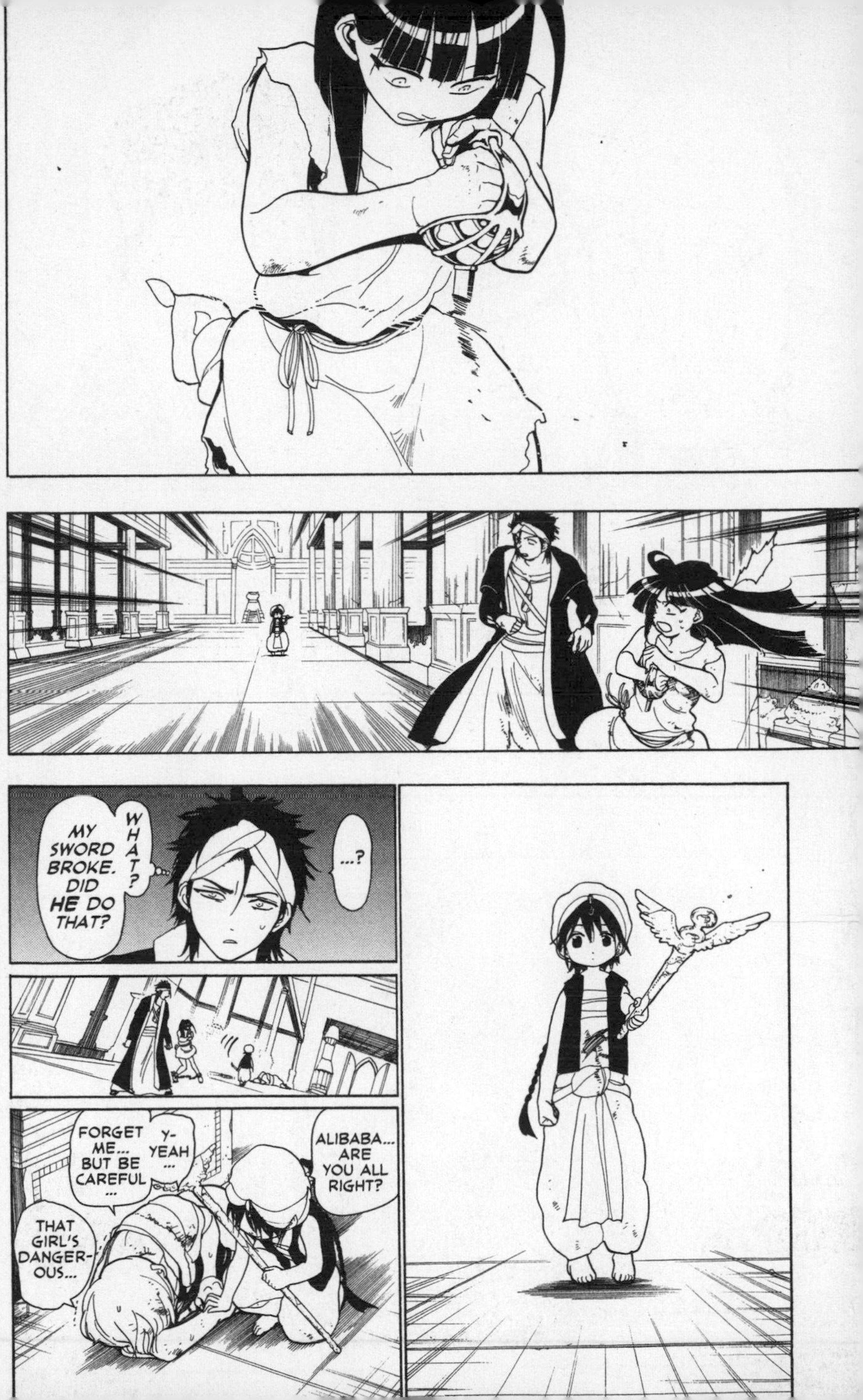
...?
WHAT?
MY SWORD BROKE. DID HE DO THAT?
ALIBABA... ARE YOU ALL RIGHT?
Y-YEAH...
FORGET ME... BUT BE CAREFUL...
THAT GIRL'S DANGER-OUS...

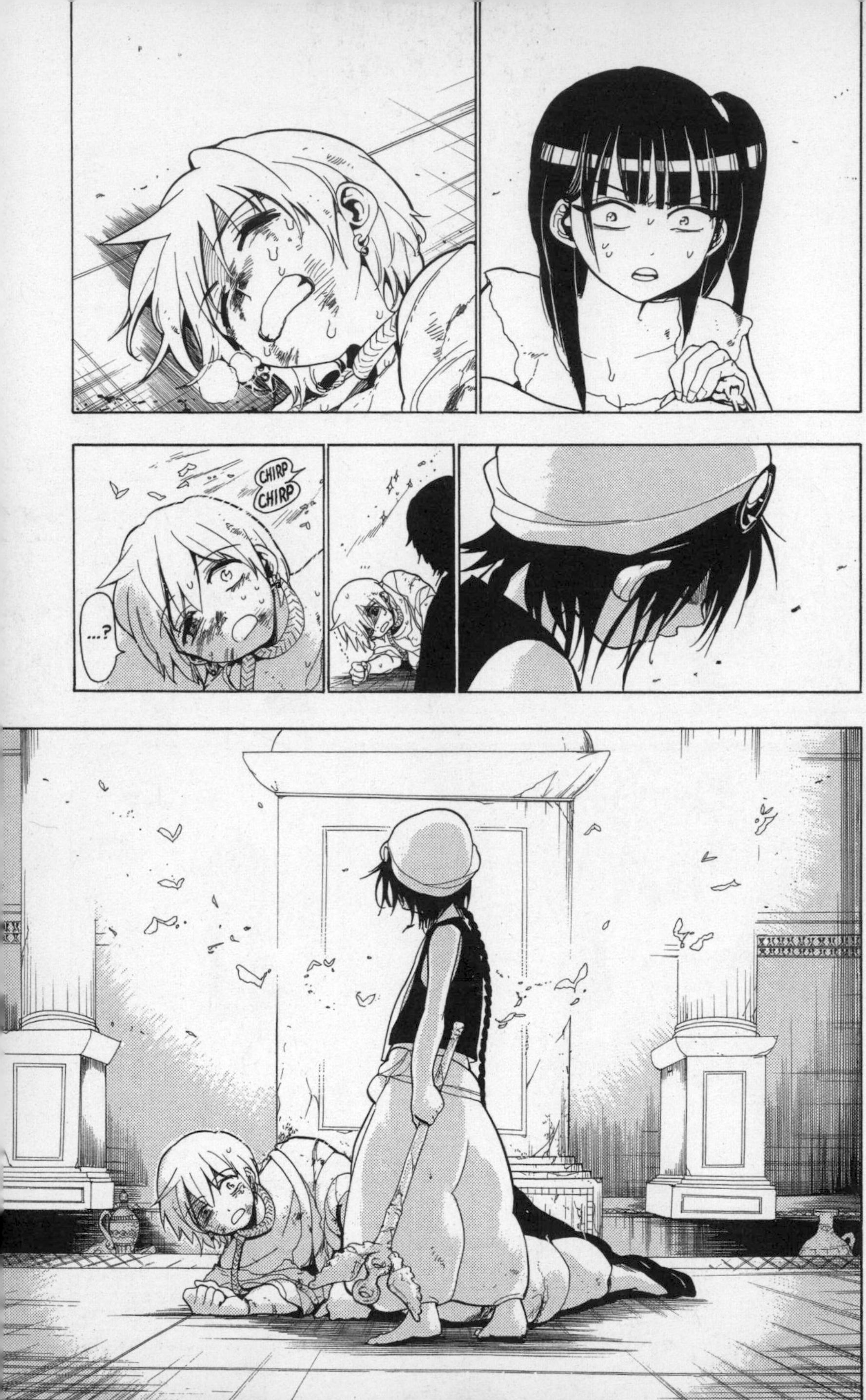
CHIRP
CHIRP
...?

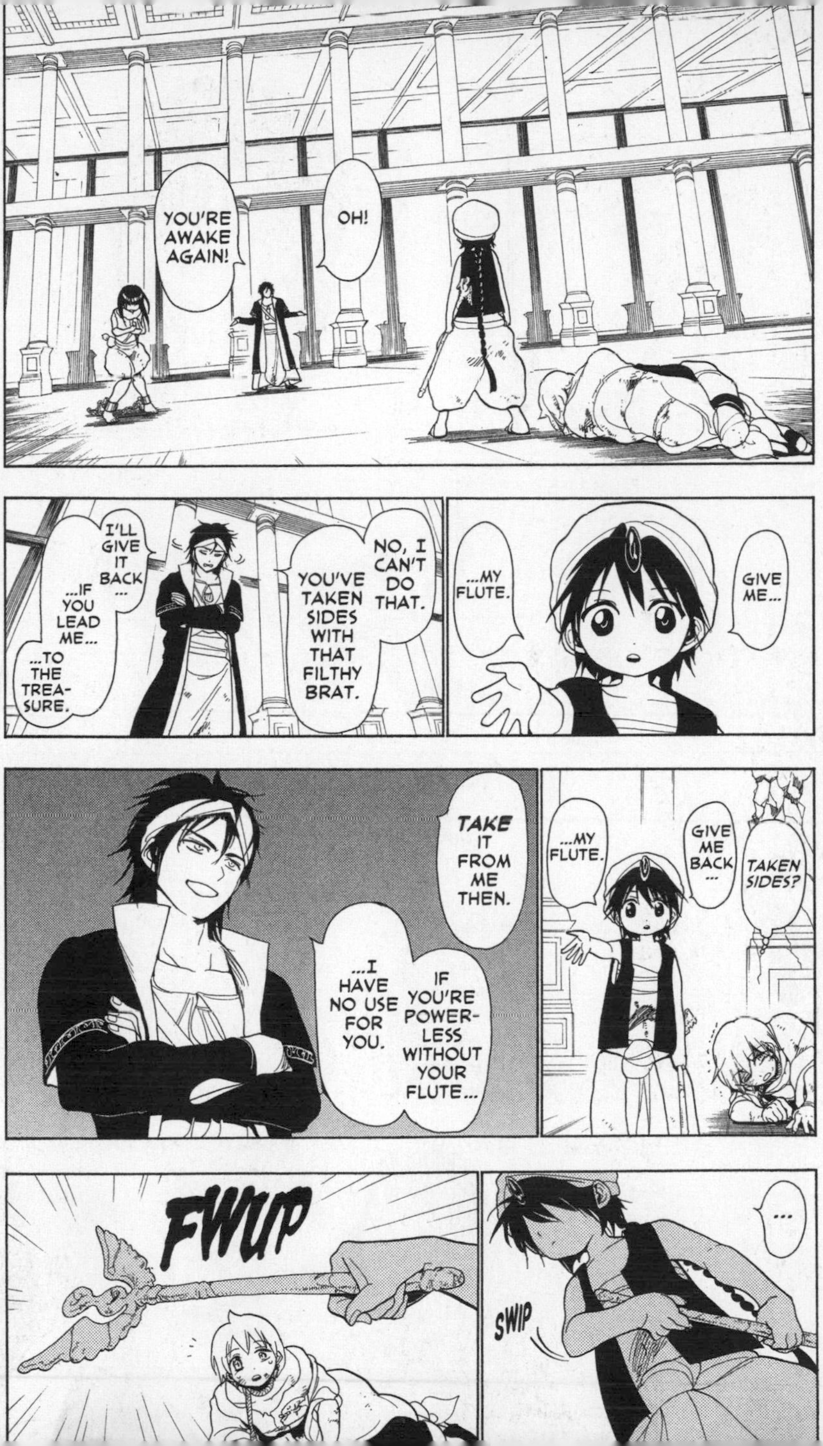
OH!
YOU'RE AWAKE AGAIN!
GIVE ME...
...MY FLUTE.
NO, I CAN'T DO THAT.
YOU'VE TAKEN SIDES WITH THAT FILTHY BRAT.
I'LL GIVE IT BACK...
...IF YOU LEAD ME...
...TO THE TREASURE.
TAKEN SIDES?
GIVE ME BACK...
...MY FLUTE.
TAKE IT FROM ME THEN.
IF YOU'RE POWERLESS WITHOUT YOUR FLUTE...
...I HAVE NO USE FOR YOU.
...
SWIP
FWUP

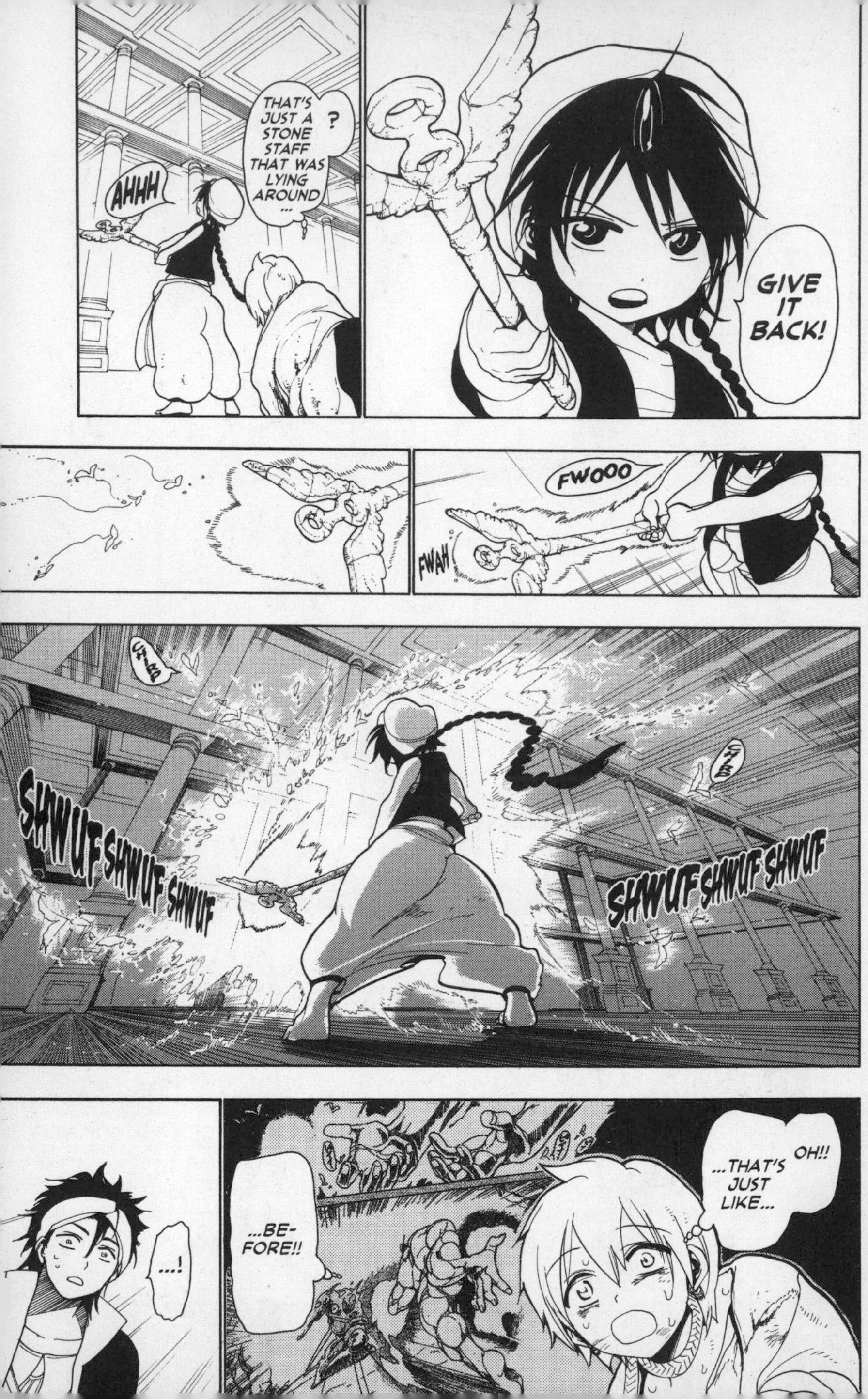
GIVE IT BACK!
?
THAT'S JUST A STONE STAFF THAT WAS LYING AROUND ...
AHHH
FWOOO
FWAH
CHIRP
SHWUF SHWUF SHWUF
CHIRP
SHWUF SHWUF SHWUF
OH!!
...THAT'S JUST LIKE...
...BE- FORE!!
...!

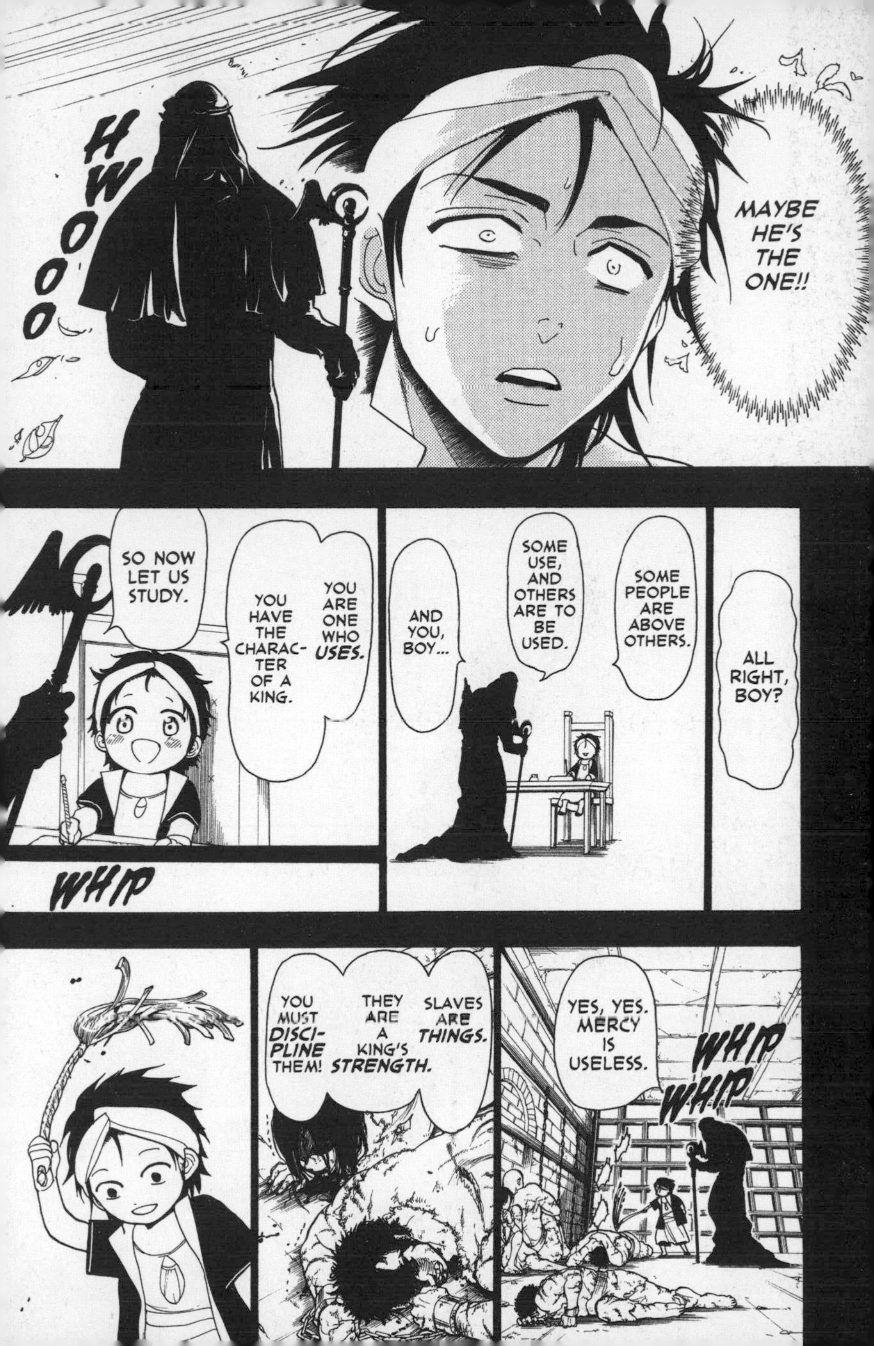
MAYBE HE'S THE ONE!!
HWOOOO
ALL RIGHT, BOY?
SOME PEOPLE ARE ABOVE OTHERS.
SOME USE, AND OTHERS ARE TO BE USED.
AND YOU, BOY...
YOU ARE ONE WHO USES.
YOU HAVE THE CHARACTER OF A KING.
SO NOW LET US STUDY.
WHIP
YES, YES. MERCY IS USELESS.
WHIP WHIP
SLAVES ARE THINGS.
THEY ARE A KING'S STRENGTH.
YOU MUST DISCIPLINE THEM!

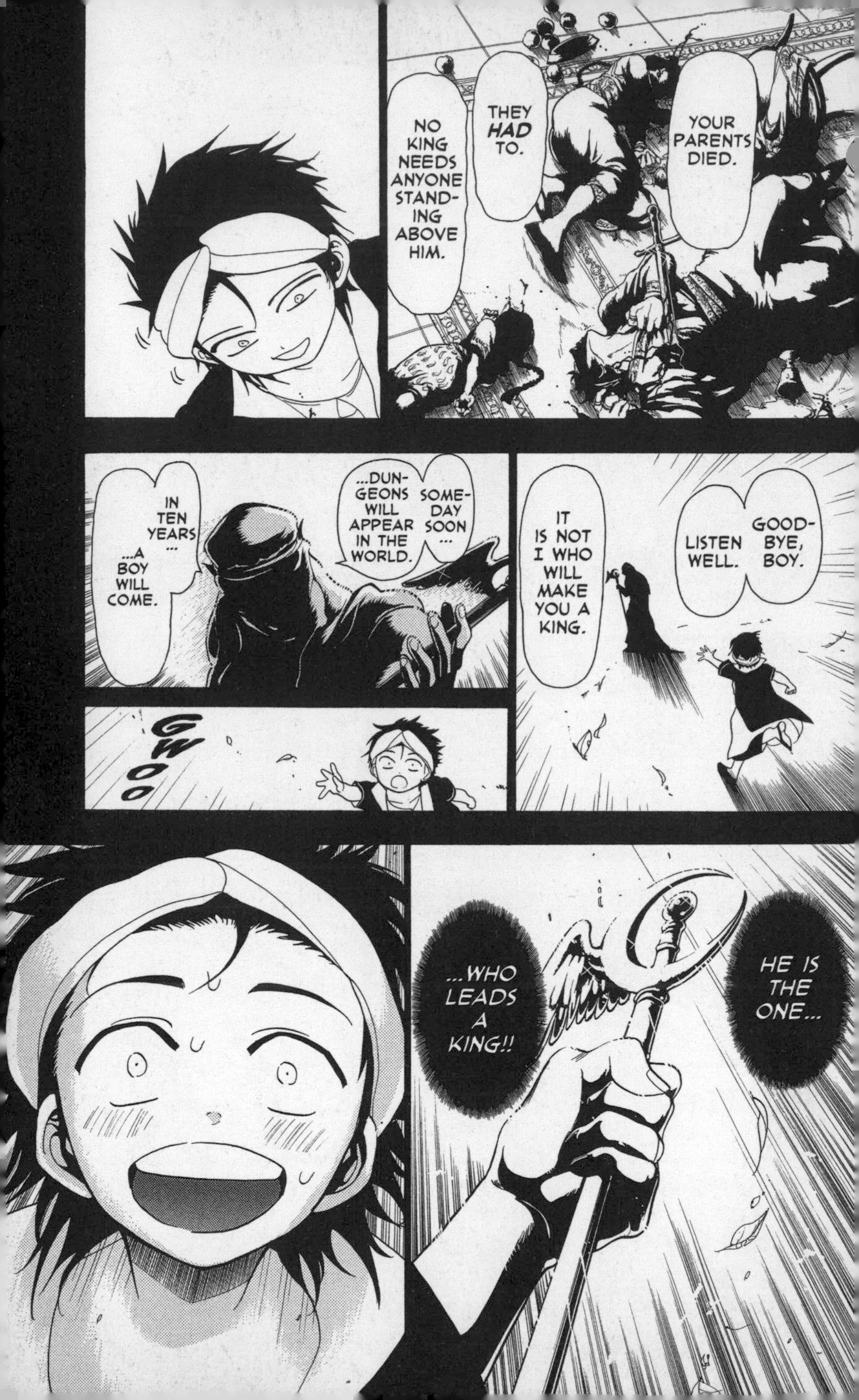
YOUR PARENTS DIED.
THEY HAD TO.
NO KING NEEDS ANYONE STAND-ING ABOVE HIM.
GOOD-BYE, BOY.
LISTEN WELL.
IT IS NOT I WHO WILL MAKE YOU A KING.
SOME-DAY SOON...
...DUN-GEONS WILL APPEAR IN THE WORLD.
IN TEN YEARS...
...A BOY WILL COME.
GWOOO
HE IS THE ONE...
...WHO LEADS A KING!!

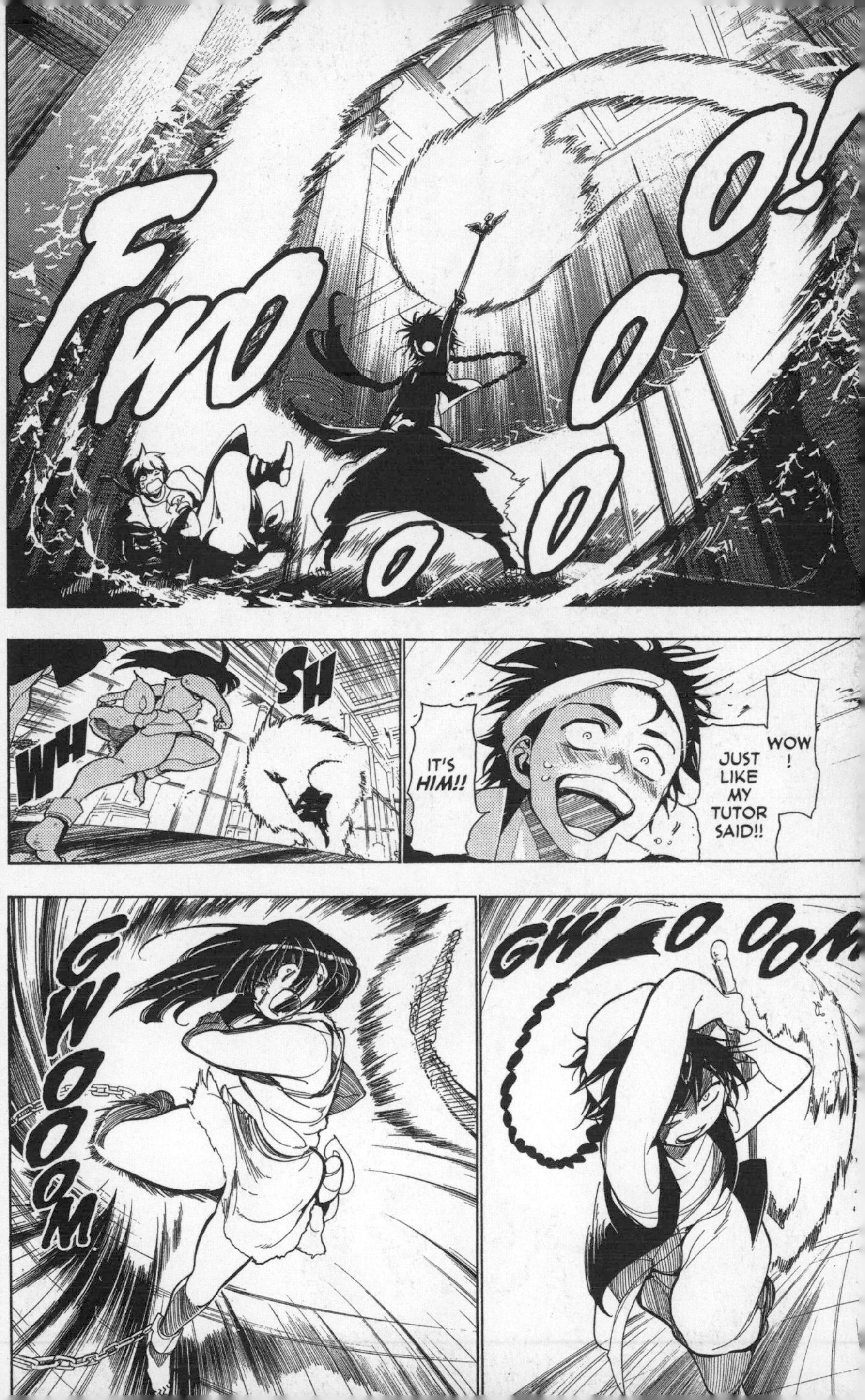
FWOOOOOOO!
WOW! JUST LIKE MY TUTOR SAID!!
IT'S HIM!!
SH
WH
GWOOOM
GWOOOOM

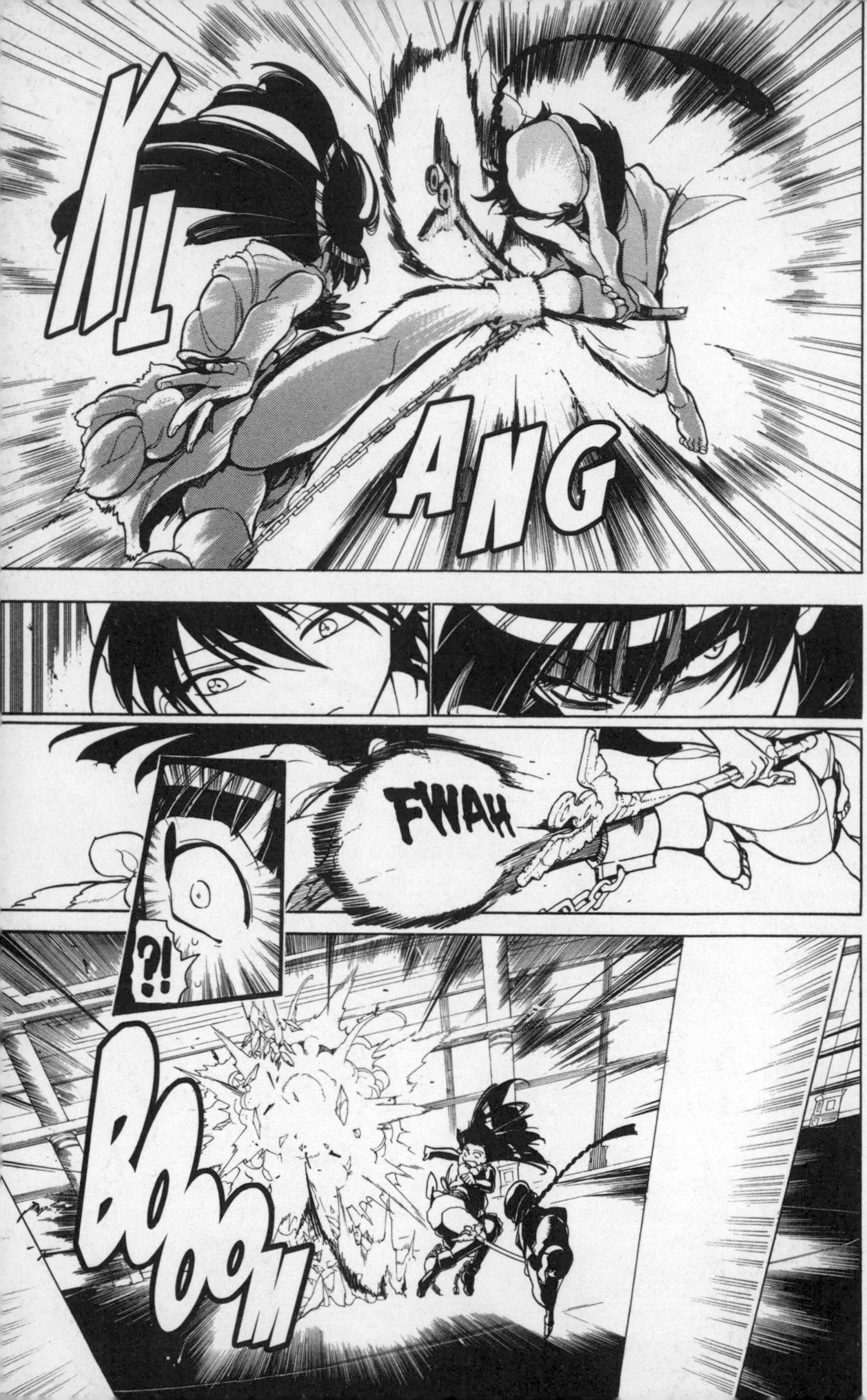
KL
ANG
FWAH
?!
BOOOM

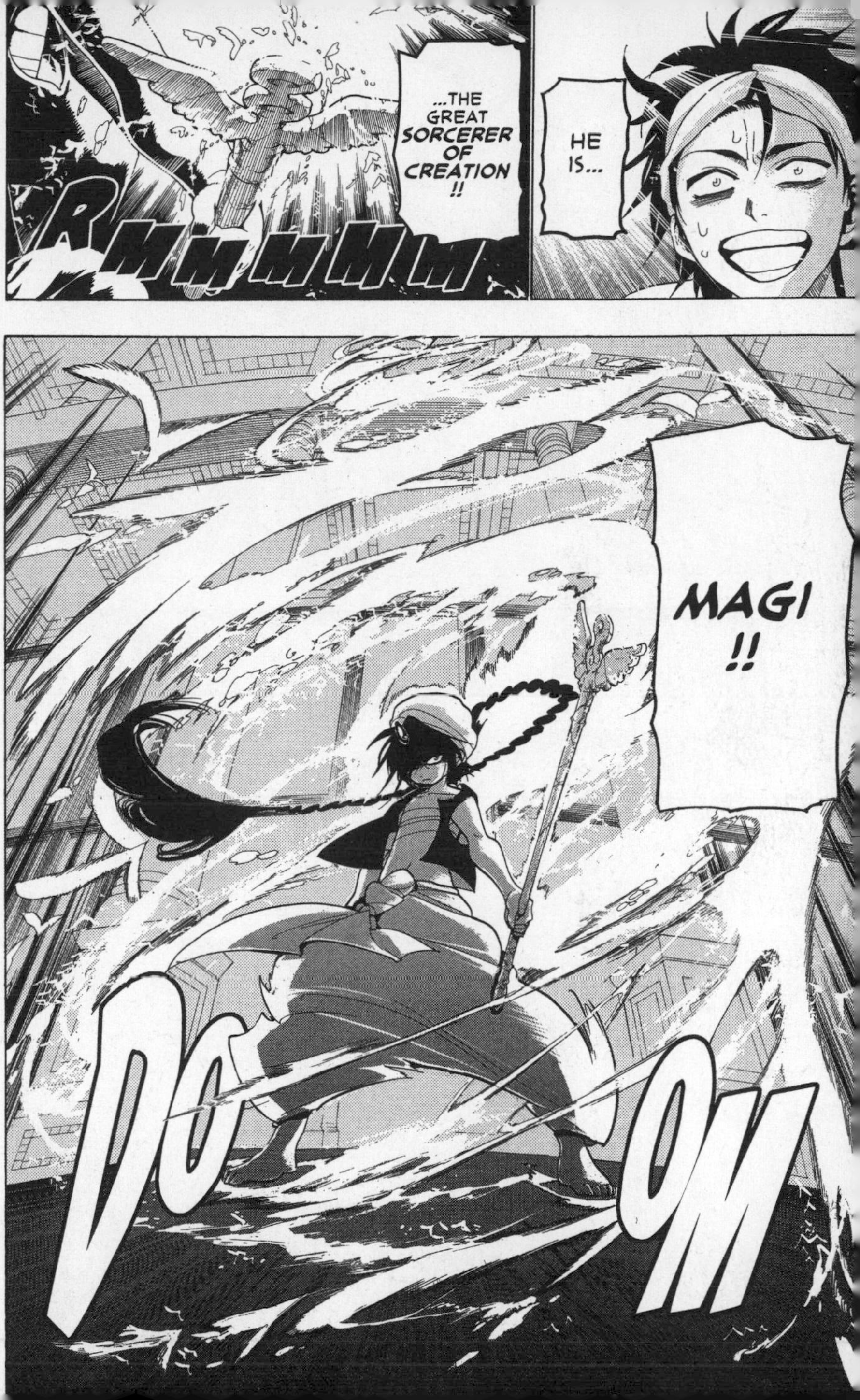
HE IS...
...THE GREAT SORCERER OF CREATION !!
RMMMMMM
MAGI !!
DOOOM

Night 14: The Lord of the Dungeon

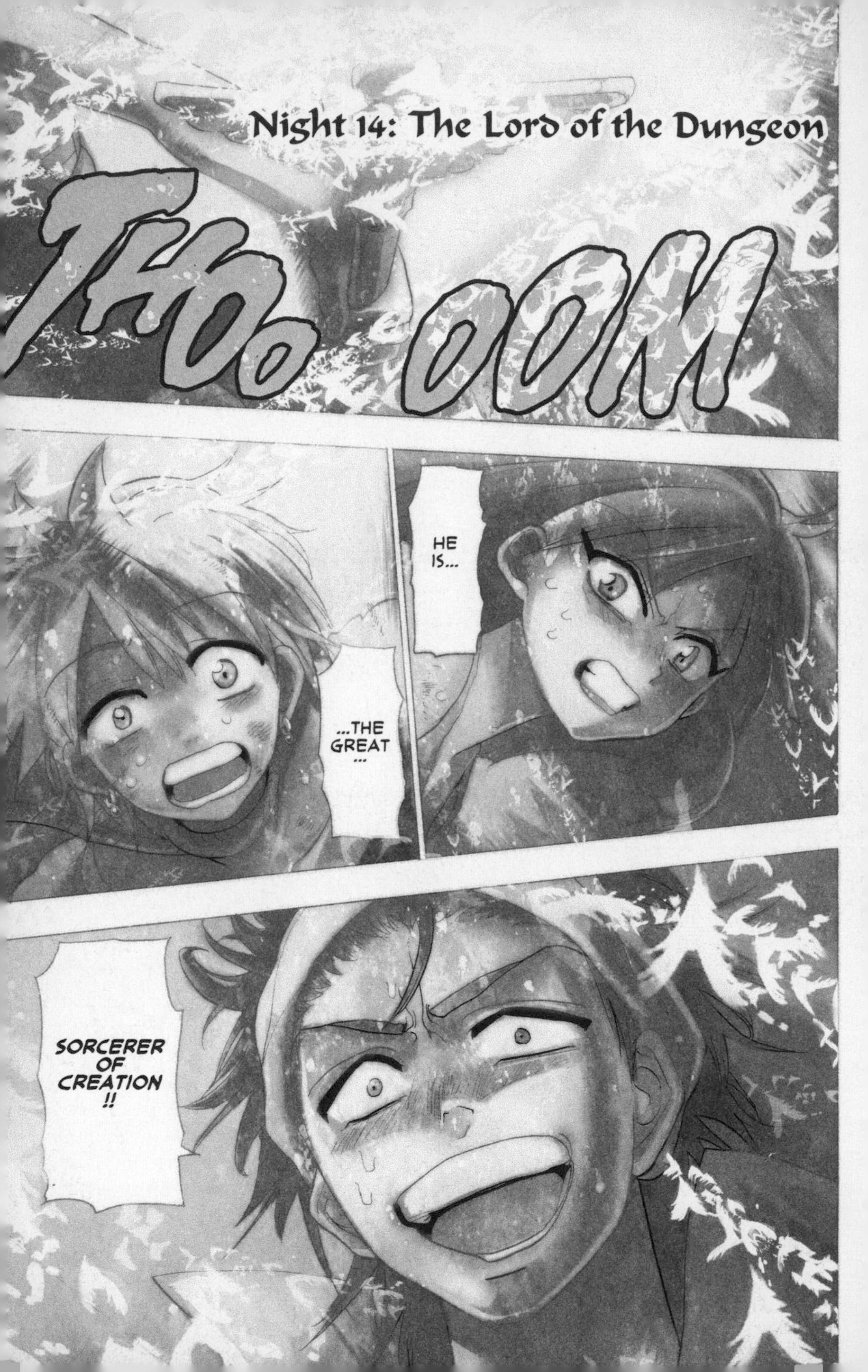
THOOOOM
HE IS...
...THE GREAT ...
SORCERER OF CREATION !!

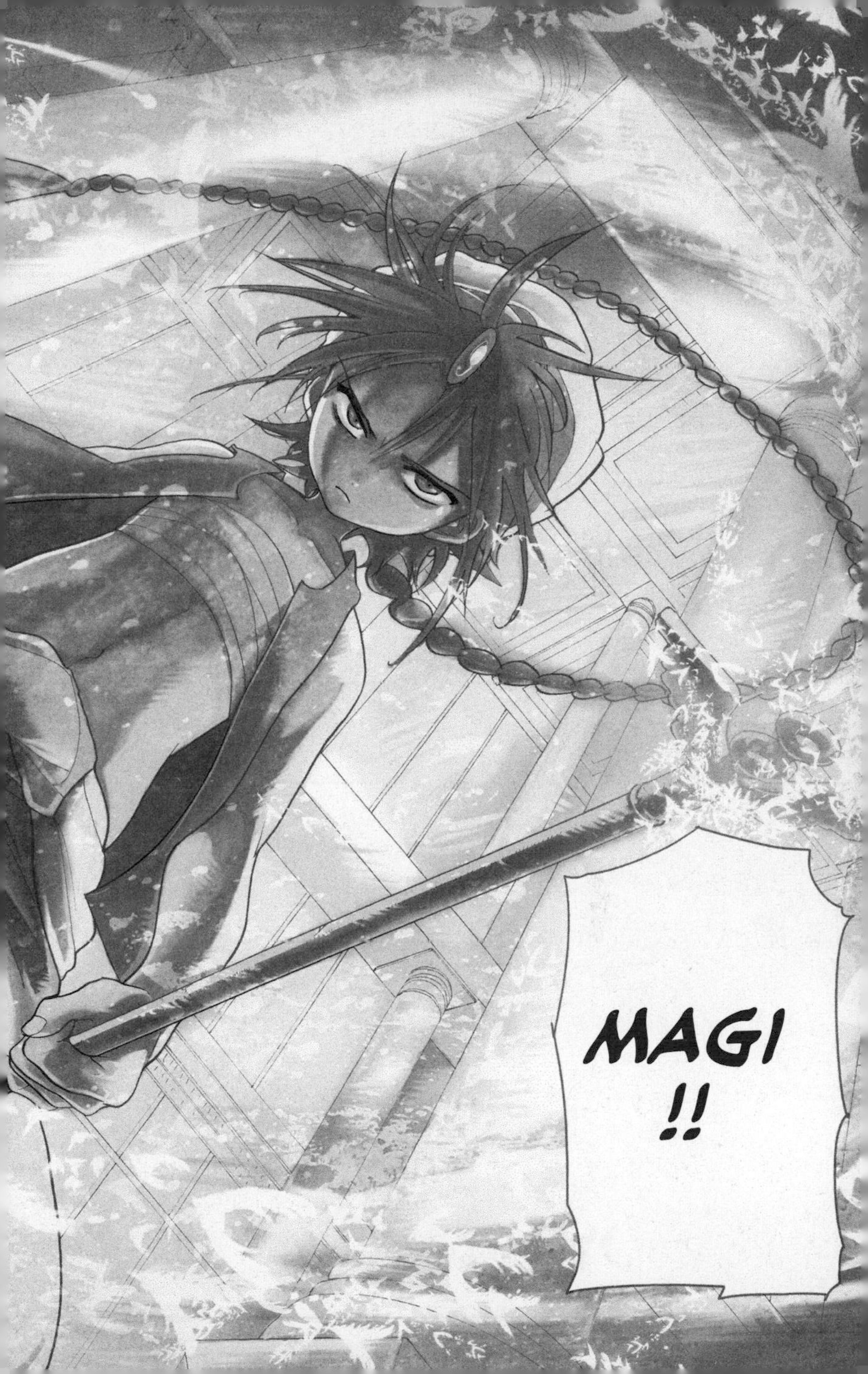
MAGI
!!

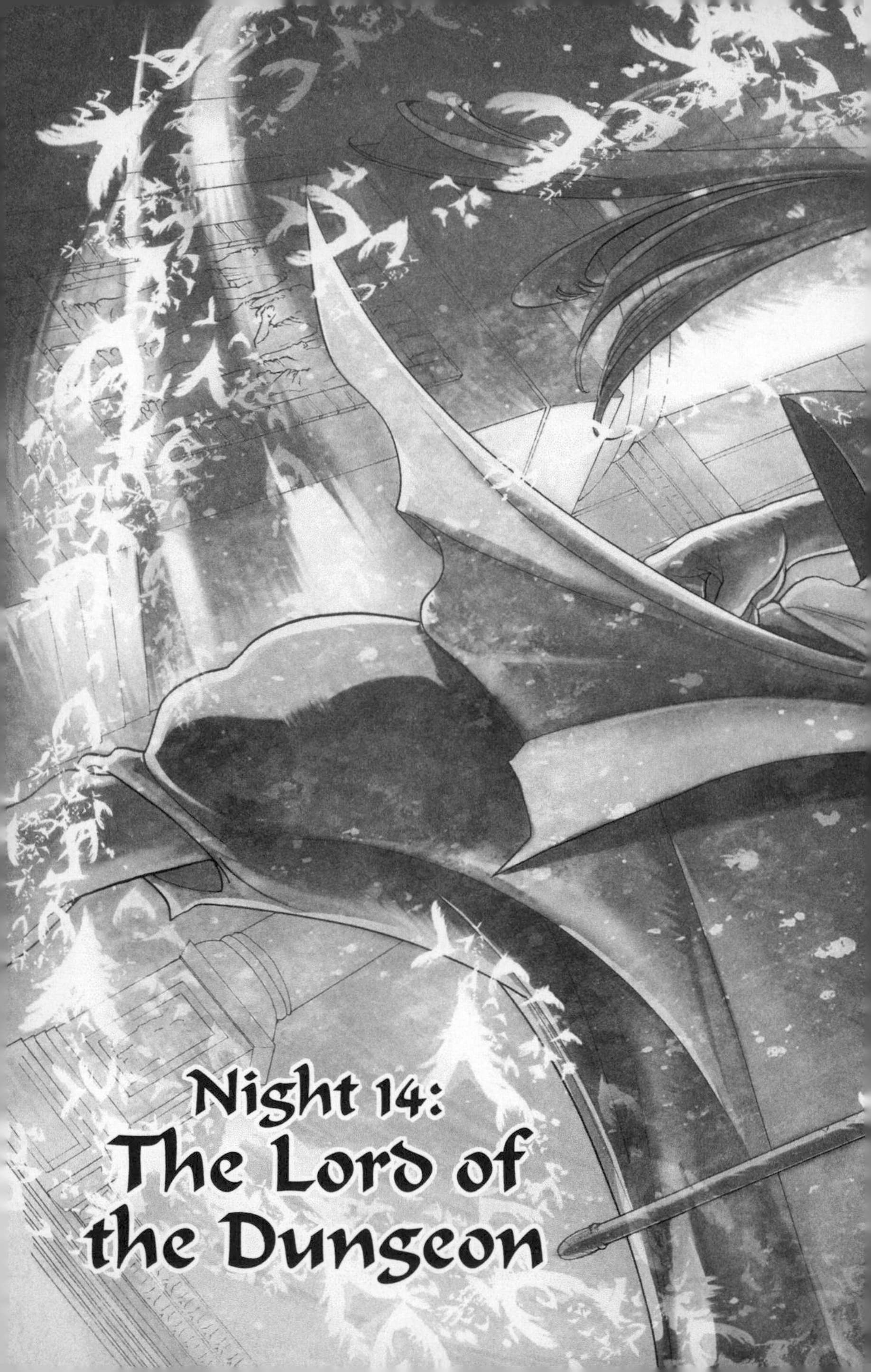
Night 14:
The Lord of the Dungeon

About Me-Shinobu Ohtaka ④

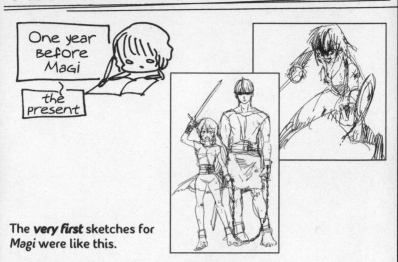

One year
Before
MaGi

the present

The **very first** sketches for Magi were like this.

Aladdin and Alibaba are super brawny, but that was the original idea. At first, I think I was planning on telling a story about **Roman gladiators.** I tend to take my manga in an extremely **bright** or extremely **dark** direction—and this was dark. After a process of **trial-and-error** to turn it into a fun manga for a shonen magazine, the result was **Magi as it is now.**

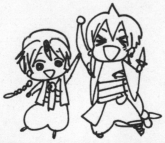

It's so much **brighter** now!

Aladdin was originally a girl. Aladdin became a boy quite a bit later on, so **the cloth around his chest is a holdover from that time.** Alibaba had a personality so dark it was like the end of the world, but I gave that up.

Continued on page 188.

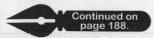

Shinobu Ohtaka History

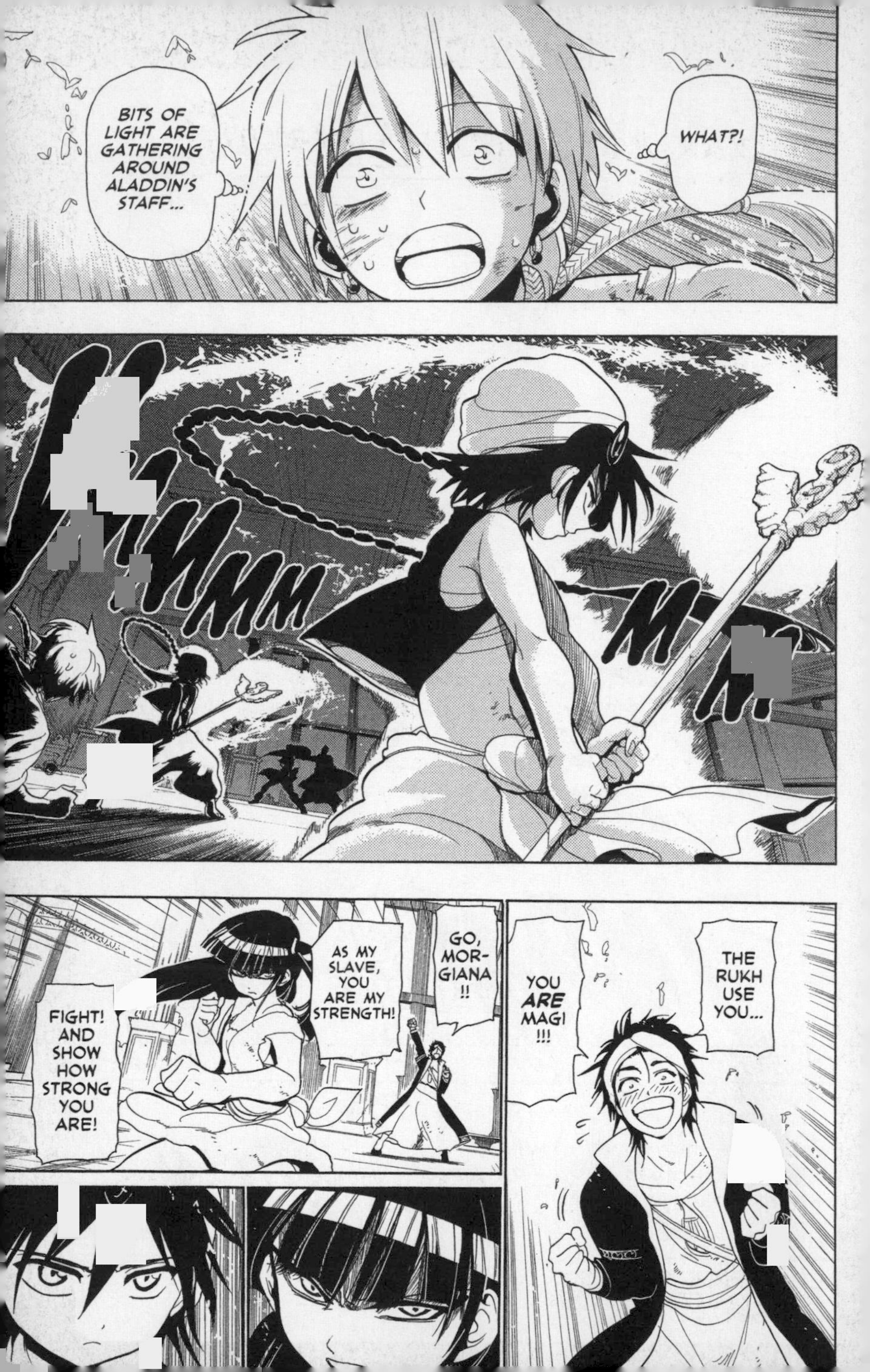
WHAT?!
BITS OF LIGHT ARE GATHERING AROUND ALADDIN'S STAFF...
THE RUKH USE YOU...
YOU ARE MAGI!!!
GO, MORGIANA!!
AS MY SLAVE, YOU ARE MY STRENGTH!
FIGHT! AND SHOW HOW STRONG YOU ARE!

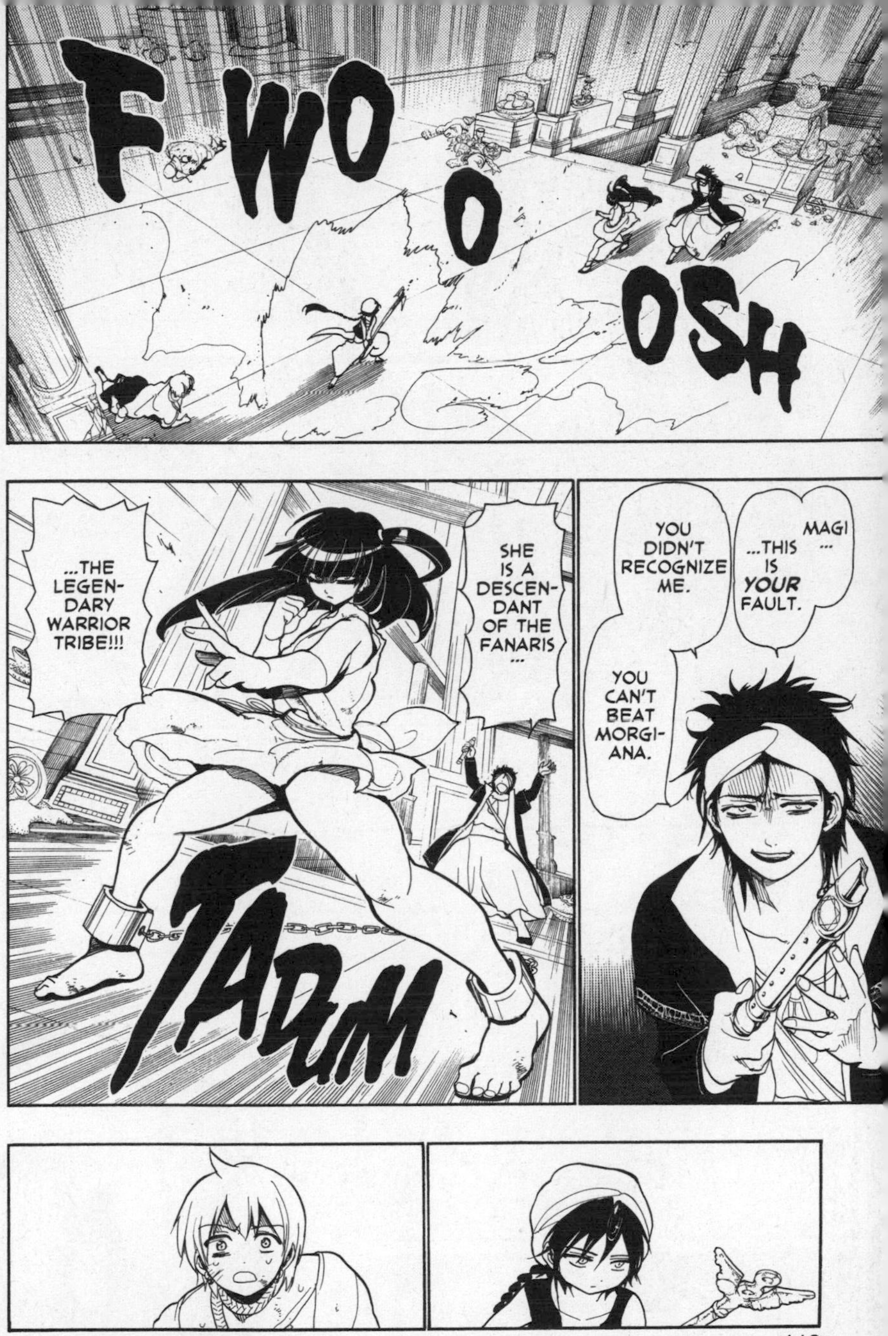
FWOOOSH
MAGI... ...THIS IS *YOUR* FAULT.
YOU DIDN'T RECOGNIZE ME.
YOU CAN'T BEAT MORGIANA.
SHE IS A DESCENDANT OF THE FANARIS...
...THE LEGENDARY WARRIOR TRIBE!!!
TARM

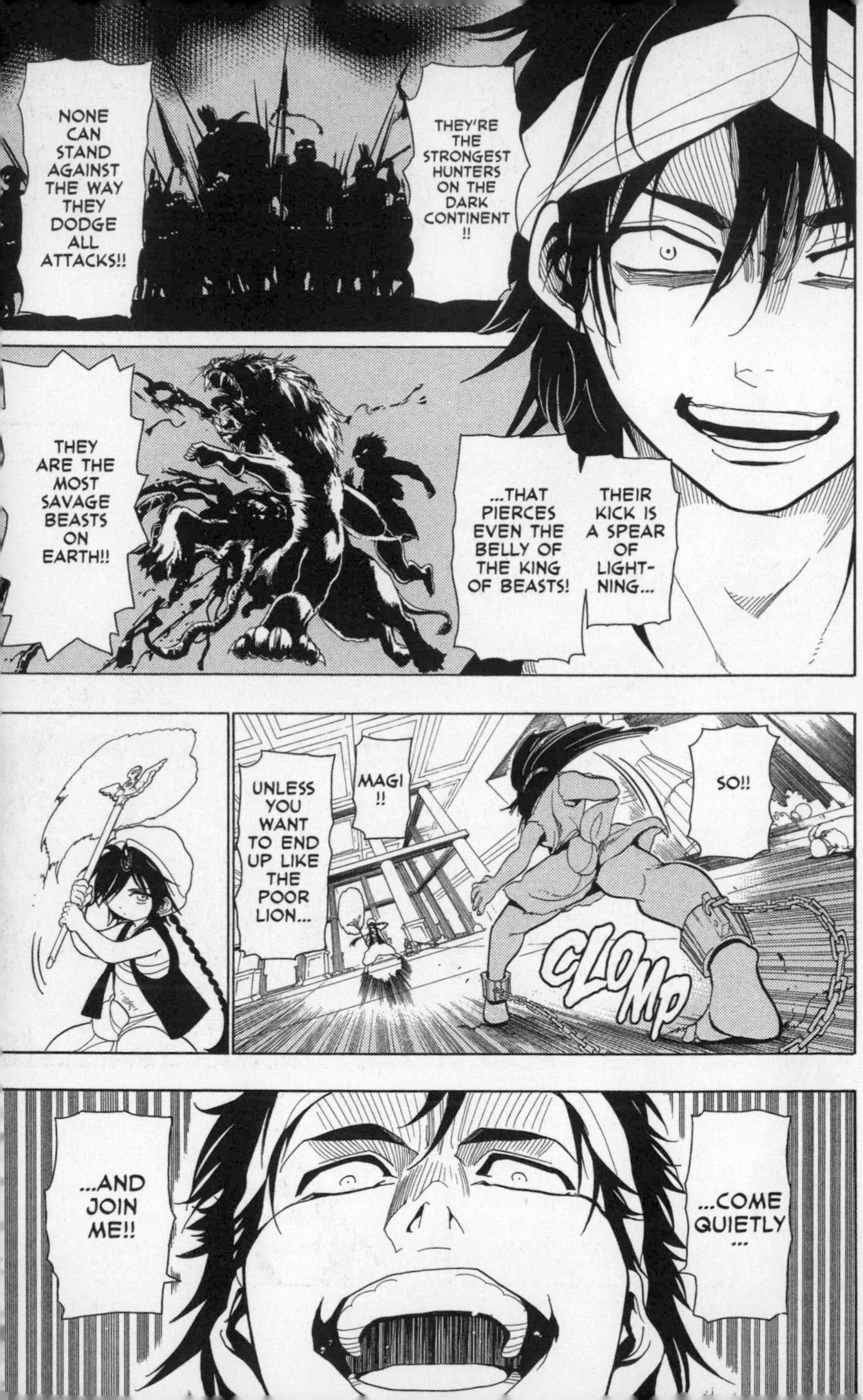
THEY'RE THE STRONGEST HUNTERS ON THE DARK CONTINENT!!
NONE CAN STAND AGAINST THE WAY THEY DODGE ALL ATTACKS!!
THEIR KICK IS A SPEAR OF LIGHT-NING...
...THAT PIERCES EVEN THE BELLY OF THE KING OF BEASTS!
THEY ARE THE MOST SAVAGE BEASTS ON EARTH!!
SO!!
MAGI!!
UNLESS YOU WANT TO END UP LIKE THE POOR LION...
CLOMP
...COME QUIETLY...
...AND JOIN ME!!

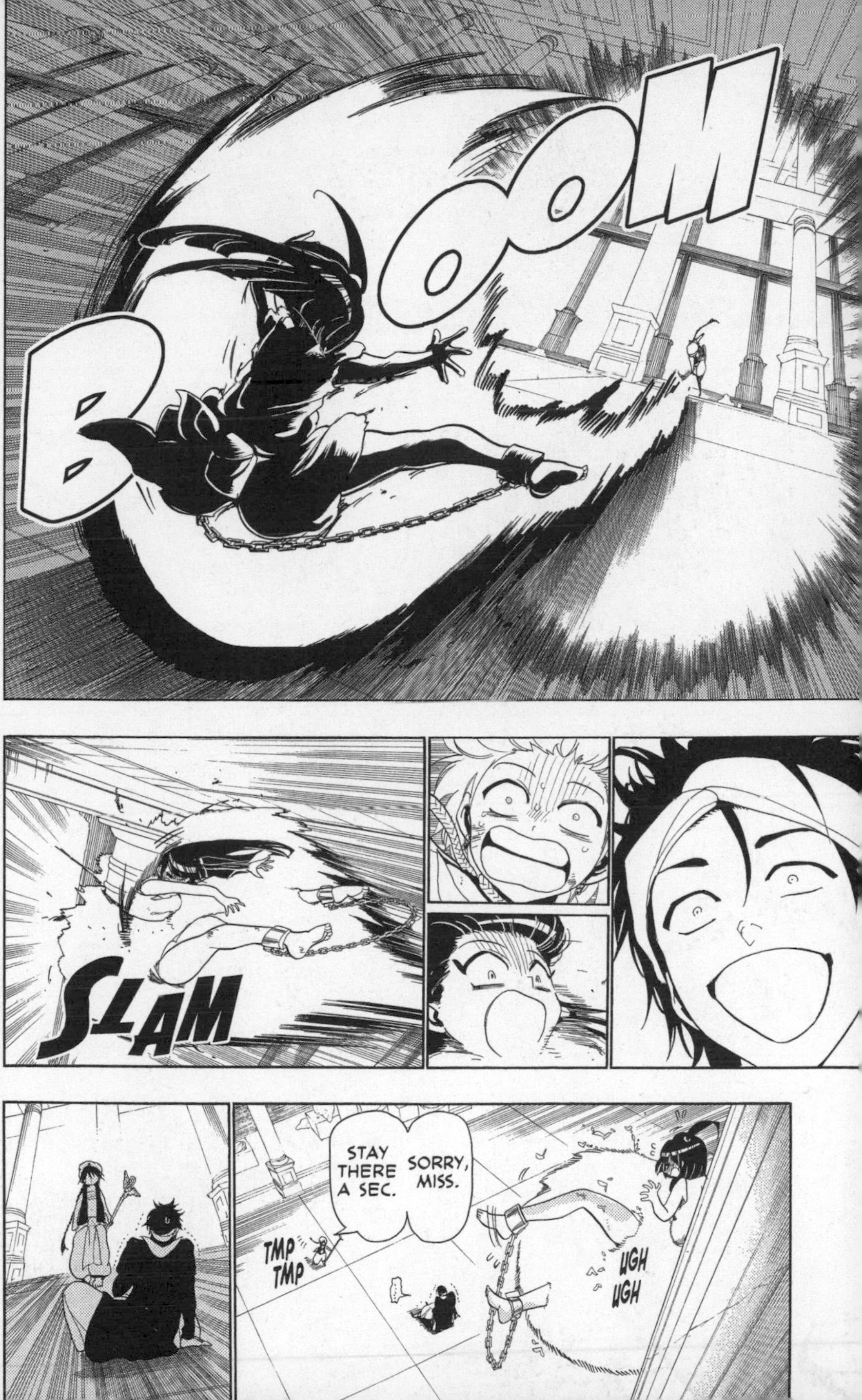
BOOM
SLAM
SORRY, MISS.
STAY THERE A SEC.
UGH UGH
TMP TMP

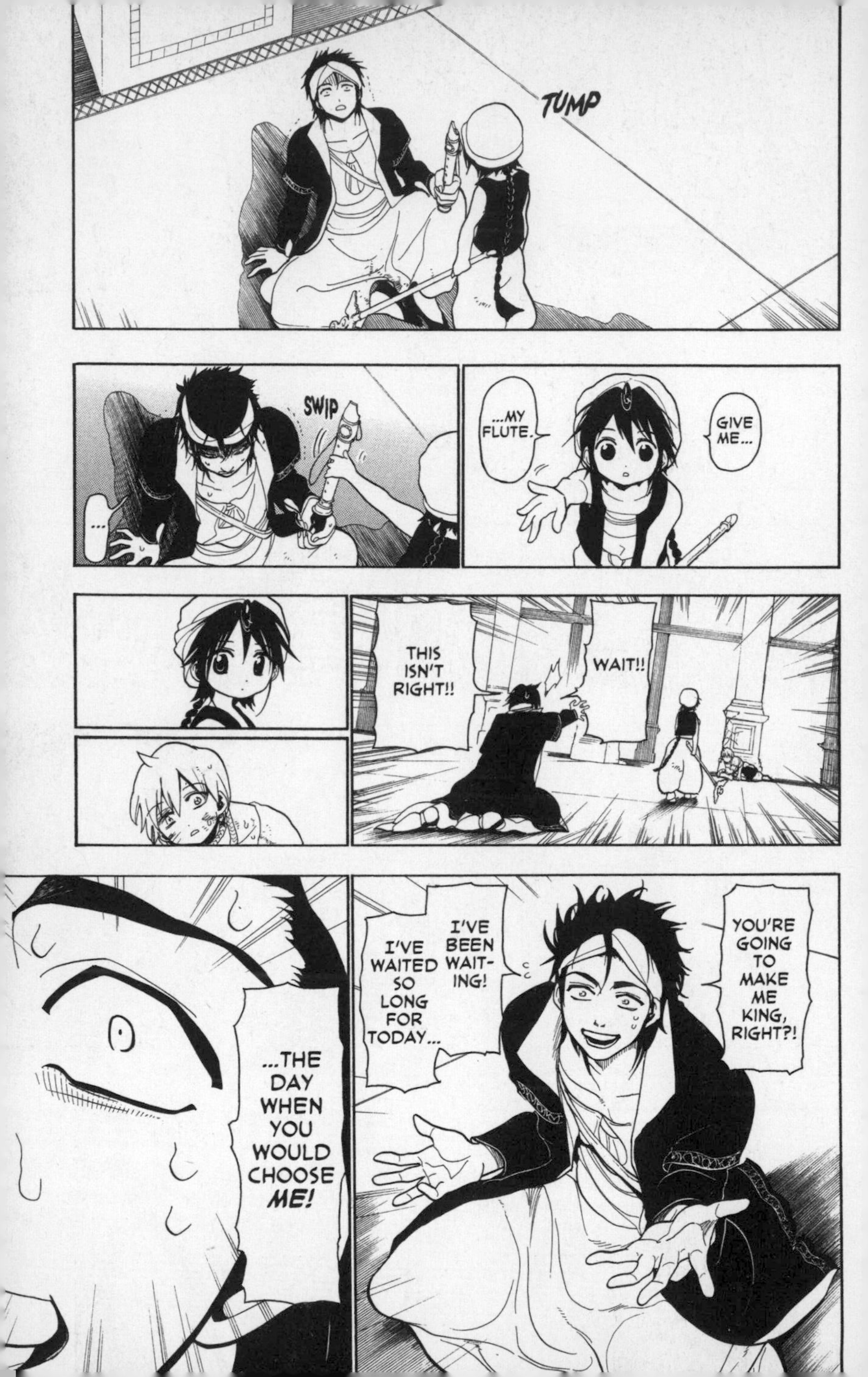
TUMP
GIVE ME...
...MY FLUTE.
SWIP
...
WAIT!!
THIS ISN'T RIGHT!!
YOU'RE GOING TO MAKE ME KING, RIGHT?!
I'VE BEEN WAIT-ING!
I'VE WAITED SO LONG FOR TODAY...
...THE DAY WHEN YOU WOULD CHOOSE *ME!*

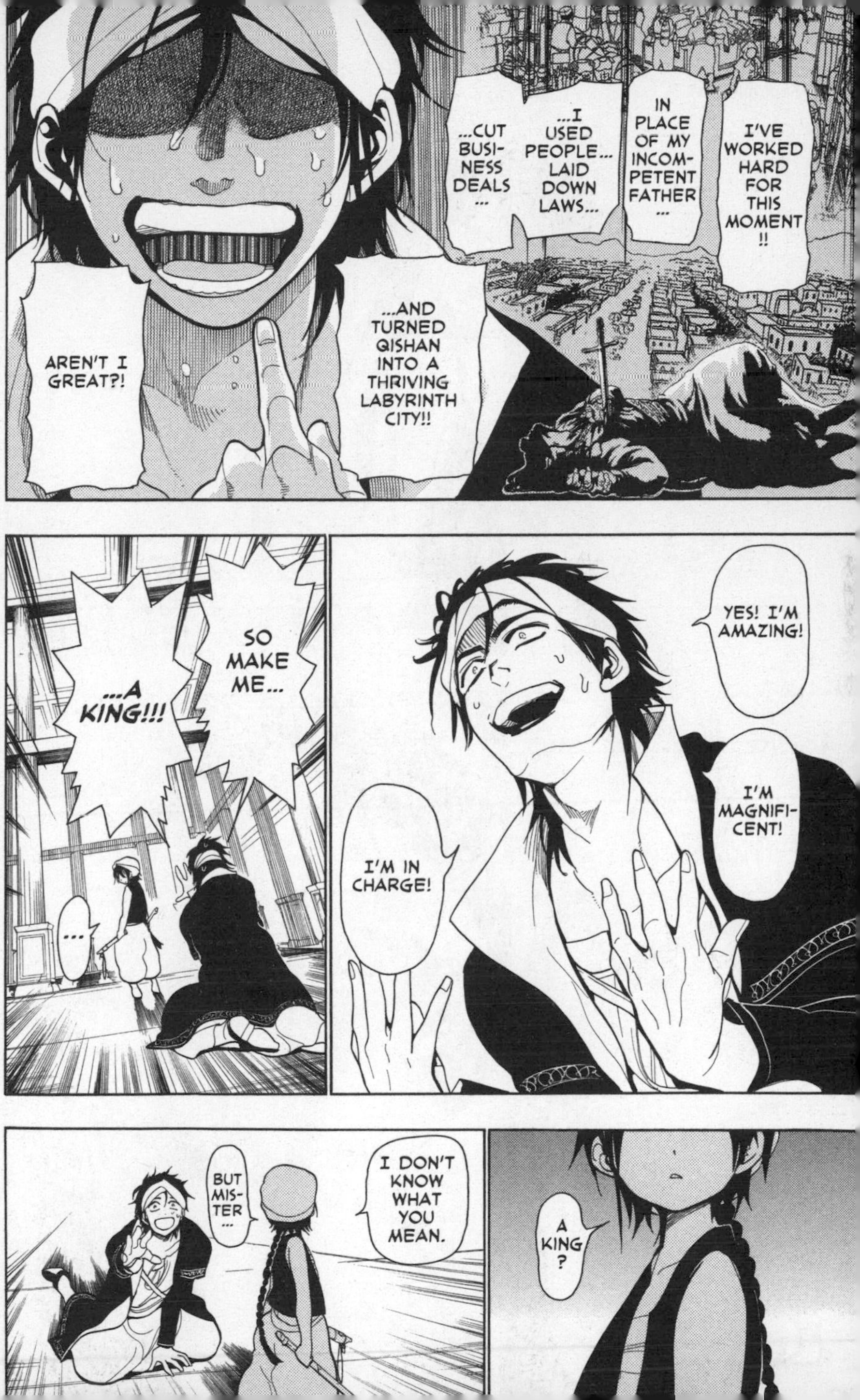
I'VE WORKED HARD FOR THIS MOMENT!!
IN PLACE OF MY INCOMPETENT FATHER...
...I USED PEOPLE... LAID DOWN LAWS...
...CUT BUSINESS DEALS...
...AND TURNED QISHAN INTO A THRIVING LABYRINTH CITY!!
AREN'T I GREAT?!
YES! I'M AMAZING!
I'M MAGNIFICENT!
I'M IN CHARGE!
SO MAKE ME...
...A KING!!!
...
A KING?
I DON'T KNOW WHAT YOU MEAN.
BUT MISTER...

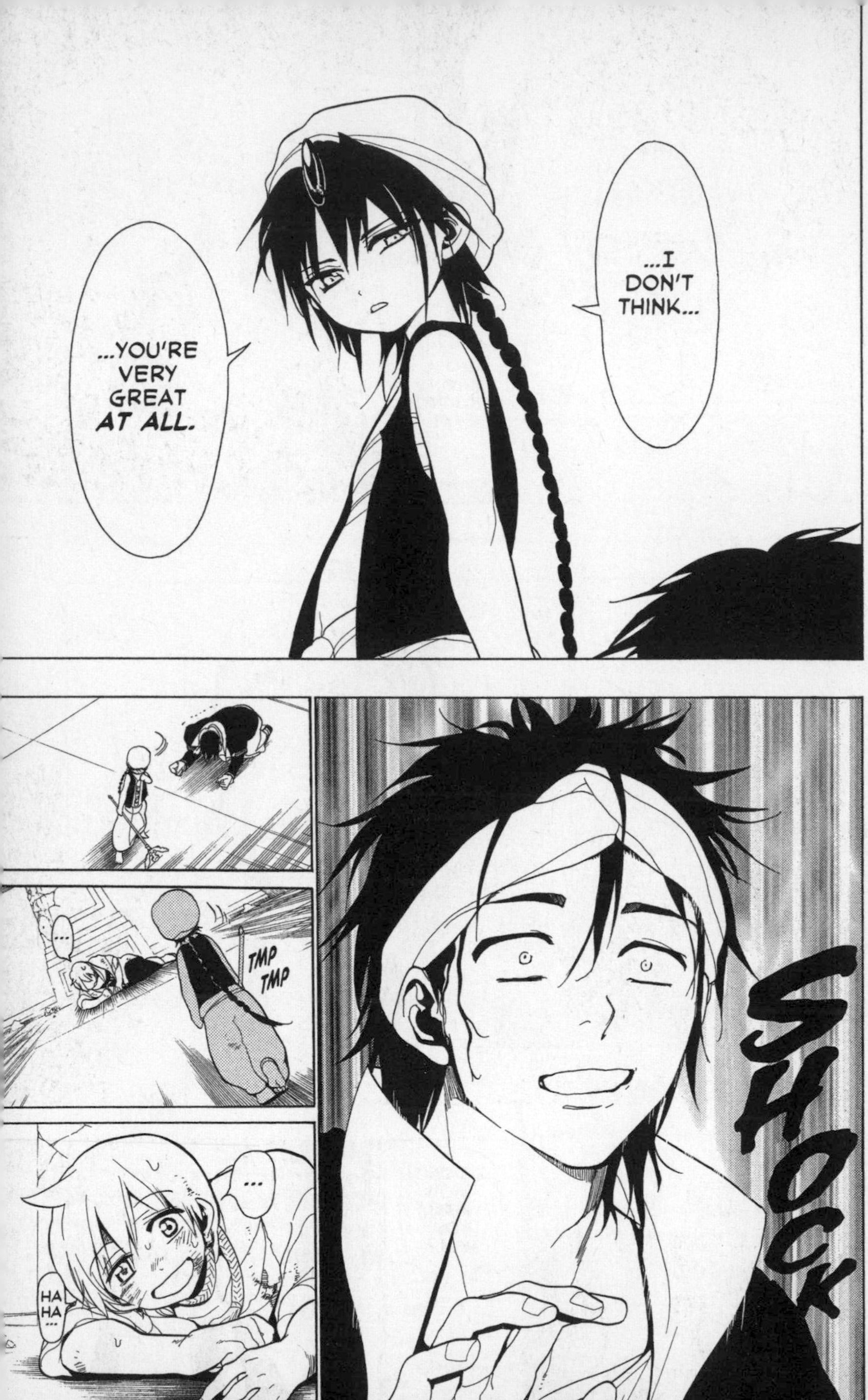
...I DON'T THINK...
...YOU'RE VERY GREAT AT ALL.
SHOCK
...
TMP TMP
...
HA HA ...

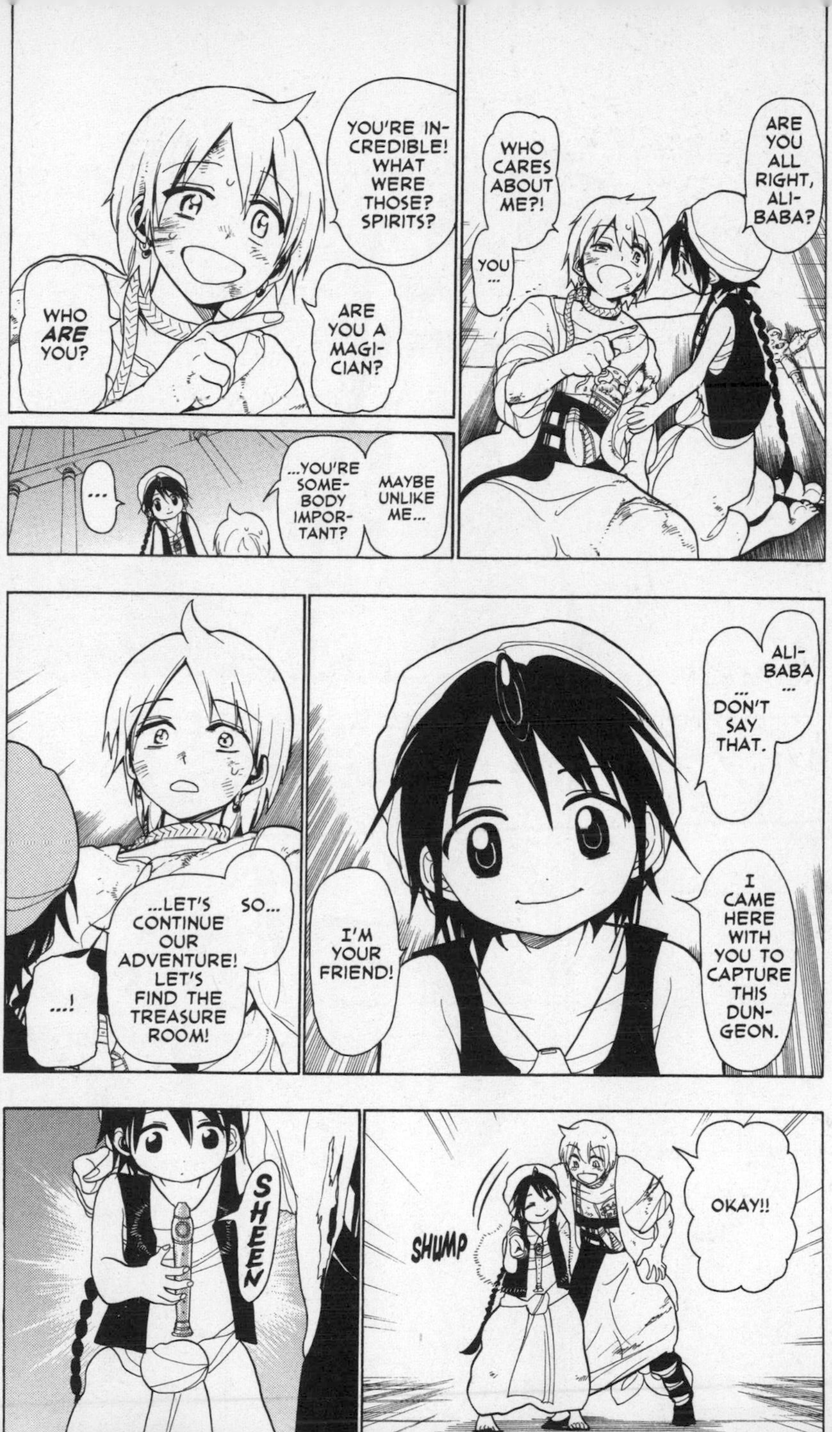
ARE YOU ALL RIGHT, ALI-BABA?
WHO CARES ABOUT ME?!
YOU ...
YOU'RE IN-CREDIBLE! WHAT WERE THOSE? SPIRITS?
ARE YOU A MAGI-CIAN?
WHO ARE YOU?
MAYBE UNLIKE ME...
...YOU'RE SOME-BODY IMPOR-TANT?
...
ALI-BABA ... DON'T SAY THAT.
I CAME HERE WITH YOU TO CAPTURE THIS DUN-GEON.
I'M YOUR FRIEND!
SO...
...LET'S CONTINUE OUR ADVENTURE! LET'S FIND THE TREASURE ROOM!
...!
OKAY!!
SHUMP
SHEEN

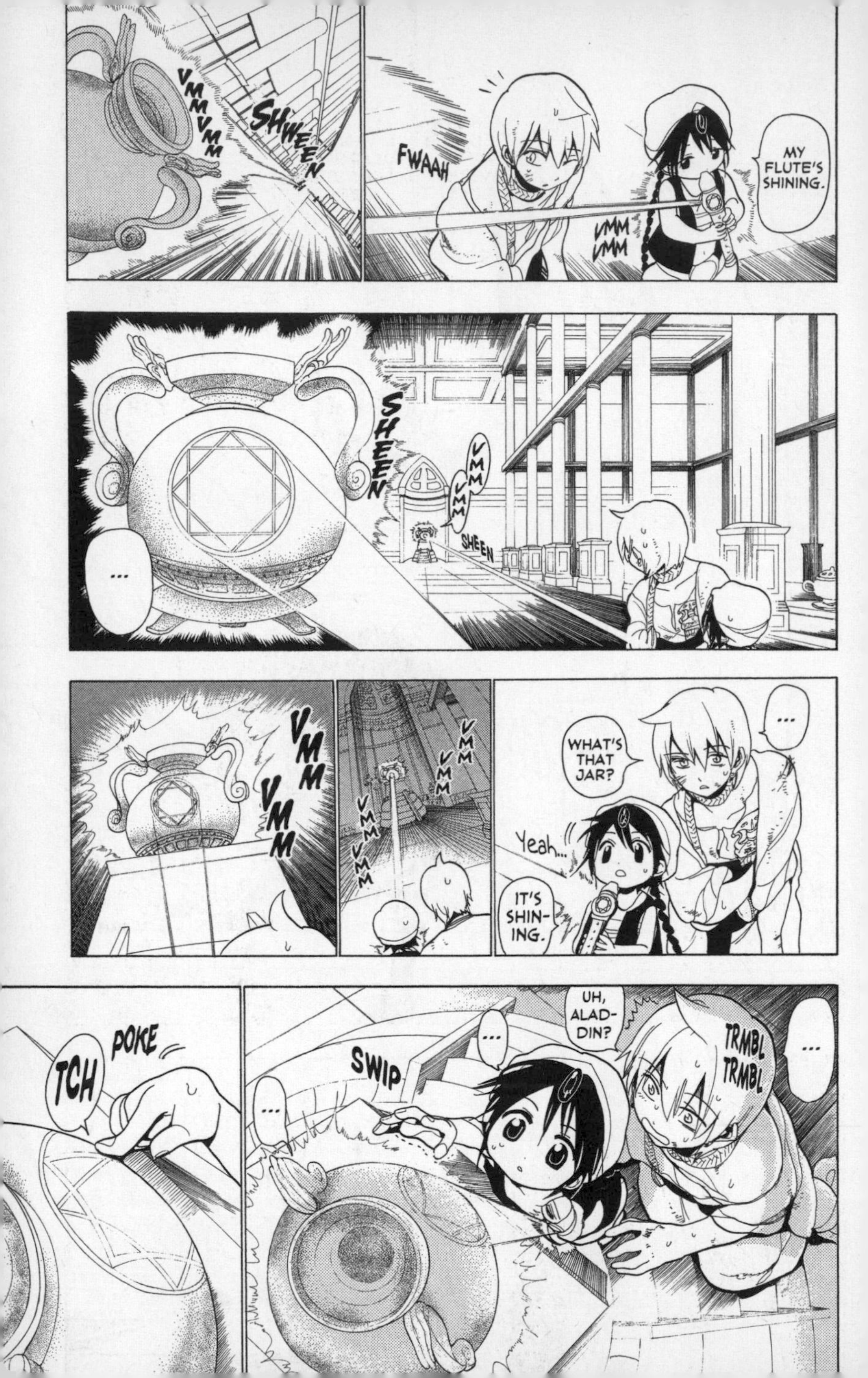
MY FLUTE'S SHINING.
FWAAH
VMM VMM
SHWEEN
VMMVMM
SHEEN
VMM VMM
SHEEN
...
...
WHAT'S THAT JAR?
Yeah...
IT'S SHIN-ING.
VMM VMM
VMM VMM VMM
VMM VMM
...
TRMBL TRMBL
UH, ALAD-DIN?
...
SWIP
...
POKE
TCH

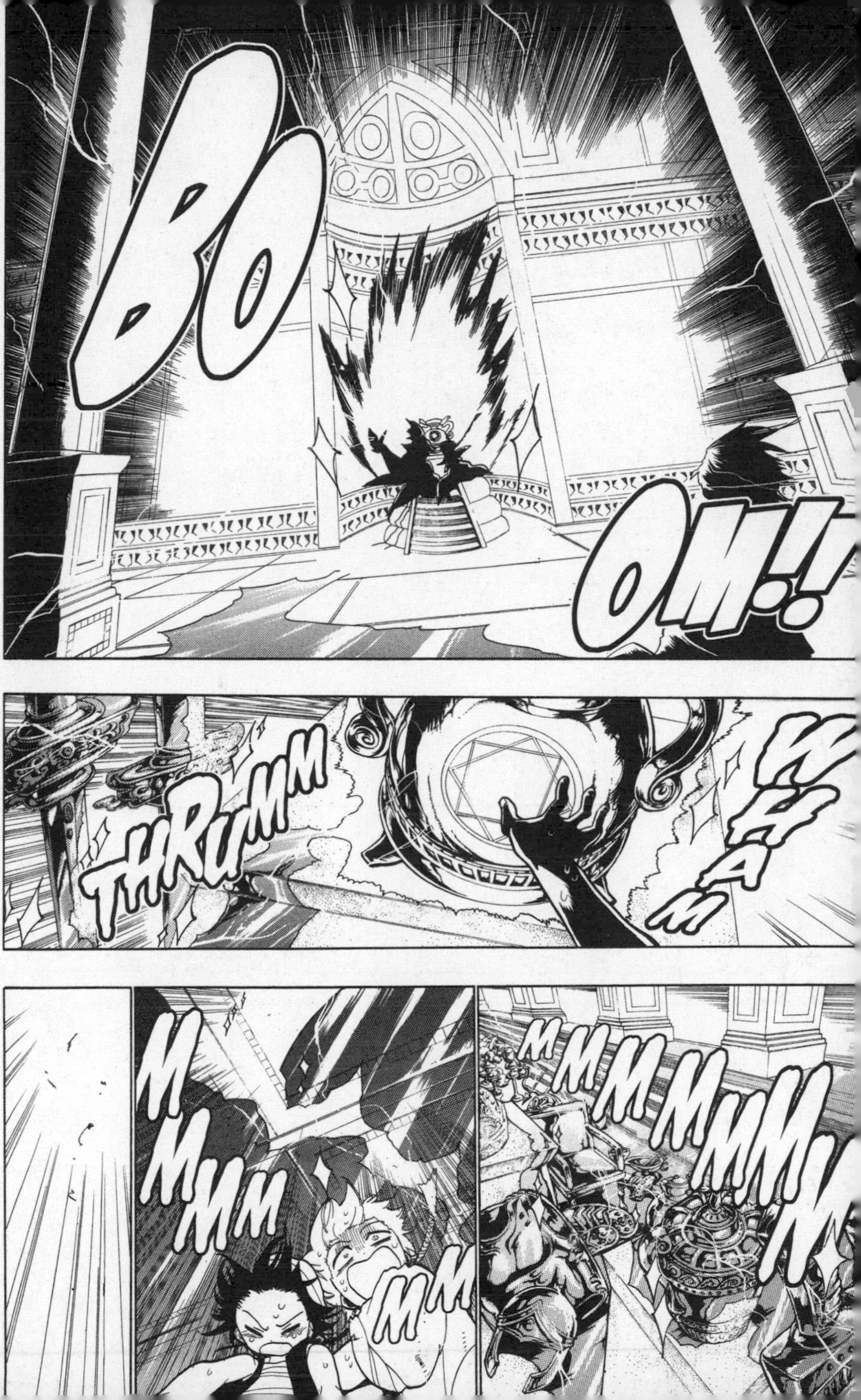
BOOM!!
WHAM
THRUMM
MMMMMMM
MMMMMM

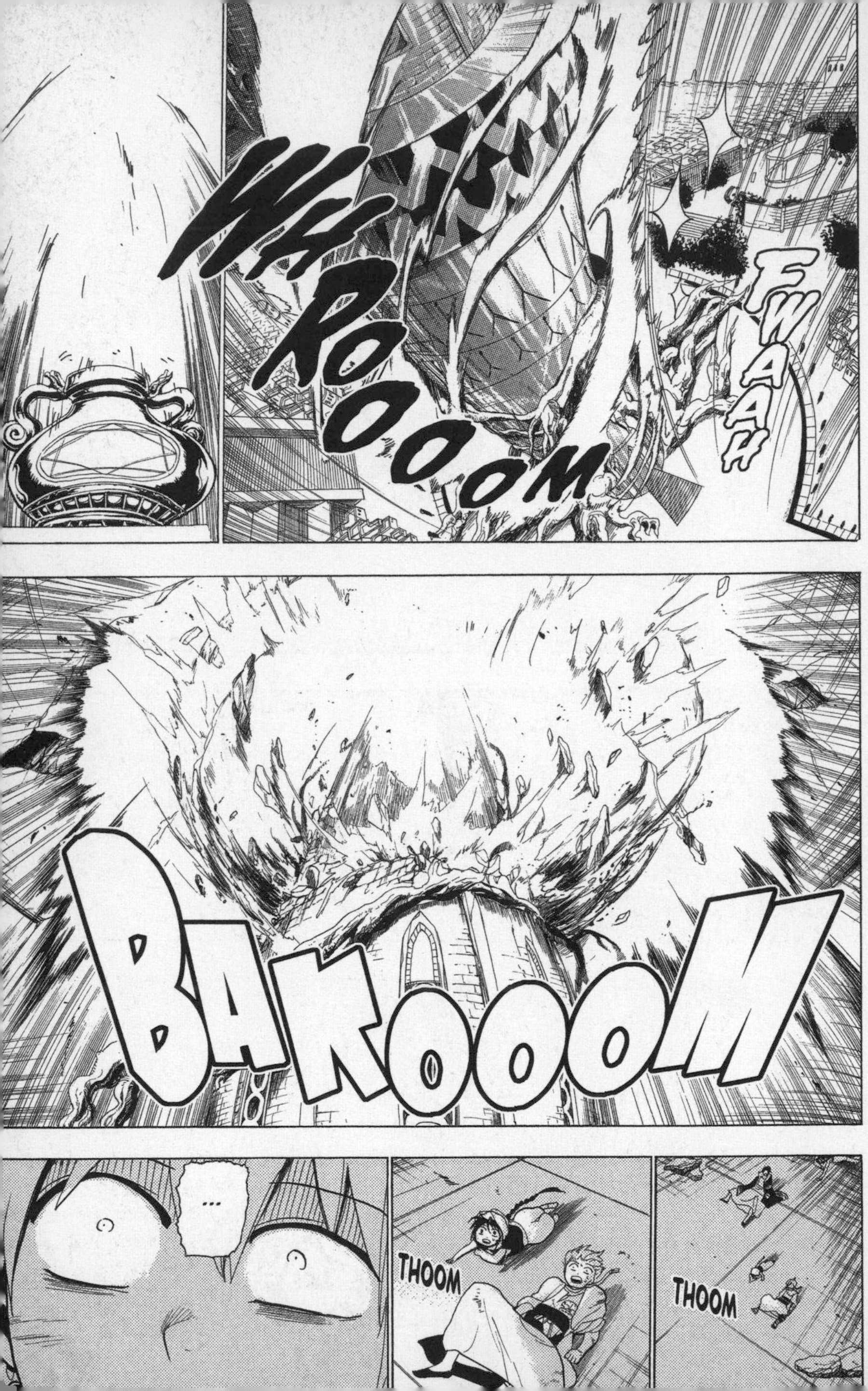
WHROOOOM
FWAAH
BAKOOOM
THOOM
THOOM
...

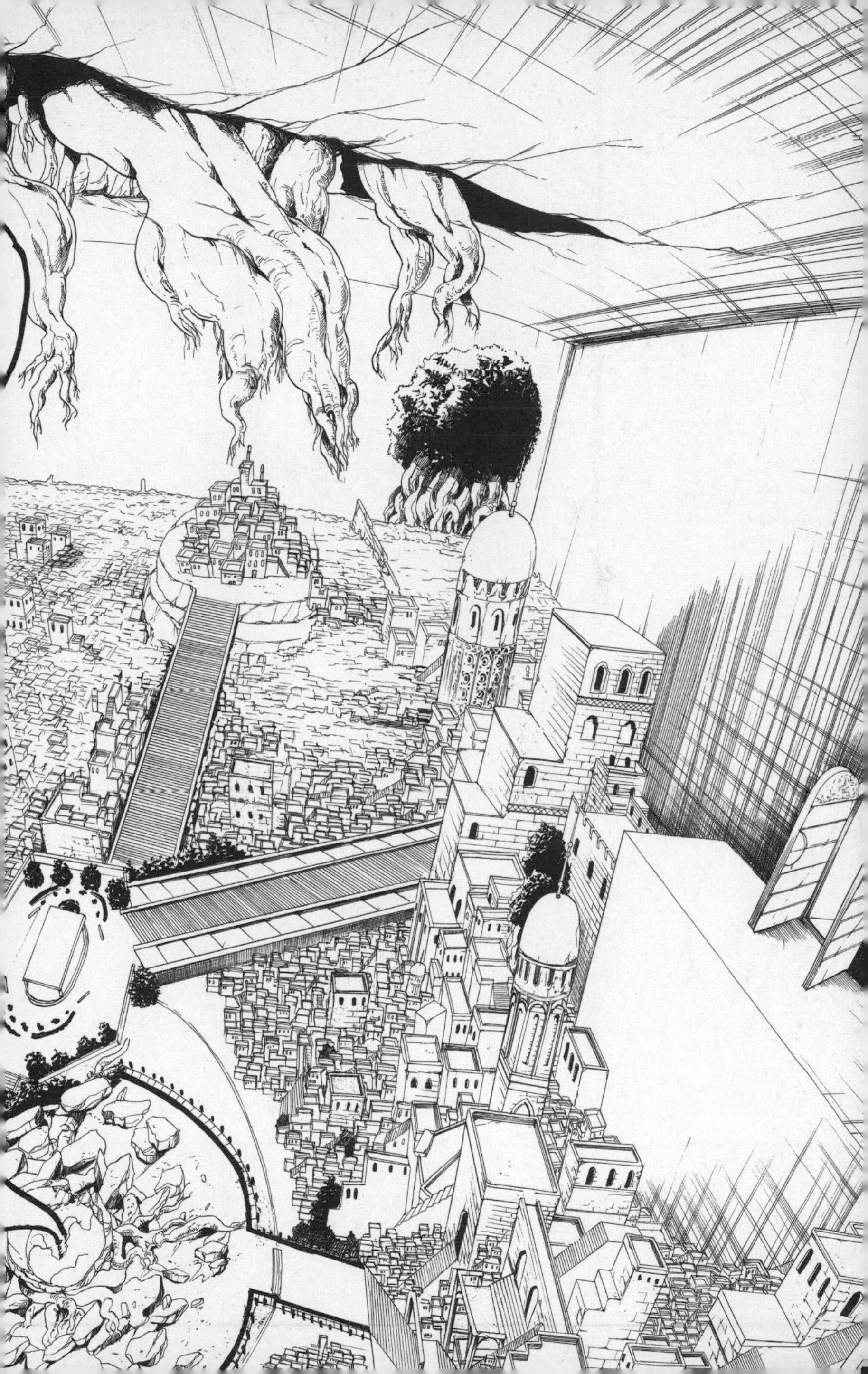

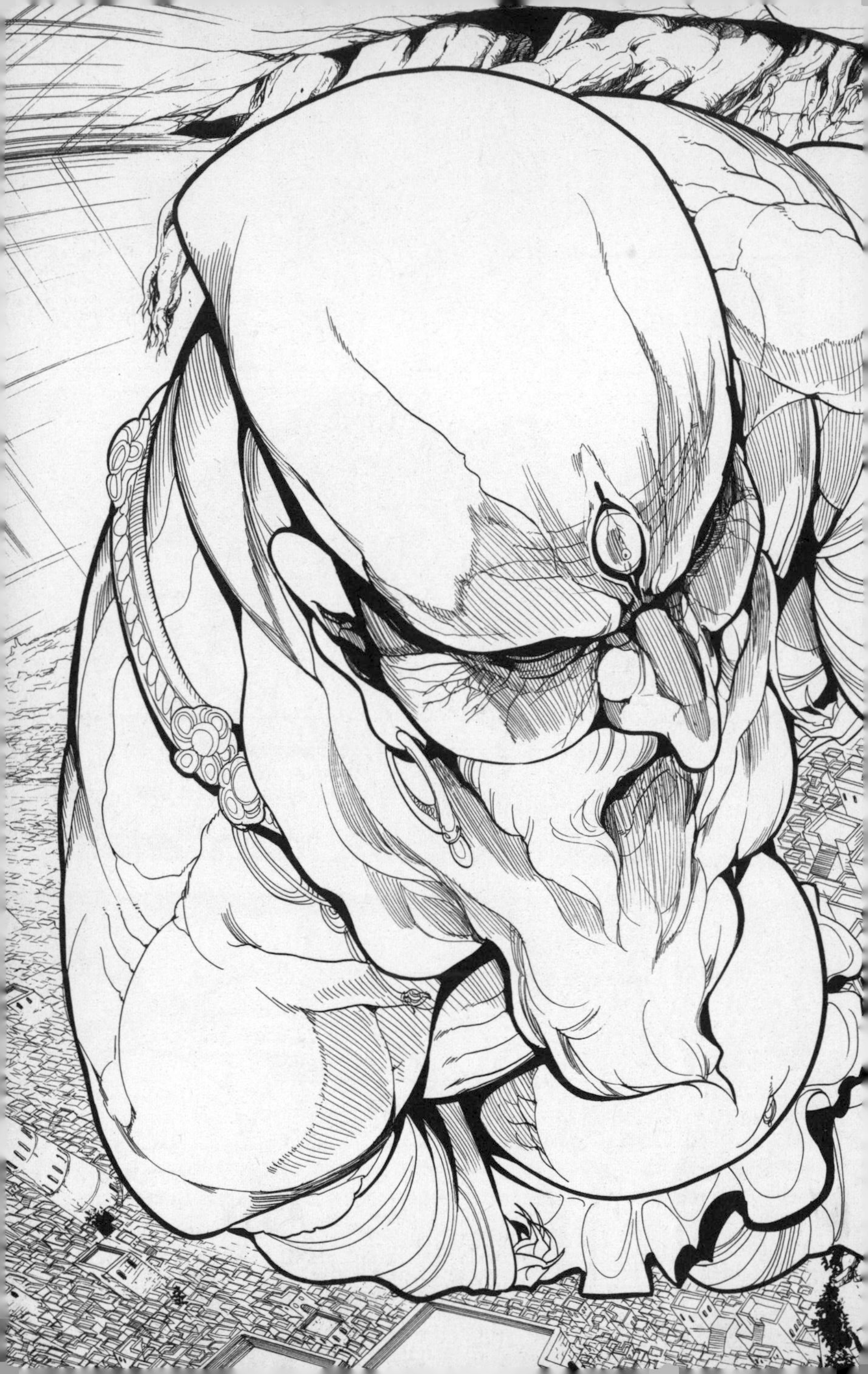

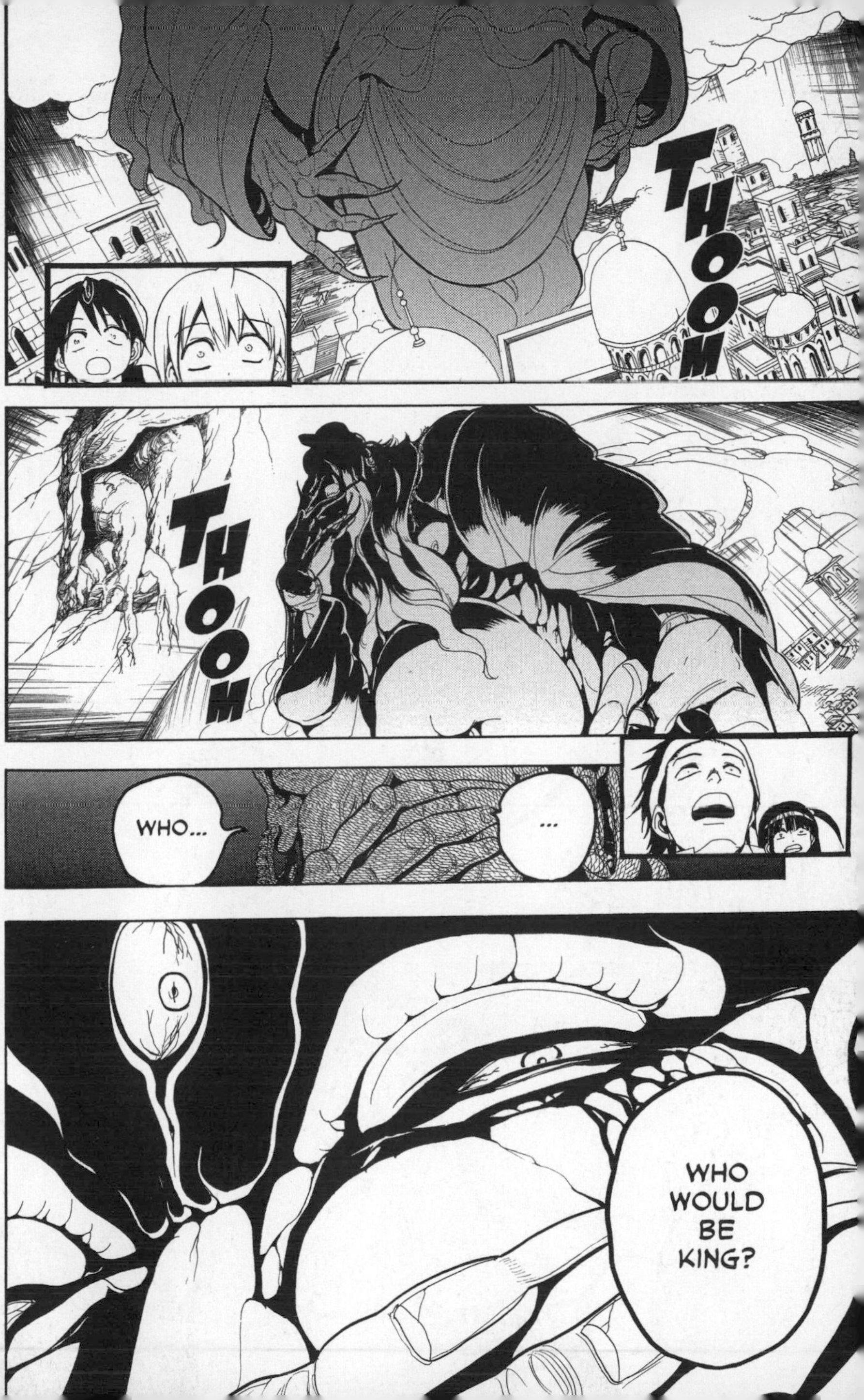
THOOM
THOOM
...
WHO...
WHO WOULD BE KING?

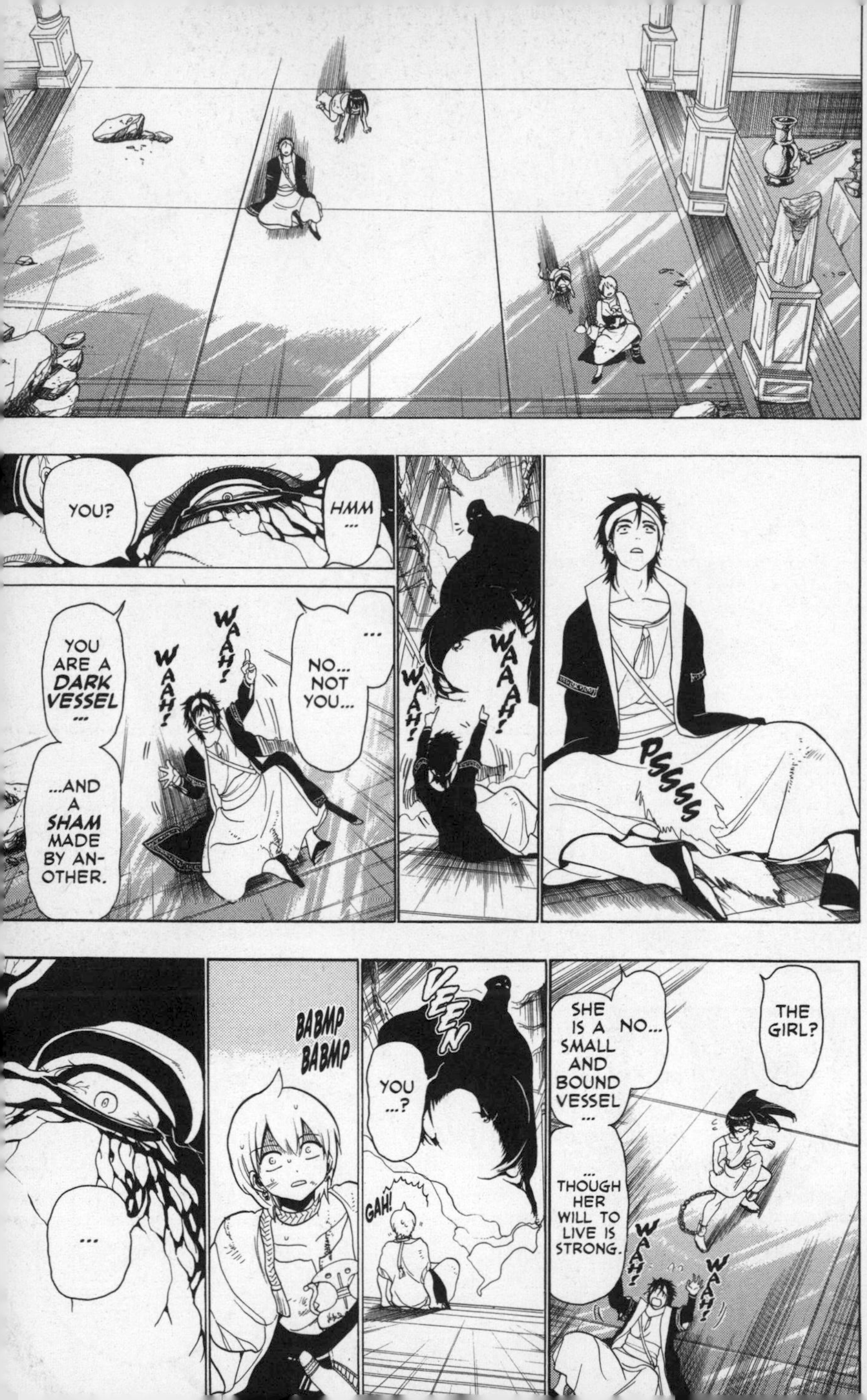
PSSSS
WAAH!
WAAAH!
HMM...
YOU?
...
NO... NOT YOU...
WAAH!
WAAH!
YOU ARE A DARK VESSEL...
...AND A SHAM MADE BY ANOTHER.
THE GIRL?
NO...
SHE IS A SMALL AND BOUND VESSEL...
...THOUGH HER WILL TO LIVE IS STRONG.
WAAH!
WAAH!
VEEN
YOU...?
GAH!
BABMP BABMP
...

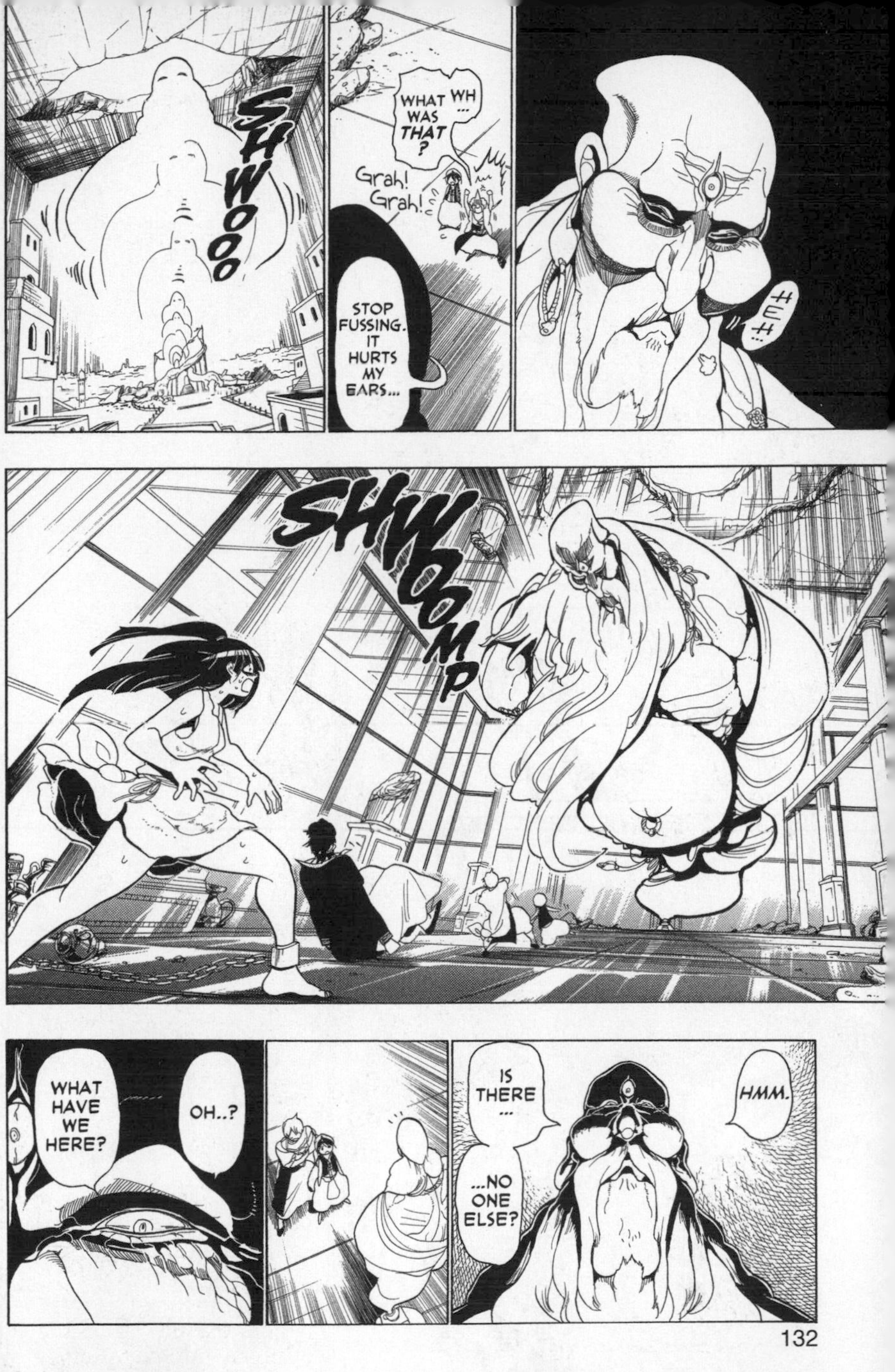
HEH...
WH ...
WHAT WAS THAT?
Grah! Grah!
STOP FUSSING. IT HURTS MY EARS...
SHWOOOO
SHWOOOMP
HMM.
IS THERE ...
...NO ONE ELSE?
OH..?
WHAT HAVE WE HERE?

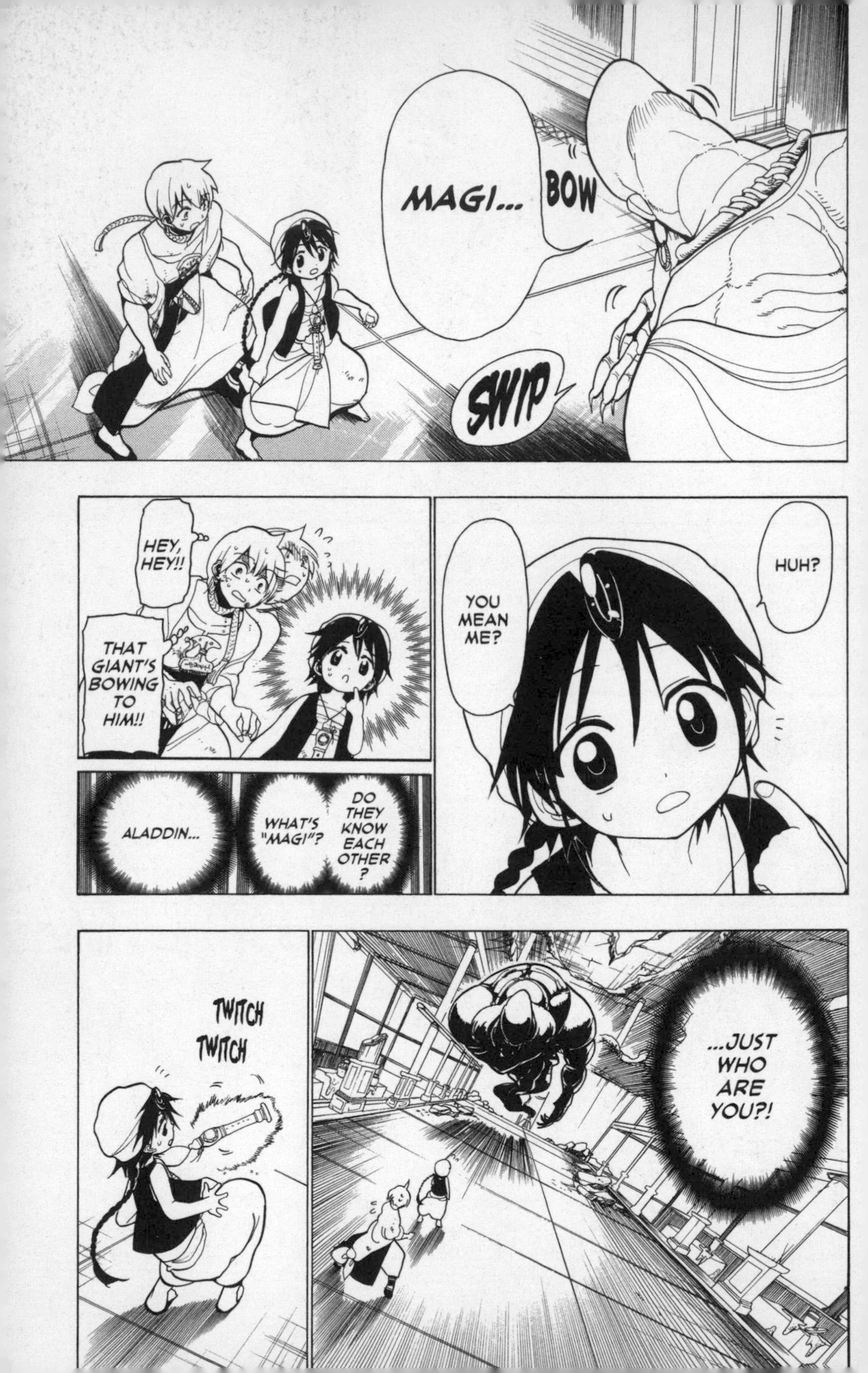
BOW
MAGI...
SWIP
HUH?
YOU MEAN ME?
HEY, HEY!!
THAT GIANT'S BOWING TO HIM!!
DO THEY KNOW EACH OTHER?
WHAT'S "MAGI"?
ALADDIN...
...JUST WHO ARE YOU?!
TWITCH TWITCH

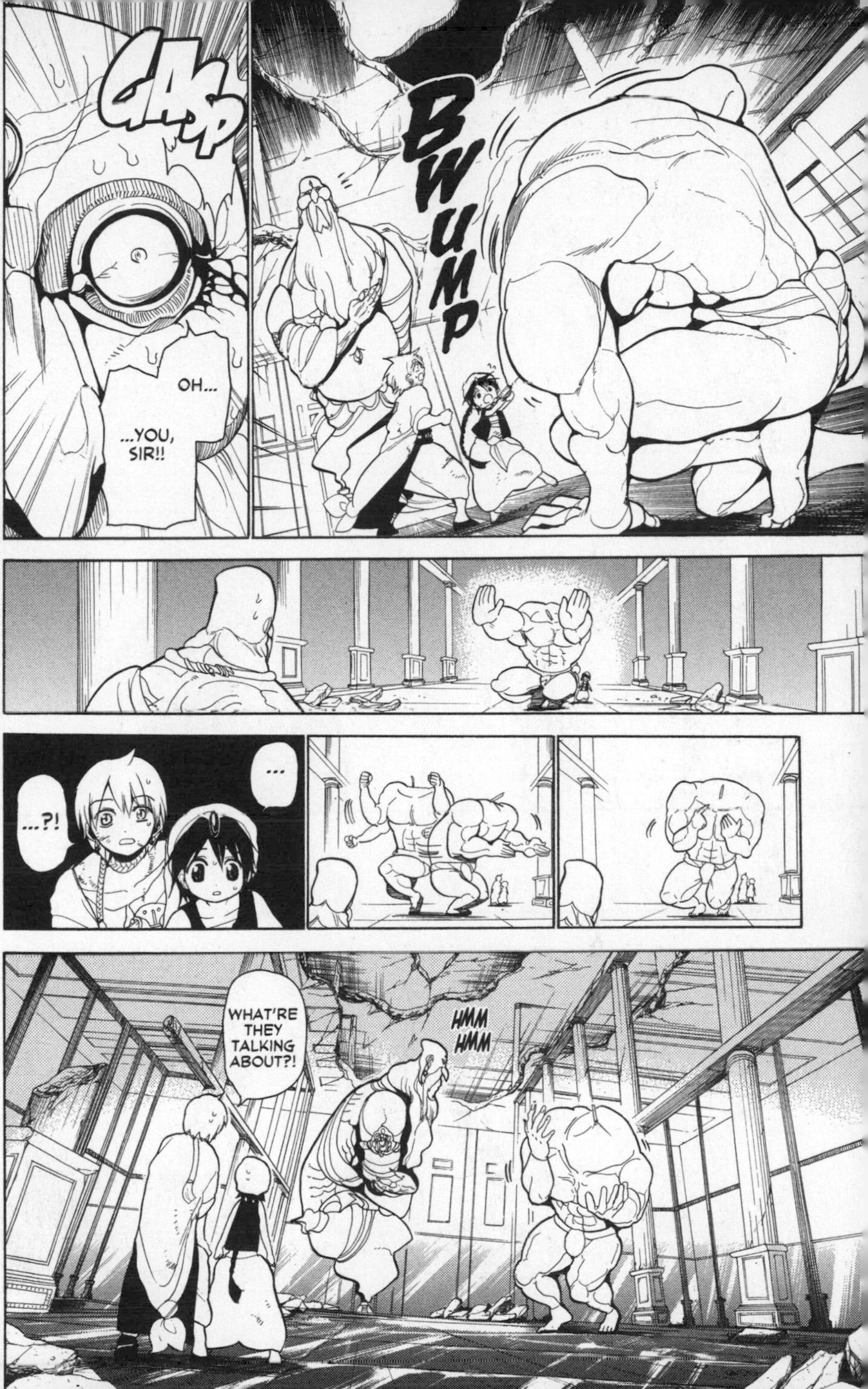
BWUMP
GASP
OH...
...YOU, SIR!!
...
...?!
HMM HMM
WHAT'RE THEY TALKING ABOUT?!

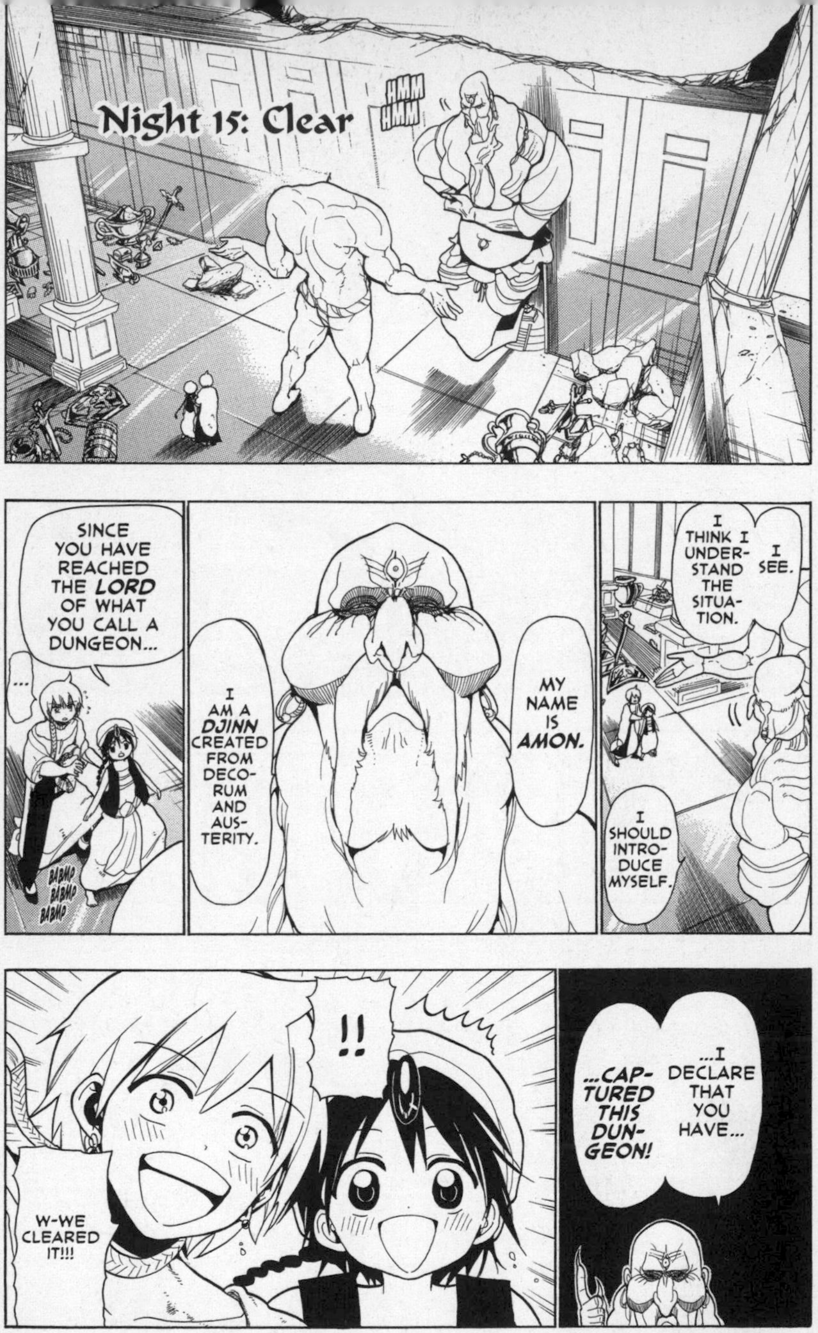
Night 15: Clear
HMM HMM
I SEE.
I THINK I UNDERSTAND THE SITUATION.
I SHOULD INTRODUCE MYSELF.
MY NAME IS AMON.
I AM A DJINN CREATED FROM DECORUM AND AUSTERITY.
SINCE YOU HAVE REACHED THE LORD OF WHAT YOU CALL A DUNGEON...
...
BABMP BABMP BABMP
...I DECLARE THAT YOU HAVE...
...CAPTURED THIS DUNGEON!
!!
W-WE CLEARED IT!!!

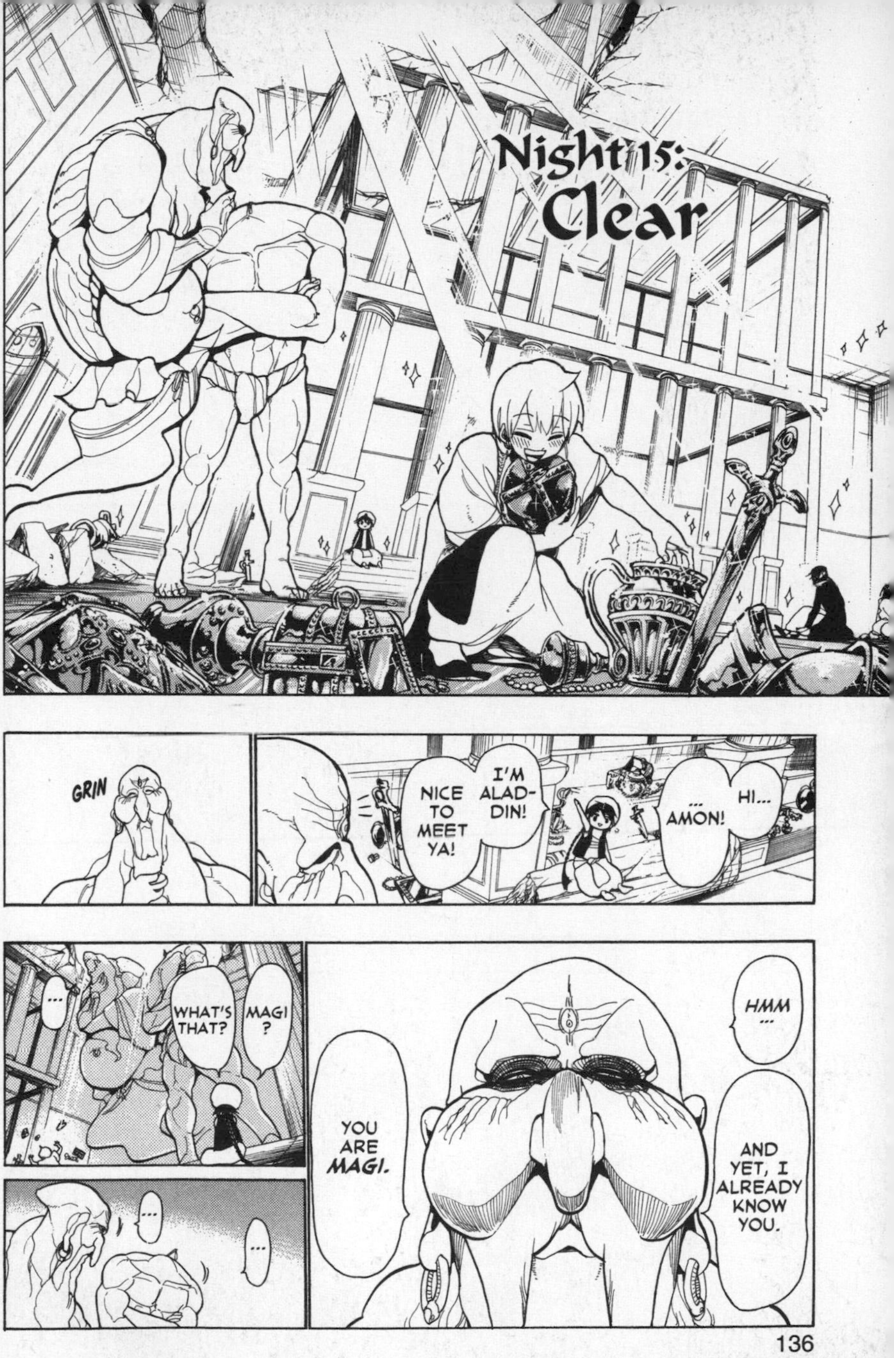
Night 15:
Clear
HI...
...AMON!
I'M ALAD-DIN!
NICE TO MEET YA!
GRIN
HMM...
AND YET, I ALREADY KNOW YOU.
YOU ARE MAGI.
MAGI?
WHAT'S THAT?
...
...
...

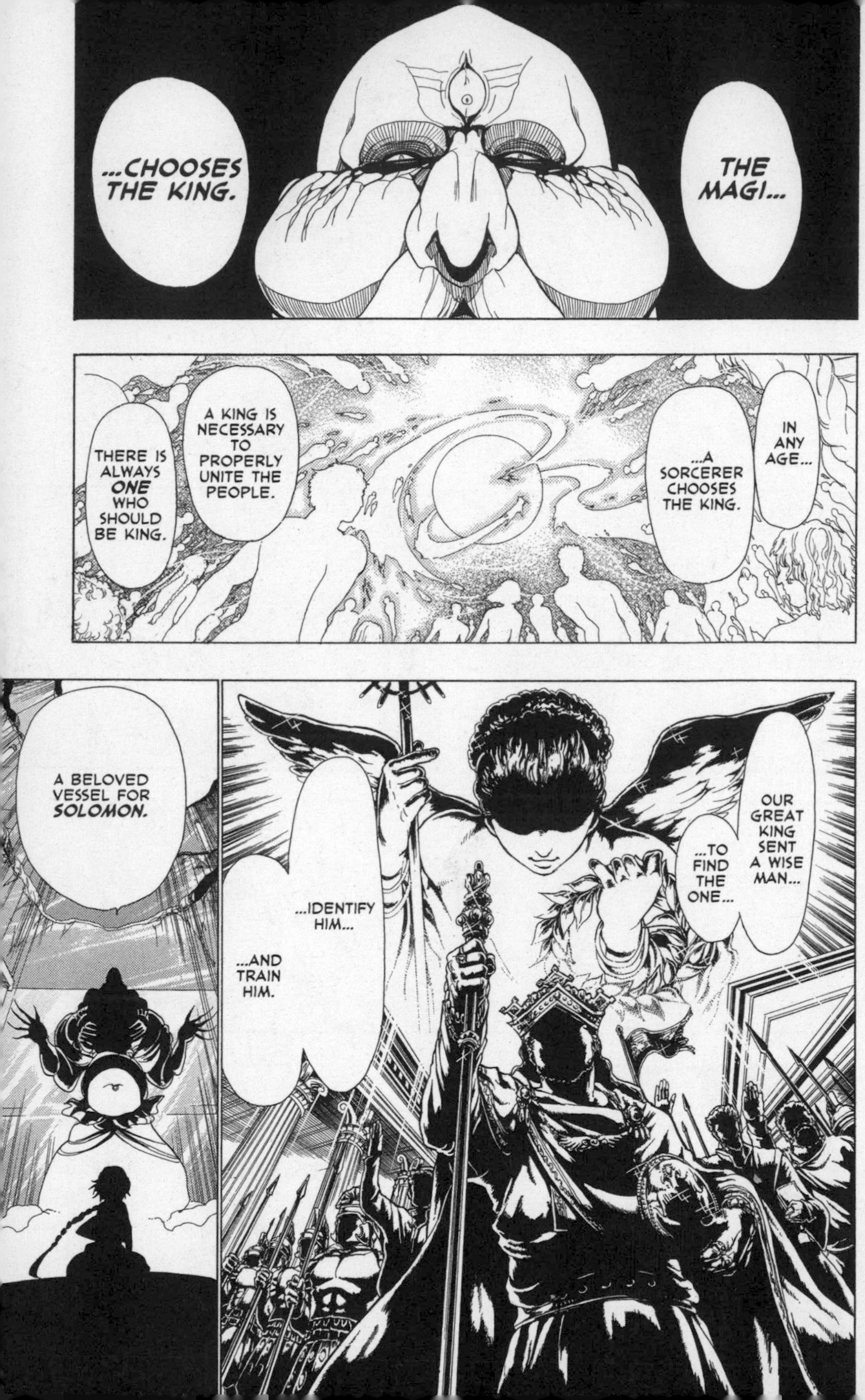
THE MAGI...
...CHOOSES THE KING.
IN ANY AGE...
...A SORCERER CHOOSES THE KING.
A KING IS NECESSARY TO PROPERLY UNITE THE PEOPLE.
THERE IS ALWAYS ONE WHO SHOULD BE KING.
OUR GREAT KING SENT A WISE MAN...
...TO FIND THE ONE...
...IDENTIFY HIM...
...AND TRAIN HIM.
A BELOVED VESSEL FOR SOLOMON.

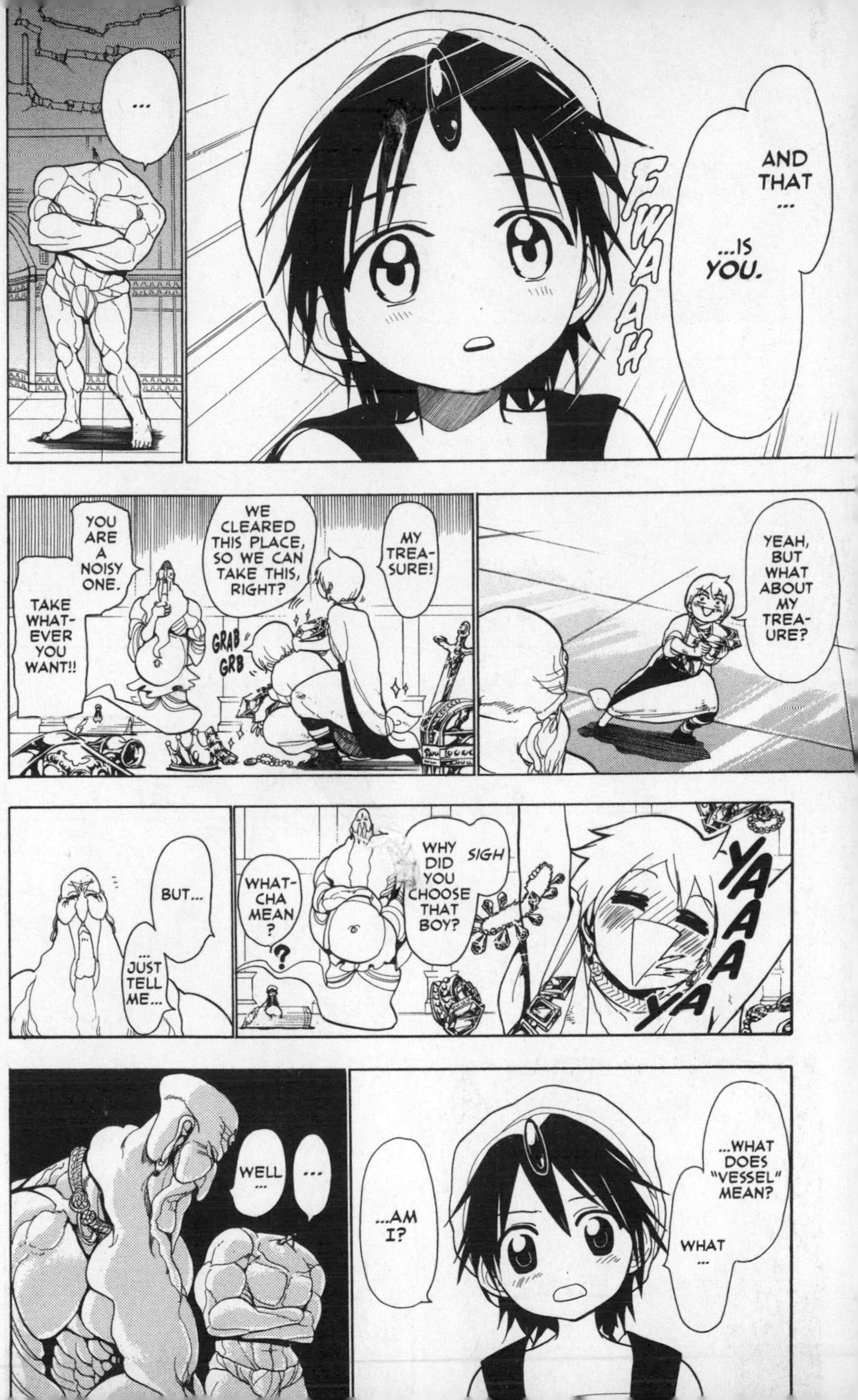
AND THAT ...
...IS YOU.
FWAAAH
...
YEAH, BUT WHAT ABOUT MY TREA-URE?
MY TREA-SURE!
WE CLEARED THIS PLACE, SO WE CAN TAKE THIS, RIGHT?
GRAB GRB
YOU ARE A NOISY ONE.
TAKE WHAT-EVER YOU WANT!!
YAAAAYA
WHY DID YOU CHOOSE THAT BOY?
SIGH
WHAT-CHA MEAN?
BUT...
...JUST TELL ME...
...WHAT DOES "VESSEL" MEAN?
WHAT ...
...AM I?
WELL ...
...

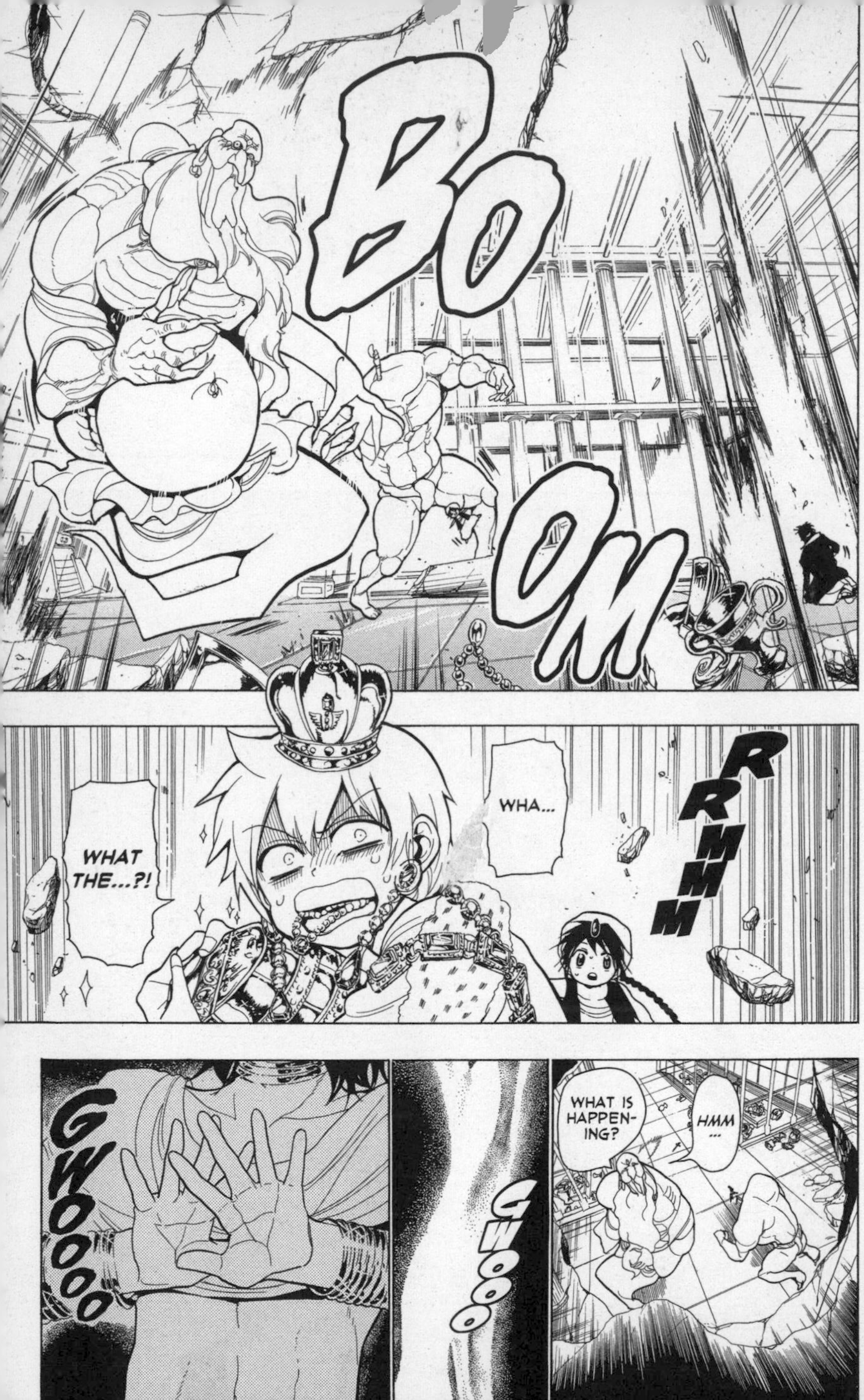
BOOM
RRMMMM
WHA...
WHAT THE...?!
HMM...
WHAT IS HAPPEN-ING?
GWOOOO
GWOOOOO

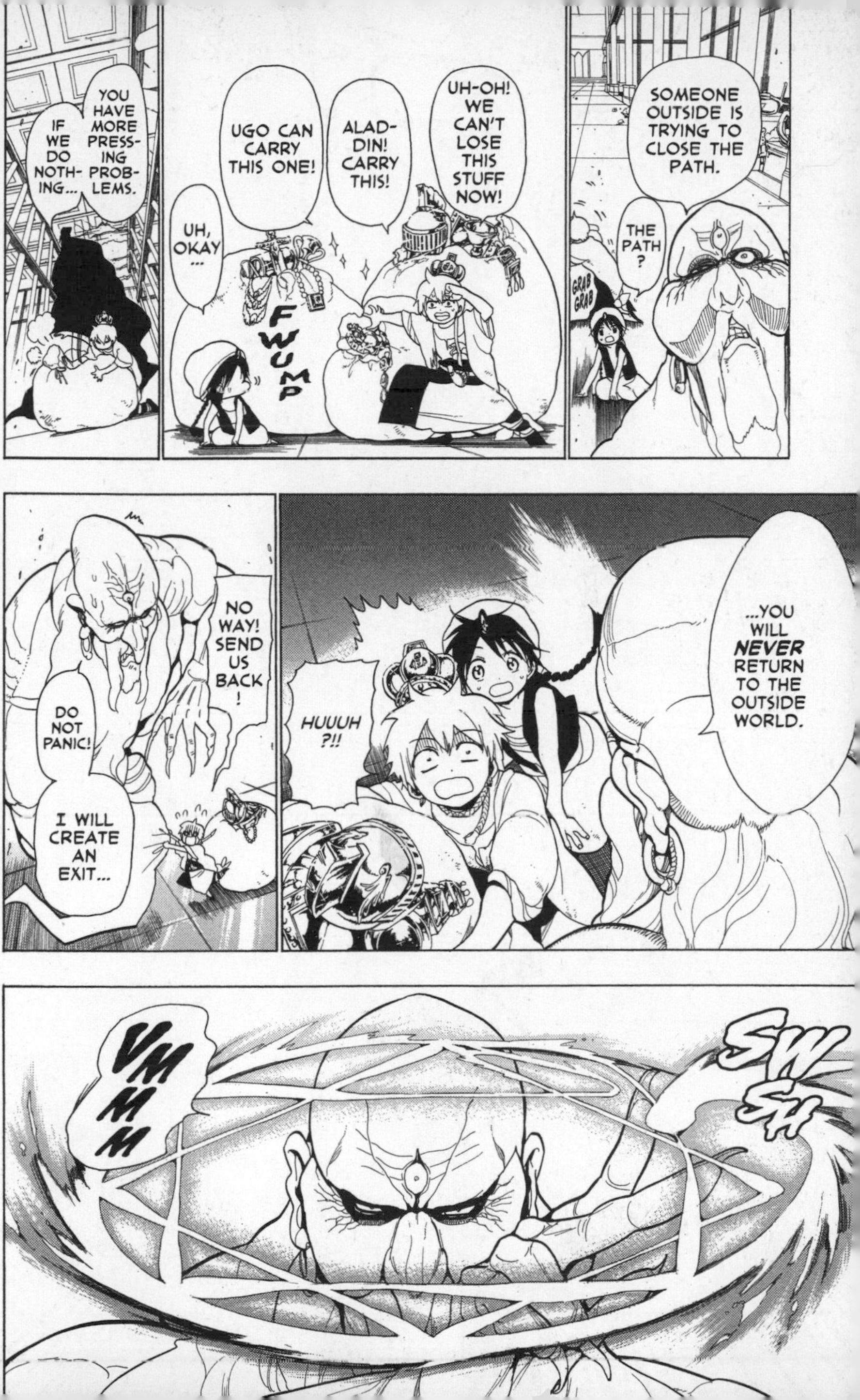
SOMEONE OUTSIDE IS TRYING TO CLOSE THE PATH.
THE PATH?
GRAB GRAB
UH-OH! WE CAN'T LOSE THIS STUFF NOW!
ALAD-DIN! CARRY THIS!
UGO CAN CARRY THIS ONE!
UH, OKAY...
FWUMP
YOU HAVE MORE PRESS-ING PROB-LEMS.
IF WE DO NOTH-ING...
...YOU WILL NEVER RETURN TO THE OUTSIDE WORLD.
HUUUH?!!
NO WAY! SEND US BACK!
DO NOT PANIC!
I WILL CREATE AN EXIT...
SWISH
VMMM

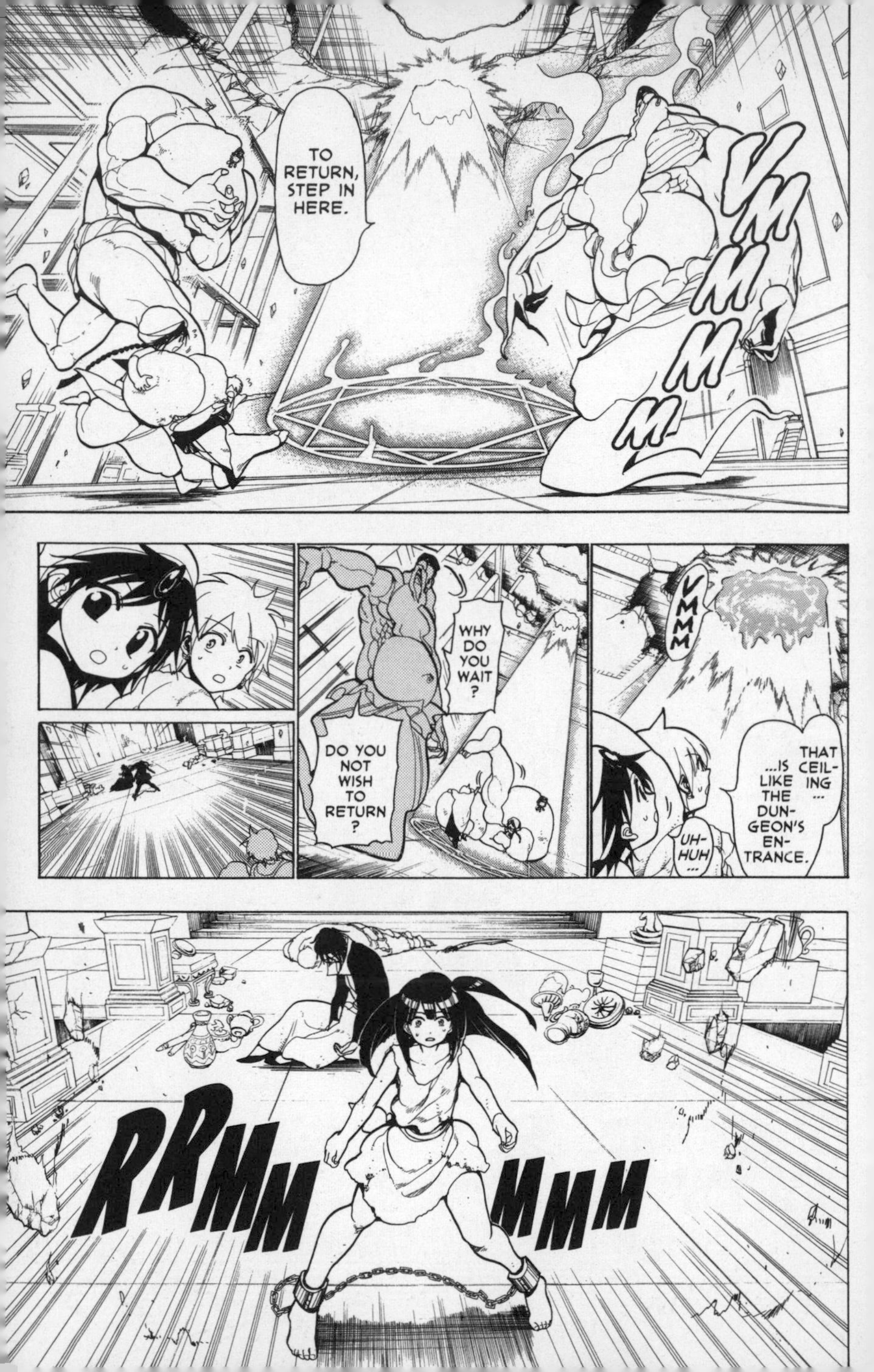
VMMMMM
TO RETURN, STEP IN HERE.
VMMM
THAT CEILING... ...IS LIKE THE DUNGEON'S ENTRANCE.
UH-HUH...
WHY DO YOU WAIT?
DO YOU NOT WISH TO RETURN?
RRMM MMM

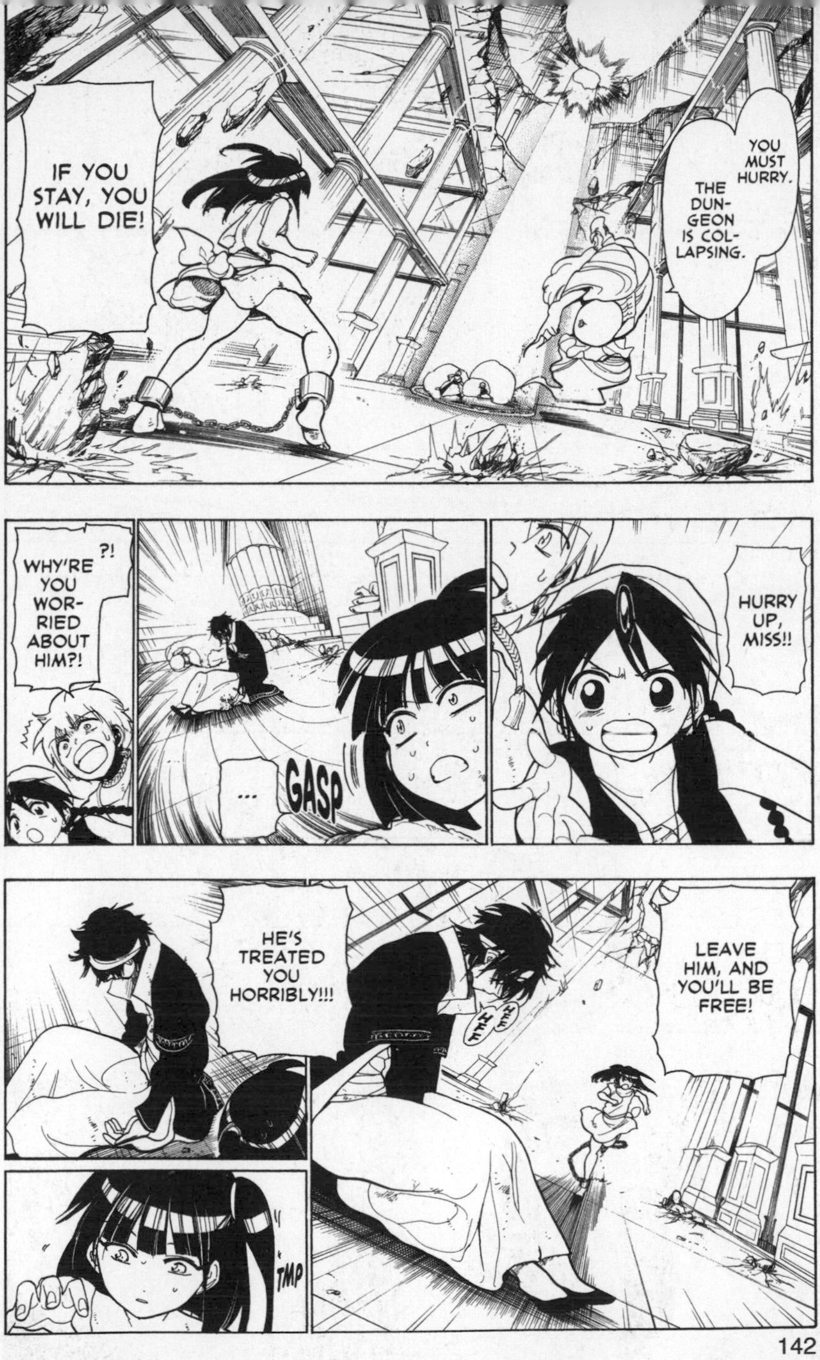
YOU MUST HURRY. THE DUNGEON IS COLLAPSING.
IF YOU STAY, YOU WILL DIE!
HURRY UP, MISS!!
GASP
...
?!
WHY'RE YOU WORRIED ABOUT HIM?!
LEAVE HIM, AND YOU'LL BE FREE!
HEFF HEFF
HE'S TREATED YOU HORRIBLY!!!
TMP

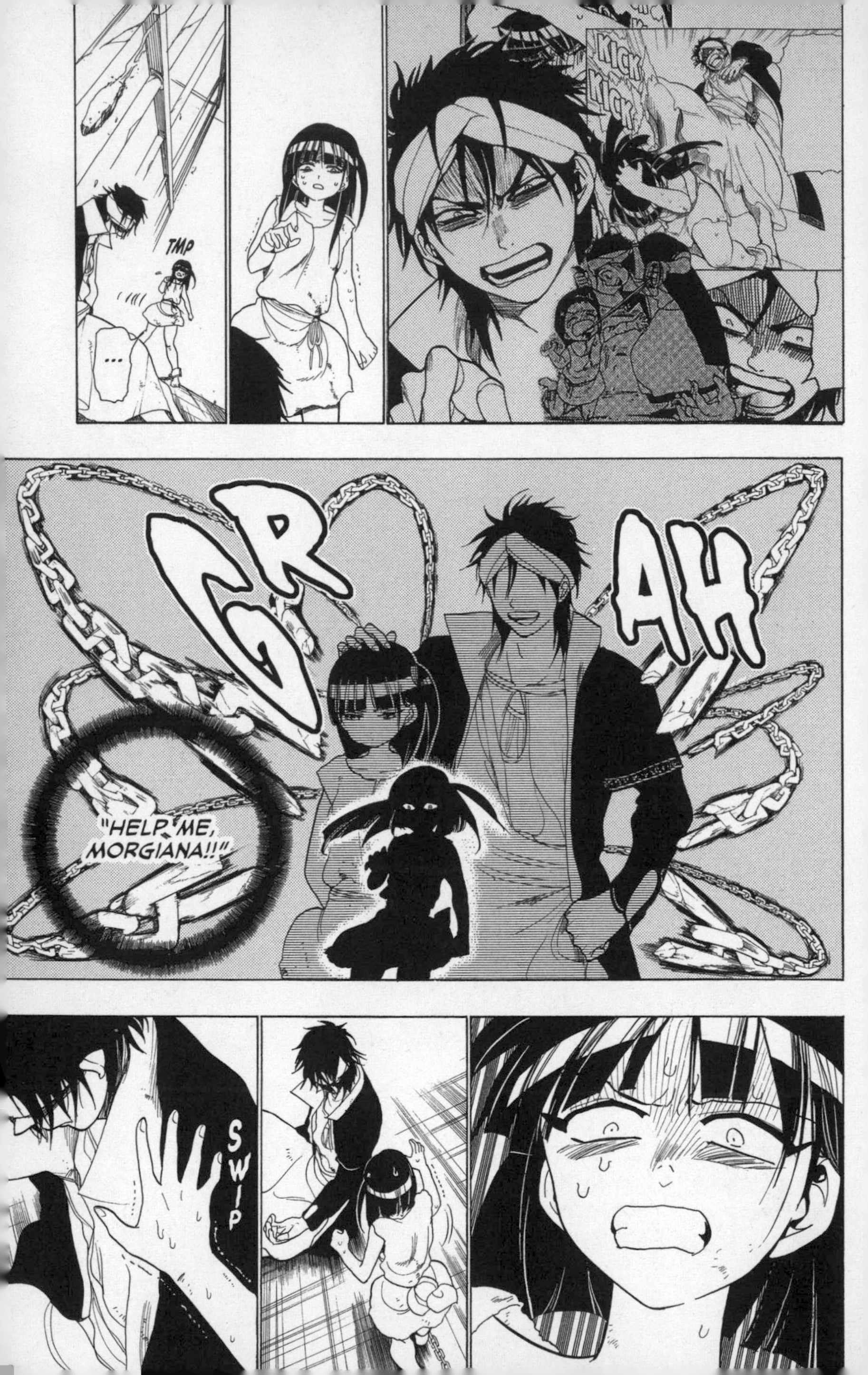
KICK
KICK
TMP
...
CRAH
"HELP ME, MORGIANA!!"
SWIP

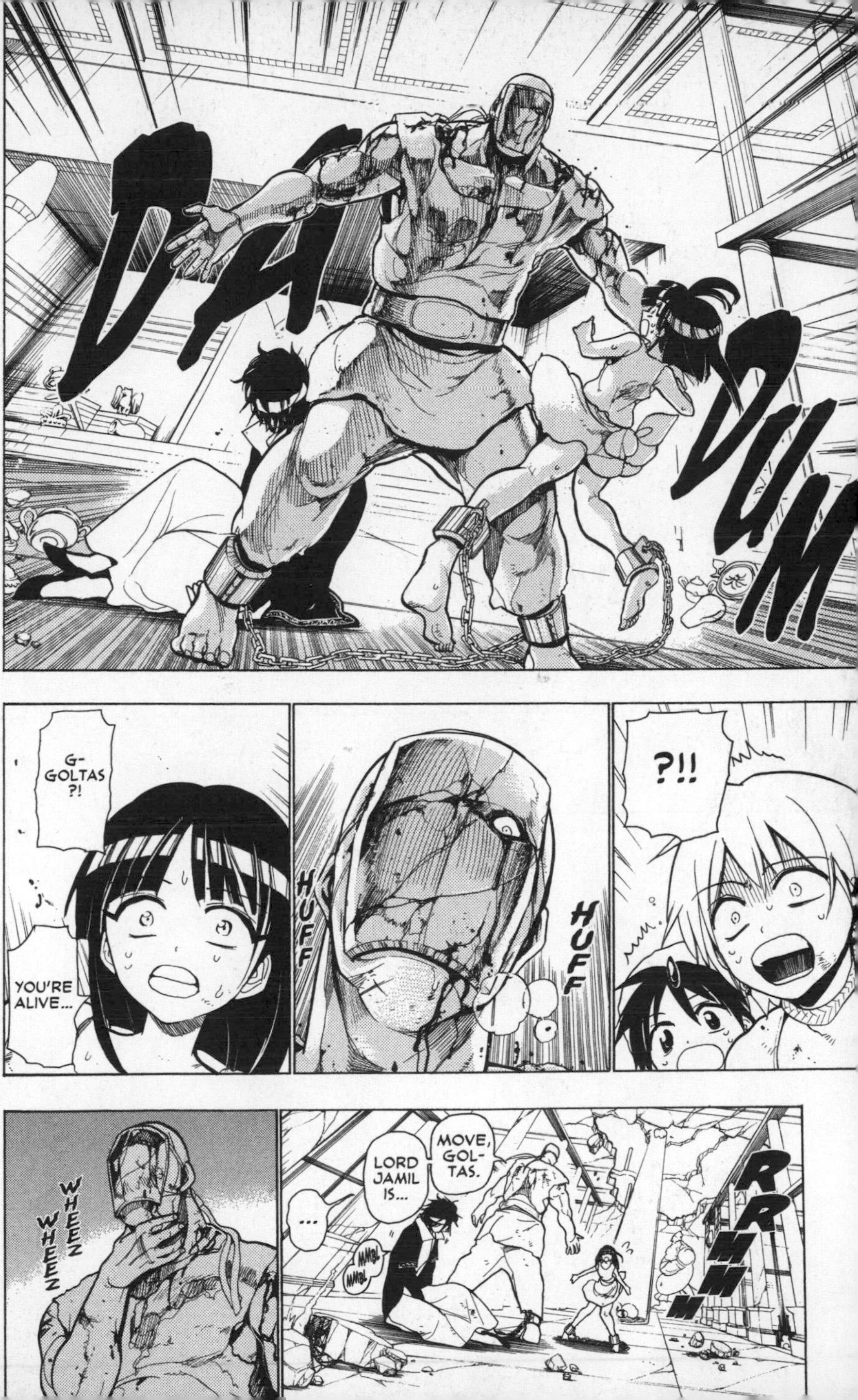
DA
DUM
?!!
HUFF
HUFF
G-GOLTAS?!
YOU'RE ALIVE...
RRMMMM
MOVE, GOL-TAS.
LORD JAMIL IS...
...
MMBL
MMBL
WHEEZ
WHEEZ

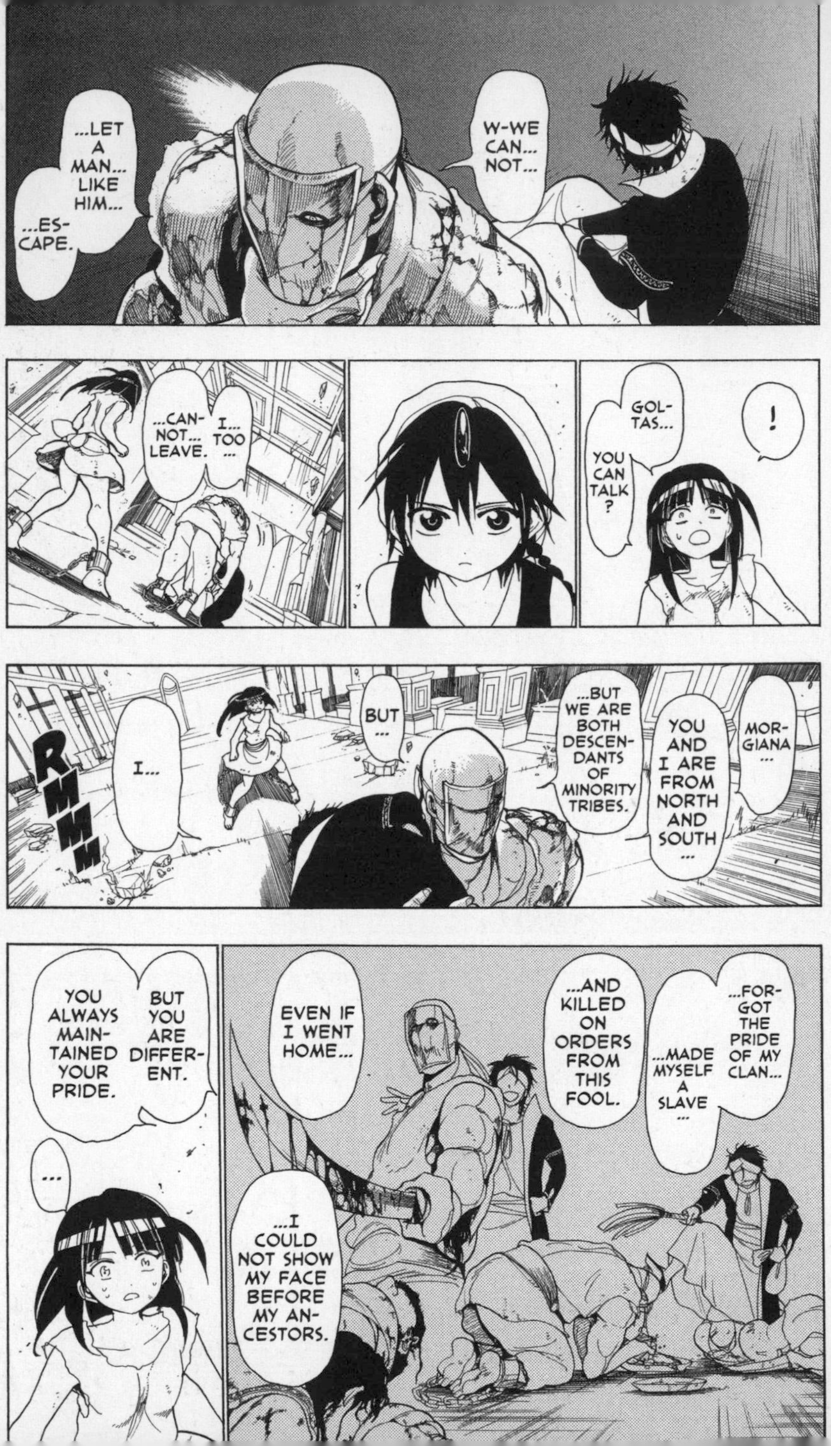
W-WE CAN... NOT...
...LET A MAN... LIKE HIM...
...ES-CAPE.
!
GOL-TAS...
YOU CAN TALK?
I... TOO ...
...CAN-NOT... LEAVE.
MOR-GIANA ...
YOU AND I ARE FROM NORTH AND SOUTH ...
...BUT WE ARE BOTH DESCEN-DANTS OF MINORITY TRIBES.
BUT ...
I...
RMMM
...FOR-GOT THE PRIDE OF MY CLAN...
...MADE MYSELF A SLAVE ...
...AND KILLED ON ORDERS FROM THIS FOOL.
EVEN IF I WENT HOME...
...I COULD NOT SHOW MY FACE BEFORE MY AN-CESTORS.
BUT YOU ARE DIFFER-ENT.
YOU ALWAYS MAIN-TAINED YOUR PRIDE.
...

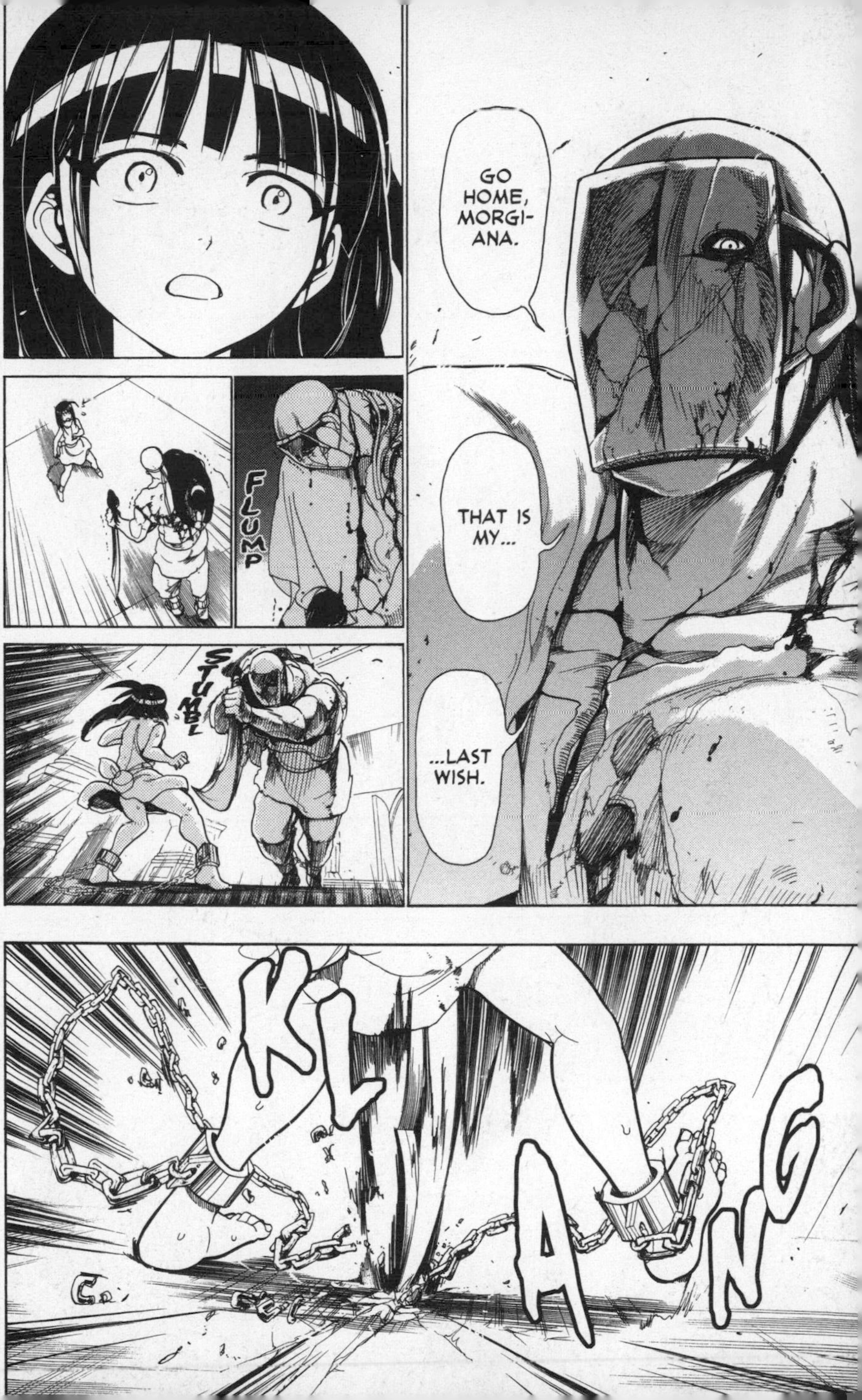
GO HOME, MORGIANA.
THAT IS MY...
...LAST WISH.
FLUMP
STUMBLE
KLANG

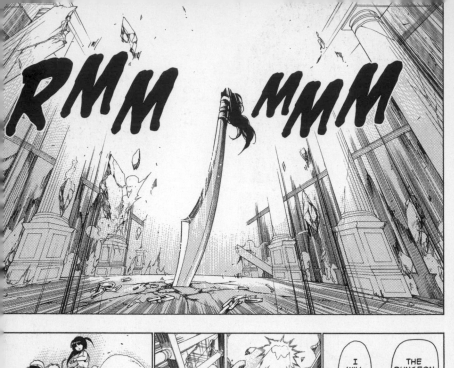

RMM MMM
THE DUNGEON IS COL-LAPSING.
I WILL SEND YOU NOW!!

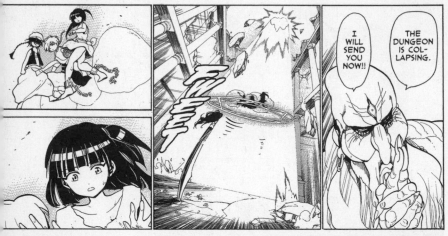

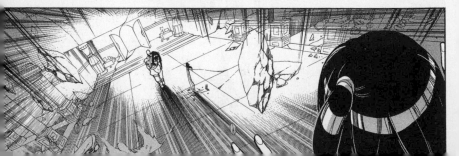

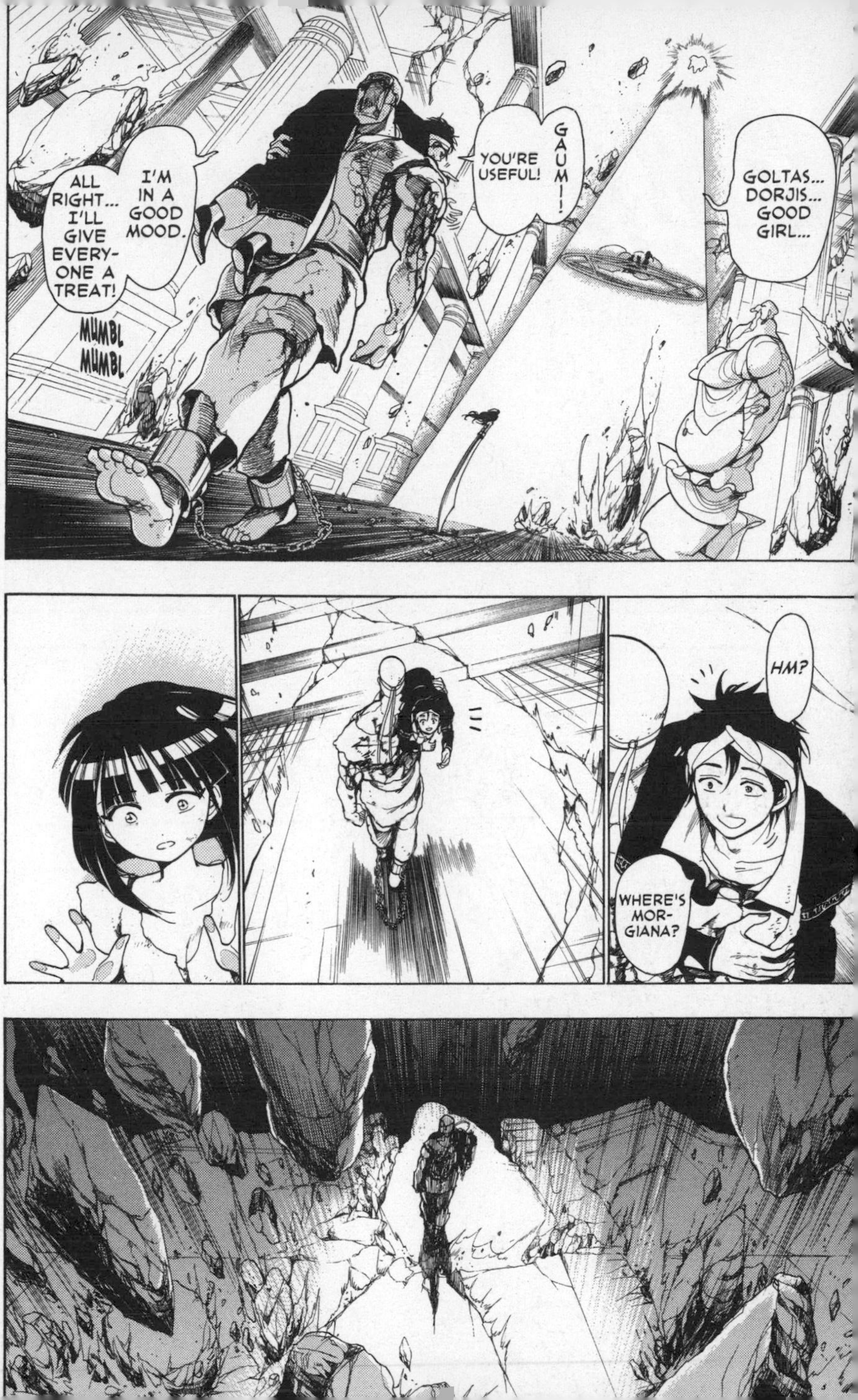
GOLTAS... DORJIS... GOOD GIRL...
GAUM!!
YOU'RE USEFUL!
I'M IN A GOOD MOOD.
ALL RIGHT... I'LL GIVE EVERYONE A TREAT!
MUMBL MUMBL
HM?
WHERE'S MORGIANA?

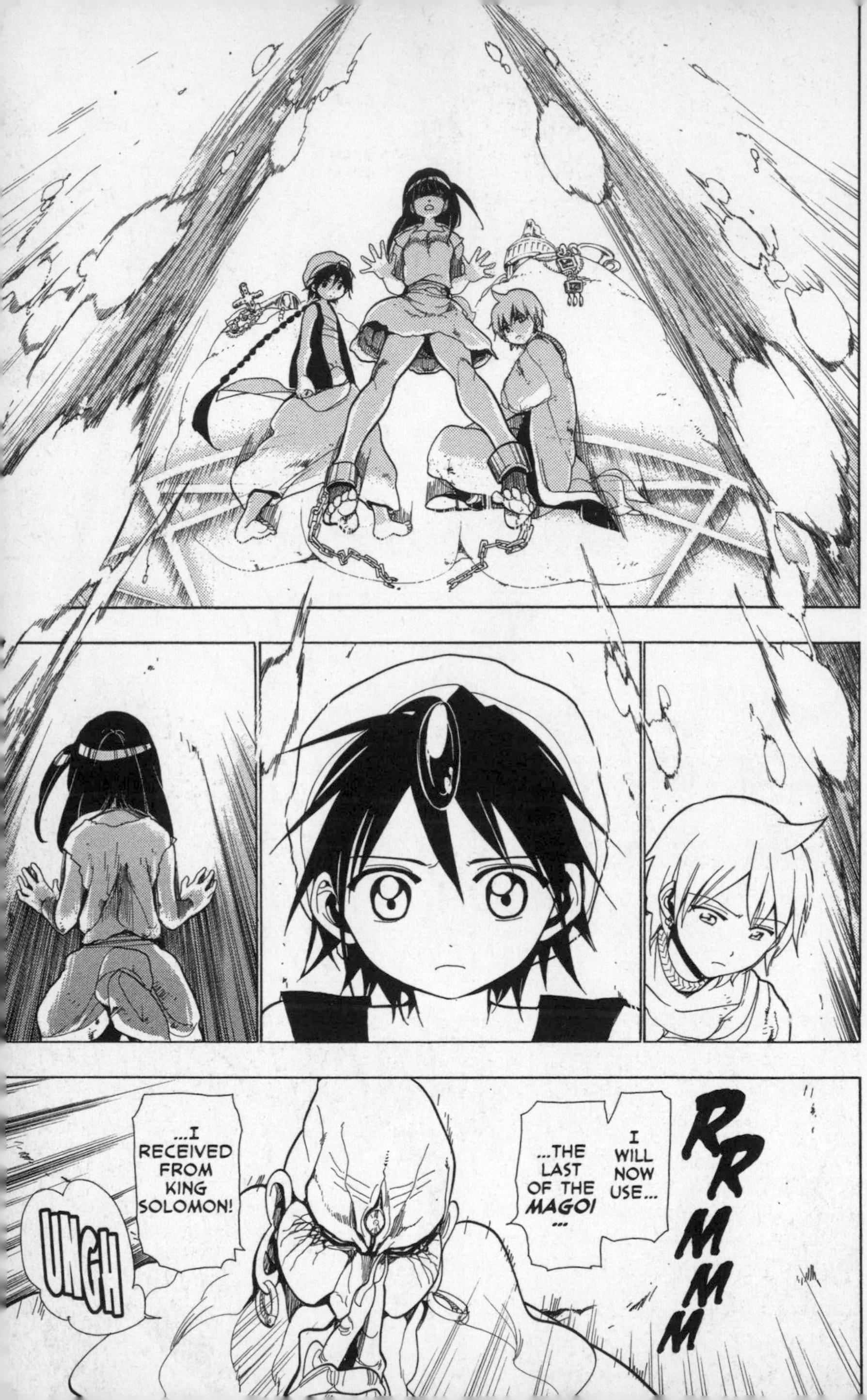
RRMMM
I WILL NOW USE...
...THE LAST OF THE *MAGOI* ...
...I RECEIVED FROM KING SOLOMON!
UNGH

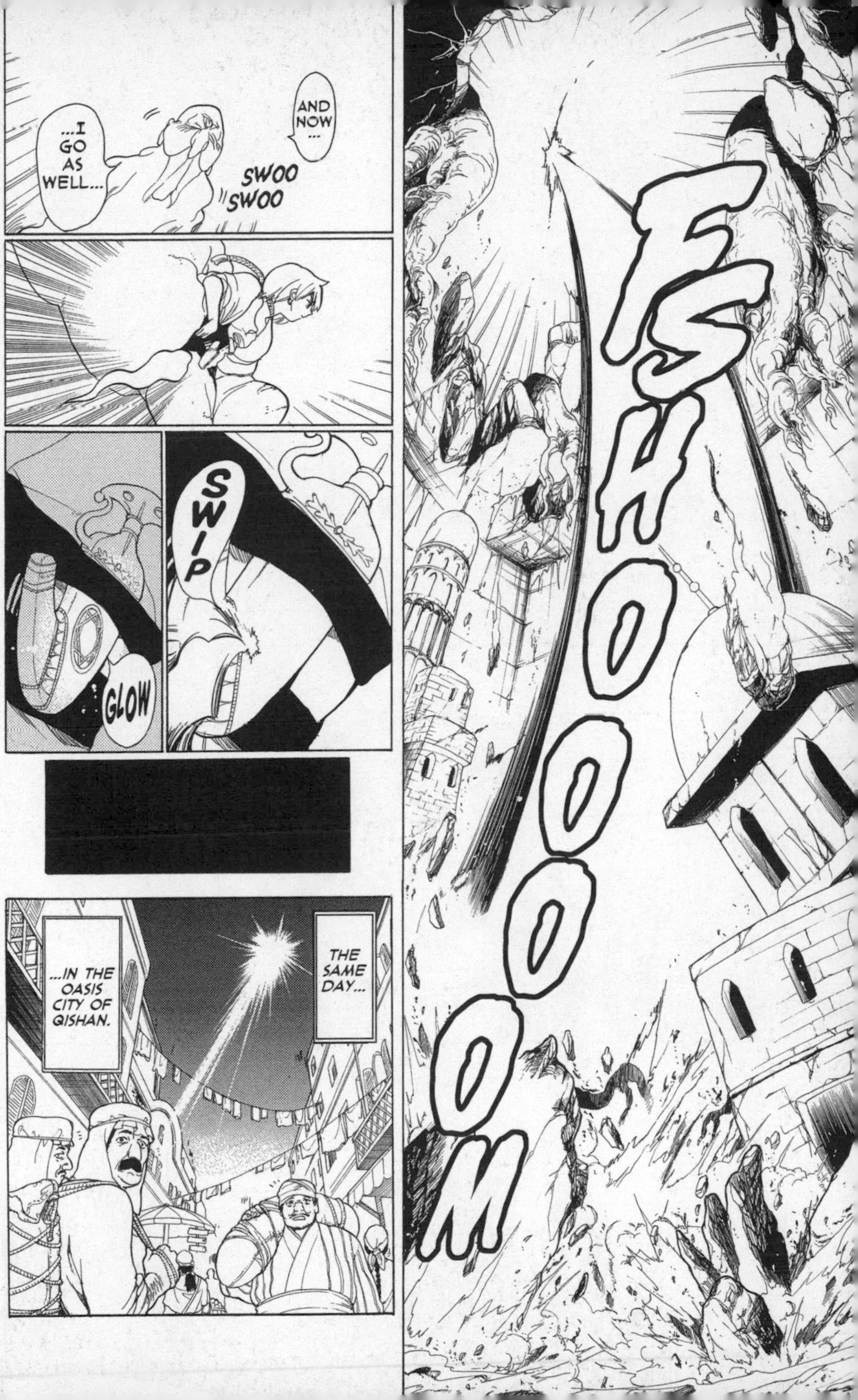
FSHOOOOOOM
AND NOW...
...I GO AS WELL...
SWOO SWOO
SWIP
GLOW
THE SAME DAY...
...IN THE OASIS CITY OF QISHAN.

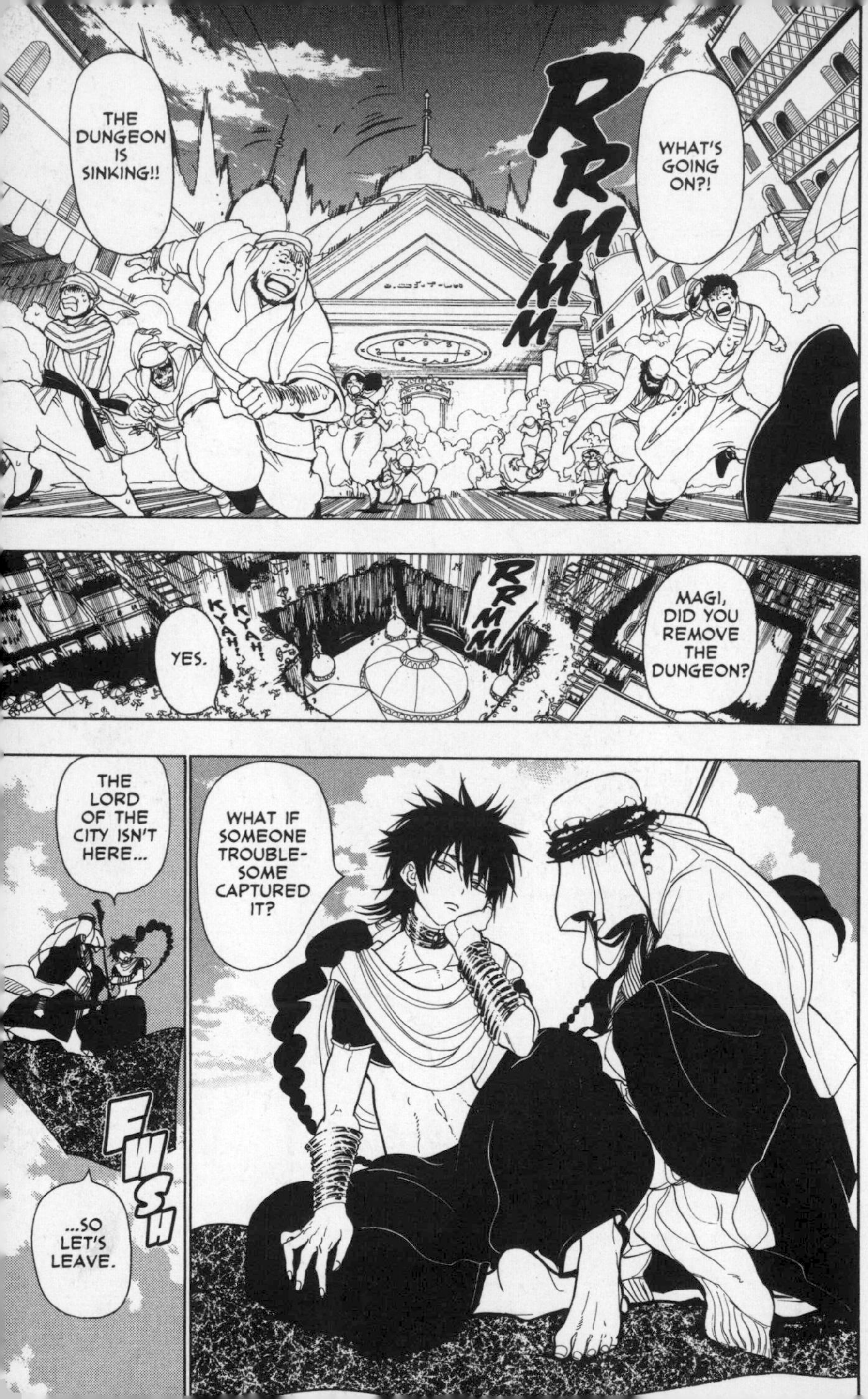
WHAT'S GOING ON?!
RRMMMM
THE DUNGEON IS SINKING!!
MAGI, DID YOU REMOVE THE DUNGEON?
RRMM
KYAH! KYAH!
YES.
WHAT IF SOMEONE TROUBLE-SOME CAPTURED IT?
THE LORD OF THE CITY ISN'T HERE...
FWSH
...SO LET'S LEAVE.

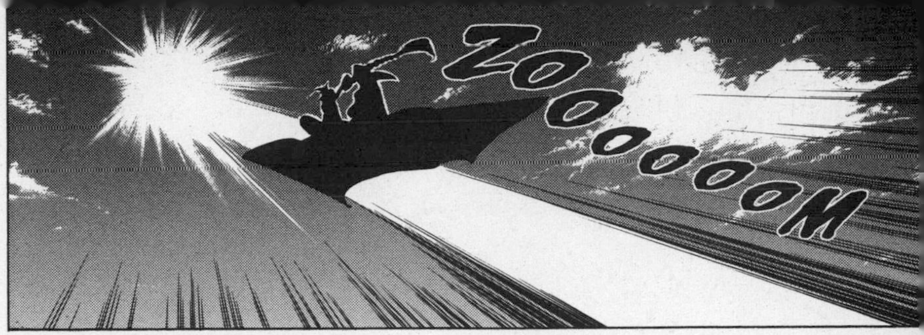
ZOOOOOOM

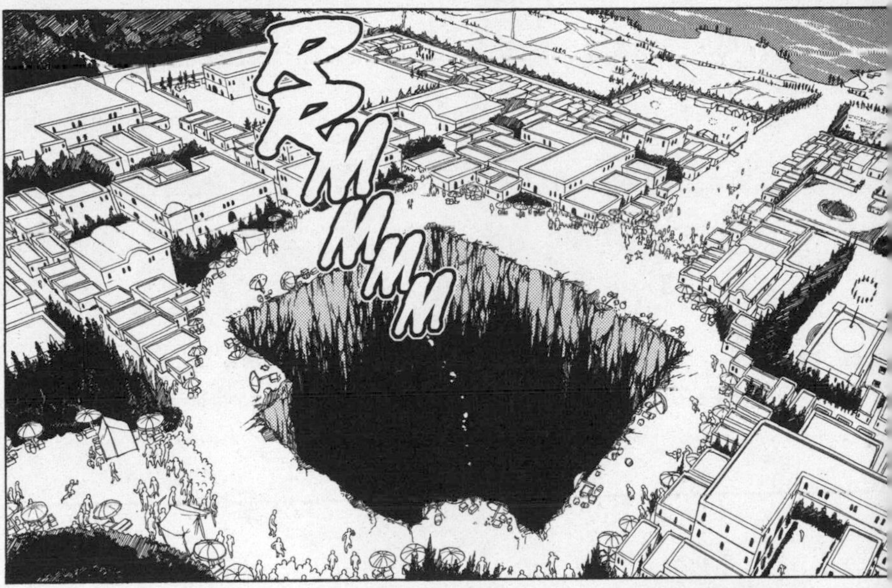
RRMMMM

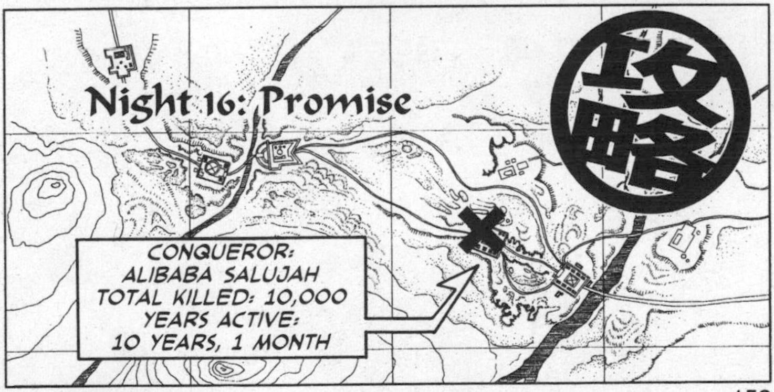
Night 16: Promise
攻略
CONQUEROR:
ALIBABA SALUJAH
TOTAL KILLED: 10,000
YEARS ACTIVE:
10 YEARS, 1 MONTH

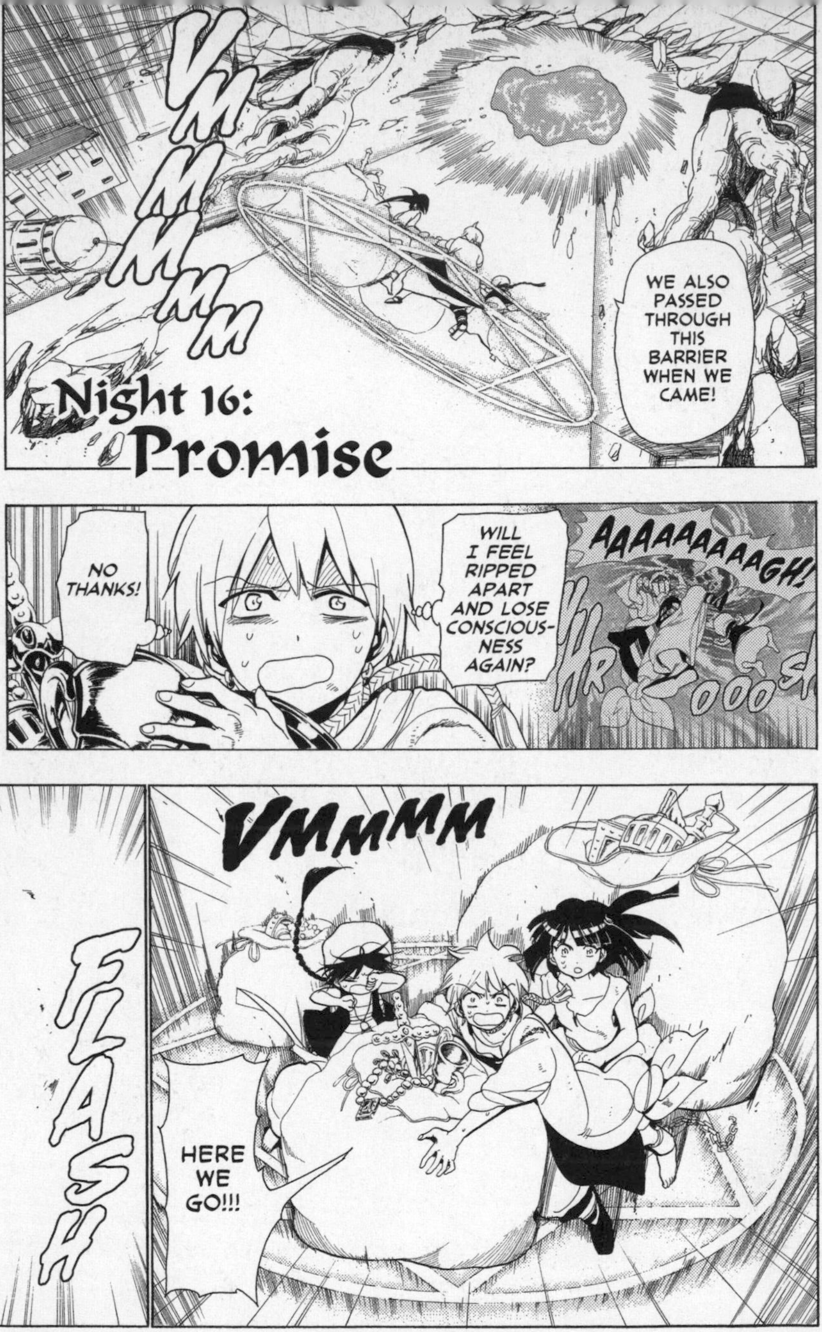
WE ALSO PASSED THROUGH THIS BARRIER WHEN WE CAME!
VMMMMMM
Night 16: Promise
AAAAAAAAAAGH!
WILL I FEEL RIPPED APART AND LOSE CONSCIOUSNESS AGAIN?
NO THANKS!
VMMMM
HERE WE GO!!!
FLASH

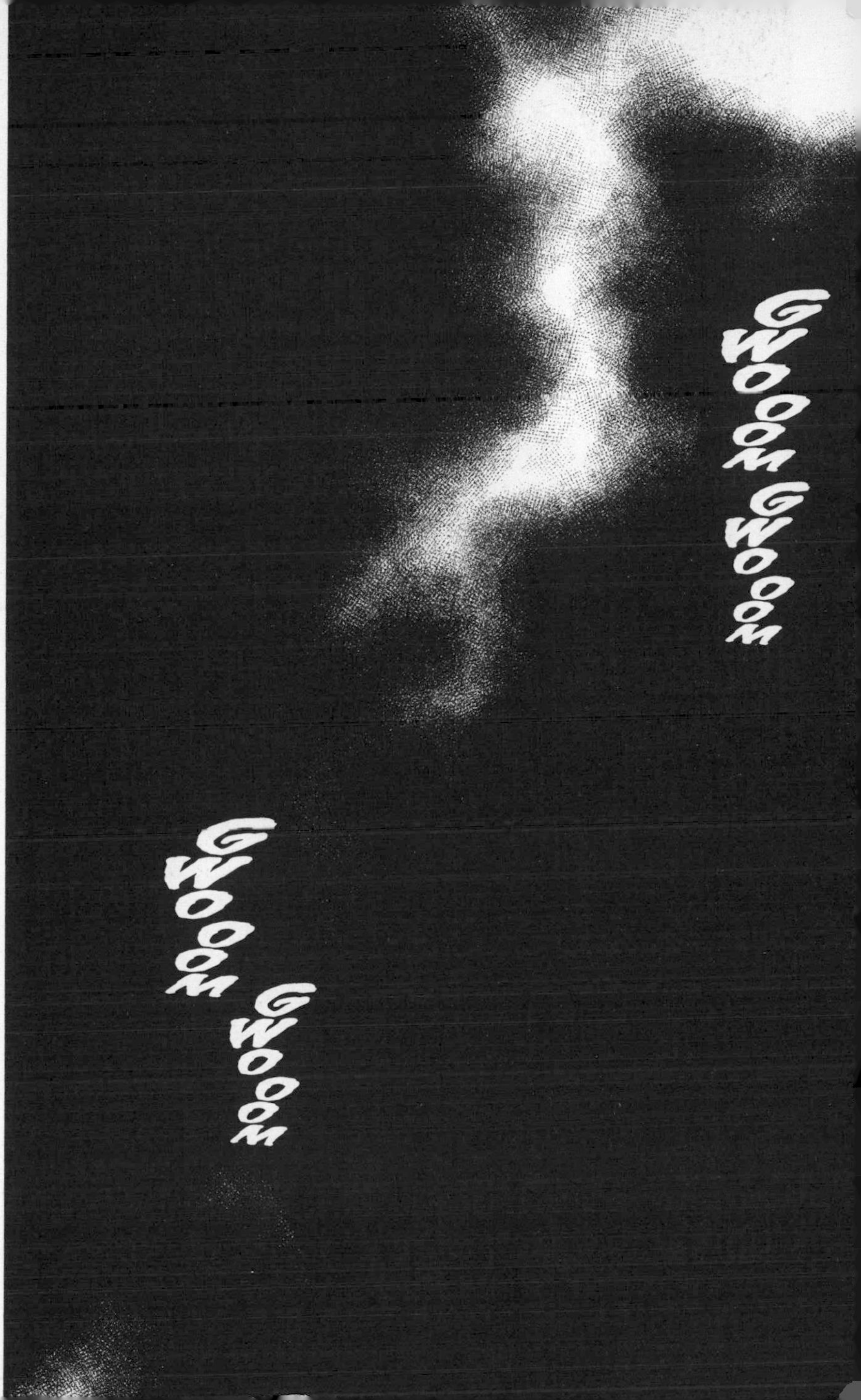
GWOOOM GWOOOM
GWOOOM GWOOOM

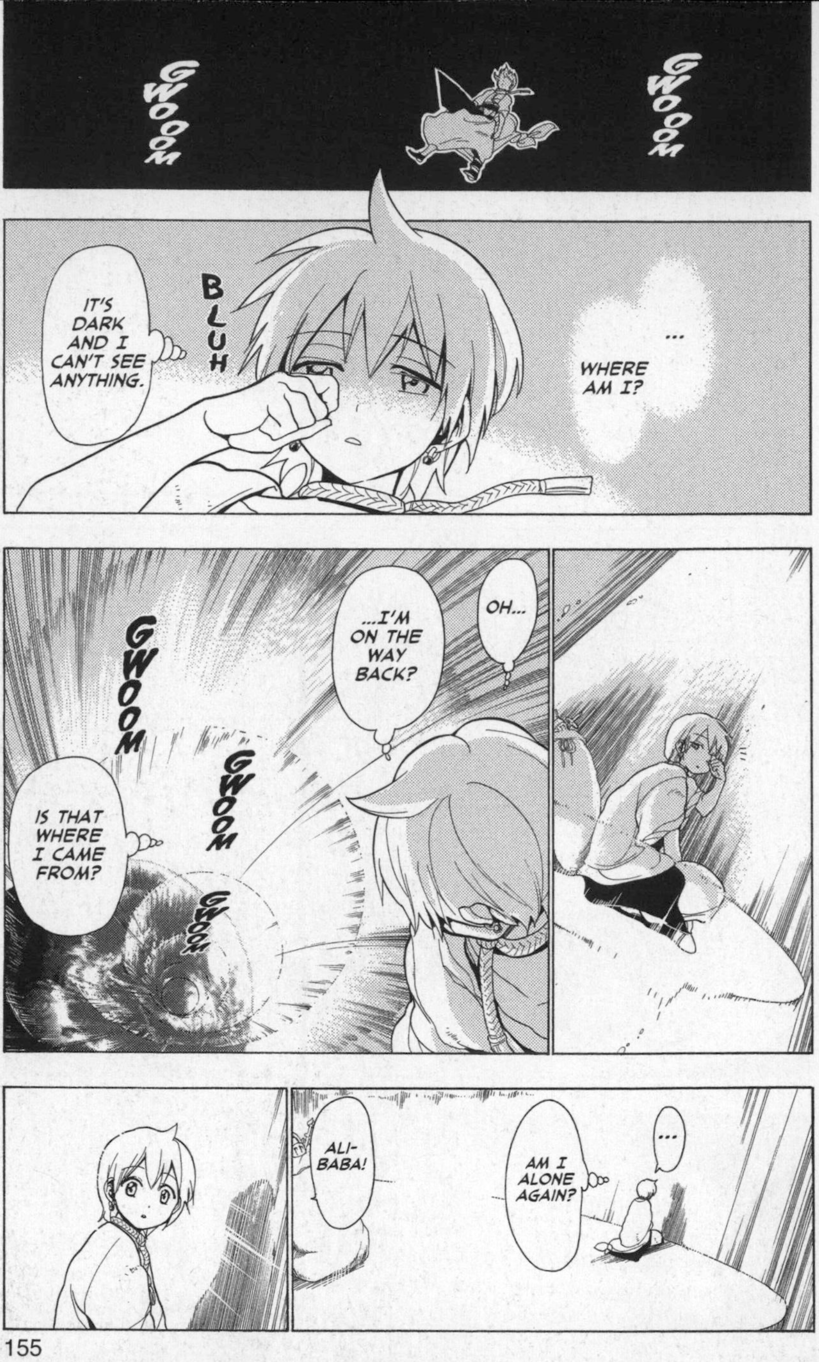
GWOOOM
GWOOOM
...
WHERE AM I?
BLUH
IT'S DARK AND I CAN'T SEE ANYTHING.
OH...
...I'M ON THE WAY BACK?
GWOOM
GWOOM
GWOOM
GWOOM
IS THAT WHERE I CAME FROM?
...
AM I ALONE AGAIN?
ALI-BABA!

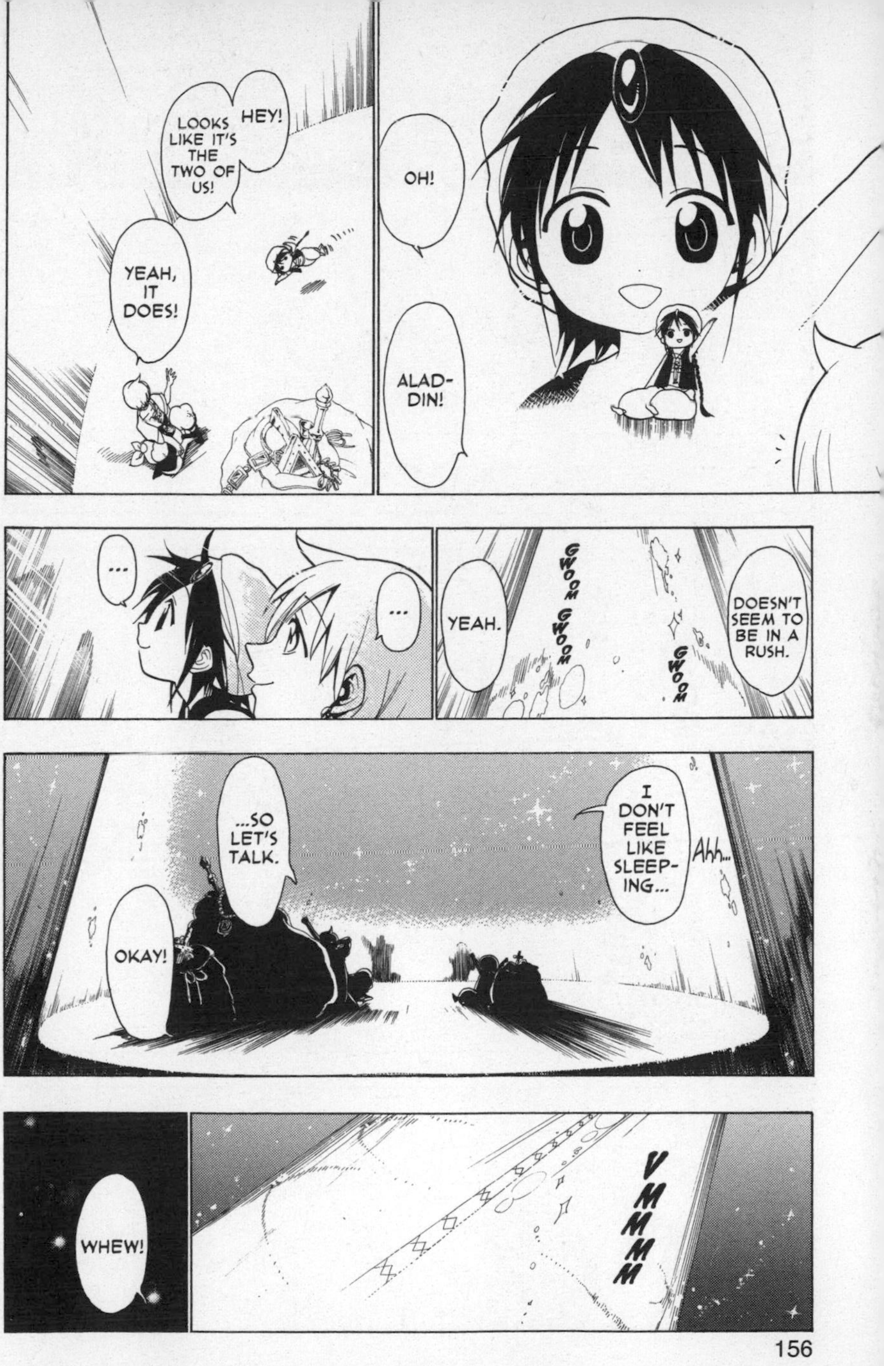
OH!
ALAD-DIN!
HEY! LOOKS LIKE IT'S THE TWO OF US!
YEAH, IT DOES!
DOESN'T SEEM TO BE IN A RUSH.
GWOOM GWOOM
GWOOM
YEAH.
...
...
I DON'T FEEL LIKE SLEEPING...
Ahh...
...SO LET'S TALK.
OKAY!
VMMMM
WHEW!

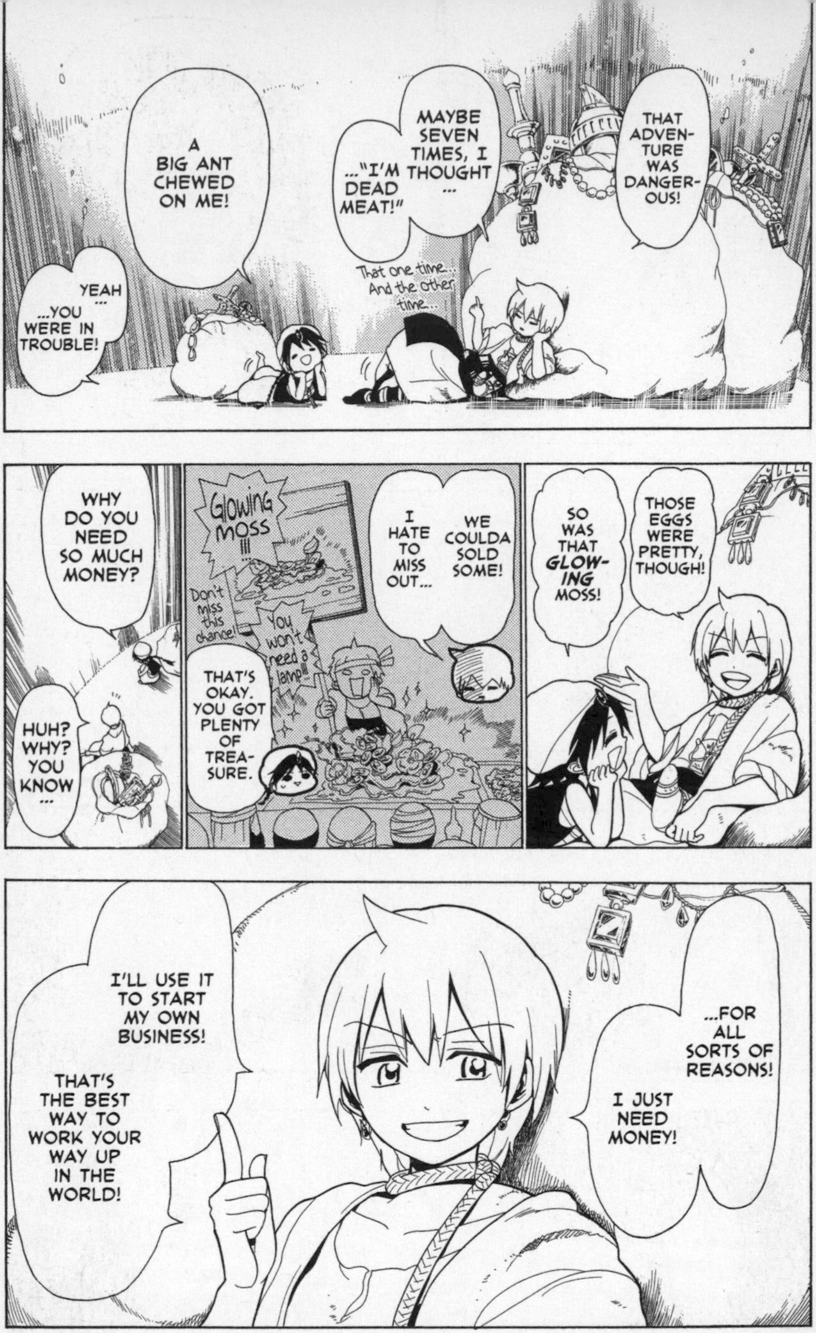
THAT ADVENTURE WAS DANGEROUS!
MAYBE SEVEN TIMES, I THOUGHT ...
..."I'M DEAD MEAT!"
That one time... And the other time...
A BIG ANT CHEWED ON ME!
YEAH ... ...YOU WERE IN TROUBLE!
THOSE EGGS WERE PRETTY, THOUGH!
SO WAS THAT GLOWING MOSS!
WE COULDA SOLD SOME!
I HATE TO MISS OUT...
Glowing moss !!!
Don't miss this chance!
You won't need a lamp!!!
THAT'S OKAY. YOU GOT PLENTY OF TREASURE.
WHY DO YOU NEED SO MUCH MONEY?
HUH? WHY? YOU KNOW ...
...FOR ALL SORTS OF REASONS!
I JUST NEED MONEY!
I'LL USE IT TO START MY OWN BUSINESS!
THAT'S THE BEST WAY TO WORK YOUR WAY UP IN THE WORLD!

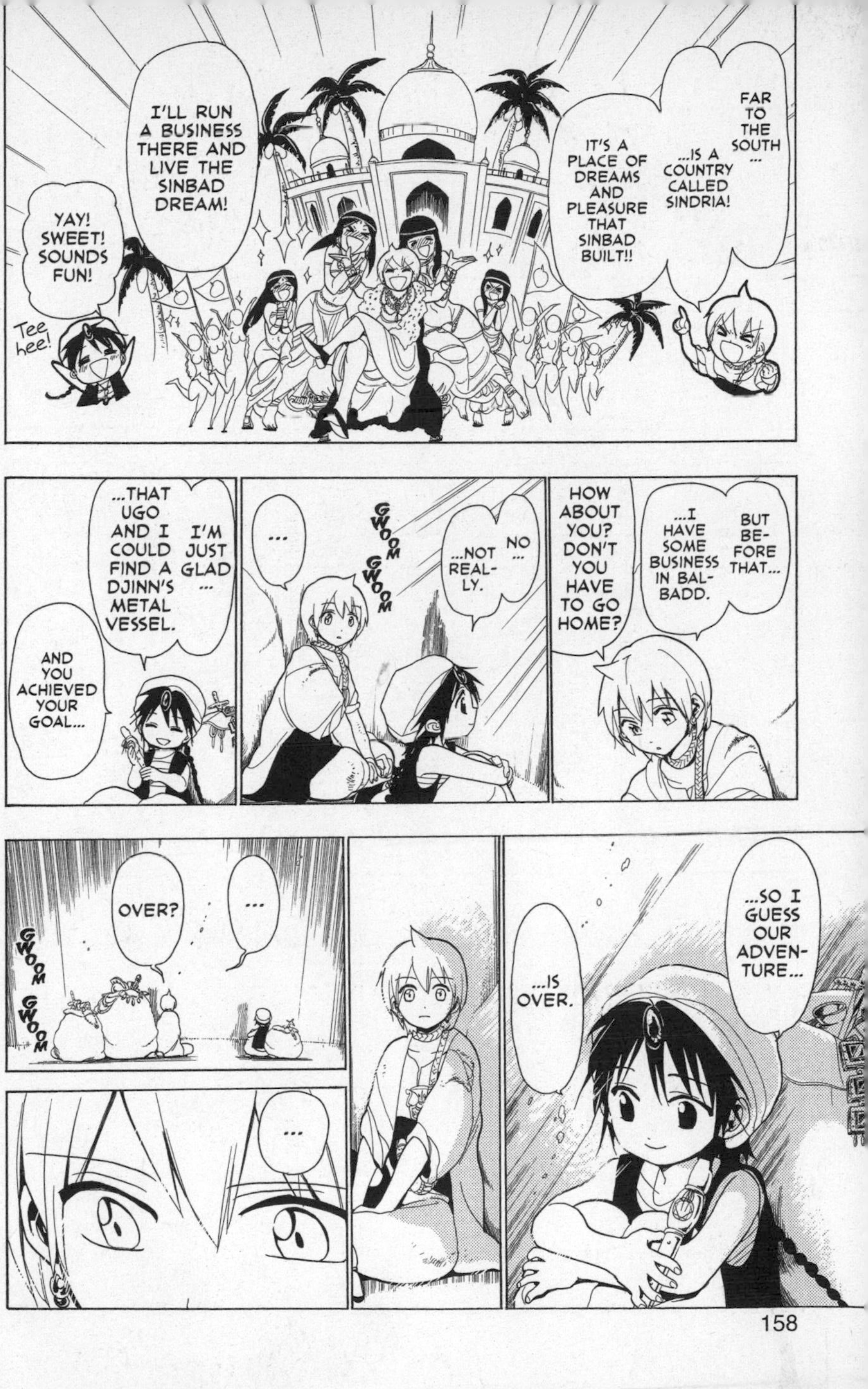
FAR TO THE SOUTH ...
...IS A COUNTRY CALLED SINDRIA!
IT'S A PLACE OF DREAMS AND PLEASURE THAT SINBAD BUILT!!
I'LL RUN A BUSINESS THERE AND LIVE THE SINBAD DREAM!
YAY! SWEET! SOUNDS FUN!
Tee hee!
BUT BEFORE THAT...
...I HAVE SOME BUSINESS IN BALBADD.
HOW ABOUT YOU? DON'T YOU HAVE TO GO HOME?
NO ...
...NOT REALLY.
GWOOM GWOOM
...
I'M JUST GLAD ...
...THAT UGO AND I COULD FIND A DJINN'S METAL VESSEL.
AND YOU ACHIEVED YOUR GOAL...
...SO I GUESS OUR ADVENTURE...
...IS OVER.
...
OVER?
GWOOM GWOOM
...

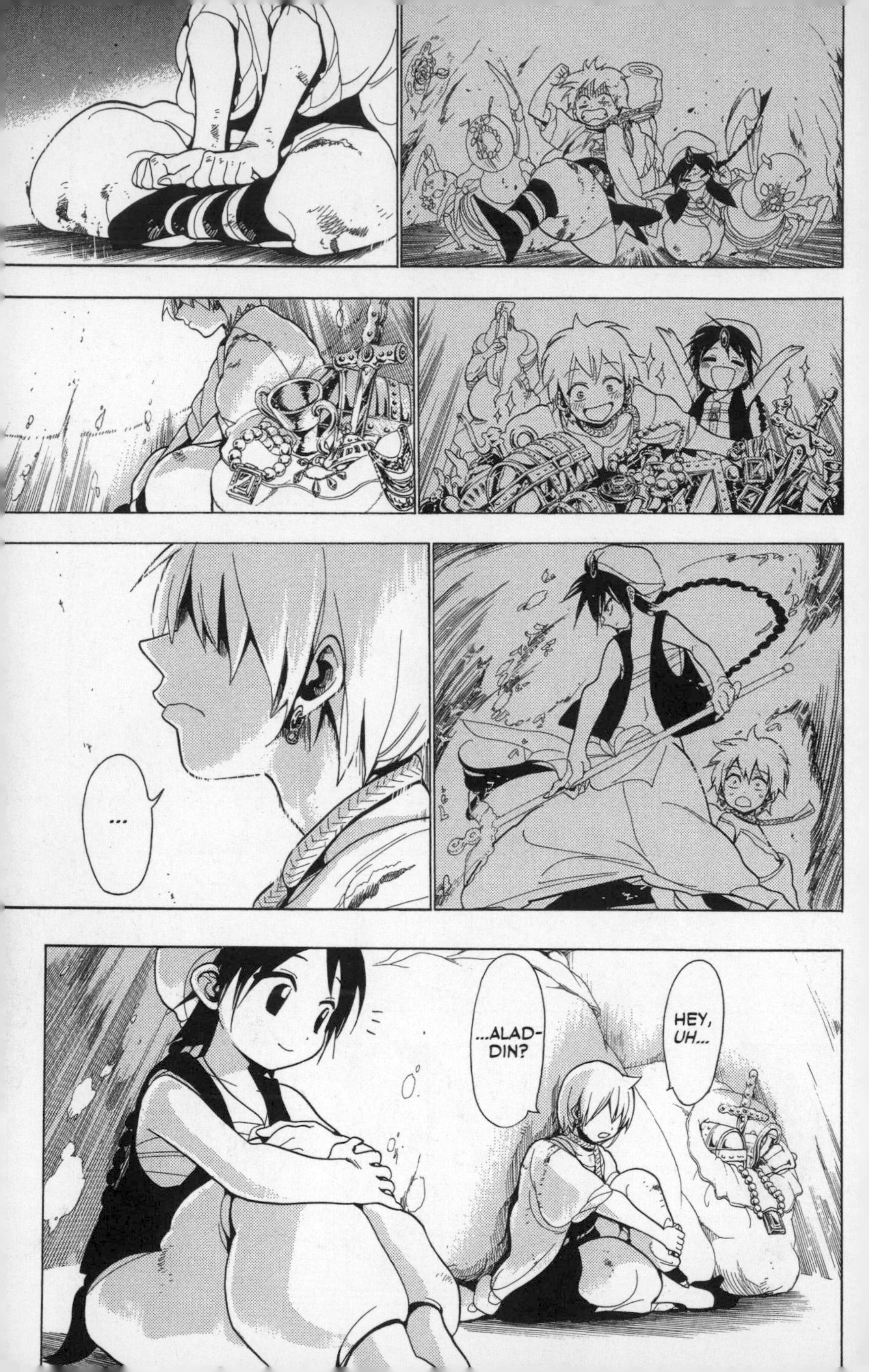
...
HEY, UH...
...ALAD-DIN?

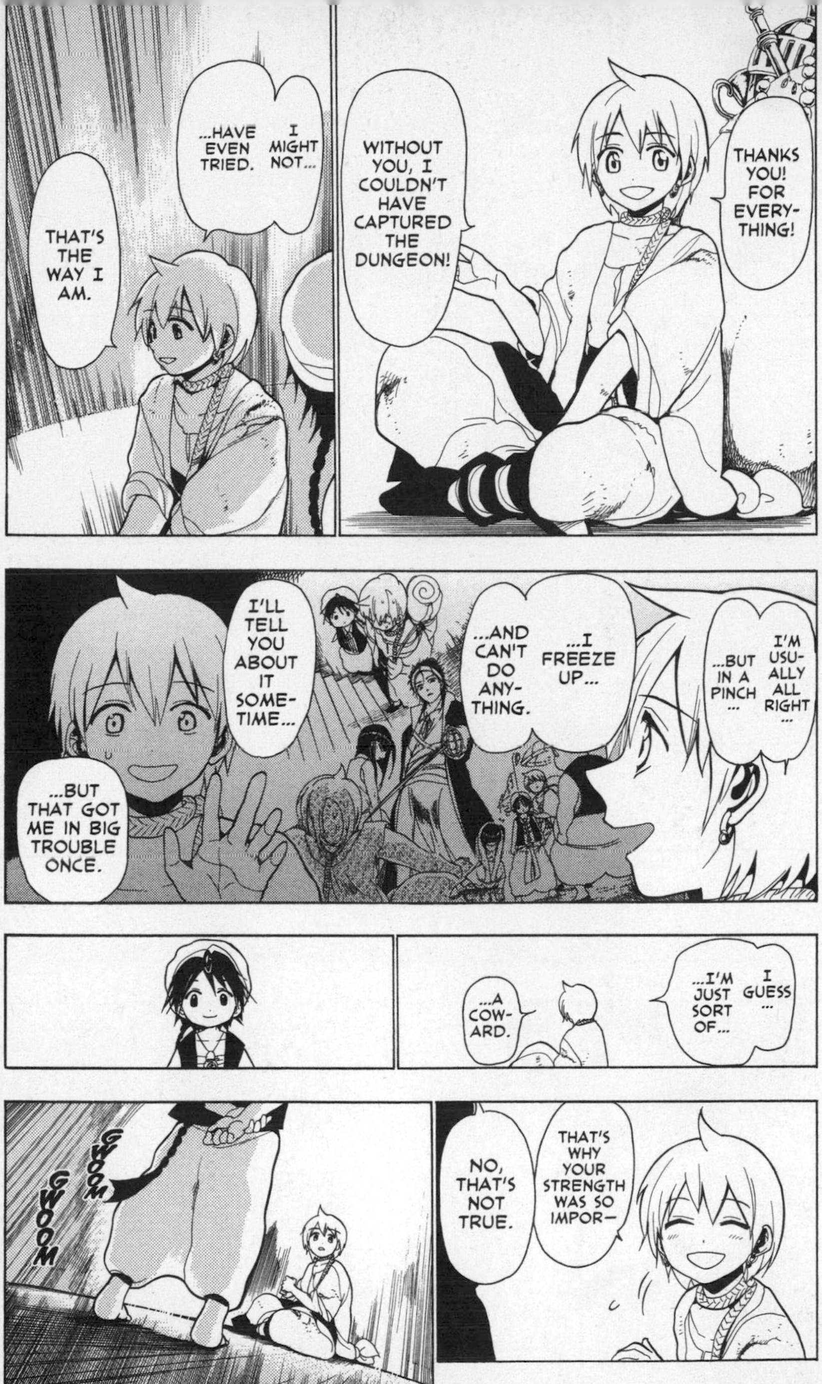
THANKS YOU! FOR EVERYTHING!
WITHOUT YOU, I COULDN'T HAVE CAPTURED THE DUNGEON!
I MIGHT NOT... ...HAVE EVEN TRIED.
THAT'S THE WAY I AM.
I'M USUALLY ALL RIGHT... ...BUT IN A PINCH...
...I FREEZE UP... ...AND CAN'T DO ANYTHING.
I'LL TELL YOU ABOUT IT SOMETIME...
...BUT THAT GOT ME IN BIG TROUBLE ONCE.
I GUESS... ...I'M JUST SORT OF...
...A COWARD.
THAT'S WHY YOUR STRENGTH WAS SO IMPOR—
NO, THAT'S NOT TRUE.
GWOOM
GWOOM

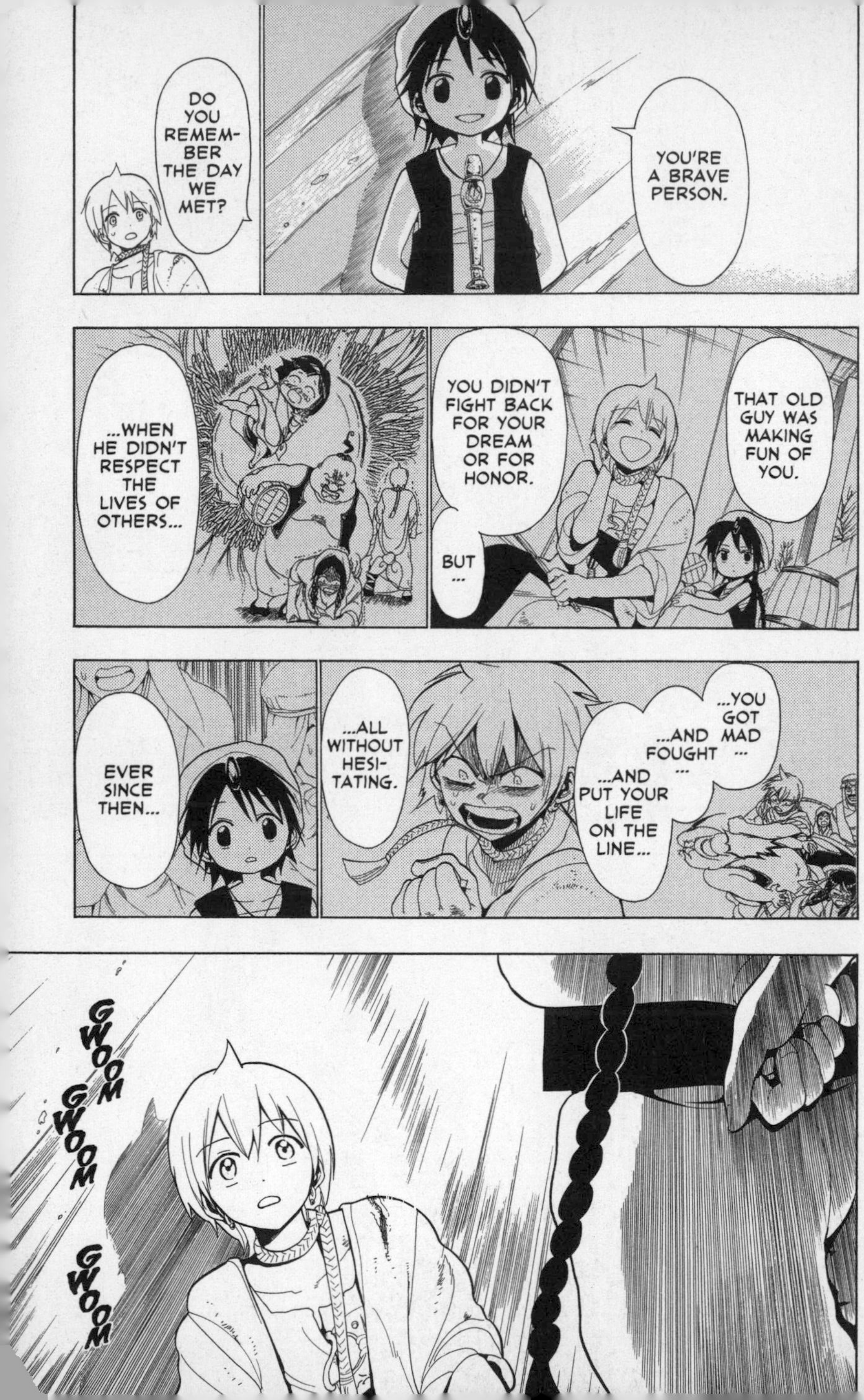
YOU'RE A BRAVE PERSON.
DO YOU REMEM-BER THE DAY WE MET?
THAT OLD GUY WAS MAKING FUN OF YOU.
YOU DIDN'T FIGHT BACK FOR YOUR DREAM OR FOR HONOR.
BUT ...
...WHEN HE DIDN'T RESPECT THE LIVES OF OTHERS...
...YOU GOT MAD ...
...AND FOUGHT ...
...AND PUT YOUR LIFE ON THE LINE...
...ALL WITHOUT HESI-TATING.
EVER SINCE THEN...
GWOOM GWOOM GWOOM
GWOOM

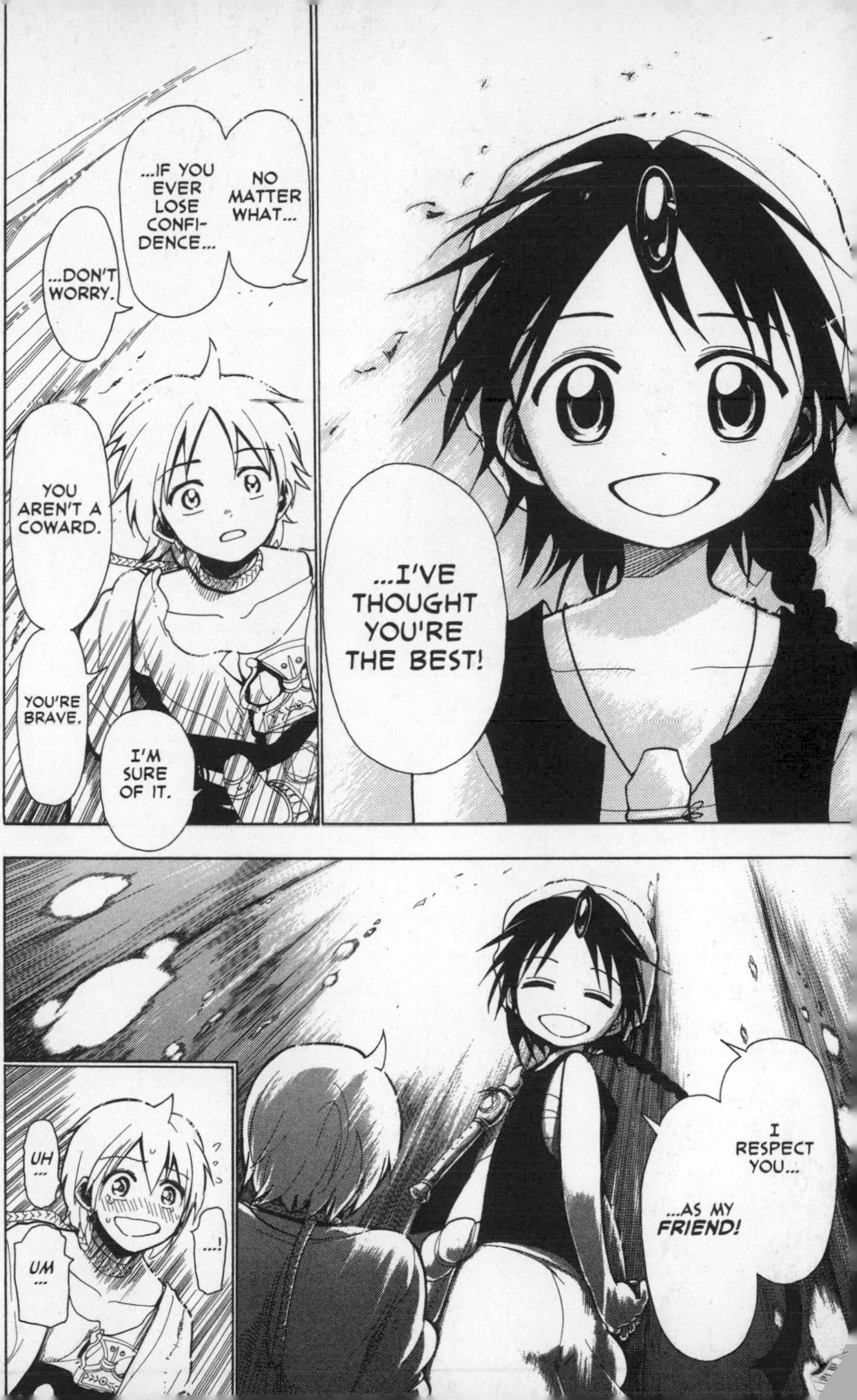
...I'VE THOUGHT YOU'RE THE BEST!
NO MATTER WHAT...
...IF YOU EVER LOSE CONFI-DENCE...
...DON'T WORRY.
YOU AREN'T A COWARD.
I'M SURE OF IT.
YOU'RE BRAVE.
I RESPECT YOU...
...AS MY FRIEND!
...!
UH ...
UM ...

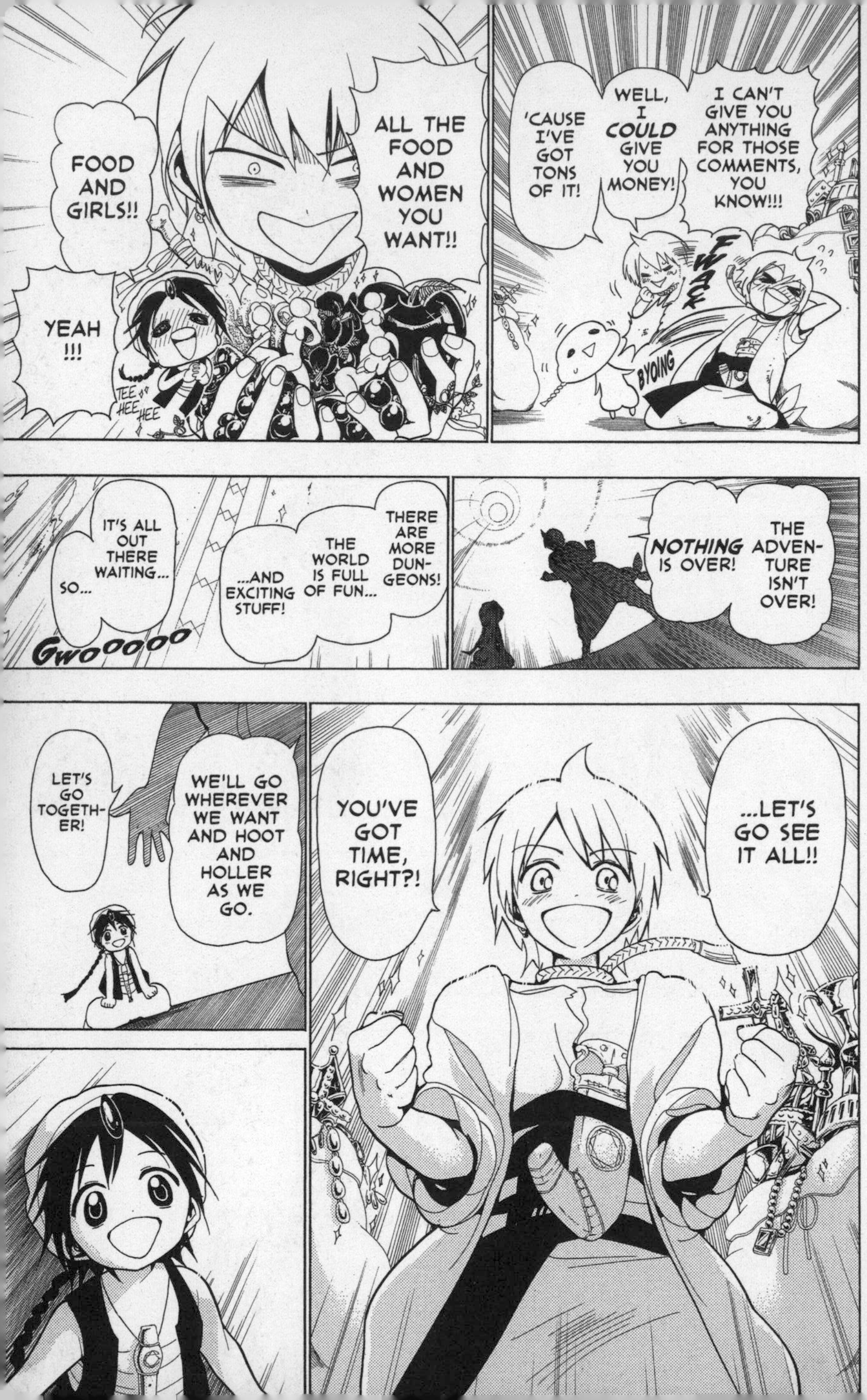
I CAN'T GIVE YOU ANYTHING FOR THOSE COMMENTS, YOU KNOW!!!
WELL, I *COULD* GIVE YOU MONEY!
'CAUSE I'VE GOT TONS OF IT!
FWACK
BYOING
ALL THE FOOD AND WOMEN YOU WANT!!
FOOD AND GIRLS!!
YEAH !!!
TEE HEE HEE
THE ADVENTURE ISN'T OVER!
NOTHING IS OVER!
THERE ARE MORE DUNGEONS!
THE WORLD IS FULL OF FUN...
...AND EXCITING STUFF!
IT'S ALL OUT THERE WAITING... SO...
GWOOOOO
...LET'S GO SEE IT ALL!!
YOU'VE GOT TIME, RIGHT?!
WE'LL GO WHEREVER WE WANT AND HOOT AND HOLLER AS WE GO.
LET'S GO TOGETHER!

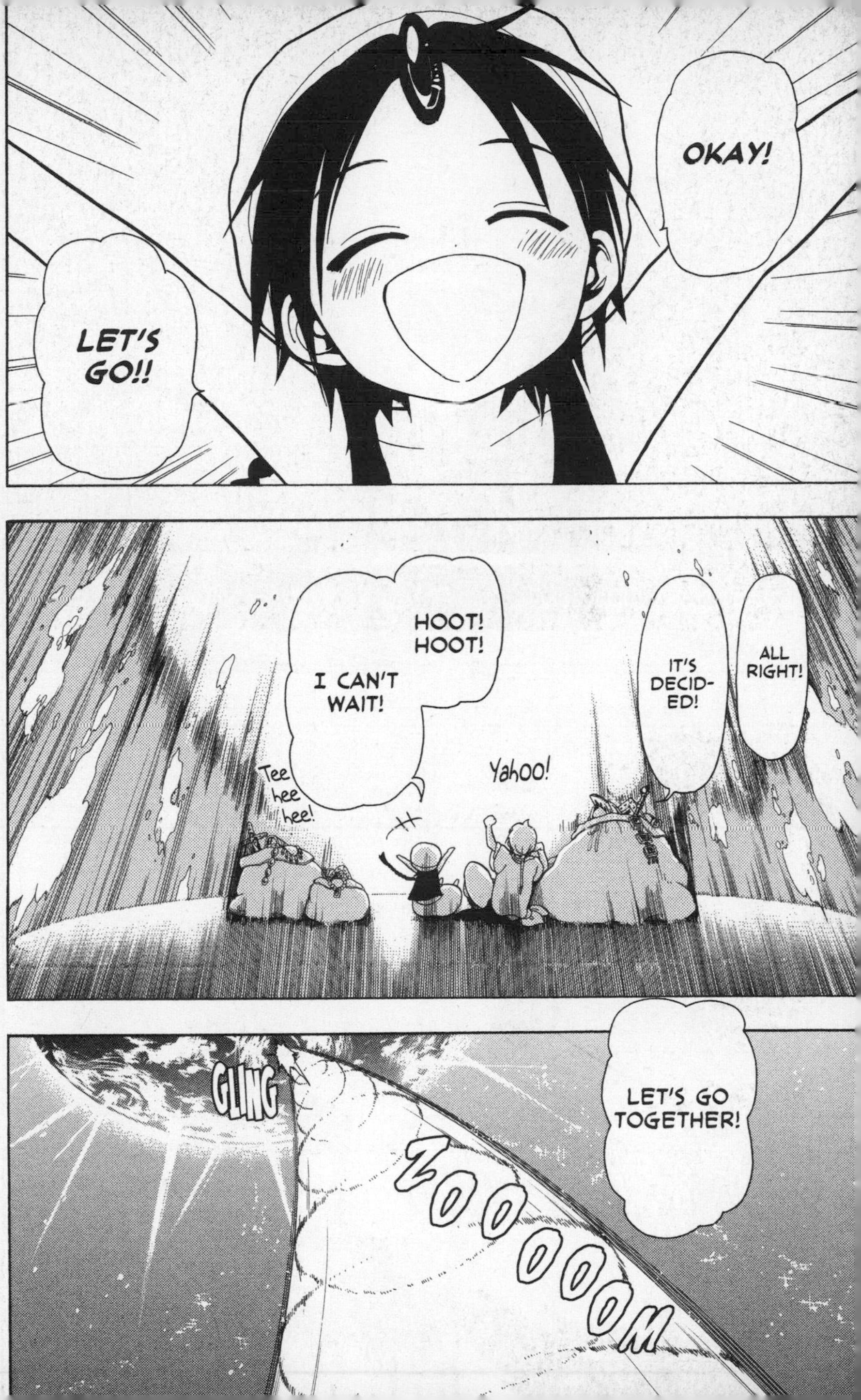
OKAY!
LET'S GO!!
ALL RIGHT!
IT'S DECID-ED!
HOOT! HOOT! I CAN'T WAIT!
Yahoo!
Tee hee hee!
LET'S GO TOGETHER!
GLING
ZOOOOOM

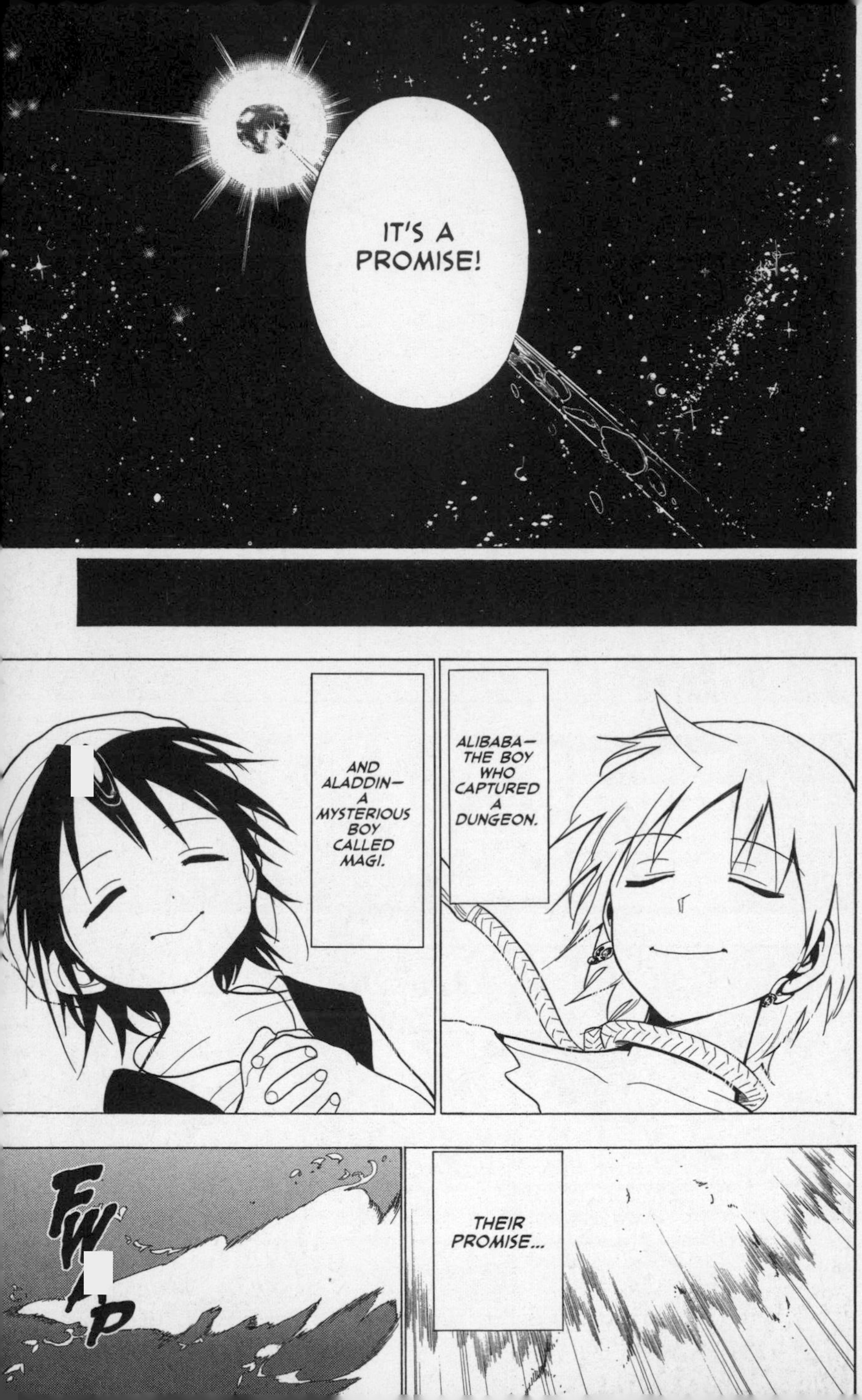
IT'S A PROMISE!
ALIBABA—THE BOY WHO CAPTURED A DUNGEON.
AND ALADDIN—A MYSTERIOUS BOY CALLED MAGI.
THEIR PROMISE...
FWAP

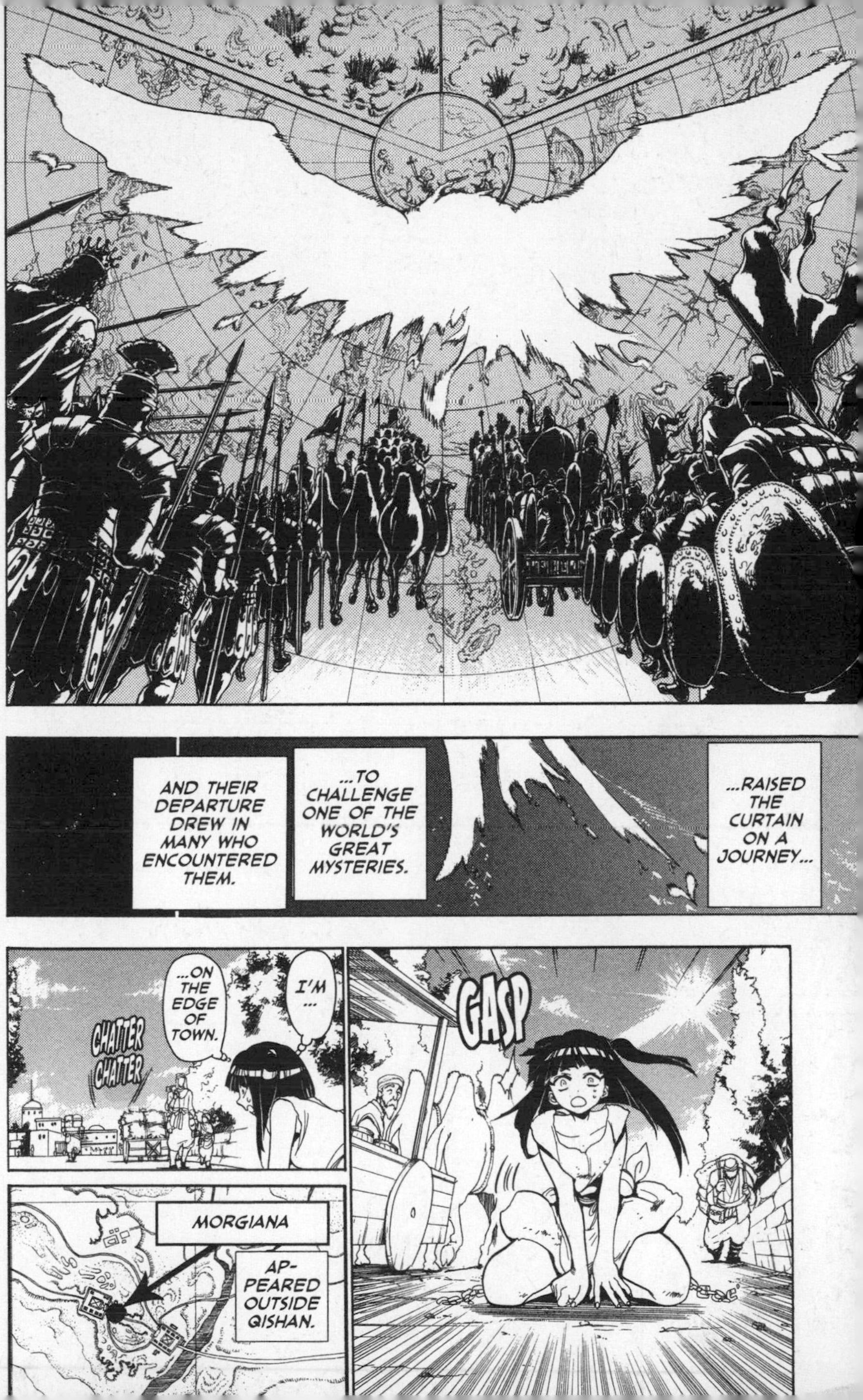
...RAISED THE CURTAIN ON A JOURNEY...
...TO CHALLENGE ONE OF THE WORLD'S GREAT MYSTERIES.
AND THEIR DEPARTURE DREW IN MANY WHO ENCOUNTERED THEM.
GASP
I'M ...
...ON THE EDGE OF TOWN.
CHATTER CHATTER
MORGIANA
AP-PEARED OUTSIDE QISHAN.

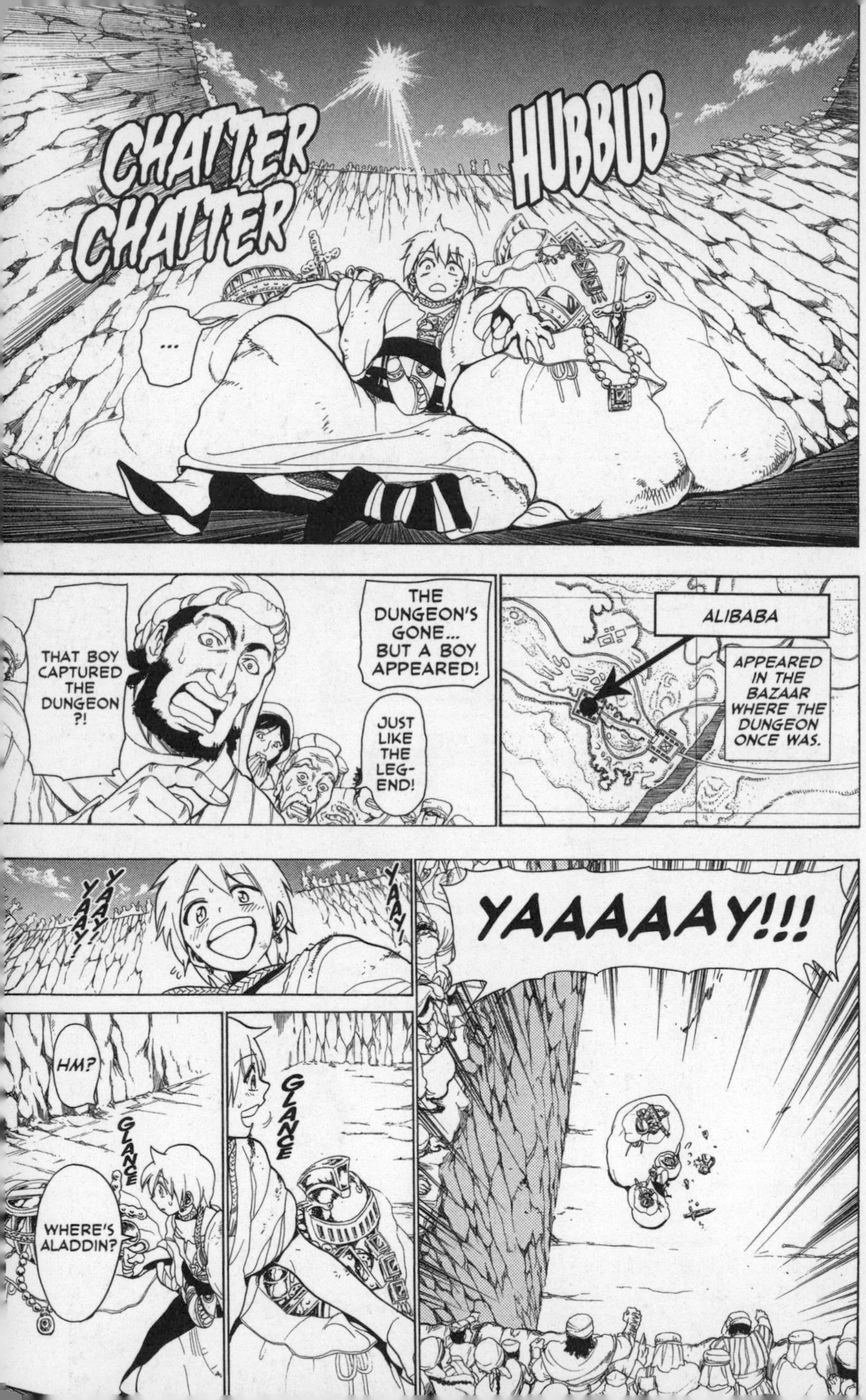
HUBBUB
CHATTER CHATTER
...
ALIBABA
APPEARED IN THE BAZAAR WHERE THE DUNGEON ONCE WAS.
THE DUNGEON'S GONE... BUT A BOY APPEARED!
JUST LIKE THE LEG-END!
THAT BOY CAPTURED THE DUNGEON ?!
YAAAAAY!!!
YAAY!
YAAAY!
YAAAY!
GLANCE
HM?
GLANCE
WHERE'S ALADDIN?

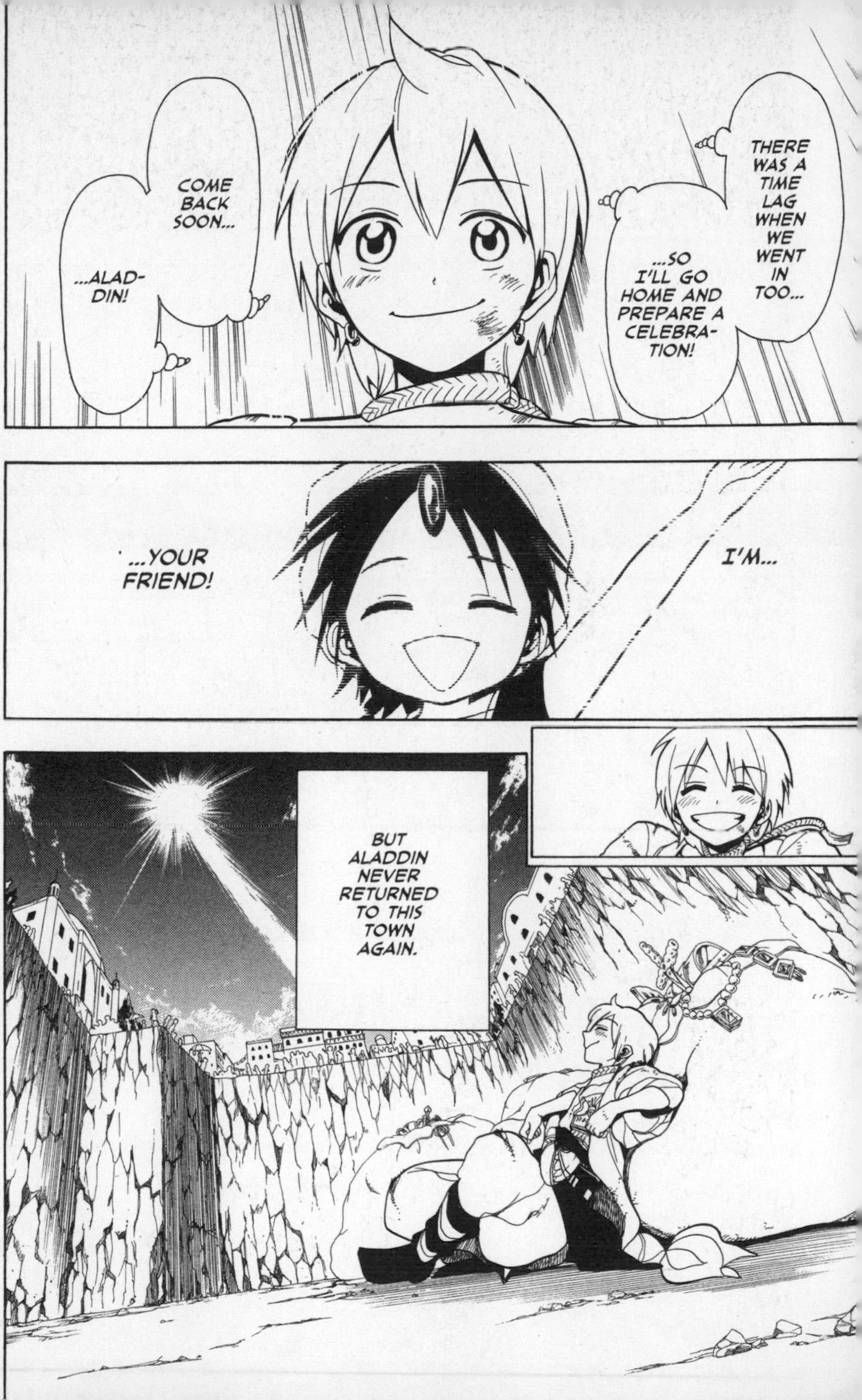
THERE WAS A TIME LAG WHEN WE WENT IN TOO...
...SO I'LL GO HOME AND PREPARE A CELEBRATION!
COME BACK SOON...
...ALAD-DIN!
I'M...
...YOUR FRIEND!
BUT ALADDIN NEVER RETURNED TO THIS TOWN AGAIN.

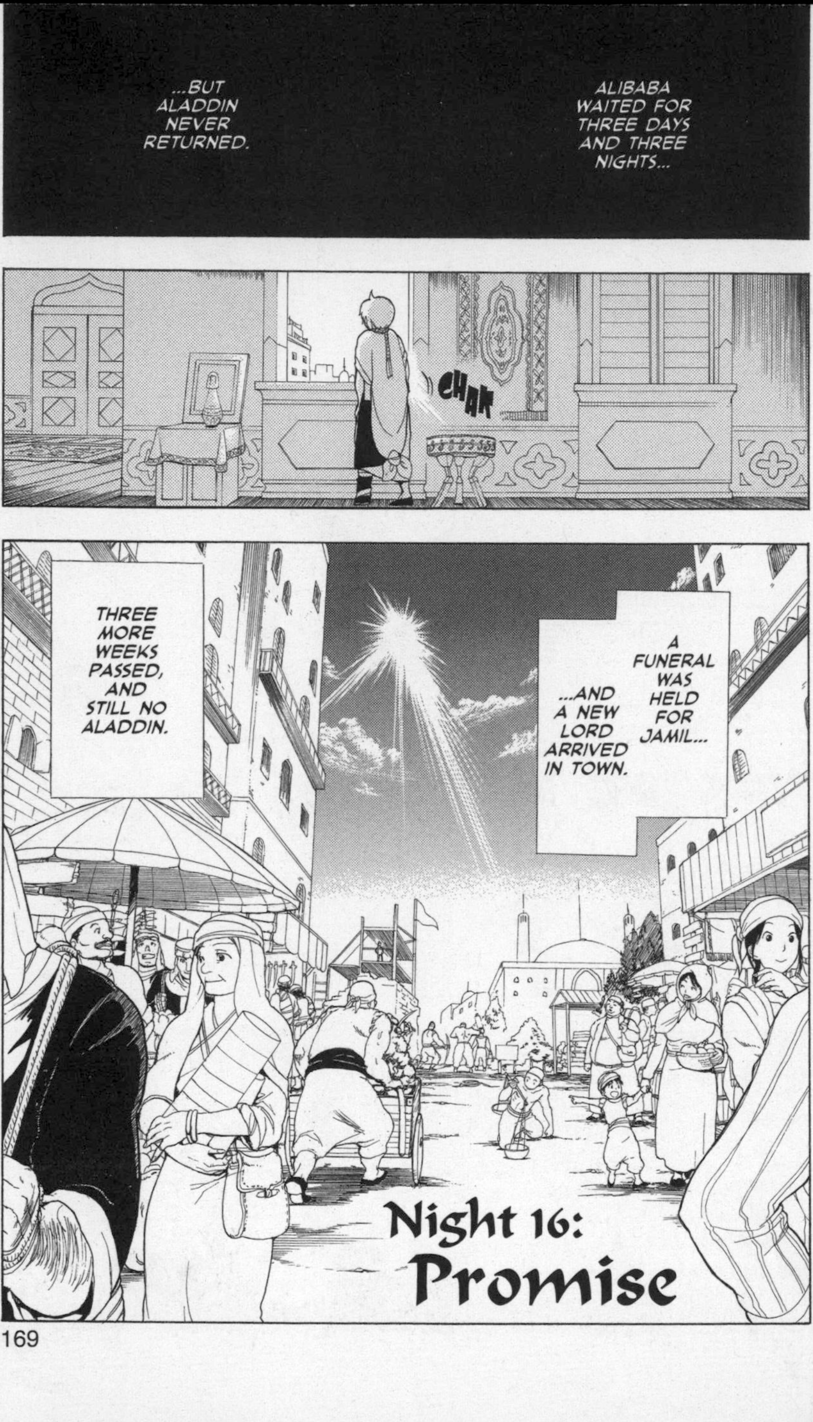
ALIBABA WAITED FOR THREE DAYS AND THREE NIGHTS...
...BUT ALADDIN NEVER RETURNED.
CHAK
A FUNERAL WAS HELD FOR JAMIL...
...AND A NEW LORD ARRIVED IN TOWN.
THREE MORE WEEKS PASSED, AND STILL NO ALADDIN.
Night 16: Promise

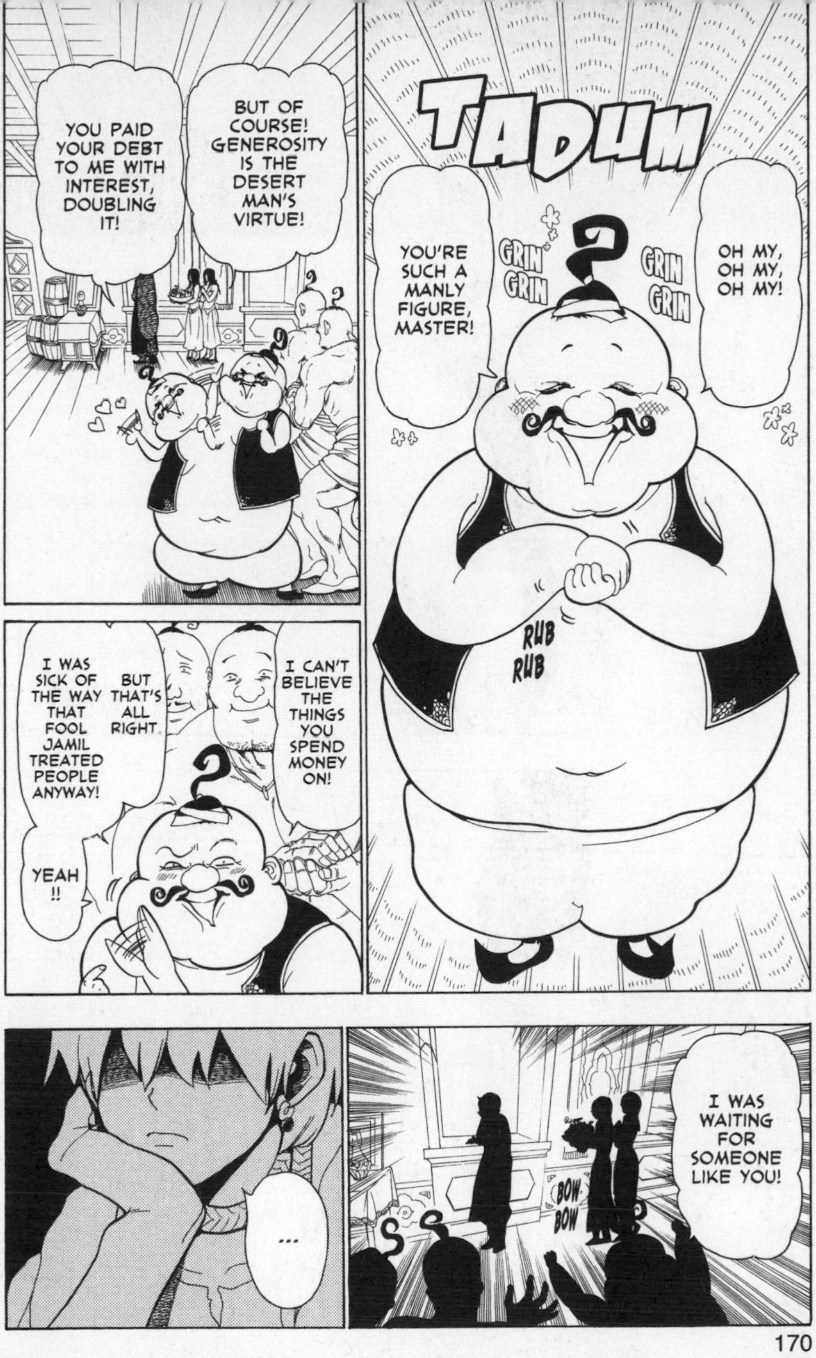
TADUM
OH MY, OH MY, OH MY!
GRIN GRIN
YOU'RE SUCH A MANLY FIGURE, MASTER!
GRIN GRIN
RUB RUB
BUT OF COURSE! GENEROSITY IS THE DESERT MAN'S VIRTUE!
YOU PAID YOUR DEBT TO ME WITH INTEREST, DOUBLING IT!
I CAN'T BELIEVE THE THINGS YOU SPEND MONEY ON!
BUT THAT'S ALL RIGHT.
I WAS SICK OF THE WAY THAT FOOL JAMIL TREATED PEOPLE ANYWAY!
YEAH !!
I WAS WAITING FOR SOMEONE LIKE YOU!
BOW BOW
...

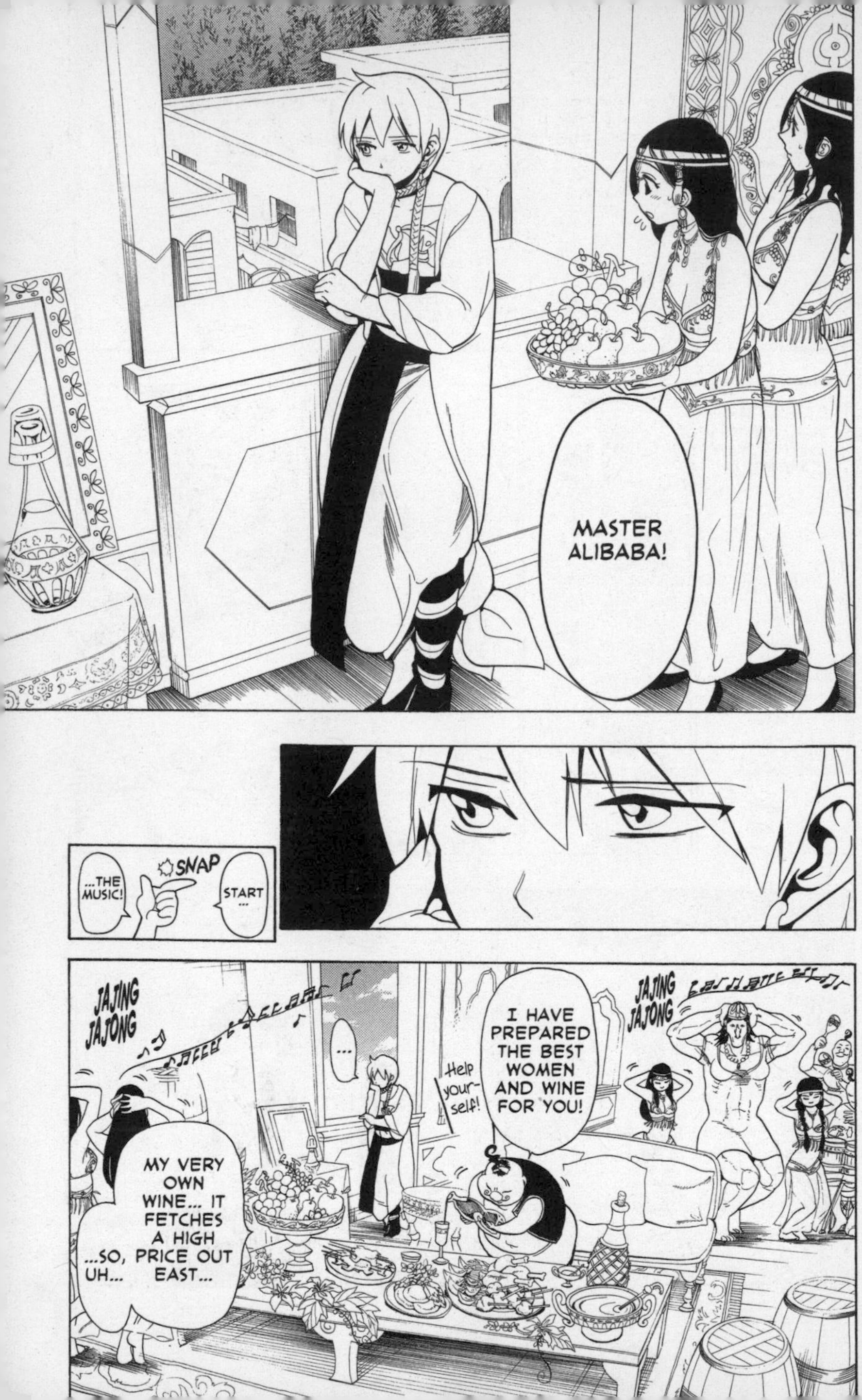
MASTER ALIBABA!
START...
SNAP
...THE MUSIC!
JAJING JAJONG
I HAVE PREPARED THE BEST WOMEN AND WINE FOR YOU!
Help your-self!
...
JAJING JAJONG
MY VERY OWN WINE... IT FETCHES A HIGH PRICE OUT EAST...
...SO, UH...

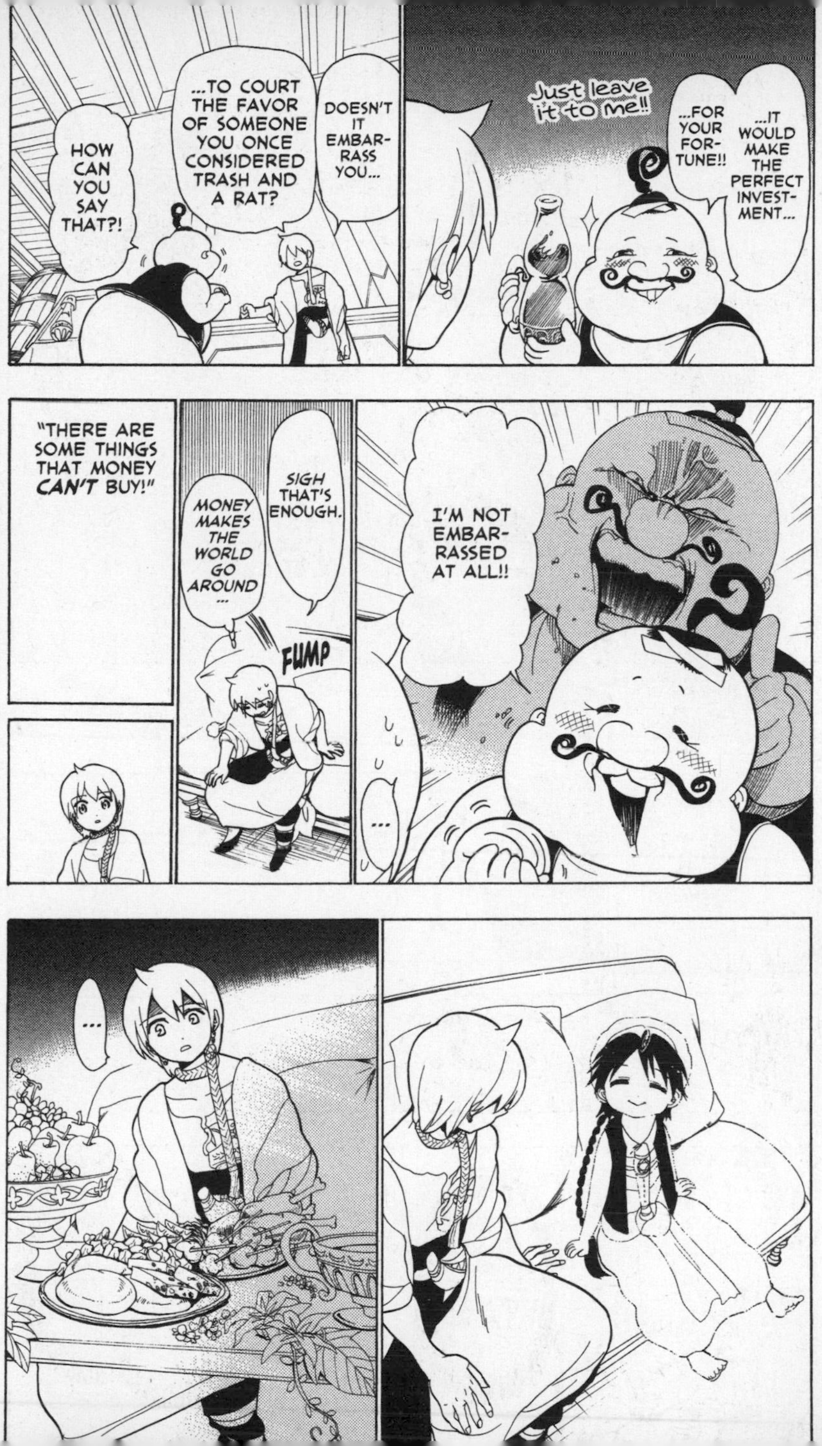

...IT WOULD MAKE THE PERFECT INVESTMENT...
...FOR YOUR FORTUNE!!
Just leave it to me!!
DOESN'T IT EMBARRASS YOU...
...TO COURT THE FAVOR OF SOMEONE YOU ONCE CONSIDERED TRASH AND A RAT?
HOW CAN YOU SAY THAT?!
I'M NOT EMBARRASSED AT ALL!!
...
SIGH THAT'S ENOUGH.
MONEY MAKES THE WORLD GO AROUND...
FUMP
"THERE ARE SOME THINGS THAT MONEY CAN'T BUY!"
...

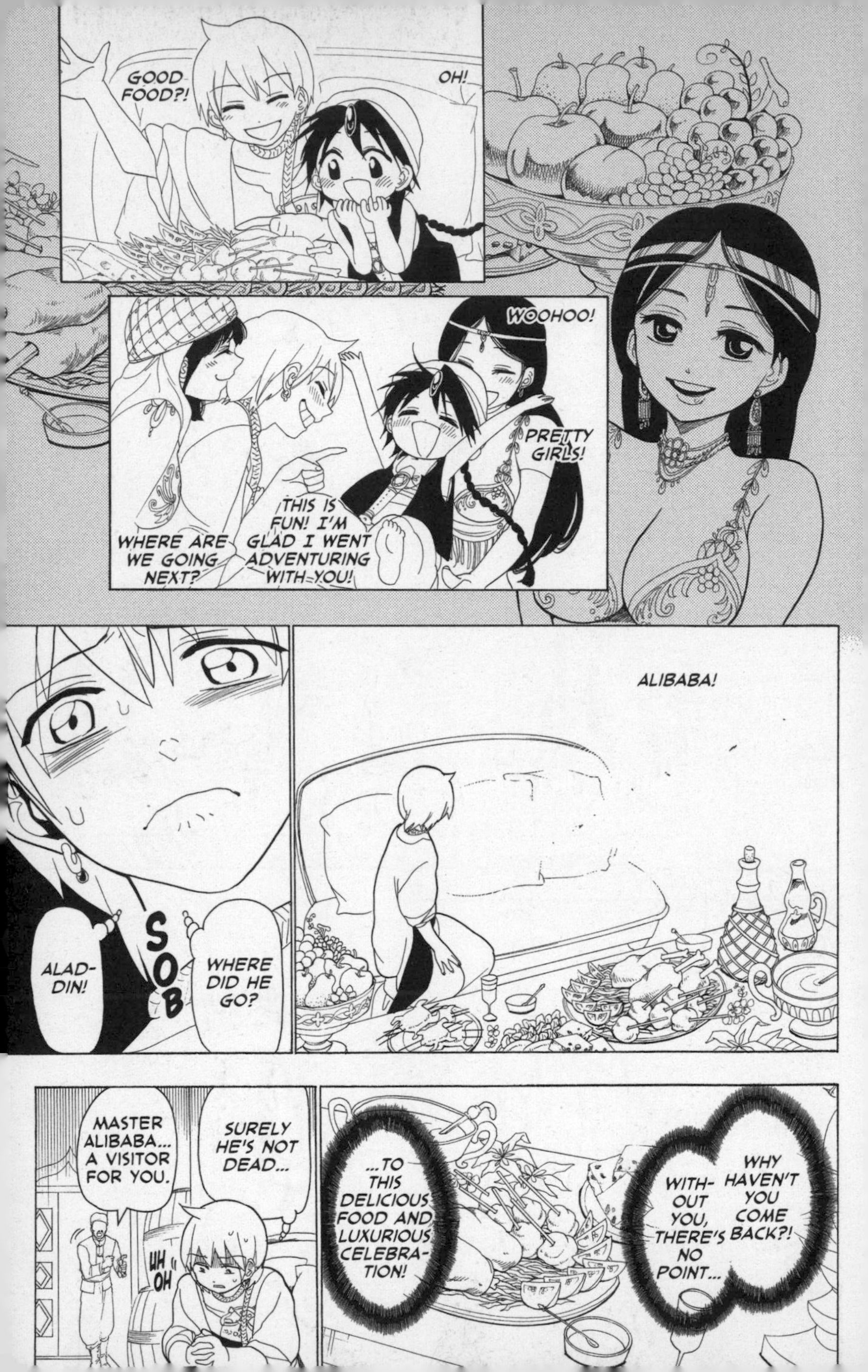
OH!
GOOD FOOD?!
WOOHOO!
PRETTY GIRLS!
THIS IS FUN! I'M GLAD I WENT ADVENTURING WITH YOU!
WHERE ARE WE GOING NEXT?
ALIBABA!
WHERE DID HE GO?
SOB
ALAD-DIN!
WHY HAVEN'T YOU COME BACK?!
WITH-OUT YOU, THERE'S NO POINT...
...TO THIS DELICIOUS FOOD AND LUXURIOUS CELEBRA-TION!
SURELY HE'S NOT DEAD...
MASTER ALIBABA... A VISITOR FOR YOU.
UH OH

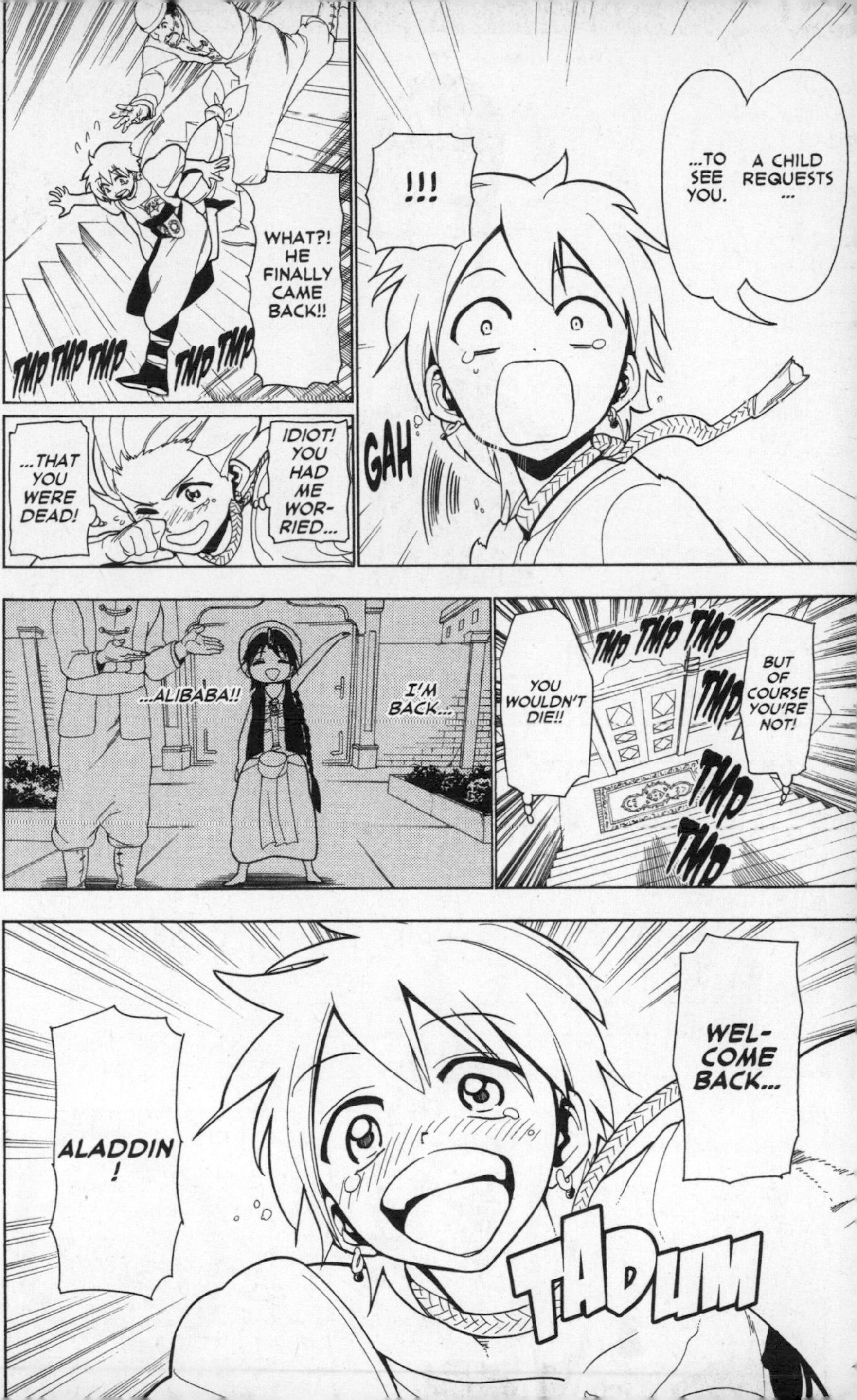
A CHILD REQUESTS ...
...TO SEE YOU.
!!!
GAH
WHAT?! HE FINALLY CAME BACK!!
TMP TMP TMP
TMP TMP
IDIOT! YOU HAD ME WOR-RIED...
...THAT YOU WERE DEAD!
BUT OF COURSE YOU'RE NOT!
YOU WOULDN'T DIE!!
TMP TMP TMP
TMP
TMP
TMP
I'M BACK...
...ALIBABA!!
WEL-COME BACK...
ALADDIN!
TADUM

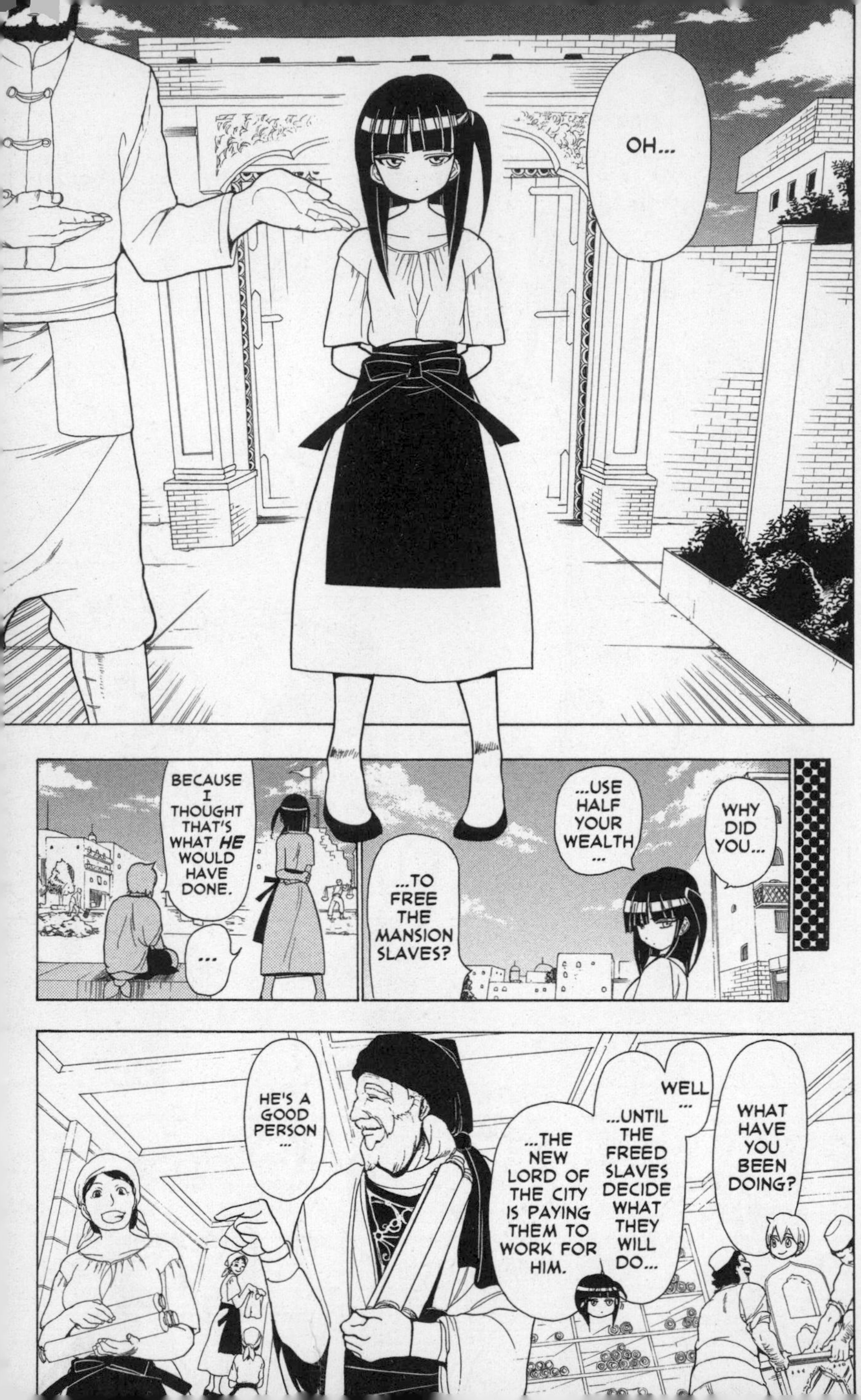
OH...
WHY DID YOU...
...USE HALF YOUR WEALTH...
...TO FREE THE MANSION SLAVES?
BECAUSE I THOUGHT THAT'S WHAT *HE* WOULD HAVE DONE.
...
WHAT HAVE YOU BEEN DOING?
WELL...
...UNTIL THE FREED SLAVES DECIDE WHAT THEY WILL DO...
...THE NEW LORD OF THE CITY IS PAYING THEM TO WORK FOR HIM.
HE'S A GOOD PERSON...

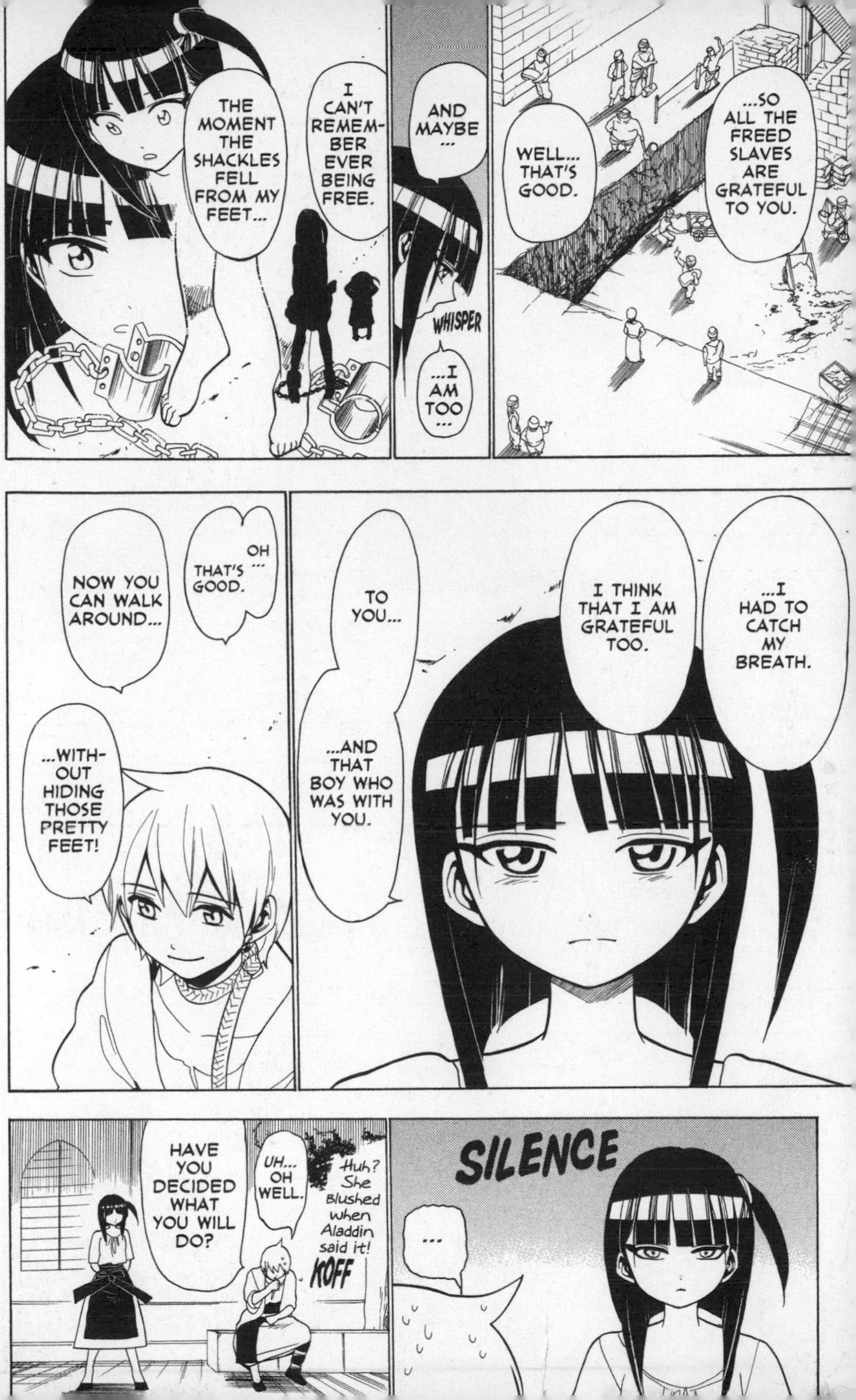
...SO ALL THE FREED SLAVES ARE GRATEFUL TO YOU.
WELL... THAT'S GOOD.
AND MAYBE ...
WHISPER
...I AM TOO ...
I CAN'T REMEMBER EVER BEING FREE.
THE MOMENT THE SHACKLES FELL FROM MY FEET...
...I HAD TO CATCH MY BREATH.
I THINK THAT I AM GRATEFUL TOO.
TO YOU...
...AND THAT BOY WHO WAS WITH YOU.
OH ... THAT'S GOOD.
NOW YOU CAN WALK AROUND...
...WITHOUT HIDING THOSE PRETTY FEET!
SILENCE
...
Huh? She Blushed when Aladdin said it!
UH... OH WELL.
KOFF
HAVE YOU DECIDED WHAT YOU WILL DO?

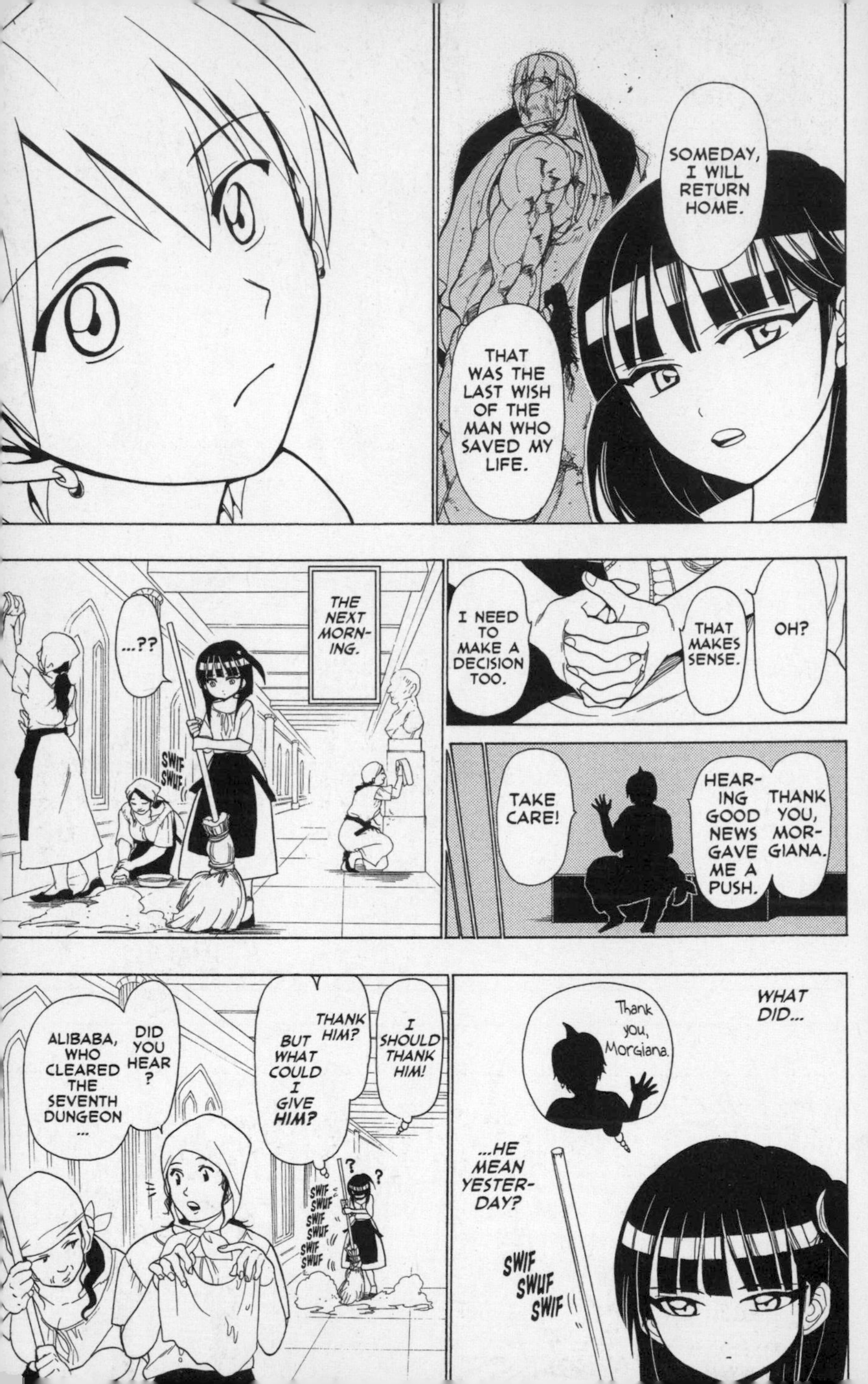
SOMEDAY, I WILL RETURN HOME.
THAT WAS THE LAST WISH OF THE MAN WHO SAVED MY LIFE.
OH?
THAT MAKES SENSE.
I NEED TO MAKE A DECISION TOO.
THANK YOU, MORGIANA.
HEARING GOOD NEWS GAVE ME A PUSH.
TAKE CARE!
THE NEXT MORNING.
...??
SWIF SWUF
WHAT DID...
Thank you, Morgiana.
...HE MEAN YESTERDAY?
SWIF SWUF SWIF
I SHOULD THANK HIM!
THANK HIM?
BUT WHAT COULD I GIVE HIM?
DID YOU HEAR?
ALIBABA, WHO CLEARED THE SEVENTH DUNGEON...
SWIF SWUF SWIF SWUF SWIF SWUF

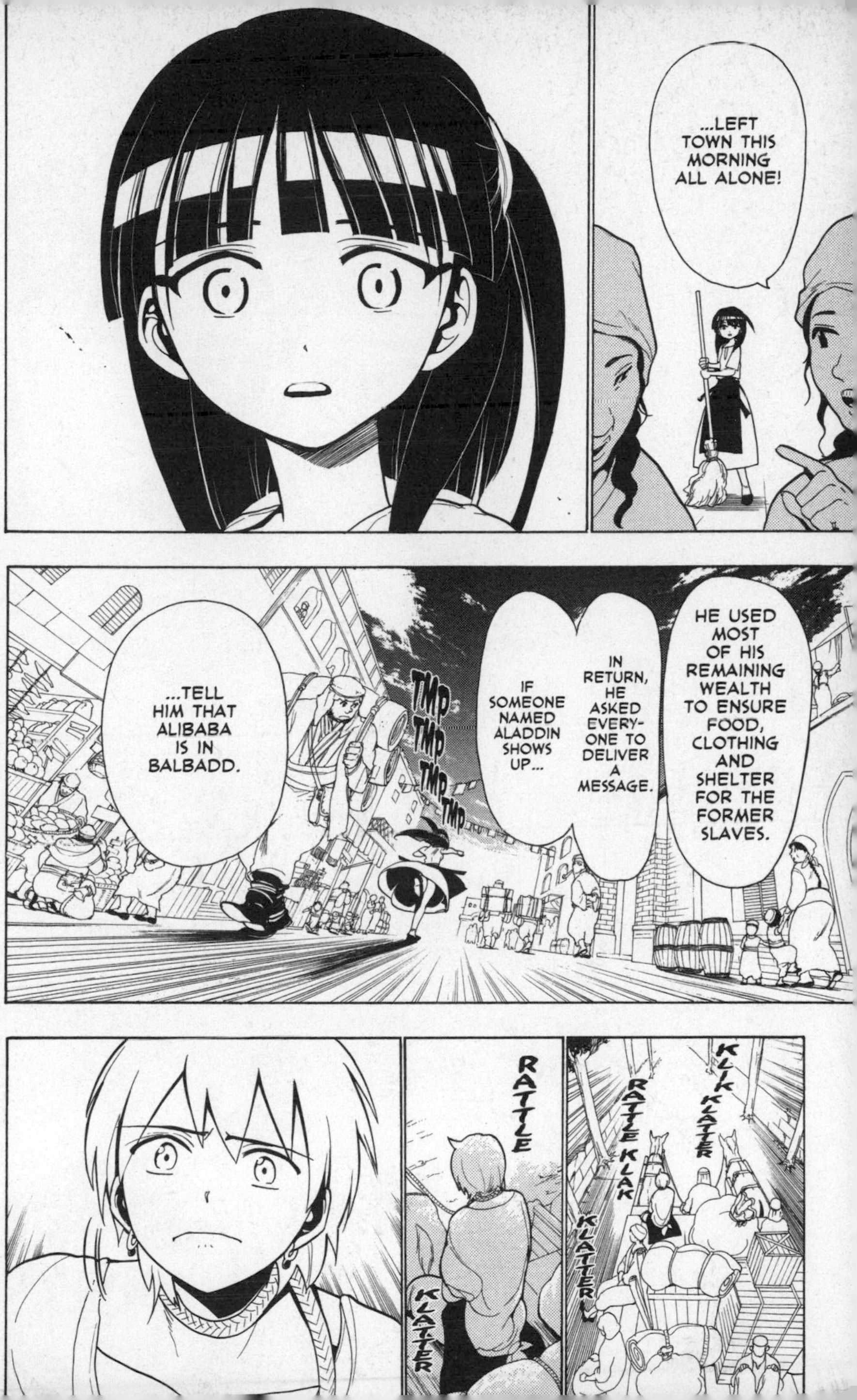
...LEFT TOWN THIS MORNING ALL ALONE!
HE USED MOST OF HIS REMAINING WEALTH TO ENSURE FOOD, CLOTHING AND SHELTER FOR THE FORMER SLAVES.
IN RETURN, HE ASKED EVERY-ONE TO DELIVER A MESSAGE.
IF SOMEONE NAMED ALADDIN SHOWS UP...
TMP TMP TMP TMP
...TELL HIM THAT ALIBABA IS IN BALBADD.
KLIK KLATTER
RATTLE KLAK
KLATTER
RATTLE
KLATTER

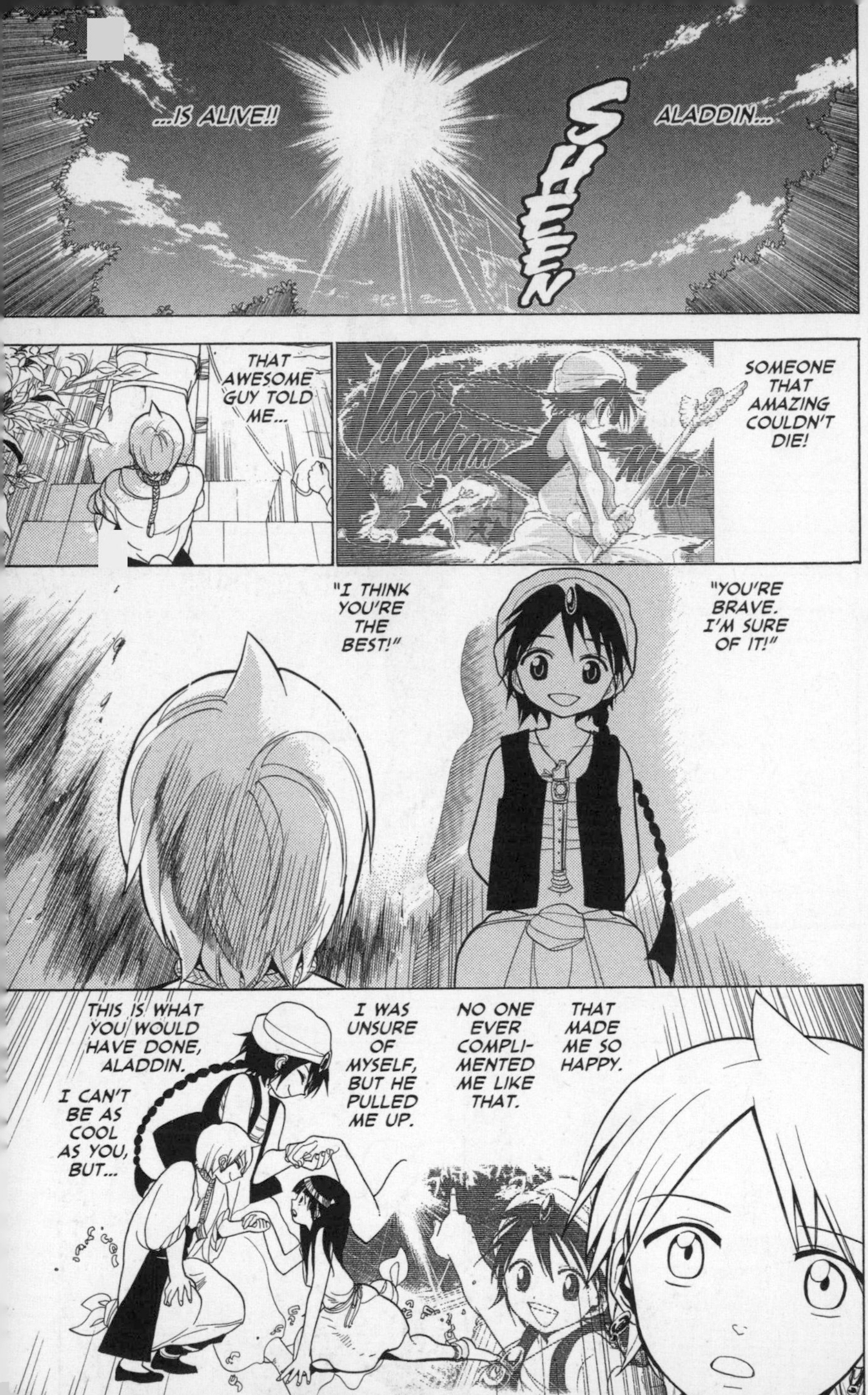
ALADDIN...
SHEEN
...IS ALIVE!!
SOMEONE THAT AMAZING COULDN'T DIE!
THAT AWESOME GUY TOLD ME...
"YOU'RE BRAVE. I'M SURE OF IT!"
"I THINK YOU'RE THE BEST!"
THAT MADE ME SO HAPPY.
NO ONE EVER COMPLI-MENTED ME LIKE THAT.
I WAS UNSURE OF MYSELF, BUT HE PULLED ME UP.
THIS IS WHAT YOU WOULD HAVE DONE, ALADDIN.
I CAN'T BE AS COOL AS YOU, BUT...

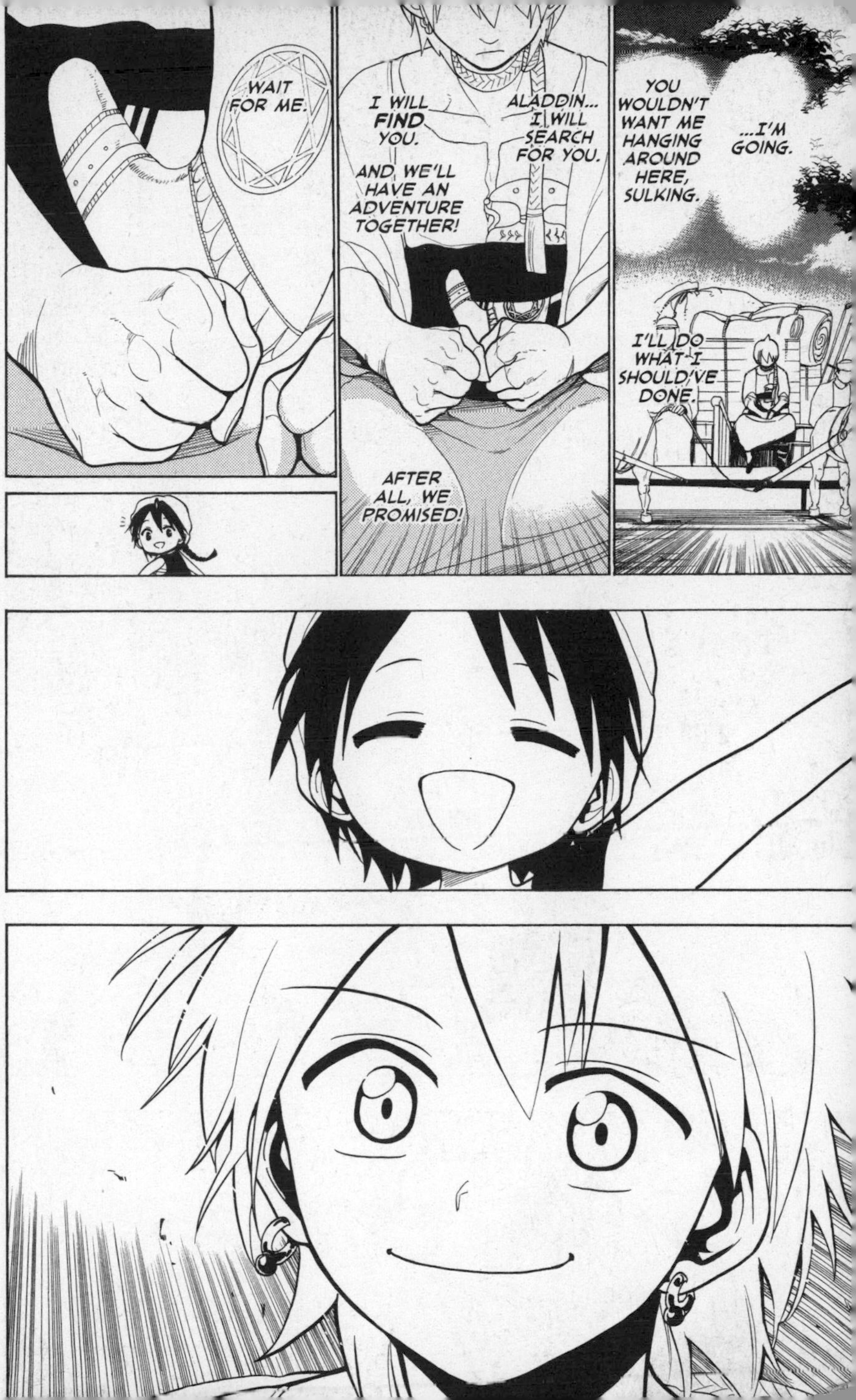
YOU WOULDN'T WANT ME HANGING AROUND HERE, SULKING.
...I'M GOING.
I'LL DO WHAT I SHOULD'VE DONE.
ALADDIN... I WILL SEARCH FOR YOU.
I WILL **FIND** YOU.
AND WE'LL HAVE AN ADVENTURE TOGETHER!
AFTER ALL, WE PROMISED!
WAIT FOR ME.

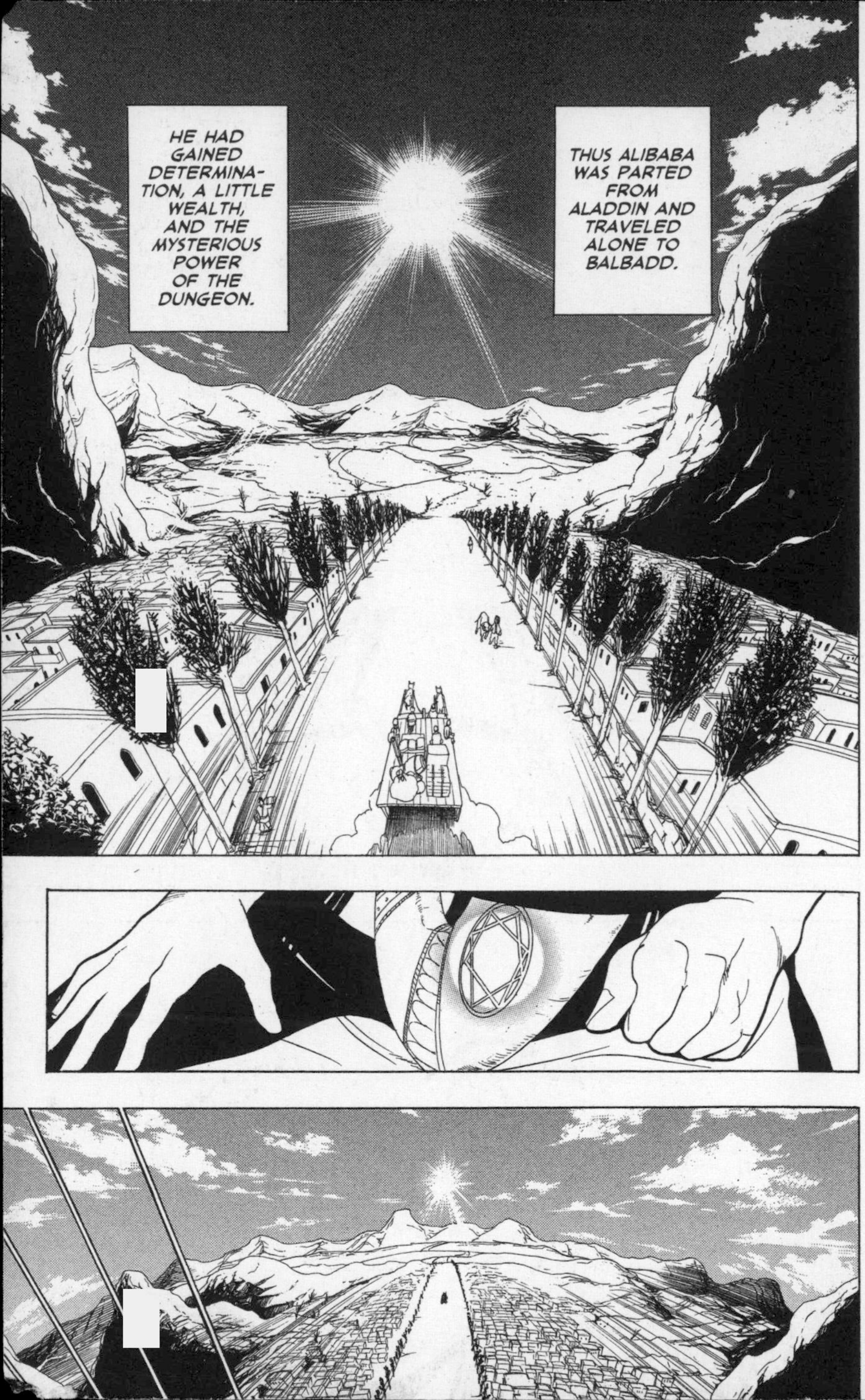
THUS ALIBABA WAS PARTED FROM ALADDIN AND TRAVELED ALONE TO BALBADD.
HE HAD GAINED DETERMINATION, A LITTLE WEALTH, AND THE MYSTERIOUS POWER OF THE DUNGEON.

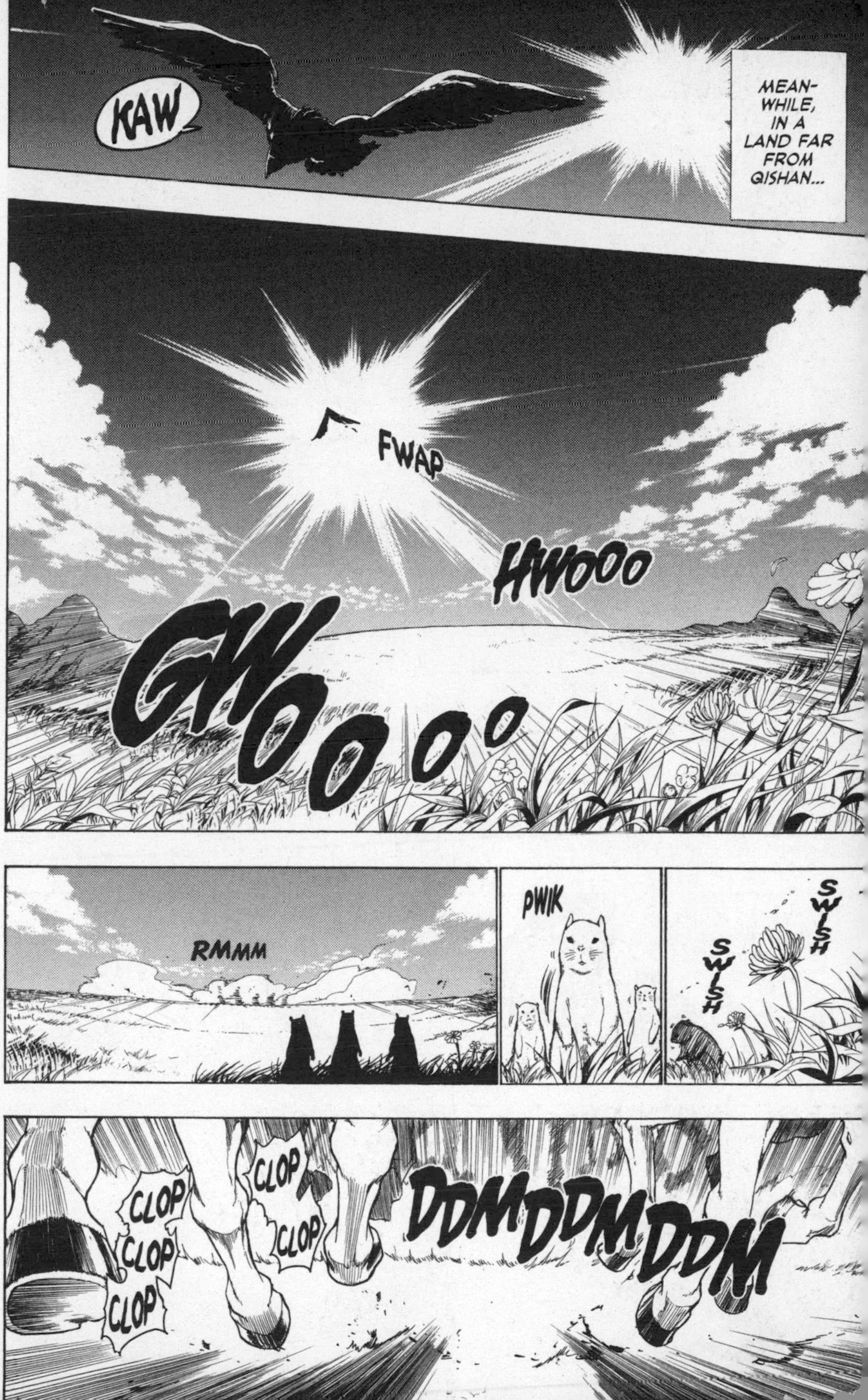
MEAN-WHILE, IN A LAND FAR FROM QISHAN...
KAW
FWAP
HWOOO
GWOOOOO
SWISH
SWISH
PWIK
RMMM
DDM DDM DDM
CLOP
CLOP
CLOP
CLOP
CLOP

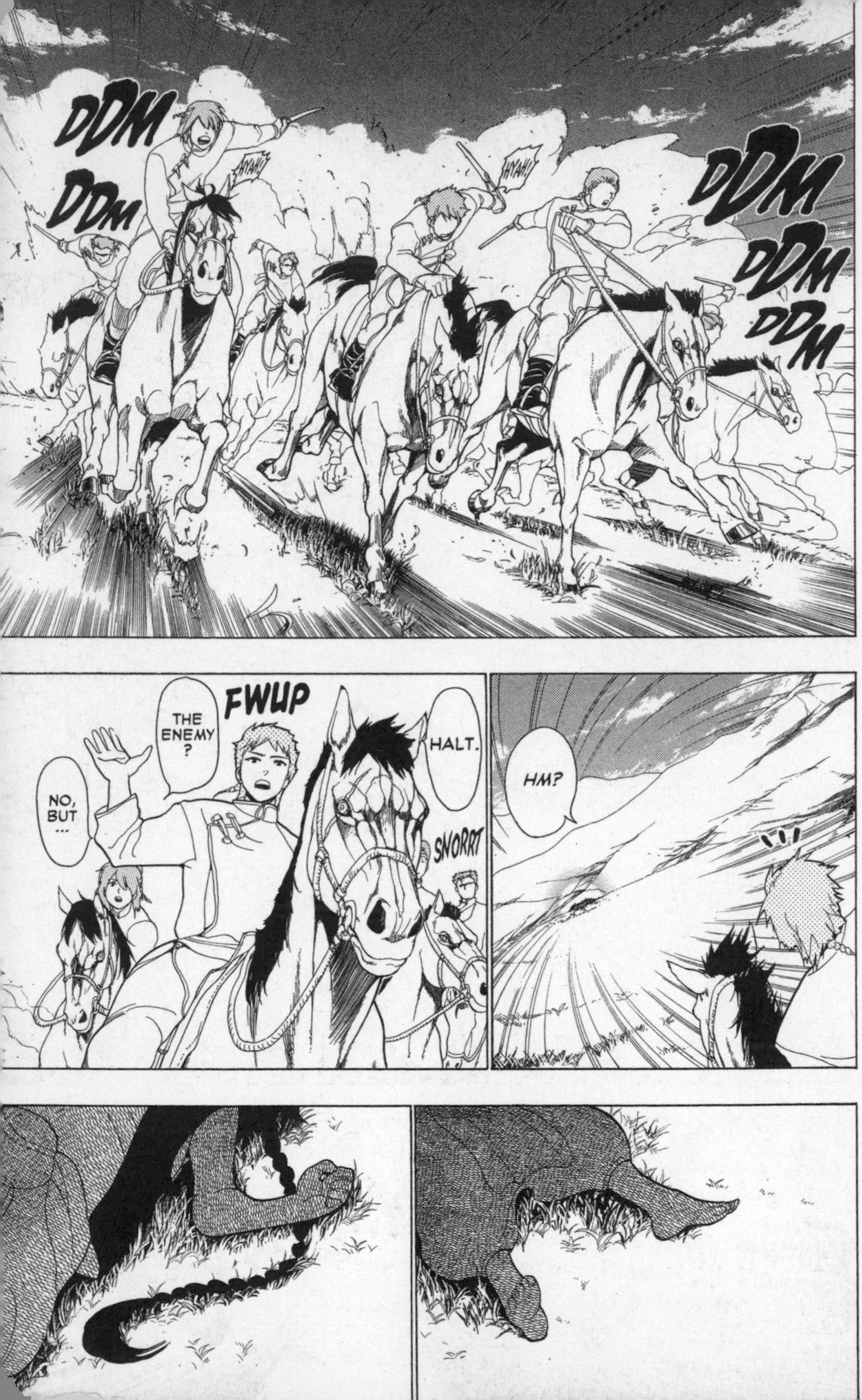
DDM
DDM
DDM
HYAH!
HYAH!
DDM
DDM
HM?
HALT.
FWUP
THE ENEMY?
NO, BUT ...
SNORRT

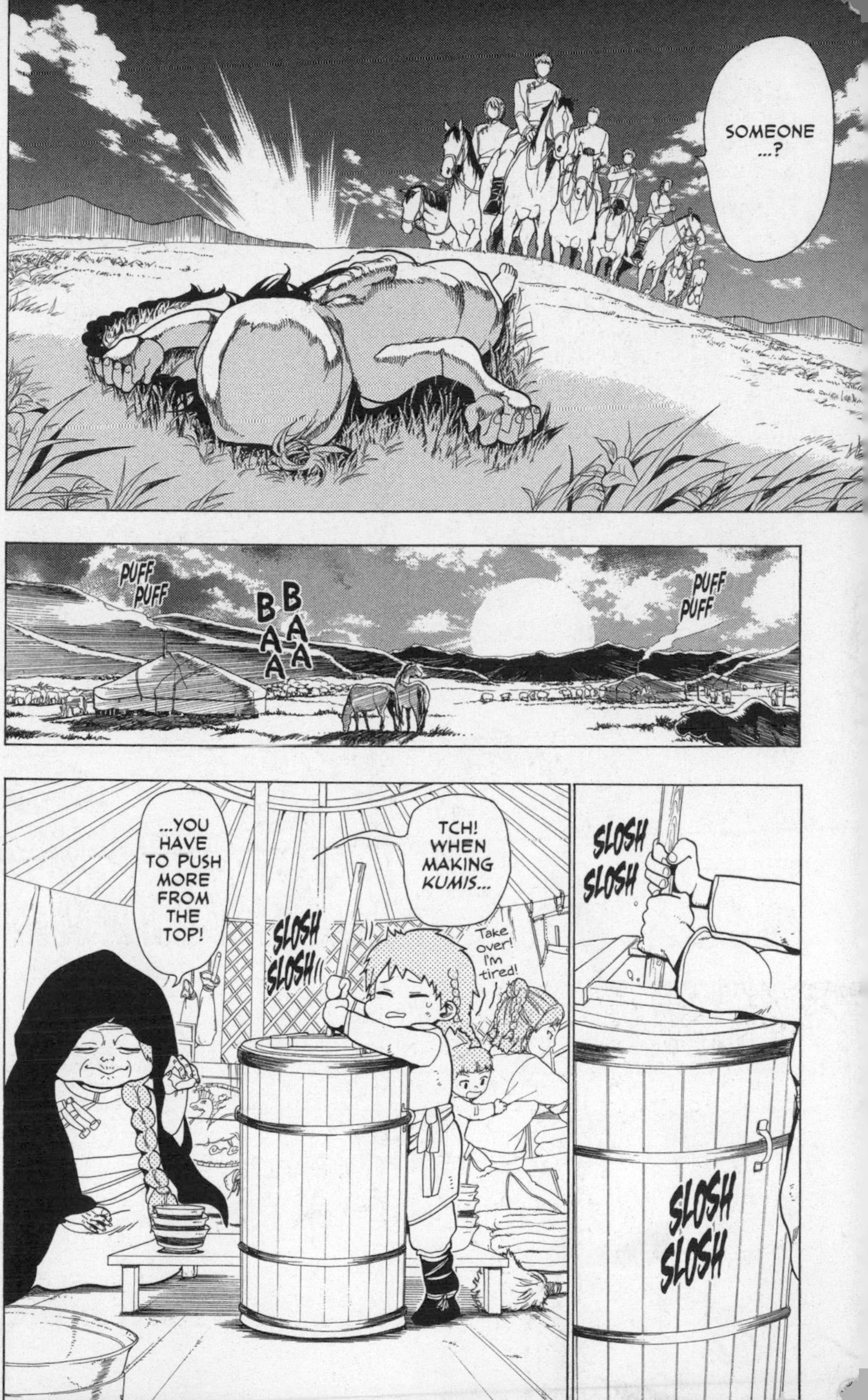
SOMEONE ...?
PUFF PUFF
BAAA BAAA
PUFF PUFF
SLOSH SLOSH
SLOSH SLOSH
TCH! WHEN MAKING KUMIS...
Take over! I'm tired!
SLOSH SLOSH
...YOU HAVE TO PUSH MORE FROM THE TOP!

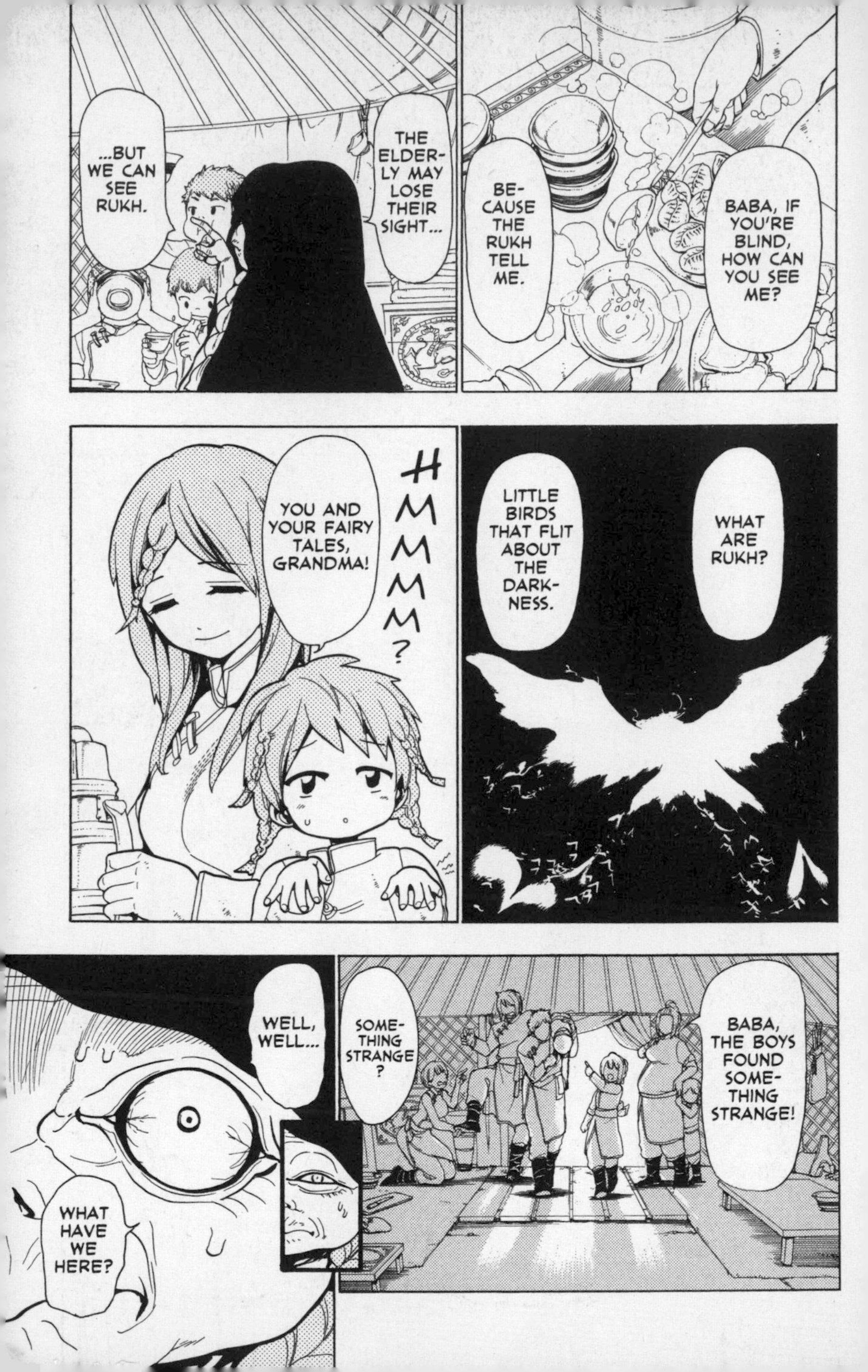
BABA, IF YOU'RE BLIND, HOW CAN YOU SEE ME?
BE-CAUSE THE RUKH TELL ME.
THE ELDER-LY MAY LOSE THEIR SIGHT...
...BUT WE CAN SEE RUKH.
WHAT ARE RUKH?
LITTLE BIRDS THAT FLIT ABOUT THE DARK-NESS.
HMMMMM?
YOU AND YOUR FAIRY TALES, GRANDMA!
BABA, THE BOYS FOUND SOME-THING STRANGE!
SOME-THING STRANGE?
WELL, WELL...
WHAT HAVE WE HERE?

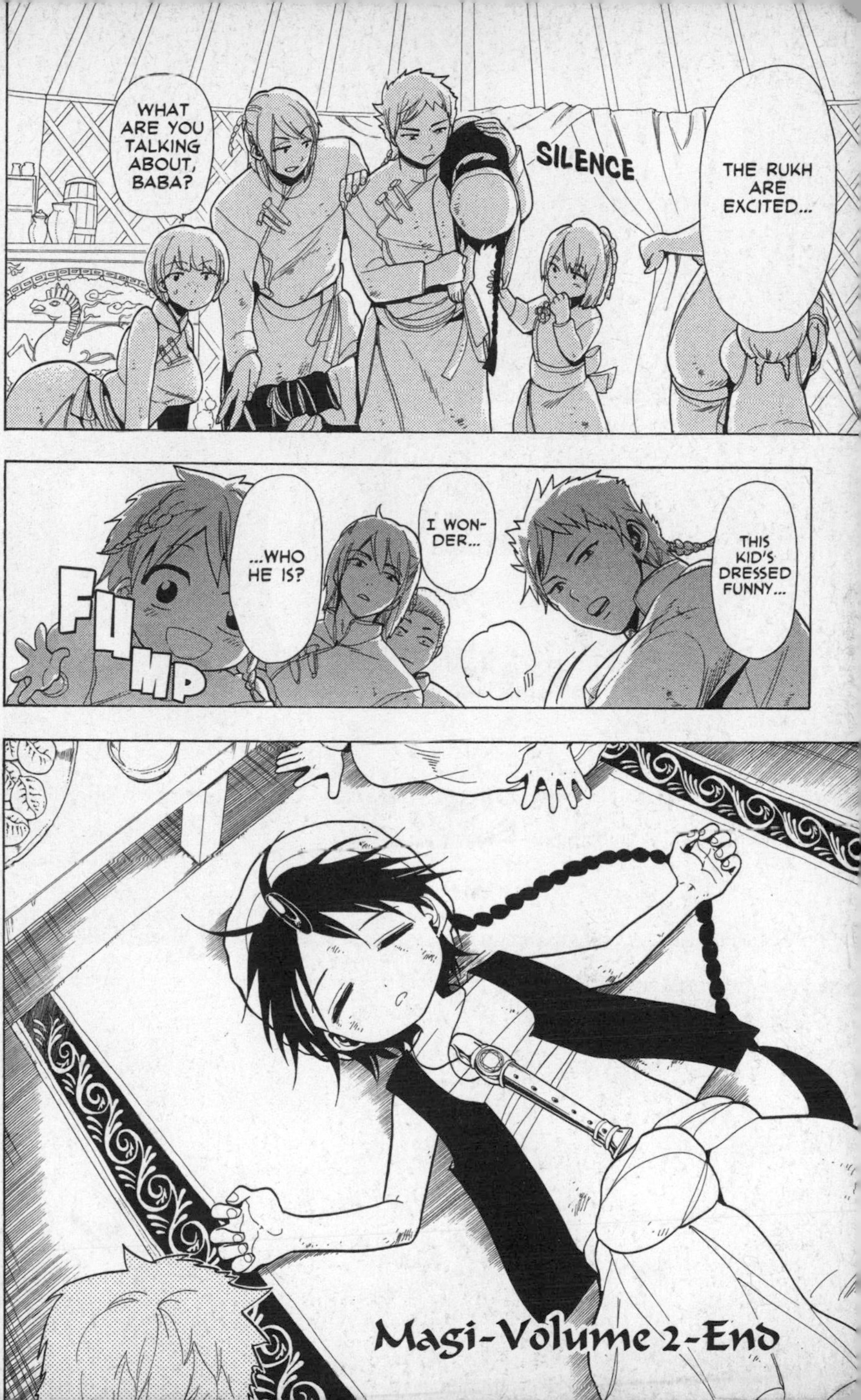
THE RUKH ARE EXCITED...
SILENCE
WHAT ARE YOU TALKING ABOUT, BABA?
THIS KID'S DRESSED FUNNY...
I WON-DER...
...WHO HE IS?
FUMP
Magi-Volume 2-End

MAGI
The labyrinth of magic
2

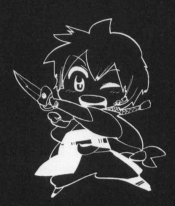

Staff

■ **Story & Art**
Shinobu Ohtaka

■ **Regular Assistants**

Matsubara

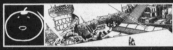

Miho Isshiki

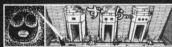

Akira Sugito

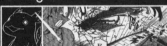

■ **Editor**
Kazuaki Ishibashi

■ **Sales & Promotion**
Akira Ozeki
Shinichirou Todaka

■ **Designers**
Yasuo Shimura + Bay Bridge Studio

■ **Special Thanks**
Mutsumi Ogasawara

About Me–Shinobu Ohtaka ⑤

Later, ***after about a year of discussions,*** we discussed changing the setting from Rome to the Middle East. And the Middle East immediately suggests—That's right!—***The Arabian Nights!*** While researching *The Arabian Nights,* I noticed that while it's fantasy, much of ***it speaks to today's world.*** I thought it would be interesting to use that as a motif.

And there's a reason I named ***the main characters*** Aladdin and Alibaba after ***famous characters.*** In portraying characters in fantasy, I thought having an original basis for them would ***make it easier for readers to get an idea*** for who they are and grow familiar with them.

Magi is not a manga that accurately depicts the story of *The Arabian Nights,* but I want to draw upon a ***mysterious atmosphere of magic and myth,*** relate tales of adventure, and write a fun manga. Also, I want to choose my motifs from ***as wide a range as possible,*** going beyond the Middle East to China, India, Europe, Africa...and someday, Japan. By the way, the setting in volume 3 resembles the grasslands of Mongolia. I hope the ***vastness of the world*** will be larger than that in *The Arabian Nights.* (If the series continues...)

Unlike the characters in the manga, I can't use magic, but by wielding my pen, I hope at the very least to create ***a manga everyone can enjoy,*** so please watch over Aladdin and Alibaba in the days ahead! ***Thank you!***

The End.

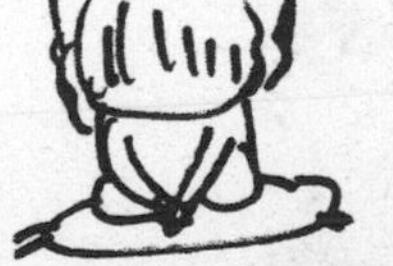

Shinobu Ohtaka

SHINOBU OHTAKA

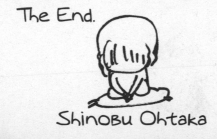

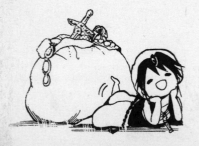

SHINOBU OHTAKA

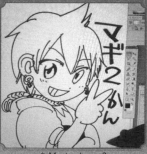

Magi volume 2

I'll do my best!

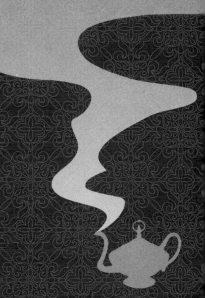

MAGI

Volume 2
Shonen Sunday Edition

Story and Art by
SHINOBU OHTAKA

MAGI Vol.2
by Shinobu OHTAKA
© 2009 Shinobu OHTAKA
All rights reserved.
Original Japanese edition published by SHOGAKUKAN.
English translation rights in the United States of America, Canada,
the United Kingdom and Ireland arranged with SHOGAKUKAN.

Translation & English Adaptation ◇ John Werry

Touch-up Art & Lettering ◇ Stephen Dutro

Editor ◇ Mike Montesa

Printed in the U.S.A.

Published by VIZ Media, LLC
P.O. Box 77010
San Francisco, CA 94107

10 9 8 7 6 5 4 3 2 1
First printing, October 2013

PARENTAL ADVISORY
MAGI is rated T for Teen.
This volume contains
suggestive themes.
ratings.viz.com

WWW.SHONENSUNDAY.COM

www.viz.com

You're reading the
WRONG WAY

MAGI reads from right to left, starting in the upper-right corner. Japanese is read from **right** to **left**, meaning that action, sound effects, and word-balloon order are completely reversed from English order.

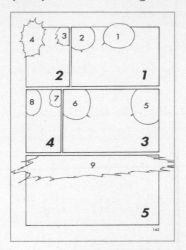